English Translation of The Holy Quran

by

Maulana Muhammad Ali

Author of the English Translation of the Holy Quran with full commentary, and several other classic works on Islam

*Pocket-size edition
With detailed Index*

Ahmadiyya Anjuman Isha'at Islam Lahore Inc.
Columbus, Ohio, U.S.A.

*Pocket-size Edition containing Translation only,
first published, March 1999*

*This translation first appeared in the Revised
Edition of Maulana Muhammad Ali's full work
(with Arabic text, Introduction and Commentary),
first printed in 1951.*

© Copyright 1999 by
Ahmadiyya Anjuman Isha'at Islam Lahore Inc.,
1315 Kingsgate Road, Columbus, Ohio 43221
U.S.A.
All Rights Reserved.

Phone: 614 457 8504
Fax: 614-457-4455
URL: http://www.muslim.org

Translator's bio-data:
Maulana Muhammad Ali
b. 1874, d. 1951 (Lahore, Pakistan)

Printed in Belgium

Library of Congress Catalog Card No. 98-72724
ISBN: 0-913321-49-4 Standard
ISBN: 0-913321-77-X Deluxe Leather

Publisher's Note

In this small-size book we are publishing the translation of the Holy Quran taken from Maulana Muhammad Ali's comprehensive and world-famous work which consists of the English Translation of the Holy Quran along with the Arabic text and a full commentary. It has been produced to meet the frequently-expressed demand for the meanings of the Holy Quran to be available in a book small enough to be easily carried, so that it may be studied at those times, such as while travelling, when it would be inconvenient to handle the larger comprehensive volume.

We have included in this pocket-size edition an enlarged Index of the Holy Quran, which should be of help in locating verses dealing with particular subjects.

Please note for information that the section titles given in this translation within chapters of the Holy Quran are not part of the text of the Holy Quran, but have been inserted by the translator to summarize the contents of the sections.

For a particular and more detailed understanding of any point in this translation, consult Maulana Muhammad Ali's full work, as referred to above.

PROSTRATION IN THE HOLY QURAN

There are fifteen occasions in the Holy Quran where the reciters are required to prostrate themselves:

7:206	27:26
13:15	32:15
16:50	38:24
17:109	41:38
19:58	53:62
22:18	84:21
22:77	96:19
25:60	

CONTENTS

Section - *Page*

Ch. 1 — Al-Fātiḥah: THE OPENING - - - - - - - - - 1

Part 1 - 1

Ch. 2 — Al-Baqarah: THE COW - - - - - - - - - - - 2
1. Fundamental Principles of Islām - - - - - - - - - 2
2. Lip-profession - 2
3. Divine Unity - 3
4. Greatness of Man - 4
5. Israelite Prophecies fulfilled - - - - - - - - - - - - 5
6. Divine favours on Israel - - - - - - - - - - - - - - - 6
7. Divine favours on Israel - - - - - - - - - - - - - - - 7
8. Israelites' Degeneration - - - - - - - - - - - - - - - 8
9. Grow in hard heartedness - - - - - - - - - - - - - 9
10. Violation of Covenant - - - - - - - - - - - - - - - 10
11. Reject the Prophet - - - - - - - - - - - - - - - - - 11
12. Enmity to the Prophet - - - - - - - - - - - - - - - 12
13. Previous Scriptures abrogated - - - - - - - - - - 13
14. Perfect guidance only in Islām - - - - - - - - - 14
15. Covenant with Abraham - - - - - - - - - - - - - 15
16. Religion of Abraham - - - - - - - - - - - - - - - - 16

Part 2 - 17
17. Ka'bah — Spiritual Centre - - - - - - - - - - - - 17
18. Ka'bah — Spiritual Centre - - - - - - - - - - - - 18
19. Hard Trials establish Truth - - - - - - - - - - - - 19
20. Unity must prevail - - - - - - - - - - - - - - - - - 20
21. Prohibited Foods - - - - - - - - - - - - - - - - - - - 21
22. Retaliation and Bequests - - - - - - - - - - - - - 21
23. Fasting - 22
24. Fighting in Defence - - - - - - - - - - - - - - - - 23
25. The Pilgrimage - 25

iii

CONTENTS

Section	Page
26. Trials and Tribulations	26
27. Miscellaneous Questions	27
28. Divorce	28
29. Divorce	29
30. Remarriage	30
31. Provision for Divorced Women and Widows	31
32. Fighting for Truth	32
33. Fighting for Truth	33

Part 3 — 33
34.	No Compulsion in Religion	34
35.	Dead Nations' Revival	34
36.	Spending for Truth	35
37.	Spending for Truth	36
38.	Usury Prohibited	37
39.	Contracts and Evidence	38
40.	Muslims' Victory Sure	39

Ch. 3 — Āl-'Imrān: THE FAMILY OF AMRAN — 40
1.	Rule of Interpretation	40
2.	Unity — Basis of all Religions	41
3.	Kingdom granted to another People	42
4.	Last Members of a Chosen Race	43
5.	Birth and Ministry of Jesus	44
6.	Jesus Cleared of False Charges	46
7.	Controversy with Jews and Christians	46
8.	Devices against Islām	47
9.	Covenant of Prophets	48

Part 4 — 50
10.	Ever-living testimony to Islām	50
11.	Muslims exhorted to remain united	50
12.	Relations of Jews with Muslims	51
13.	Battle of Uḥud	53
14.	Success meant for Muslims	53
15.	Perseverance in Sufferings	54
16.	Causes of Misfortune in Uḥud Battle	55
17.	Uḥud made a distinction	56

CONTENTS

Section	Page
18. No Gain to Enemy	58
19. Carpings of People of Book	59
20. Ultimate Triumph of Faithful	60

Ch. 4 — Al-Nisā': THE WOMEN — 62
1. Orphans' Guardians	62
2. Law of Inheritance	63
3. Treatment of Women	64
4. Women who may be married	65

Part 5 — 65
5. Women's Rights over their Earnings	66
6. Disagreement of Husband and Wife	67
7. Purification of Soul	68
8. Kingdom for Abraham's Descendants	69
9. Prophet must be obeyed	70
10. Believers must defend	71
11. Hypocrites' Attitude	72
12. How to deal with Hypocrites	73
13. Murderer of a Muslim	74
14. Muslims among enemy	75
15. Prayer when Fighting	75
16. Hypocrites are Dishonest	76
17. Secret Counsels of Hypocrites	77
18. Idolatry condemned	77
19. Equitable Dealings	78
20. Hypocrisy Condemned	79
21. End of Hypocrites	80

Part 6 — 81
22. The Transgressions of the Jews	81
23. Previous Revelations Attest Qur'ān	83
24. Prophethood of Jesus	84

Ch. 5 — Al-Mā'idah: THE FOOD — 85
1. Perfection of Religion in Islām	85
2. Duty of Uprightness	86
3. Christian Violation of Covenant	87

CONTENTS

Section	Page
4. Israelites' Violation of Covenant	88
5. Cain and Abel	89
6. Punishment of Offenders	90
7. Qur'ān and Previous Scriptures	91
8. Relations with Enemies	93
9. The Mockers	93
10. Christian Deviation	95
11. Christian Nearness to Islām	96

Part 7 — 96

12. A Warning	97
13. Inviolability of Ka'bah	98
14. Some Directions for Muslims	99
15. Christian Love of this Life	100
16. False Doctrines introduced	101

Ch. 6 — Al-An'ām: THE CATTLE — 103

1. Ultimate Triumph of Unity	103
2. Greatness of Divine Mercy	104
3. Polytheists' witness against self	105
4. Rejection of Truth	106
5. Consequences of Rejection	107
6. Reward of Believers	108
7. Divine Judgment	108
8. Divine Judgment	109
9. Abraham's Argument for Divine Unity	110
10. Prophets among Abraham's Line	111
11. Truth of Revelation	112
12. Ultimate Triumph of Truth	113
13. Gradual Progress	114

Part 8 — 115

14. Polytheists' Opposition	115
15. The Chief Opponents	116
16. Evils of Idolatry	117
17. Idolaters' Self-imposed Prohibitions	118
18. Prohibited Foods	119
19. Guiding Rules of Life	120

CONTENTS

vii

Section — *Page*

20.	Goal for the Faithful	121

Ch. 7 — Al-A'rāf: THE ELEVATED PLACES — — 123

1.	Opponents' Doom	123
2.	Devil's Opposition to Man	123
3.	Warning against Devil's Insinuations	125
4.	Messengers to uplift Humanity	125
5.	Acceptors of Message	127
6.	Helplessness of Opponents	128
7.	Righteous will prosper	128
8.	Noah	129
9.	Hūd	129
10.	Ṣāliḥ and Lot	130
11.	Shu'aib	131

Part 9 — 132

12.	Makkans warned	133
13.	Moses sent to Pharaoh	133
14.	Pharaoh summons Enchanters	134
15.	Israelites' Persecution	135
16.	*Moses shows Signs*	135
17.	Moses receives Law	136
18.	Israelites worship a calf	137
19.	Torah and the Prophet's Advent	138
20.	Divine Favours on Israelites	139
21.	Israelites' Transgressions	140
22.	Divine Impress on Man's Nature	141
23.	Coming of Doom	142
24.	The Final Word	143

Ch. 8 — Al-Anfāl: VOLUNTARY GIFTS — — — — — 145

1.	The Battle of Badr	145
2.	The Battle of Badr	146
3.	The Way to Success	147
4.	Muslims to be Guardians of the Sacred Mosque	147
5.	Badr a Sign of Prophet's Truth	148

CONTENTS

Section	Page

Part 10 — 149
6. Success does not depend on Numbers — 149
7. Enemy's Strength weakened — 150
8. Peace to be secured by Strength — 151
9. Muslims to meet Overwhelming Numbers — 151
10. Relations of Muslim State with others — 152

Ch. 9 — Al-Barā'at: THE IMMUNITY — 154
1. Declaration of Immunity — 154
2. Reasons for the Immunity — 154
3. Idolaters' Service of the Sacred House — 156
4. Islām will Triumph in Arabia — 156
5. Islām will Triumph in the World — 157
6. The Tabūk Expedition — 158
7. The Hypocrites — 159
8. The Hypocrites — 161
9. The Hypocrites — 162
10. The Hypocrites — 162
11. The Hypocrites — 163
12. The Hypocrites — 164

Part 11 — 165
13. The Hypocrites — 166
14. The Faithful — 167
15. What Faithful should do — 168
16. Prophet's Great Anxiety — 169

Ch. 10 — Yūnus: JONAH — 170
1. Truth of Revelation — 170
2. Punishment of Rejection — 171
3. Merciful Dealing — 172
4. Uniqueness of Divine Gifts — 173
5. Reprobates' Punishment — 175
6. Mercy takes Precedence of Punishment — 176
7. Good News for Faithful — 176
8. Noah and Moses — 177
9. End of Opposition to Moses — 178
10. Warning benefits the Heedful — 179

CONTENTS ix

Section	Page
11. Divine Judgment	180

Ch. 11 — Hūd — 182
1. A Warning — 182

Part 12 — 182
2. Truth of Revelation — 183
3. History of Noah — 184
4. History of Noah — 185
5. History of Hūd — 187
6. History of Ṣāliḥ — 188
7. Abraham and Lot — 189
8. History of Shu'aib — 190
9. Iniquitous and Righteous — 191
10. Believers comforted — 192

Ch. 12 — Yūsuf: JOSEPH — 194
1. Joseph's Vision — 194
2. Brothers' plot against Joseph — 194
3. Joseph's Firmness under Temptation — 195
4. Joseph is Imprisoned — 196
5. Joseph Preaches in Prison — 197
6. Joseph interprets King's Vision — 198
7. Joseph cleared of Charges — 199

Part 13 — 199
8. Joseph helps his Brothers — 199
9. The youngest brother — 201
10. Joseph discloses his Identity — 201
11. Israel goes to Egypt — 203
12. Lesson for Prophet's Opponents — 204

Ch. 13 — Al-Ra'd: THE THUNDER — 205
1. Truth of Revelation — 205
2. Fall and Rise of Nations — 206
3. Good and Evil bear Reward — 207
4. Revolution to be brought about by Qur'ān — 208
5. Opposition will fail — 209
6. Steady Progress of Truth — 209

CONTENTS

Section — — — — — — — — — — — — — — — — — — — *Page*

Ch. 14 — Ibrāhīm: ABRAHAM — — — — 211
1. Revelation dispels darkness — — — — — 211
2. Truth is rejected first — — — — — — — 211
3. Opposition is at last destroyed — — — — 212
4. Truth is Confirmed — — — — — — — — 213
5. Man's injustice in rejecting Truth — — — 214
6. Abraham's prayer — — — — — — — — 214
7. End of Opposition — — — — — — — — 215

Ch. 15 — Al-Ḥijr: THE ROCK — — — — — 217
1. The Qur'ān is guarded — — — — — — — 217

Part 14 — — — — — — — — — — — — — — — 217
2. Evil will be destroyed — — — — — — — 218
3. Devil's Opposition to Righteous — — — — 218
4. Mercy for the Righteous — Abraham — — 219
5. Lot and Shu'aib — — — — — — — — — 220
6. Warning to Dwellers of Rock — — — — — 221

Ch. 16 — Al-Naḥl: THE BEE — — — — — 223
1. Revelation testified by Nature — — — — 223
2. Nature upholds Unity — — — — — — — 223
3. Denial due to Ignorance — — — — — — 224
4. Wicked meet Disgrace — — — — — — — 225
5. Prophets raised to explain — — — — — — 226
6. Opponents' Doom — — — — — — — — 226
7. Human Nature revolts against Polytheism — 227
8. Iniquity of Deniers — — — — — — — — 228
9. Parables showing Truth of Revelation — — 228
10. Recipient of Revelation — — — — — — 229
11. Punishment withheld — — — — — — — 230
12. Prophets testify — — — — — — — — — 230
13. Revelation enjoins Good — — — — — — 231
14. Qur'ān not a Forgery — — — — — — — 232
15. Fate of Opponents — — — — — — — — 233
16. Way to Greatness — — — — — — — — 234

CONTENTS

Section	Page

Part 15 — 235

Ch. 17 — Banī Isrā'īl: THE ISRAELITES — 235
1. Israelites Punished Twice — 235
2. Every deed has a consequence — 236
3. Moral Precepts — 237
4. Moral Precepts — 238
5. Disbelievers grow harder — 238
6. Punishment must follow — 239
7. Devil's Opposition to the Righteous — 240
8. Opposition to the Prophet — 241
9. Truth will prevail — 242
10. Qur'ān — a unique Guidance — 242
11. Justice of Retribution — 243
12. Comparison with Moses — 244

Ch. 18 — Al-Kahf: THE CAVE — 246
1. A Warning to Christians — 246
2. Dwellers in the Cave — 247
3. Dwellers in the Cave — 247
4. Qur'ān as a Guidance — 248
5. A Parable — 249
6. Guilty are judged — 250
7. Their Helplessness — 251
8. Warning is disregarded — 251
9. Moses' search of Knowledge — 252
10. Moses' search of Knowledge — 253

Part 16 — 253
11. <u>Dh</u>u-l-qarnian — Gog and Magog — 254
12. Christian Nations — 255

Ch. 19 — Maryam: MARY — 257
1. Zacharias and John — 257
2. Mary and Jesus — 258
3. Abraham — 259
4. Other Prophets are raised — 260
5. How Opponents were dealt with — 261

CONTENTS

Section — *Page*

6. False doctrine of Sonship — 262

Ch. 20 — Ṭā Hā — 264
1. Moses is called — 264
2. Moses and Aaron go to Pharaoh — 265
3. Moses and Enchanters — 267
4. Israelites worship Calf — 268
5. End of Calf-worship — 269
6. The Prophet's Opponents — 270
7. The Devil's misleading — 271
8. Punishment is certain — 272

Part 17 — 274

Ch. 21 — Al-Anbiyā': THE PROPHETS — 274
1. Judgment approaches — 274
2. Truth triumphed always — 274
3. Truth of revelation — 276
4. Allāh deals Mercifully — 277
5. Abraham is Delivered — 277
6. Allāh always delivers Prophets — 279
7. Righteous will inherit land — 280

Ch. 22 — Al-Ḥajj: THE PILGRIMAGE — 282
1. The Judgment — 282
2. Certainty of Divine Help — 283
3. Believers are Triumphant — 284
4. Pilgrimage — 284
5. Sacrifices — 285
6. Believers permitted to fight — 286
7. Opposition to the Prophet — 287
8. Faithful shall be established — 288
9. Divine mercy to men — 288
10. Polytheism will be uprooted — 289

Part 18 — 291

Ch. 23 — Al-Mu'minūn: THE BELIEVERS — 291
1. Success of the Faithful — 291

CONTENTS

Section — *Page*

2. Noah — 292
3. Prophets after Noah — 293
4. Higher Values of Life — 294
5. Polytheism is self-condemned — 296
6. Regrets of the Wicked — 296

Ch. 24 — Al-Nūr: THE LIGHT — 299
1. Law relating to Adultery — 299
2. 'Ā'ishah's Slanderers — 300
3. Slanderers of Women — 301
4. Preventive Measures — 301
5. Manifestation of Divine Light — 303
6. Manifestation of Divine Power — 303
7. Establishment of the Kingdom of Islām — 304
8. Respect for Privacy — 305
9. State matters take Precedence — 306

Ch. 25 — Al-Furqān: THE DISCRIMINATION — 308
1. A Warner for all Nations — 308
2. Truth of Warning — 309

Part 19 — 310
3. Day of Discrimination — 310
4. Lesson in Fate of Former People — 311
5. A lesson from Nature — 311
6. The Transformation wrought — 313

Ch. 26 — Al-Shu'arā': THE POETS — 315
1. The Prophet is consoled — 315
2. Moses called and sent to Pharaoh — 315
3. Moses and Enchanters — 316
4. Moses delivered, Pharaoh drowned — 317
5. History of Abraham — 318
6. History of Noah — 319
7. History of Hūd — 320
8. History of Ṣāliḥ — 321
9. History of Lot — 322
10. History of Shu'aib — 322

Section	Page
11. Prophet's Opponents warned	323

Ch. 27 — Al-Naml: THE NAML
1. Reference to Moses' History	326
2. History of Solomon	327
3. History of Solomon	328
4. Ṣāliḥ and Lot	329
5. The Faithful will be exalted	330

Part 20
	330
6. The Spiritual Resurrection	331
7. Passing away of Opposition	332

Ch. 28 — Al-Qaṣaṣ: THE NARRATIVE
1. History of Moses	334
2. History of Moses	335
3. History of Moses	336
4. History of Moses	337
5. A Prophet like Moses	338
6. Truth of Revelation	339
7. Opponents shall be brought low	340
8. Korah's wealth ruins him	341
9. The Prophet will return to Makkah	342

Ch. 29 — Al-'Ankabūt: THE SPIDER
1. Trials purify	344
2. Noah and Abraham	345
3. Abraham and Lot	346
4. Opposition to Truth ever a Failure	346

Part 21
	348
5. Qur'ān is a Purifier	348
6. Warning and Consolation	348
7. Triumph of the Faithful	349

Ch. 30 — Al-Rūm: THE ROMANS
1. A Great Prophecy	351
2. The two Parties	352
3. Manifestation of Divine Power in Nature	352

CONTENTS

Section — *Page*

4. Appeal to Human Nature	353
5. A Transformation	354
6. Overthrow of Opposition	355

Ch. 31 — Luqmān — 357
1. Believers will be Successful — 357
2. Luqmān's Advice to his Son — 358
3. Greatness of Divine Power — 358
4. The Doom comes — 360

Ch. 32 — Al-Sajdah: THE ADORATION — 361
1. Islām will be established — 361
2. Believers and Disbelievers compared — 362
3. Dead Earth will receive life — 363

Ch. 33 — Al-Aḥzāb: THE ALLIES — 364
1. Spiritual and Physical Relationship — 364
2. Allies' Attack on Madīnah — 365
3. Allies' Flight: Quraizah punished — 366
4. Prophet's Domestic Simplicity — 367

Part 22 — 367
5. Prophet's Marriage with Zainab — 368
6. Prophet's Marriages — 369
7. Rules of Conduct in Domestic Relations — 370
8. Spreading Evil Reports — 371
9. Exhortation to the Faithful — 372

Ch. 34 — Al-Saba': THE SABA' — 373
1. Judgment is certain — 373
2. Favours followed by Retribution — 374
3. A Victory for Muslims — 375
4. Leaders of Evil — 376
5. Wealth stands not for Greatness — 377
6. Truth will prosper — 377

Ch. 35 — Al-Fāṭir: THE ORIGINATOR — 379
1. Divine Favours — 379
2. Truth will prevail — 379

CONTENTS

Section	Page
3. A New Generation will be raised	380
4. The Elect	381
5. Punishment due to evil deeds	382

Ch. 36 — Yā Sīn — 384
1. Truth of the Qur'ān --- 384
2. Confirmation of the Truth --- 384

Part 23 --- 385
3. Signs of the Truth --- 386
4. Reward and Punishment --- 387
5. The Resurrection --- 388

Ch. 37 — Al-Ṣāffāt: THOSE RANGING IN RANKS 390
1. Unity will prevail --- 390
2. The Judgment --- 391
3. Noah and Abraham --- 393
4. Moses, Aaron, Elias and Lot --- 394
5. Jonah and the Prophet's Triumph --- 395

Ch. 38 — Ṣād --- 398
1. The Enemy's Discomfiture --- 398
2. David's Enemies --- 399
3. Solomon and his Enemies --- 400
4. Job — Triumph of the Righteous --- 400
5. Opposition to Prophets --- 402

Ch. 39 — Al-Zumar: THE COMPANIES --- 404
1. Obedience to Allāh --- 404
2. Believers and Disbelievers --- 405
3. A Perfect Guidance --- 406

Part 24 --- 407
4. Rejectors will be abased --- 407
5. Punishment cannot be averted --- 408
6. Divine Mercy --- 409
7. The Final Judgment --- 410
8. Each Party meets its Desert --- 410

CONTENTS xvii

Section — *Page*

Ch. 40 — Al-Mu'min: THE BELIEVER — 412
1. Protection of the Faithful — 412
2. Failure of Opponents — 413
3. A Warning in Moses' History — 414
4. A Believer of Pharaoh's People — 414
5. End of Pharaoh — 415
6. Messengers Receive Divine Help — 416
7. Power of Allāh — 417
8. End of Opposition — 418
9. End of Opposition — 419

Ch. 41 — Hā Mīm — 420
1. Invitation to Truth — 420
2. The Warning — 420
3. Man's Evidence against Himself — 421
4. Believers strengthened — 422
5. Effect of Revelation — 423
6. Gradual Spread of Truth — 424

Part 25 — 424

Ch. 42 — Al-Shūrā: THE COUNSEL — 426
1. Divine mercy in giving warning — 426
2. Judgment is given — 426
3. Allāh's Dealing is Just — 428
4. Believers should be Patient — 429
5. Revelation guides aright — 430

Ch. 43 — Zukhruf: GOLD — 432
1. Revelation is a Divine Favour — 432
2. Polytheism condemned — 433
3. Allāh's Choice of a Prophet — 433
4. Opposition to Truth is punished — 434
5. Pharaoh's Opposition to Moses — 435
6. Jesus as a Prophet — 436
7. The Two Parties — 436

Ch. 44 — Al-Dukhān: THE DROUGHT — 439
1. Lighter Punishment followed by Severer — 439

Section	Page
2. Good and Evil Rewarded	440
3. Good and Evil Rewarded	441

Ch. 45 — Al-Jāthiyah: THE KNEELING — 442
1. Denial of Revelation — 442
2. Truth of the Revelation — 443
3. Denial of Judgment — 443
4. The Doom — 444

Part 26 — 446

Ch. 46 — Al-Aḥqāf: THE SANDHILLS — 446
1. Truth of Revelation — 446
2. Witness of Truth — 447
3. The Fate of 'Ād — 448
4. A Warning — 449

Ch. 47 — Muḥammad — 451
1. Opponents will perish in War — 451
2. Oppressors brought low — 452
3. The Weak-hearted Ones — 453
4. An Exhortation — 453

Ch. 48 — Al-Fatḥ: THE VICTORY — 455
1. Ḥudaibiyah Truce — a Victory — 455
2. The Defaulters — 456
3. More Victories for Islām — 457
4. Ultimate Triumph of Islām — 458

Ch. 49 — Al-Ḥujurāt: THE APARTMENTS — 459
1. Respect for the Prophet — 459
2. Respect for Muslim Brotherhood — 460

Ch. 50 — Qāf — 462
1. The Resurrection — 462
2. The Resurrection — 463
3. The Resurrection — 463

Ch. 51 — Al-Dhāriyāt: THE SCATTERERS — 465
1. Falsehood is doomed — 465

CONTENTS xix

Section	Page
2. Fate of Previous Nations	466

Part 27 — 466
3. Judgment is sure — 467

Ch. 52 — Al-Ṭūr: THE MOUNTAIN — 468
1. Success of the Faithful — 468
2. Opponents are doomed — 469

Ch. 53 — Al-Najm: THE STAR — 471
1. Eminence attained by the Prophet — 471
2. Nothing avails against Truth — 472
3. Allāh's Power manifested — 472

Ch. 54 — Al-Qamar: THE MOON — 474
1. Judgment to overtake Opponents — 474
2. Thamūd and Lot's People — 475
3. Pharaoh and the Prophet's Opponents — 476

Ch. 55 — Al-Raḥmān: THE BENEFICENT — 477
1. Divine Beneficence — 477
2. Judgment of the Guilty — 478
3. Reward for the Righteous — 479

Ch. 56 — Al-Wāqi'ah: THE EVENT — 481
1. Three Classes of Men — 481
2. The Guilty — 482
3. Judgment is Inevitable — 483

Ch. 57 — Al-Ḥadīd: IRON — 485
1. Establishment of God's Kingdom — 485
2. Light and Life given by Prophet — 486
3. Truth shall be established — 487
4. Double Reward for Believers — 488

Part 28 — 489

Ch. 58 — Al-Mujādilah: THE PLEADING WOMAN — 489
1. Safeguarding Women's Rights — 489
2. Secret Counsels condemned — 490

CONTENTS

Section	Page
3. Guard against Internal Enemy	491

Ch. 59 — Al-Ḥashr: THE BANISHMENT — 493
1. The Exiled Jews — 493
2. Hypocrites deceive Jews — 494
3. An Exhortation — 495

Ch. 60 — Al-Mumtaḥanah: THE WOMAN WHO IS EXAMINED — 497
1. Friendly Relations with Enemies — 497
2. Friendly Relations with non-Muslims — 498

Ch. 61 — Al-Ṣaff: THE RANKS — 500
1. Triumph of Islām — 500
2. Establish Truth by Sacrifices — 501

Ch. 62 — Al-Jumu'ah: THE CONGREGATION — 502
1. Muslims chosen for Divine Favours — 502
2. Friday Prayer — 503

Ch. 63 — Al-Munāfiqūn: THE HYPOCRITES — 504
1. The Hypocrites — 504
2. An Exhortation — 505

Ch. 64 — Al-Taghābun: THE MANIFESTATION OF LOSSES — 506
1. Disbelievers Warned — 506
2. An Exhortation — 507

Ch. 65 — Al-Ṭalāq: THE DIVORCE — 508
1. Supplementary Divorce Rules — 508
2. Makkah warned — 509

Ch. 66 — Al-Taḥrim: THE PROHIBITION — 510
1. Prophet's Domestic Relations — 510
2. Progress of Faithful — 511

Part 29 — 512

Ch. 67 — Al-Mulk: THE KINGDOM — 512
1. The Kingdom of God — 512

CONTENTS xxi

Section — *Page*

2. The Disbelievers' Doom — 513

Ch. 68 — Al-Qalam: THE PEN — 515
1. Not a Madman's Message — 515
2. A Reminder for Nations — 516

Ch. 69 — Al-Ḥāqqah: THE SURE TRUTH — 518
1. The Doom — 518
2. False Allegations refuted — 519

Ch. 70 — Al-Ma'ārij: THE WAYS OF ASCENT — 521
1. Certainty of the Punishment — 521
2. A New Nation to be raised — 522

Ch. 71 — Nūḥ: NOAH — 524
1. Noah preaches — 524
2. Destruction of Transgressors — 525

Ch. 72 — Al-Jinn: THE JINN — 526
1. Foreign Believers — 526
2. Protection of Revelation — 527

Ch. 73 — Al-Muzzammil: THE ONE COVERING HIMSELF UP — 528
1. Prophet enjoined to pray — 528
2. Prayer enjoined on Muslims — 529

Ch. 74 — Al-Muddaththir: THE ONE WRAPPING HIMSELF UP — 530
1. The Prophet enjoined to warn — 530
2. The Warning — 531

Ch. 75 — Al-Qiyāmah: THE RESURRECTION — 533
1. Truth of the Resurrection — 533
2. The Dead Rise — 534

Ch. 76 — Al-Insān: THE MAN — 535
1. Attainment of Perfection — 535
2. Another Generation raised — 536

CONTENTS

Section	Page

Ch. 77 — Al-Mursalāt: THOSE SENT FORTH — 537
1. Consequences of Rejection — 537
2. Consequences of Rejection — 538

Part 30 — 539

Ch. 78 — Al-Naba': THE ANNOUNCEMENT — 539
1. The Day of Decision — 539
2. The Day of Decision — 540

Ch. 79 — Al-Nāzi'āt: THOSE WHO YEARN — 541
1. The Great Commotion — 541
2. The Great Calamity — 542

Ch. 80 — 'Abasa: HE FROWNED — 543

Ch. 81 — Al-Takwir: THE FOLDING UP — 545

Ch. 82 — Al-Infiṭār: THE CLEAVING — 547

Ch. 83 — Al-Taṭfīf: DEFAULT IN DUTY — 548

Ch. 84 — Al-Inshiqāq: THE BURSTING ASUNDER — 550

Ch. 85 — Al-Burūj: THE STARS — 552

Ch. 86 — Al-Ṭāriq: THE COMER BY NIGHT — 553

Ch. 87 — Al-A'lā: THE MOST HIGH — 554

Ch. 88 — Al-Ghāshiyah: THE OVERWHELMING EVENT — 555

Ch. 89 — Al-Fajr: THE DAYBREAK — 556

Ch. 90 — Al-Balad: THE CITY — 558

Ch. 91 — Al-Shams: THE SUN — 559

Ch. 92 — Al-Lail: THE NIGHT — 560

Ch. 93 — Al-Ḍuḥā: THE BRIGHTNESS OF THE DAY — 561

CONTENTS xxiii

Section -------- *Page*

Ch. 94 — Al-Inshirāḥ: THE EXPANSION ----- 562

Ch. 95 — Al-Tīn: THE FIG -------------- 562

Ch. 96 — Al-'Alaq: THE CLOT ----------- 563

Ch. 97 — Al-Qadr: THE MAJESTY --------- 564

Ch. 98 — Al-Bayyinah: THE CLEAR EVIDENCE 565

Ch. 99 — Al-Zilzāl: THE SHAKING -------- 566

Ch. 100 — Al-'Ādiyāt: THE ASSAULTERS --- 567

Ch. 101 — Al-Qāri'ah: THE CALAMITY ----- 568

Ch. 102 — Al-Takāthur: THE ABUNDANCE
    OF WEALTH ---------------------- 569

Ch. 103 — Al-'Aṣr: THE TIME ------------ 570

Ch. 104 — Al-Humazah: THE SLANDERER --- 570

Ch. 105 — Al-Fīl: THE ELEPHANT --------- 571

Ch. 106 — Al-Quraish: THE QURAISH ----- 571

Ch. 107 — Al-Mā'ūn: ACTS OF KINDNESS --- 572

Ch. 108 — Al-Kauthar: THE ABUNDANCE
    OF GOOD ------------------------ 572

Ch. 109 — Al-Kāfirūn: THE DISBELIEVERS -- 573

Ch. 110 — Al-Naṣr: THE HELP ------------ 573

Ch. 111 — Al-Lahab: THE FLAME --------- 574

Ch. 112 — Al-Ikhlāṣ: THE UNITY --------- 574

Ch. 113 — Al-Falaq: THE DAWN ---------- 575

Ch. 114 — Al-Nās: THE MEN ------------- 575

Index -------------------------------- 576

سُورَةُ الْفَاتِحَةِ مَكِّيَّةٌ

بِسْمِ اللهِ الرَّحْمٰنِ الرَّحِيمِ ۞

اَلْحَمْدُ لِلّٰهِ رَبِّ الْعٰلَمِينَ ۞

الرَّحْمٰنِ الرَّحِيمِ ۞

مٰلِكِ يَوْمِ الدِّينِ ۞

اِيَّاكَ نَعْبُدُ وَاِيَّاكَ نَسْتَعِينُ ۞

اِهْدِنَا الصِّرَاطَ الْمُسْتَقِيمَ ۞

صِرَاطَ الَّذِينَ اَنْعَمْتَ عَلَيْهِمْ غَيْرِ

الْمَغْضُوبِ عَلَيْهِمْ وَلَا الضَّالِّينَ ۞

CHAPTER 1
Al-Fātiḥah: **The Opening**

(REVEALED AT MAKKAH: 7 *verses*)

In the name of Allāh, the Beneficent, the Merciful.

1 Praise be to Allāh, the Lord of the worlds,
2 The Beneficent, the Merciful,
3 Master of the day of Requital.
4 Thee do we serve and Thee do we beseech for help.
5 *Guide us on the right path,*
6 The path of those upon whom Thou hast bestowed favours,
7 Not those upon whom wrath is brought down, nor those who go astray.

Part 1

CHAPTER 2

Al-Baqarah: **The Cow**

(REVEALED AT MADĪNAH: 40 *sections*; 286 *verses*)

SECTION 1:
Fundamental Principles of Islām

In the name of Allāh, the Beneficent, the Merciful.

1 I, Allāh, am the best Knower.

2 This Book, there is no doubt in it, is a guide to those who keep their duty,

3 Who believe in the Unseen and keep up prayer and spend out of what We have given them,

4 And who believe in that which has been revealed to thee and that which was revealed before thee, and of the Hereafter they are sure.

5 These are on a right course from their Lord and these it is that are successful.

6 Those who disbelieve — it being alike to them whether thou warn them or warn them not — they will not believe.

7 Allāh has sealed their hearts and their hearing; and there is a covering on their eyes, and for them is a grievous chastisement.

SECTION 2:
Lip-profession

8 And there are some people who say: We believe in Allāh and the Last Day; and they are not believers.

9 They seek to deceive Allāh and those who believe, and they deceive only themselves and they perceive not.

10 In their hearts is a disease, so Allāh increased their disease, and for them is a painful chastisement because they lie.

11 And when it is said to them, Make not mischief in the land, they say: We are but peacemakers.

12 Now surely they are

THE COW

13 And when it is said to them, Believe as the people believe, they say: Shall we believe as the fools believe? Now surely they are the fools, but they know not.

14 And when they meet those who believe, they say, We believe; and when they are alone with their devils, they say: Surely we are with you, we were only mocking.

15 Allāh will pay them back their mockery, and He leaves them alone in their inordinacy, blindly wandering on.

16 These are they who buy error for guidance, so their bargain brings no gain, nor are they guided.

17 Their parable is as the parable of one who kindles a fire, but when it illumines all around him, Allāh takes away their light, and leaves them in darkness — they cannot see.

18 Deaf, dumb, (and) blind, so they return not:

19 Or like abundant rain from the cloud in which is darkness, and thunder and lightning; they put their fingers into their ears because of the thunder-peal, for fear of death. And Allāh encompasses the disbelievers.

20 The lightning almost takes away their sight. Whenever it shines on them they walk in it, and when it becomes dark to them they stand still. And if Allāh had pleased, He would have taken away their hearing and their sight. Surely Allāh is Possessor of power over all things.

SECTION 3:
Divine Unity

21 O men, serve your Lord Who created you and those before you, so that you may guard against evil,

22 Who made the earth a resting-place for you and the heaven a structure, and sends down rain from the clouds then brings forth with its fruits for your sustenance; so do not set up rivals to Allāh while you know.

23 And if you are in doubt as to that which We have revealed to Our servant, then produce a chapter like it and call on your helpers besides Allāh if you are truthful.

24 But if you do (it) not — and you can never do (it) — then be on your guard against the fire whose fuel is men and stones; it is prepared for the disbelievers.

25 And give good news to those who believe and do good deeds, that for them are Gardens in which rivers flow. Whenever they are given a portion of the fruit thereof, they will say: This is what was given to us before; and they are given the like of it. And for them therein are pure companions and therein they will abide.

26 Surely Allāh disdains not to set forth any parable — a gnat or anything above that. Then as for those who believe, they know that it is *the truth from their Lord*; and as for those who disbelieve, they say: What is it that Allāh means by this parable? Many He leaves in error by it and many He leads aright by it. And He leaves in error by it only the transgressors.

27 Who break the covenant of Allāh after its confirmation and cut asunder what Allāh has ordered to be joined, and make mischief in the land. These it is that are the losers.

28 How can you deny Allāh and you were without life and He gave you life? Again, He will cause you to die and again bring you to life, then you shall be brought back to Him.

29 He it is Who created for you all that is in the earth. And He directed Himself to the heaven, so He made them complete seven heavens; and He is Knower of all things.

SECTION 4:
Greatness of Man and Need for Revelation

30 And when thy Lord said to the angels, I am going to place a ruler in the earth, they said: Wilt Thou place in it such as make mischief in it and shed blood? And we celebrate Thy praise and extol Thy holiness. He said: Surely I know what you know not.

31 And He taught Adam all the names, then present-

THE COW

ed them to the angels; He said: Tell Me the names of those if you are right.

32 They said: *Glory be to Thee! we have no knowledge but that which Thou hast taught us. Surely Thou art the Knowing, the Wise.*

33 He said: O Adam, inform them of their names. So when he informed them of their names, He said: Did I not say to you that I know what is unseen in the heavens and the earth? And I know what you manifest and what you hide.

34 And when We said to the angels, Be submissive to Adam, they submitted, but Iblīs (did not). He refused and was proud, and he was one of the disbelievers.

35 And We said: O Adam, dwell thou and thy wife in the garden, and eat from it a plenteous (food) wherever you wish, and approach not this tree, lest you be of the unjust.

36 But the devil made them slip from it, and caused them to depart from the state in which they were. And We said: Go forth, some of you are the enemies of others. And there is for you in the earth an abode and a provision *for a time.*

37 Then Adam received (revealed) words from his Lord, and He turned to him (mercifully). Surely He is Oft-returning (to mercy), the Merciful.

38 We said: Go forth from this (state) all. Surely there will come to you a guidance from Me, then whoever follows My guidance, no fear shall come upon them, nor shall they grieve.

39 And (as to) those who disbelieve in and reject Our messages, they are the companions of the Fire; in it they will abide.

SECTION 5:
Israelite Prophecies fulfilled in Qur'ān

40 O Children of Israel, call to mind My favour which I bestowed on you and be faithful to (your) covenant with Me, I shall fulfil (My) covenant with you; and Me, Me alone, should you fear.

41 And believe in that

which I have revealed, verifying that which is with you, and be not the first to deny it; neither take a mean price for My messages; and keep your duty to Me, Me alone.

42 And mix not up truth with falsehood, nor hide the truth while you know.

43 And keep up prayer and pay the poor-rate and bow down with those who bow down.

44 Do you enjoin men to be good and neglect your own souls while you read the Book? Have you then no sense?

45 And seek assistance through patience and prayer, and this is hard except for the humble ones,

46 Who know that they will meet their Lord and that to Him they will return.

SECTION 6:
Divine Favours on Israel

47 O Children of Israel, call to mind My favour which I bestowed on you and that I made you excel the nations.

48 And guard yourselves against a day when no soul will avail another in the least, neither will intercession be accepted on its behalf, nor will compensation be taken from it, nor will they be helped.

49 And when We delivered you from Pharaoh's people, who subjected you to severe torment, killing your sons and sparing your women, and in this there was a great trial from your Lord.

50 And when We parted the sea for you, so We saved you and drowned the people of Pharaoh while you saw.

51 And when We appointed a time of forty nights with Moses, then you took the calf (for a god) after him, and you were unjust.

52 Then We pardoned you after that so that you might give thanks.

53 And when We gave Moses the Book and the Discrimination that you might walk aright.

54 And when Moses said to his people: O my people, you have surely wronged yourselves by taking the calf (for a god), so turn to your Creator (penitently), and kill your passions. That is best for you with your Creator. So He turned to you (mercifully). Surely He is the Oft-returning (to mercy), the Merciful.

55 And when you said: O Moses, we will not believe in thee till we see Allāh manifestly, so the punishment overtook you while you looked on.

56 Then We raised you up after your stupor that you might give thanks.

57 And We made the clouds to give shade over you and We sent to you manna and quails. Eat of the good things that We have given you. And they did not do Us any harm, but they wronged their own souls.

58 And when We said: Enter this city, then eat from it a plenteous (food) whence you wish, and enter the gate submissively, and make petition for forgiveness. We will forgive you your wrongs and increase the reward of those who do good (to others).

59 But those who were unjust changed the word which had been spoken to them, for another saying, so We sent upon the wrongdoers a pestilence from heaven, because they transgressed.

SECTION 7:
Divine Favours on Israel

60 And when Moses prayed for water for his people, We said: March on to the rock with thy staff. So there flowed from it twelve springs. Each tribe knew their drinking-place. Eat and drink of the provisions of Allāh, and act not corruptly, making mischief in the land.

61 And when you said: O Moses, we cannot endure one food, so pray thy Lord on our behalf to bring forth for us out of what the earth grows, of its herbs and its cucumbers and its garlic and its lentils and its onions. He said: Would you exchange that which is better for that which is worse? Enter a city, so you will have what you ask for. And abasement and humiliation were stamped upon them, and they incurred Allāh's wrath. That was so because they disbelieved in the messages of Allāh and would kill the prophets unjustly. That was so because they disobeyed and exceeded the limits.

SECTION 8:
Israelites' Degeneration

62 Surely those who believe, and those who are Jews, and the Christians, and the Sabians, whoever believes in Allāh and the Last Day and does good, they have their reward with their Lord, and there is no fear for them, nor shall they grieve.

63 And when We made a covenant with you and raised the mountain above you: Hold fast that which We have given you, and bear in mind what is in it, so that you may guard against evil.

64 Then after that you turned back; and had it not been for the grace of Allāh and His mercy on you, you had certainly been among the losers.

65 And indeed you know those among you who violated the Sabbath, so We said to them: Be (as) apes, despised and hated.

66 So We made them an example to those who witnessed it and those who came after it and an admonition to those who guard against evil.

67 And when Moses said to his people: Surely Allāh commands you to sacrifice a cow. They said: Dost thou ridicule us? He said: I seek refuge with Allāh from being one of the ignorant.

68 They said: Call on thy Lord for our sake to make it plain to us what she is. (Moses) said: He says, Surely she is a cow neither advanced in age nor too young, of middle age between these (two); so do what you are commanded.

69 They said: Call on thy Lord for our sake to make it clear to us what her colour is. (Moses) said: He says, She is a yellow cow; her colour is intensely yellow delighting the beholders.

70 They said: Call on thy Lord for our sake to make it

clear to us what she is, for surely to us the cows are all alike, and if Allāh please we shall surely be guided aright.

71 (Moses) said: He says: She is a cow not made submissive to plough the land, nor does she water the tilth, sound, without a blemish in her. They said: Now thou hast brought the truth. So they slaughtered her, though they had not the mind to do (it).

SECTION 9:
They grow in Hard-heartedness

72 And when you (almost) killed a man, then you disagreed about it. And Allāh was to bring forth that which you were going to hide.

73 So We said: Smite him with it partially. Thus Allāh brings the dead to life, and He shows you His signs that you may understand.

74 Then your hearts hardened after that, so that they were like rocks, rather worse in hardness. And surely there are some rocks from which streams burst forth; and there are some of them which split asunder so water flows from them; and there are some of them which fall down for the fear of Allāh. And Allāh is not heedless of what you do.

75 Do you then hope that they would believe in you, and a party from among them indeed used to hear the word of Allāh, then altered it after they had understood it, and they know (this).

76 And when they meet those who believe they say, We believe, and when they are apart one with another they say: Do you talk to *them* of what Allāh has disclosed to you that they may contend with you by this before your Lord? Do you not understand?

77 Do they not know that Allāh knows what they keep secret and what they make known?

78 And some of them are illiterate; they know not the Book but only (from) hearsay, and they do but conjecture.

79 Woe! then to those who write the Book with

their hands then say, This is from Allāh; so that they may take for it a small price. So woe! to them for what their hands write and woe! to them for what they earn.

80 And they say: Fire will not touch us but for a few days. Say: Have you received a promise from Allāh? Then Allāh will not fail to perform His promise. Or do you speak against Allāh what you know not?

81 Yea, whoever earns evil and his sins beset him on every side, those are the companions of the Fire; therein they abide.

82 And those who believe and do good deeds, these are the owners of the Garden; therein they abide.

SECTION 10:
Their Covenant and its Violation

83 And when We made a covenant with the Children of Israel: You shall serve none but Allāh. And do good to (your) parents, and to the near of kin and to orphans and the needy, and speak good (words) to (all) men, and keep up prayer and pay the poor-rate. Then you turned back except a few of you, and you are averse.

84 And when We made a covenant with you: You shall not shed your blood, nor turn your people out of your cities; then you promised and you bear witness.

85 Yet you it is who would slay your people and turn a party from among you out of their homes, backing each other up against them unlawfully and exceeding the limits. And if they should come to you as captives you would ransom them, whereas their turning out itself was unlawful for you. Do you then believe in a part of the Book and disbelieve in the other? What then is the reward of such among you as do this but disgrace in the life of this world, and on the day of Resurrection they shall be sent back to the most grievous chastisement. And Allāh is not heedless of what you do.

86 These are they who buy the life of this world for

THE COW

the Hereafter, so their chastisement shall not be lightened, nor shall they be helped.

SECTION 11:
They reject the Prophet

87 And We indeed gave Moses the Book and We sent messengers after him one after another; and We gave Jesus, son of Mary, clear arguments and strengthened him with the Holy Spirit. Is it then that whenever there came to you a messenger with what your souls desired not, you were arrogant? And some you gave the lie to and others you would slay.

88 And they say: Our hearts are repositories. Nay, Allāh has cursed them on account of their unbelief; so little it is that they believe.

89 And when there came to them a Book from Allāh verifying that which they have, and aforetime they used to pray for victory against those who disbelieved — but when there came to them that which they recognized, they disbelieved in it; so Allāh's curse is on the disbelievers.

90 Evil is that for which they sell their souls — that they should deny that which Allāh has revealed, out of envy that Allāh should send down of His grace on whomsoever of His servants He pleases; so they incur wrath upon wrath. And there is an abasing chastisement for the disbelievers.

91 And when it is said to them, Believe in that which Allāh has revealed, they say: We believe in that which was revealed to us. And they deny what is besides that, while it is the Truth verifying that which they have. Say: Why then did you kill Allāh's prophets before (this) if you were believers?

92 And Moses indeed came to you with clear arguments, then you took the calf (for a god) in his absence and you were wrongdoers.

93 And when We made a covenant with you and raised the mountain above you: Take hold of that which We have given you with firmness and obey.

They said: We hear and disobey. And they were made to imbibe (the love of) the calf into their hearts on account of their disbelief. Say: Evil is that which your faith bids you if you are believers.

94 Say: If the abode of the Hereafter with Allāh is specially for you to the exclusion of the people, then invoke death if you are truthful.

95 And they will never invoke it on account of what their hands have sent on before, and Allāh knows the wrongdoers.

96 And thou wilt certainly find them the greediest of men for life, (greedier) even than those who set up gods (with God). One of them loves to be granted a life of a thousand years, and his being granted a long life will in no way remove him further off from the chastisement. And Allāh is Seer of what they do.

SECTION 12:
Their Enmity to the Prophet

97 Say: Whoever is an enemy to Gabriel — for surely he revealed it to thy heart by Allāh's command, verifying that which is before it and a guidance and glad tidings for the believers.

98 Whoever is an enemy to Allāh and His angels and His messengers and Gabriel and Michael, then surely Allāh is an enemy to disbelievers.

99 And We indeed have revealed to thee clear messages, and none disbelieve in them except the transgressors.

100 Is it that whenever they make a covenant, a party of them cast it aside? Nay, most of them have no faith.

101 And when there came to them a messenger from Allāh verifying that which they have, a party of those who were given the Book threw the Book of Allāh behind their backs as if they knew nothing.

102 And they follow what the devils fabricated against the kingdom of Solomon. And Solomon disbelieved not, but the devils disbelieved, teaching men enchantment. And it was not revealed to the two angels in Babel, Hārūt and Mārūt. Nor did they teach (it to) anyone, so that they should have said, We are only a trial, so disbelieve not. But they learn from these two (sources) that by which they make a distinction between a man and his wife. And they cannot hurt with it anyone except with Allāh's permission. And they learn that which harms them and profits them not. And certainly they know that he who buys it has no share of good in the Hereafter. And surely evil is the *price for which* they have sold their souls, did they but know!

103 And if they had believed and kept their duty, reward from Allāh would certainly have been better; did they but know!

SECTION 13:
Previous Scriptures are abrogated

104 O you who believe, say not *Rā'i-nā* and say *Unẓur-nā*, and listen. And for the disbelievers there is a painful chastisement.

105 Neither those who disbelieve from among the people of the Book, nor the polytheists, like that any good should be sent down to you from your Lord. And Allāh chooses whom He pleases for His Mercy; and Allāh is the Lord of mighty grace.

106 Whatever message We abrogate or cause to be forgotten, We bring one better than it or one like it. Knowest thou not that Allāh is Possessor of power over all things?

107 Knowest thou not that Allāh's is the kingdom of the heavens and the earth, and that besides Allāh you have not any friend or helper?

108 Rather you wish to put questions to your Messenger, as Moses was questioned before. And whoever adopts disbelief instead of faith he indeed has lost the right direction of the way.

109 Many of the people of the Book wish that they could turn you back into disbelievers after you have believed, out of envy from themselves, after truth has become manifest to them. But pardon and forgive, till Allāh bring about His command. Surely Allāh is Possessor of power over all things.

110 And keep up prayer and pay the poor-rate. And whatever good you send before for yourselves, you will find it with Allāh. Surely Allāh is Seer of what you do.

111 And they say: None shall enter the Garden except he who is a Jew, or the Christians. These are their vain desires. Say: Bring your proof if you are truthful.

112 Nay, whoever submits himself entirely to Allāh and he is the doer of good (to others), he has his reward from his Lord, and there is no fear for such nor shall they grieve.

SECTION 14: Perfect Guidance is only in Islām

113 And the Jews say, The Christians follow nothing (good), and the Christians say, The Jews follow nothing (good), while they recite the (same) Book. Even thus say those who have no knowledge, like what they say. So Allāh will judge between them on the day of Resurrection in that wherein they differ.

114 And who is more unjust than he who prevents (men) from the mosques of Allāh, from His name being remembered therein, and strives to ruin them? (As for) these, it was not proper for them to enter them except in fear. For them is disgrace in this world, and theirs is a grievous chastisement in the Hereafter.

115 And Allāh's is the East and the West, so whither you turn thither is Allāh's purpose. Surely Allāh is Ample-giving, Knowing.

116 And they say: Allāh has taken to Himself a son — glory be to Him! Rather, whatever is in the heavens and the earth is His. All are obedient to Him.

117 Wonderful Originator of the heavens and the earth! And when He decrees an affair, He says to it only, Be, and it is.

118 And those who have

no knowledge say: Why does not Allāh speak to us or a sign come to us? Even thus said those before them, the like of what they say. Their hearts are all alike. Indeed We have made the messages clear for a people who are sure.

119 Surely We have sent thee with the Truth as a bearer of good news and as a warner, and thou wilt not be called upon to answer for the companions of the flaming Fire.

120 And the Jews will not be pleased with thee, nor the Christians, unless thou follow their religion. Say: Surely Allāh's guidance — that is the (perfect) guidance. And if thou follow their desires after the knowledge that has come to thee thou shalt have from Allāh no friend, nor helper.

121 Those to whom We have given the Book follow it as it ought to be followed. These believe in it. And whoever disbelieves in it, these it is that are the losers.

SECTION 15:
Covenant with Abraham

122 O Children of Israel, call to mind My favour which I bestowed on you and that I made you excel the nations.

123 And be on your guard against a day when no soul will avail another in the least, neither will any compensation be accepted from it, nor will intercession profit it, nor will they be helped.

124 And when his Lord tried Abraham with certain commands he fulfilled them. He said: Surely I will make thee a leader of men. (Abraham) said: And of my offspring? My covenant does not include the wrong-doers, said He.

125 And when We made the House a resort for men and a (place of) security. And: Take ye the place of Abraham for a place of prayer. And We enjoined Abraham and Ishmael, saying: Purify My House for those who visit (it) and those who abide (in it) for devotion and those who bow down (and) those who prostrate themselves.

126 And when Abraham said: My Lord, make this a secure town and provide its people with fruits, such of them as believe in Allāh and the Last Day. He said: And whoever disbelieves, I shall grant him enjoyment for a short while, then I shall drive him to the chastisement of the Fire. And it is an evil destination.

127 And when Abraham and Ishmael raised the foundations of the House: Our Lord, accept from us; surely Thou art the Hearing, the Knowing.

128 Our Lord, and make us both submissive to Thee, and (raise) from our offspring, a nation submissive to Thee, and show us our ways of devotion and turn to us (mercifully); surely Thou art the Oft-returning (to mercy), the Merciful.

129 Our Lord, and raise up in them a Messenger from among them who shall recite to them Thy messages and teach them the Book and the Wisdom, and purify them. Surely Thou art the Mighty, the Wise.

SECTION 16:
The Religion of Abraham

130 And who forsakes the religion of Abraham but he who makes a fool of himself. And certainly We made him pure in this world and in the Hereafter he is surely among the righteous.

131 When his Lord said to him, Submit, he said: I submit myself to the Lord of the worlds.

132 And the same did Abraham enjoin on his sons, and (so did) Jacob: O my sons, surely Allāh has chosen for you (this) religion, so die not unless you are submitting ones.

133 Or were you witnesses when death visited Jacob, when he said to his sons: What will you serve after me? They said: We shall serve thy God and the God of thy fathers, Abraham and Ishmael and Isaac, one God only, and to Him do we submit.

134 Those are a people that have passed away; for them is what they earned and for you what you earn; and you will not be asked of what they did.

THE COW

135 And they say: Be Jews or Christians, you will be on the right course. Say: Nay, (we follow) the religion of Abraham, the upright one, and he was not one of the polytheists.

136 Say: We believe in Allāh and (in) that which has been revealed to us, and (in) that which was revealed to Abraham, and Ishmael and Isaac and Jacob and the tribes, and (in) that which was given to Moses and Jesus, and (in) that which was given to the prophets from their Lord, we do not make any distinction between any of them and to Him do we submit.

137 So if they believe as you believe, they are indeed on the right course; and if they turn back, then they are only in opposition. But Allāh will suffice thee against them; and He is the Hearing, the Knowing.

138 (We take) Allāh's colour, and who is better than Allāh at colouring, and we are His worshippers.

139 Say: Do you dispute with us about Allāh, and He is our Lord and your Lord, and for us are our deeds and for you your deeds; and we are sincere to Him?

140 Or do you say that Abraham and Ishmael and Isaac and Jacob and the tribes were Jews or Christians? Say: Do you know better or Allāh? And who is more unjust than he who conceals a testimony that he has from Allāh? And Allāh is not heedless of what you do.

141 Those are a people that have passed away; and for them is what they earned and for you what you earn; and you will not be asked of what they did.

Part 2
SECTION 17:
The Ka'bah as the Spiritual Centre

142 The fools among the people will say: "What has turned them from their *qiblah* which they had?" Say: The East and the West belong only to Allāh; He guides whom He pleases to the right path.

143 And thus We have made you an exalted nation that you may be the bearers of witness to the people and (that) the Messenger may be a bearer of witness to you. And We did not make that which thou wouldst have to be the *qiblah* but that We might distinguish him who follows the Messenger from him who turns back upon his heels. And it was indeed a hard test except for those whom Allāh has guided. Nor was Allāh going to make your faith to be fruitless. Surely Allāh is Compassionate, Merciful, to the people.

144 Indeed We see the turning of the face to heaven, so We shall surely make thee master of the *qiblah* which thou likest; turn then thy face towards the Sacred Mosque. And wherever you are turn your faces towards it. And those who have been given the Book certainly know that it is the truth from their Lord. And Allāh is not heedless of what they do.

145 And even if thou shouldst bring to those who have been given the Book every sign they would not follow thy *qiblah*, nor canst thou be a follower of their *qiblah*, neither are they the followers of each other's *qiblah*. And if thou shouldst follow their desires after the knowledge that has come to thee, then thou wouldst indeed be of the wrong-doers.

146 Those whom We have given the Book recognize him as they recognize their sons. And a party of them surely conceal the truth while they know.

147 The truth is from thy Lord, so be thou not of the doubters.

SECTION 18:
The Ka'bah as the Spritual Centre

148 And everyone has a goal to which he turns (himself), so vie with one another in good works. Wherever you are, Allāh will bring you all together. Surely Allāh is Possessor of power *over all things*.

149 And from whatsoever place thou comest forth, turn thy face towards the Sacred Mosque. And surely it is the truth from thy Lord. And Allāh is not heedless of what you do.

150 And from whatsoever place thou comest forth turn thy face towards the Sacred Mosque. And wherever you are turn your faces towards it, so that people may have no plea against you except such of them as are unjust — so fear them not and fear Me — and that I may complete My favour to you and that you may go aright.

151 Even as We have sent among you a Messenger from among you, who recites to you Our messages and purifies you and teaches you the Book and the Wisdom and teaches you that which you did not know.

152 Therefore glorify Me, I will make you eminent, and give thanks to Me and be not ungrateful to Me.

SECTION 19:
Hard Trials necessary to establish Truth

153 O you who believe, seek assistance through patience and prayer; surely Allāh is with the patient.

154 And speak not of those who are slain in Allāh's way as dead. Nay, (they are) alive, but you perceive not.

155 And We shall certainly try you with something of fear and hunger and loss of property and lives and fruits. And give good news to the patient,

156 Who, when a misfortune befalls them, say: Surely we are Allāh's, and to Him we shall return.

157 Those are they on whom are blessings and mercy from their Lord; and those are the followers of the right course.

158 The Ṣafā and the Marwah are truly among the signs of Allāh; so whoever makes a pilgrimage to the House or pays a visit (to it), there is no blame on him if he goes round them. And whoever does good spontaneously — surely Allāh is Bountiful in rewarding, Knowing.

159 Those who conceal the clear proofs and the guidance that We revealed after We have made it clear in the Book for men, these it is whom Allāh curses, and those who curse, curse them (too).

160 Except those who repent and amend and make manifest (the truth), these it is to whom I turn (mercifully); and I am the Oft-returning (to mercy), the Merciful.

161 Those who disbelieve and die while they are disbelievers, these it is on whom is the curse of Allāh and the angels and men, of all (of them):

162 Abiding therein; their chastisement shall not be lightened nor shall they be given respite.

163 And your God is one God; there is no God but He! He is the Beneficent, the Merciful.

SECTION 20:
Unity must prevail

164 In the creation of the heavens and the earth, and the alternation of night and day, and the ships that run in the sea with that which profits men, and the water that Allāh sends down from the sky, then gives life therewith to the earth after its death and spreads in it all (kinds of) animals, and the changing of the winds and the clouds made subservient between heaven and earth, there are surely signs for a people who understand.

165 Yet there are some men who take for themselves objects of worship besides Allāh, whom they love as they should love Allāh. And those who believe are stronger in (their) love for Allāh. And O that the wrongdoers had seen, when they see the chastisement, that power is wholly Allāh's, and that Allāh is Severe in chastising!

166 When those who were followed renounce those who followed (them), and they see the chastisement and their ties are cut asunder.

167 And those who followed will say: If we could but return, we would renounce them as they have renounced us. Thus will Allāh show them their deeds to be intense regret to them, and they will not escape from the Fire.

THE COW

SECTION 21:
Prohibited Foods

168 O men, eat the lawful and good things from what is in the earth, and follow not the footsteps of the devil. Surely he is an open enemy to you.

169 He enjoins on you only evil and indecency, and that you speak against Allāh what you know not.

170 And when it is said to them, Follow what Allāh has revealed, they say: Nay, we follow that wherein we found our fathers. What! Even though their fathers had no sense at all, nor did they follow the right way.

171 *And the parable of those who disbelieve is as the parable of one who calls out to that which hears no more than a call and a cry.* Deaf, dumb, blind, so they have no sense.

172 O you who believe, eat of the good things that We have provided you with, and give thanks to Allāh if He it is Whom you serve.

173 He has forbidden you only what dies of itself, and blood, and the flesh of swine, and that over which any other (name) than (that of) Allāh has been invoked. *Then whoever is driven by necessity, not desiring, nor exceeding the limit, no sin is upon him.* Surely Allāh is Forgiving, Merciful.

174 Those who conceal aught of the Book that Allāh has revealed and take for it a small price, they eat nothing but fire into their bellies, and Allāh will not speak to them on the day of Resurrection, nor will He purify them; and for them is a painful chastisement.

175 Those are they who buy error for guidance and chastisement for forgiveness; how bold they are to challenge the Fire!

176 That is because Allāh has revealed the Book with truth. And surely those who disagree about the Book go far in opposition.

SECTION 22:
Retaliation and Bequests

177 It is not righteousness that you turn your faces towards the East and the West, but righteous is the one who believes in Allāh, and the Last Day, and the angels and the Book and the prophets, and gives away wealth out of love for Him to the near of kin and the orphans and the needy and the wayfarer and to those who ask and to set slaves free and keeps up prayer and pays the poor-rate; and the performers of their promise when they make a promise, and the patient in distress and affliction and in the time of conflict. These are they who are truthful; and these are they who keep their duty.

178 O you who believe, retaliation is prescribed for you in the matter of the slain: the free for the free, and the slave for the slave, and the female for the female. But if remission is made to one by his (aggrieved) brother, prosecution (for blood-money) should be according to usage, and payment to him in a good manner. This is an alleviation from your Lord and a mercy. Whoever exceeds the limit after this, will have a painful chastisement.

179 And there is life for you in retaliation, O men of understanding, that you may guard yourselves.

180 It is prescribed for you, when death approaches one of you, if he leaves behind wealth for parents and near relatives, to make a bequest in a kindly manner; it is incumbent upon the dutiful.

181 Then whoever changes it after he has heard it, the sin of it is only upon those who change it. Surely Allāh is Hearing, Knowing.

182 But if one fears a wrong or a sinful course on the part of the testator, and effects an agreement between the parties, there is no blame on him. Surely Allāh is Forgiving, Merciful.

SECTION 23: Fasting

183 O you who believe, fasting is prescribed for you, as it was prescribed for those before you, so that you may guard against evil.

184 For a certain number of days. But whoever among you is sick or on a journey, (he shall fast) a (like) number of other days. And those who find it extremely hard may effect redemption by feeding a poor man. So whoever does good spontaneously, it is *better for him; and that you fast is better for you if you know.*

185 The month of Ramaḍān is that in which the Qur'ān was revealed, a guidance to men and clear proofs of the guidance and the Criterion. So whoever of you is present in the month, he shall fast therein, and whoever is sick or on a journey, (he shall fast) a (like) number of other days. Allāh desires ease for you, and He desires not hardship for you, and (He desires) that you should complete the number and that you should exalt the greatness of Allāh for having guided you and you that you may give thanks.

186 And when My servants ask thee concerning Me, surely I am nigh. I answer the prayer of the suppliant when he calls on Me, so they should hear My call and believe in Me that they may walk in the right way.

187 It is made lawful for you to go in to your wives on the night of the fast. They are an apparel for you and you are an apparel for them. *Allāh knows that you acted unjustly to yourselves, so He turned to you in mercy and removed (the burden) from you.* So now be in contact with them and seek what Allāh has ordained for you, and eat and drink until the whiteness of the day becomes distinct from the blackness of the night at dawn, then complete the fast till nightfall, and touch them not while you keep to the mosques. These are the limits of Allāh, so go not near them. Thus does Allāh make clear His messages for men that they may keep their duty.

188 And swallow not up your property among yourselves by false means, nor seek to gain access thereby to the judges, so that you may swallow up a part of the property of men wrongfully while you know.

SECTION 24:
Fighting in Defence

189 They ask thee of the new moons. Say: They are times appointed for men, and (for) the pilgrimage. And it is not righteousness that you enter the houses by their backs, but he is righteous who keeps his duty. And go into the houses by their doors; and keep your duty to Allāh, that you may be successful.

190 And fight in the way of Allāh against those who fight against you but be not aggressive. Surely Allāh loves not the aggressors.

191 And kill them wherever you find them, and drive them out from where they drove you out, and persecution is worse than slaughter. And fight not with them at the Sacred Mosque until they fight with you in it; so if they fight you (in it), slay them. Such is the recompense of the disbelievers.

192 But if they desist, then surely Allāh is Forgiving, Merciful.

193 And fight them until there is no persecution, and religion is only for Allāh. But if they desist, then there should be no hostility except against the oppressors.

194 The sacred month for the sacred month, and retaliation (is allowed) in sacred things. Whoever then acts aggressively against you, inflict injury on him according to the injury he has inflicted on you and keep your duty to Allāh, and know that Allāh is with those who keep their duty.

195 And spend in the way of Allāh and cast not yourselves to perdition with your own hands and do good (to others). Surely Allāh loves the doers of good.

196 And accomplish the pilgrimage and the visit for Allāh. But if you are prevented, (send) whatever offering is easy to obtain; and shave not your heads until the offering reaches its destination. Then whoever among you is sick or has an ailment of the head, he (may effect) a compensation by fasting or alms or sacrificing. And when you are secure, whoever profits by combining the visit with the pilgrimage (should take) whatever offering is easy to obtain. But he who cannot find (an offering) should fast for three days during the pilgrimage and

THE COW

for seven days when you return. These are ten (days) complete. This is for him whose family is not present in the Sacred Mosque. And keep your duty to Allāh, and know that Allāh is Severe in requiting (evil).

SECTION 25:
The Pilgrimage

197 The months of the pilgrimage are well known; so whoever determines to perform pilgrimage therein there shall be no immodest speech, nor abusing, nor altercation in the pilgrimage. And whatever good you do, Allāh knows it. And make provision for yourselves, the best provision being to keep one's duty. And keep your duty to Me, O men of understanding.

198 It is no sin for you that you seek the bounty of your Lord. So when you press on from 'Arafāt, remember Allāh near the Holy Monument, and remember Him as He has guided you, though before that you were certainly of the erring ones.

199 Then hasten on from where the people hasten on, and ask the forgiveness of Allāh. Surely Allāh is Forgiving, Merciful.

200 And when you have performed your devotions, laud Allāh as you lauded your fathers, rather a more hearty lauding. But there are some people who say, Our Lord, give us in the world. And for such there is no portion in the Hereafter.

201 And there are some among them who say: Our Lord, grant us good in this world and good in the Hereafter, and save us from the chastisement of the Fire.

202 For those there is a portion on account of what they have earned. And Allāh is Swift in reckoning.

203 And remember Allāh during the appointed days. Then whoever hastens off in two days, it is no sin for him; and whoever stays behind, it is no sin for him, for one who keeps his duty. And keep your duty to Allāh, and know that you will be gathered together to Him.

204 And of men is he whose speech about the life

of this world pleases thee, and he calls Allāh to witness as to that which is in his heart, yet he is the most violent of adversaries.

205 And when he holds authority, he makes effort in the land to cause mischief in it and destroy tilth and offspring; and Allāh loves not mischief.

206 And when it is said to him, Be careful of thy duty to Allāh, pride carries him off to sin — so hell is sufficient for him. And certainly evil is the resting-place.

207 And of men is he who sells himself to seek the pleasure of Allāh. And Allāh is Compassionate to the servants.

208 O you who believe, enter into complete peace and follow not the footsteps of the devil. Surely he is your open enemy.

209 But if you slip after clear arguments have come to you, then know that Allāh is Mighty, Wise.

210 They wait for naught but that Allāh should come to them in the shadows of the clouds with angels, and the matter has (already) been decided. And to Allāh are (all) matters returned.

SECTION 26:
Trials and Tribulations

211 Ask of the Children of Israel how many a clear sign We gave them! And whoever changes the favour of Allāh after it has come to him, then surely Allāh is Severe in requiting (evil).

212 The life of this world is made to seem fair to those who disbelieve, and they mock those who believe. And those who keep their duty will be above them on the Day of Resurrection. And Allāh gives to whom He pleases without measure.

213 Mankind is a single nation. So Allāh raised prophets as bearers of good news and as warners, and He revealed with them the Book with truth, that it might judge between people concerning that in which they differed. And none but the very people who were given it differed about it after clear arguments had come to them, envying one another. So Allāh has guided by His will those who believe to the truth about which they differed. And Allāh guides whom He pleases to the right path.

214 Or do you think that you will enter the Garden, while there has not yet befallen you the like of what befell those who have passed away before you. Distress and affliction befell them and they were shaken violently, so that the Messenger and those who believed with him said: When will the help of Allāh come? Now surely the help of Allāh is nigh!

215 They ask thee as to what they should spend. Say: Whatever wealth you spend, it is for the parents and the near of kin and the orphans and the needy and the wayfarer. And whatever good you do, Allāh surely is Knower of it.

216 Fighting is enjoined on you, though it is disliked by you; and it may be that you dislike a thing while it is good for you, and it may be that you love a thing while it is evil for you; and Allāh knows while you know not.

SECTION 27:
Miscellaneous Questions

217 They ask thee about fighting in the sacred month. Say: Fighting in it is a grave (offence). And hindering (men) from Allāh's way and denying Him and the Sacred Mosque and turning its people out of it, are still graver with Allāh; and persecution is graver than slaughter. And they will not cease fighting you until they turn you back from your religion, if they can. And whoever of you turns back from his religion, then he dies while an unbeliever — these it is whose works go for nothing in this world and the Hereafter. And they are the companions of the Fire: therein they will abide.

218 Those who believed and those who fled (their homes) and strove hard in Allāh's way — these surely hope for the mercy of Allāh. And Allāh is Forgiving, Merciful.

219 They ask thee about

intoxicants and games of chance. Say: In both of them is a great sin and (some) advantage for men, and their sin is greater than their advantage. And they ask thee as to what they should spend. Say: What you can spare. Thus does Allāh make clear to you the messages that you may ponder,

220 On this world and the Hereafter. And they ask thee concerning the orphans. Say: To set right their (affairs) is good; and if you mix with them, they are your brethren. And Allāh knows him who makes mischief from him who sets right. And if Allāh pleased, He would have made matters difficult for you. Surely Allāh is Mighty, Wise.

221 And marry not the idolatresses until they believe; and certainly a believing maid is better than an idolatress even though she please you. Nor give (believing women) in marriage to idolaters until they believe, and certainly a believing slave is better than an idolater, even though he please you.

These invite to the Fire and Allāh invites to the Garden and to forgiveness by His will and He makes clear His messages to men that they may be mindful.

SECTION 28: Divorce

222 And they ask thee about menstruation. Say: It is harmful; so keep aloof from women during menstrual discharge and go not near them until they are clean. But when they have cleansed themselves, go in to them as Allāh has commanded you. Surely Allāh loves those who turn much (to Him), and He loves those who purify themselves.

223 Your wives are a tilth for you, so go in to your tilth when you like, and send (good) beforehand for yourselves. And keep your duty to Allāh, and know that you will meet Him. And give good news to the believers.

224 And make not Allāh by your oaths a hindrance to your doing good and keeping your duty and making peace between men.

THE COW

And Allāh is Hearing, Knowing.

225 Allāh will not call you to account for what is vain in your oaths, but He will call you to account for what your hearts have earned. And Allāh is Forgiving, Forbearing.

226 Those who swear that they will not go in to their wives should wait four months; then if they go back, Allāh is surely Forgiving, Merciful.

227 And if they resolve on a divorce, Allāh is surely Hearing, Knowing.

228 And the divorced women should keep themselves in waiting for three courses. And it is not lawful for them to conceal that which Allāh has created in their wombs, if they believe in Allāh and the Last Day. And their husbands have a better right to take them back in the meanwhile if they wish for reconciliation. And women have rights similar to those against them in a just manner, and men are a degree above them. And Allāh is Mighty, Wise.

SECTION 29: Divorce

229 Divorce may be (pronounced) twice; then keep (them) in good fellowship or let (them) go with kindness. And it is not lawful for you to take any part of what you have given them, unless both fear that they cannot keep within the limits of Allāh. Then if you fear that they cannot keep within the limits of Allāh, there is no blame on them for what she gives up to become free thereby. These are the limits of Allāh, so exceed them not; and whoever exceeds the limits of Allāh, these are the wrongdoers.

230 So if he divorces her (the third time), she shall not be lawful to him afterwards until she marries another husband. If he divorces her, there is no blame on them both if they return to each other (by marriage), if they think that they can keep within the limits of Allāh. And these are the limits of Allāh which He makes clear for a people who know.

231 And when you divorce women and they reach their prescribed time, then retain them in kindness or set them free with kindness and retain them not for injury so that you exceed the limits. And whoever does this, he indeed wrongs his own soul. And take not Allāh's messages for a mockery, and remember Allāh's favour to you, and that which He has revealed to you of the Book and the Wisdom, admonishing you thereby. And keep your duty to Allāh, and know that Allāh is the Knower of all things.

SECTION 30:
Remarriage of Divorced Women and Widows

232 And when you divorce women and they end their term, prevent them not from marrying their husbands if they agree among themselves in a lawful manner. With this is admonished he among you who believes in Allāh and the Last Day. This is more profitable for you and purer. And Allāh knows while you know not.

233 And mothers shall suckle their children for two whole years, for him who desires to complete the time of suckling. And their maintenance and their clothing must be borne by the father according to usage. No soul shall be burdened beyond its capacity. Neither shall a mother be made to suffer harm on account of her child, nor a father on account of his child; and a similar duty (devolves) on the (father's) heir. But if both desire weaning by mutual consent and counsel, there is no blame on them. And if you wish to engage a wet-nurse for your children, there is no blame on you so long as you pay what you promised according to usage. And keep your duty to Allāh and know Allāh is Seer of what you do.

234 And (as for) those of you who die and leave wives behind, such women should keep themselves in waiting for four months and ten days; when they reach their term, there is no blame on you for what they do for themselves in a lawful manner. And Allāh is Aware of what you do.

235 And there is no

blame on you respecting that which you speak indirectly in the asking of (such) women in marriage or keep (the proposal) concealed within your minds. Allāh knows that you will have them in your minds, but give them not a promise in secret unless you speak in a lawful manner. And confirm not the marriage tie until the prescribed period reaches its end. And know that Allāh knows what is in your minds, so beware of Him; and know that Allāh is Forgiving, Forbearing.

SECTION 31:
Provision for Divorced Women and Widows

236 There is no blame on you if you divorce women while yet you have not touched them, nor appointed for them a portion. And provide for them, the wealthy according to his means and the straitened according to his means, a provision according to usage. (This is) a duty on the doers of good.

237 And if you divorce them before you have touched them and you have appointed for them a portion, (pay) half of what you have appointed unless they forgo or he forgoes in whose hand is the marriage tie. And it is nearer to dutifulness that you forgo. Nor neglect the giving of free gifts between you. Surely Allāh is Seer of what you do.

238 Guard the prayers and the most excellent prayer, and stand up truly obedient to Allāh.

239 But if you are in danger (say your prayers) on foot or on horseback. And when you are secure, remember Allāh as He has taught you what you knew not.

240 And those of you who die and leave wives behind, should make a bequest in favour of their wives of maintenance for a year without turning (them) out. Then if they themselves go away, there is no blame on you for what they do of lawful deeds concerning themselves. And Allāh is Mighty, Wise.

241 And for the divorced women, provision (must be made) in kindness. This is incumbent on those who have regard for duty.

242 Allāh thus makes clear to you His messages that you may understand.

SECTION 32:
Fighting in the Cause of Truth

243 Hast thou not considered those who went forth from their homes, and they were thousands, for fear of death. Then Allāh said to them, Die. Then He gave them life. Surely Allāh is Gracious to people, but most people are not grateful.

244 And fight in the way of Allāh, and know that Allāh is Hearing, Knowing.

245 Who is it that will offer to Allāh a goodly gift, so He multiplies it to him manifold? And Allāh receives and amplifies, and to Him you shall be returned.

246 Hast thou not thought of the leaders of the Children of Israel after Moses? When they said to a prophet of theirs: Raise up for us a king, that we may fight in the way of Allāh. He said: May it not be that you will not fight if fighting is ordained for you? They said: And what reason have we that we should not fight in Allāh's way and we have indeed been deprived of our homes and our children? But when fighting was ordained for them, they turned back, except a few of them. And Allāh is Knower of the wrongdoers.

247 And their prophet said to them: Surely Allāh has raised Saul to be a king over you. They said: How can he have kingdom over us while we have a greater right to kingdom than he, and he has not been granted abundance of wealth? He said: Surely Allāh has chosen him above you, and has increased him abundantly in knowledge and physique. And Allāh grants His kingdom to whom He pleases. And Allāh is Ample-giving, Knowing.

248 And their prophet said to them: Surely the sign of his kingdom is that there shall come to you the heart in which there is tranquillity from your Lord and the best of what the followers of Moses and the followers of Aaron have left, the angels bearing it. Surely *there is a sign in this for you if you are believers.*

SECTION 33:
Fighting in the Cause of Truth

249 So when Saul set out with the forces, he said: Surely Allāh will try you with a river. Whoever drinks from it, he is not of me, and whoever tastes it not, he is surely of me, except he who takes a handful with his hand. But they drank of it save a few of them. So when he had crossed it, he and those who believed with him, they said: We have today no power against Goliath and his forces. Those who were sure that they would meet their Lord said: How often has a small party vanquished a numerous host by Allāh's permission! And Allāh is with the steadfast.

250 And when they went out against Goliath and his forces, they said: Our Lord, pour out patience on us and make our steps firm and help us against the disbelieving people.

251 So they put them to flight by Allāh's permission. *And David slew Goliath,* and Allāh gave him kingdom and wisdom, and taught him of what He pleased. And were it not for Allāh's repelling some men by others, the earth would certainly be in a state of disorder; but Allāh is Full of grace to the worlds.

252 These are the messages of Allāh — We recite them to thee with truth; and surely thou art of the messengers.

Part 3

253 We have made some of these messengers to excel others. Among them are they to whom Allāh spoke, and some of them He exalted by (many) degrees of rank. And We gave clear arguments to Jesus son of Mary, and strengthened him with the Holy Spirit. And if Allāh had pleased, those after them would not have fought one with another after clear arguments had come to them, but they disagreed; so some of them believed and some of them denied. And if Allāh had pleased they would not have fought one with another, but Allāh does what He intends.

SECTION 34:
Compulsion in Religion Forbidden

254 O you who believe, spend out of what We have given you before the day comes in which there is no bargaining, nor friendship, nor intercession. And the disbelievers — they are the wrongdoers.

255 Allāh — there is no god but He, the Ever-living, the Self-subsisting by Whom all subsist. Slumber overtakes Him not, nor sleep. To Him belongs whatever is in the heavens and whatever is in the earth. Who is he that can intercede with Him but by His permission? He knows what is before them and what is behind them. And they encompass nothing of His knowledge except what He pleases. His knowledge extends over the heavens and the earth, and the preservation of them both tires Him not. And He is the Most High, the Great.

256 There is no compulsion in religion — the right way is indeed clearly distinct from error. So whoever disbelieves in the devil and believes in Allāh, he indeed lays hold on the firmest handle which shall never break. And Allāh is Hearing, Knowing.

257 Allāh is the Friend of those who believe — He brings them out of darkness into light. And those who disbelieve, their friends are the devils who take them out of light into darkness. They are the companions of the Fire; therein they abide.

SECTION 35:
How Dead Nations are Raised to Life

258 Hast thou not thought of him who disputed with Abraham about his Lord, because Allāh had given him kingdom? When Abraham said, My Lord is He Who gives life and causes to die, he said: I give life and cause death. Abraham said: Surely Allāh causes the sun to rise from the East, so do thou make it rise from the West. Thus he who disbelieved was confounded. And Allāh guides not the unjust people.

259 Or like him who passed by a town, and it had fallen in upon its roofs. He said: When will Allāh give it life after its death? So Allāh caused him to die for a hundred years, then raised him. He said: How long hast thou tarried? He said: I have tarried a day, or part of a day. He said: Nay, thou hast tarried a hundred years; but look at thy food and drink — years have not passed over it! And look at thy ass! And that We may make thee a sign to men. And look at the bones, how We set them together then clothe them with flesh. So when it became clear to him, he said: I know that Allāh is Possessor of power over all things.

260 And when Abraham said, My Lord, show me how Thou givest life to the dead, He said: Dost thou not believe? He said: Yes, but that my heart may be at ease. He said: Then take four birds, then tame them to incline to thee, then place on every mountain a part of them, then call them, they will come to thee flying; and know that Allāh is Mighty, Wise.

SECTION 36:
Spending Money in the Cause of Truth

261 The parable of those who spend their wealth in the way of Allāh is as the parable of a grain growing seven ears, in every ear a hundred grains. And Allāh multiplies (further) for whom He pleases. And Allāh is Ample-giving, Knowing.

262 Those who spend their wealth in the way of Allāh, then follow not up what they have spent with reproach or injury, their reward is with their Lord, and they shall have no fear nor shall they grieve.

263 A kind word with forgiveness is better than charity followed by injury. And Allāh is Self-sufficient, Forbearing.

264 O you who believe, make not your charity worthless by reproach and injury, like him who spends his wealth to be seen of men and believes not in Allāh and the Last Day. So his parable is as the parable of a smooth rock with earth upon it, then heavy rain falls upon it, so it leaves it bare! They are not able to gain anything of that which they earn. And Allāh guides not the disbelieving people.

265 And the parable of those who spend their wealth to seek Allāh's pleasure and for the strengthening of their souls is as the parable of a garden on elevated ground, upon which heavy rain falls, so it brings forth its fruit twofold; but if heavy rain falls not on it, light rain (suffices). And Allāh is Seer of what you do.

266 Does one of you like to have a garden of palms and vines with streams flowing in it — he has therein all kinds of fruits — and old age has overtaken *him and he has weak* offspring; when (lo!) a whirlwind with fire in it smites it so it becomes blasted. Thus Allāh makes the messages clear to you that you may reflect.

SECTION 37:
Spending in the Cause of Truth

267 O you who believe, spend of the good things that you earn and of that which We bring forth for you out of the earth, and aim not at the bad to spend thereof, while you would not take it yourselves unless you connive at it. And know that Allāh is Self-sufficient, Praiseworthy.

268 The devil threatens you with poverty and enjoins you to be niggardly, and Allāh promises you forgiveness from Himself and abundance. And Allāh is Ample-giving, Knowing:

269 He grants wisdom to whom He pleases. And whoever is granted wisdom, he indeed is given a great good. And none mind but men of understanding.

270 And whatever alms you give or (whatever) vow you vow, Allāh surely knows it. And the wrongdoers shall have no helpers.

271 If you manifest charity, how excellent it is! And if you hide it and give it to the poor, it is good for you.

THE COW

And it will do away with *some of your evil deeds;* and Allāh is Aware of what you do.

272 Their guidance is not thy duty, but Allāh guides whom He pleases. And whatever good thing you spend, it is to your good. And you spend not but to seek Allāh's pleasure. And whatever good thing you spend, it will be paid back to you in full, and you will not be wronged.

273 (Charity) is for the poor who are confined in the way of Allāh, they cannot go about in the land; the ignorant man thinks them to be rich on account of (their) abstaining (from begging). Thou canst recognize them by their mark — they beg not of men importunately. And whatever good thing you spend, surely Allāh is Knower of it.

SECTION 38:
Usury Prohibited

274 *Those who spend their wealth by night and day, privately and publicly, their reward is with their Lord; and they have no fear,* nor shall they grieve.

275 *Those who swallow usury cannot arise except as he arises whom the devil prostrates by (his) touch. That is because they say, Trading is only like usury. And Allāh has allowed trading and forbidden usury. To whomsoever then the admonition has come from his Lord, and he desists, he shall have what has already passed. And his affair is in the hands of Allāh. And whoever returns (to it) — these are the companions of the Fire: therein they will abide.*

276 Allāh will blot out usury, and He causes charity to prosper. And Allāh loves not any ungrateful sinner.

277 *Those who believe and do good deeds and keep up prayer and pay the poor-rate — their reward is with their Lord; and they have no fear, nor shall they grieve.*

278 O you who believe, keep your duty to Allāh and relinquish what remains (due) from usury, if you are believers.

279 But if you do (it) not,

then be apprised of war from Allāh and His Messenger; and if you repent, then you shall have your capital. Wrong not, and you shall not be wronged.

280 And if (the debtor) is in straitness, let there be postponement till (he is in) ease. And that you remit (it) as alms is better for you, if you only knew.

281 And guard yourselves against a day in which you will be returned to Allāh. Then every soul will be paid in full what it has earned, and they will not be wronged.

SECTION 39:
Contracts and Evidence

282 O you who believe, when you contract a debt for a fixed time, write it down. And let a scribe write it down between you with fairness; nor should the scribe refuse to write as Allāh has taught him, so let him write. And let him who owes the debt dictate, and he should observe his duty to Allāh, his Lord, and not diminish anything from it. But if he who owes the debt is unsound in understanding or weak, or (if) he is not able to dictate himself, let his guardian dictate with fairness. And call to witness from among your men two witnesses; but if there are not two men, then one man and two women from among those whom you choose to be witnesses, so that if one of the two errs, the one may remind the other. And the witnesses must not refuse when they are summoned. And be not averse to writing it whether it is small or large along with the time of its falling due. This is more equitable in the sight of Allāh and makes testimony surer and the best way to keep away from doubts. But when it is ready merchandise which you give and take among yourselves from hand to hand, there is no blame on you in not writing it down. And have witnesses when you sell one to another. And let no harm be done to the scribe or to the witnesses. And if you do (it), then surely it is a transgression on your part. And keep your duty to Allāh. And Allāh teaches you. And Allāh is

THE COW

Knower of all things.

283 And if you are on a journey and you cannot find a scribe, a security may be taken into possession. But if one of you trusts another, then he who is trusted should deliver his trust, and let him keep his duty to Allāh, his Lord. And conceal not testimony. And whoever conceals it, his heart is surely sinful. And Allāh is Knower of what you do.

SECTION 40:
Muslims Shall be Made Victorious

284 To Allāh belongs whatever is in the heavens and whatever is in the earth. And whether you manifest what is in your minds or hide it, Allāh will call you to account according to it. So He forgives whom He pleases and chastises whom He pleases. And Allāh is Possessor of power over all things.

285 The Messenger believes in what has been revealed to him from his Lord, and (so do) the believers. They all believe in Allāh and His angels and His Books and His messengers. We make no difference between any of His messengers. And they say: We hear and obey; our Lord, Thy forgiveness (do we crave), and to Thee is the eventual course.

286 Allāh imposes not on any soul a duty beyond its scope. For, it is that which it earns (of good), and against it that which it works (of evil). Our Lord, punish us not if we forget or make a mistake. Our Lord, do not lay on us a burden as Thou didst lay on those before us. Our Lord, impose not on us (afflictions) which we have not the strength to bear. And pardon us! And grant us protection! And have mercy on us! Thou art our Patron, so grant us victory over the disbelieving people.

Chapter 3
Al 'Imrān: **The Family of Amran**

(Revealed at Madīnah: 20 *sections*; 200 *verses*)

SECTION 1:
Rule of Interpretation

In the name of Allāh, the Beneficent, the Merciful.

1 I, Allāh, am the best Knower,

2 Allāh, (there is) no god but He, the Ever-living, the Self-subsisting, by Whom all subsist.

3 He has revealed to thee the Book with truth, verifying that which is before it, and He revealed the Torah and the Gospel

4 Aforetime, a guidance for the people, and He sent the Discrimination. Those who disbelieve in the messages of Allāh — for them is a severe chastisement. And Allāh is Mighty, the Lord of retribution.

5 Surely nothing in the earth or in the heaven is hidden from Allāh.

6 He it is Who shapes you in the wombs as He pleases. There is no god but He, the Mighty, the Wise.

7 He it is Who has revealed the Book to thee; some of its verses are decisive — they are the basis of the Book — and others are allegorical. Then those in whose hearts is perversity follow the part of it which is allegorical, seeking to mislead, and seeking to give it (their own) interpretation. And none knows its interpretation save Allāh, and those firmly rooted in knowledge. They say: We believe in it, it is all from our Lord. And none mind except men of understanding.

8 Our Lord, make not our hearts to deviate after Thou hast guided us and grant us mercy from Thee; surely Thou art the most liberal Giver.

9 Our Lord, surely Thou

THE FAMILY OF AMRAN

art the Gatherer of men on a day about which there is no doubt. Surely Allāh will not fail in (His) promise.

SECTION 2:
Unity the Basis of all Religions

10 Those who disbelieve, neither their wealth nor their children will avail them aught against Allāh. And they will be fuel for fire —

11 As was the case of the people of Pharaoh, and those before them! They rejected Our messages, so Allāh destroyed them on account of their sins. And Allāh is Severe in requiting (evil).

12 Say to those who disbelieve: You shall be vanquished, and driven together to hell; and evil is the resting-place.

13 Indeed there was a sign for you in the two hosts (which) met together in encounter — one party fighting in the way of Allāh and the other disbelieving, whom they saw twice as many as themselves with the sight of the eye. And Allāh strengthens with His aid whom He pleases. There is a lesson in this for those who have eyes.

14 Fair-seeming to men is made the love of desires, of women and sons and hoarded treasures of gold and silver and well-bred horses and cattle and tilth. This is the provision of the life of this world. And Allāh — with Him is the good goal (of life).

15 Say: Shall I tell you of what is better than these? For those who guard against evil are Gardens with their Lord, in which rivers flow, to abide in them, and pure companions and Allāh's goodly pleasure. And Allāh is Seer of the servants.

16 Those who say: Our Lord, we believe, so forgive our sins and save us from the chastisement of the fire.

17 The patient and the truthful, and the obedient, and those who spend and those who ask Divine protection in the morning times.

18 Allāh bears witness that there is no god but He, and (so do) the angels and those possessed of knowledge, maintaining justice. There is no god but He, the Mighty, the Wise.

19 Surely the (true) religion with Allāh is Islām. And those who were given the Book differed only after knowledge had come to them, out of envy among themselves. And whoever disbelieves in the messages of Allāh — Allāh indeed is Quick at reckoning.

20 But if they dispute with thee say: I submit myself entirely to Allāh and (so does) he who follows me. And say to those who have been given the Book and the Unlearned (people): Do you submit yourselves? If they submit, then indeed they follow the right way; and if they turn back, thy duty is only to deliver the message. And Allāh is Seer of the servants.

SECTION 3:
The Kingdom is Granted to Another People

21 Those who disbelieve in the messages of Allāh and would slay the prophets unjustly and slay those among men who enjoin justice, announce to them a painful chastisement.

22 Those are they whose works will be of no avail in this world and the Hereafter, and they will have no helpers.

23 Hast thou not seen those who are given a portion of the Book? They are invited to the Book of Allāh that it may decide between them, then a party of them turn back and they withdraw.

24 This is because they say: The Fire shall not touch us but for a few days; and that which they forge deceives them regarding their religion.

25 Then how will it be when We gather them together on a day about which there is no doubt. And every soul shall be fully paid what it has earned, and they shall not be wronged?

26 Say: O Allāh, Owner of the Kingdom, Thou givest the kingdom to whom Thou pleasest, and takest away the kingdom from whom Thou pleasest,

THE FAMILY OF AMRAN

and Thou exaltest whom *Thou pleasest* and abasest whom Thou pleasest. In Thine hand is the good. Surely, Thou art Possessor of power over all things.

27 Thou makest the night to pass into the day and Thou makest the day to pass into the night; and Thou bringest forth the living from the dead and Thou bringest forth the dead from the living; and Thou givest sustenance to whom Thou pleasest without measure.

28 Let not the believers take the disbelievers for friends rather than believers. And whoever does this has no connection with Allāh — except that you guard yourselves against them, guarding carefully. And Allāh cautions you against His retribution. And to Allāh is the eventual coming.

29 Say: Whether you hide what is in your hearts or manifest it, Allāh knows it. And He knows whatever is in the heavens and whatever is in the earth. And Allāh is Possessor of power over all things.

30 On the day when every soul will find present that *which it has done* of good; and that which it has done of evil — it will wish that between it and that (evil) there were a long distance. And Allāh cautions you against His retribution. And Allāh is Compassionate to the servants.

SECTION 4:
Last Members of a Chosen Race

31 Say: If you love Allāh, follow me: Allāh will love you, and grant you protection from your sins. And Allāh is Forgiving, Merciful.

32 Say: Obey Allāh and the Messenger; but if they turn back, Allāh surely loves not the disbelievers.

33 Truly Allāh chose Adam and Noah and the descendants of Abraham and the descendants of Amran above the nations,

34 Offspring, one of the other. And Allāh is Hearing, Knowing.

35 When a woman of Amran said: My Lord, I vow to Thee what is in my womb, to be devoted (to Thy service), so accept (it)

from me; surely Thou, only Thou, art the Hearing, the Knowing.

36 So when she brought it forth, she said: My Lord, I have brought it forth a female — and Allāh knew best what she brought forth — and the male is not like the female, and I have named it Mary, and I commend her and her offspring into Thy protection from the accursed devil.

37 So her Lord accepted her with a goodly acceptance and made her grow up a goodly growing, and gave her into the charge of Zacharias. Whenever Zacharias entered the sanctuary to (see) her, he found food with her. He said: O Mary, whence comes this to thee? She said: It is from Allāh. Surely Allāh gives to whom He pleases without measure.

38 *There did Zacharias pray to his Lord.* He said: My Lord, grant me from Thee goodly offspring; surely Thou art the Hearer of prayer.

39 So the angels called to him as he stood praying in the sanctuary: Allāh gives thee the good news of John, verifying a word from Allāh, and honourable and chaste and a prophet from among the good ones.

40 He said: My Lord, how can I have a son when old age has already come upon me, and my wife is barren? He said: Even thus does Allāh do what He pleases.

41 He said: My Lord, appoint a sign for me. Said He: Thy sign is that thou speak not to men for three days except by signs. And remember thy Lord much and glorify (Him) in the evening and early morning.

SECTION 5:
Birth of Jesus and His Ministry

42 And when the angels said: O Mary, surely Allāh has chosen thee and purified thee and chosen thee above the women of the world.

43 O Mary, be obedient to thy Lord and humble thyself and bow down with those who bow.

44 This is of the tidings of things unseen which We reveal to thee. And thou wast not with them when they cast their pens (to decide) which of them should have Mary in his charge, and thou wast not with them when they contended one with another.

45 When the angels said: O Mary, surely Allāh gives thee good news with a word from Him (of one) whose name is the Messiah, Jesus, son of Mary, worthy of regard in this world and the Hereafter, and of those who are drawn nigh (to Allāh),

46 And he will speak to the people when in the cradle and when of old age, and (he will be) one of the *good ones*.

47 She said: My Lord, how can I have a son and man has not yet touched me? He said: Even so; Allāh creates what He pleases. When He decrees a matter, He only says to it, Be, and it is.

48 And He will teach him the Book and the Wisdom and the Torah and the Gospel:

49 And (make him) a messenger to the Children of Israel (saying): I have come to you with a sign from your Lord, that I determine for you out of dust the form of a bird, then I breathe into it and it becomes a bird with Allāh's permission, and I heal the blind and the leprous, and bring the dead to life with Allāh's permission; and I inform you of what you should eat and what you should store in your houses. Surely there is a sign in this for you, if you are believers.

50 And (I am) a verifier of that which is before me of the Torah, and I allow you part of that which was forbidden to you; and I have come to you with a sign from your Lord, so keep your duty to Allāh and obey me.

51 Surely Allāh is my Lord and your Lord, so serve Him. This is the right path.

52 But when Jesus perceived disbelief on their part, he said: Who will be my helpers in Allāh's way? The disciples said: We are Allāh's helpers: we believe in Allāh, and bear thou witness that we are submitting ones.

53 Our Lord, we believe in that which Thou hast revealed and we follow the messenger, so write us down with those who bear witness.

54 And (the Jews) planned and Allāh (also) planned. And Allāh is the best of planners.

SECTION 6:
Jesus Cleared of False Charges

55 When Allāh said: O Jesus, I will cause thee to die and exalt thee in My presence and clear thee of those who disbelieve and make those who follow thee above those who disbelieve to the day of Resurrection. Then to Me is your return, so I shall decide between you concerning that wherein you differ.

56 Then as to those who *disbelieve*, I shall chastise them with severe chastisement in this world and the Hereafter, and they will have no helpers.

57 And as to those who believe and do good deeds, He will pay them fully their rewards. And Allāh loves not the unjust.

58 This We recite to thee of the messages and the Reminder full of wisdom.

59 The likeness of Jesus with Allāh is truly as the likeness of Adam. He created him from dust, then said to him, Be, and he was.

60 (This is) the truth from thy Lord, so be not of the disputers.

61 Whoever then disputes with thee in this matter after the knowledge that has come to thee, say: Come! Let us call our sons and your sons and our women and your women and our people and your people, then let us be earnest in prayer, and invoke the curse of Allāh on the liars.

62 Surely this is the true account, and there is no god but Allāh. And Allāh! He surely is the Mighty, the Wise.

63 But if they turn away, then surely Allāh knows the mischief-makers.

SECTION 7:
Controversy with Jews and Christians

64 Say: O People of the

Book, come to an equitable *word between us and you*, that we shall serve none but Allāh and that we shall not associate aught with Him, and that some of us shall not take others for lords besides Allāh. But if they turn away, then say: Bear witness, we are Muslims.

65 O People of the Book, why do you dispute about Abraham, when the Torah and the Gospel were not revealed till after him? Do you not understand?

66 Behold! You are they who disputed about that of which you had knowledge; why then do you dispute *about that of* which you have no knowledge? And Allāh knows while you know not.

67 Abraham was not a Jew nor a Christian, but he was (an) upright (man), a Muslim; and he was not one of the polytheists.

68 The nearest of people to Abraham are surely those who follow him and this Prophet and those who believe. And Allāh is the Friend of the believers.

69 A party of the People of the Book desire that they should lead you astray; and they lead not astray but themselves, and they perceive not.

70 O People of the Book, why do you disbelieve in the messages of Allāh while you witness (their truth)?

71 O People of the Book, why do you confound the truth with falsehood, and hide the truth while you know?

SECTION 8:
Machinations to Discredit Islām

72 And a party of the People of the Book say: Avow belief in that which has been revealed to those who believe, in the first part of the day, and disbelieve in the latter part of it, perhaps they may turn back.

73 And believe not but in him who follows your religion. Say: True guidance — Allāh's guidance — is that one may be given the like of what you were given; or they would prevail on you in argument before your Lord. Say: Grace is surely in Allāh's hand. He gives it to whom

He pleases. And Allāh is Ample-giving, Knowing.

74 He specially chooses for His mercy whom He pleases. And Allāh is the Lord of mighty grace.

75 And among the People of the Book there is he who, *if thou entrust him with a heap of wealth*, would pay it back to thee; and among them is he who, if thou entrust him with a dīnār would not pay it back to thee, unless thou kept on demanding it. This is because they say there is no blame on us in the matter of the unlearned people and they forge a lie against Allāh while they know.

76 Yea, whoever fulfils his promise and keeps his duty — then Allāh surely loves the dutiful.

77 Those who take a *small* price for the covenant of Allāh and their own oaths — they have no portion in the Hereafter, and Allāh will not speak to them, nor will He look upon them on the day of Resurrection, nor will He purify them, and for them is a painful chastisement.

78 And there is certainly a party of them who lie about the Book that you may consider it to be (a part) of the Book while it is not (a part) of the Book; and they say, It is from Allāh, while it is not from Allāh; and they forge a lie against Allāh whilst they know.

79 It is not meet for a mortal that Allāh should give him the Book and the judgment and the prophethood, then he should say to men: Be my servants besides Allāh's; but (he would say): Be worshippers of the Lord because you teach the Book and because you study (it);

80 Nor would he enjoin you to take the angels and the prophets for lords. Would he enjoin you to disbelieve after you submit?

SECTION 9:
Covenant of the Prophets

81 And when Allāh made a covenant through the prophets: Certainly what I have given you of Book and Wisdom — then a Messenger comes to you verifying that which is with you, you shall believe in him, and you shall aid him. He said: Do you affirm and accept My compact in this (matter)? They said: We do affirm. He said: Then bear witness, and I (too) am of the bearers of witness with you.

82 Whoever then turns back after this, these are the transgressors.

83 Seek they then other than Allāh's religion? And to Him submits whoever is in the heavens and the earth, willingly or unwillingly, and to Him they will be returned.

84 Say: We believe in Allāh and that which is revealed to us, and that which was revealed to Abraham and Ishmael and Isaac and Jacob and the tribes, and that which was given to Moses and Jesus and to the prophets from their Lord; we make no distinction between any of them, and to Him we submit.

85 And whoever seeks a religion other than Islām, it will not be accepted from him, and in the Hereafter he will be one of the losers.

86 How shall Allāh guide a people who disbelieved after their believing, and (after) they had borne witness that the Messenger was true, and clear arguments had come to them? And Allāh guides not the unjust people.

87 As for these, their reward is that on them is the curse of Allāh and the angels and of men, all together —

88 Abiding therein. Their chastisement shall not be lightened, nor shall they be respited —

89 Except those who repent after that and amend, for surely Allāh is Forgiving, Merciful.

90 Those who disbelieve after their believing, then increase in disbelief, their repentance is not accepted, and these are they that go astray.

91 Those who disbelieve and die while they are disbelievers, the earth full of gold will not be accepted from one of them, though he should offer it as ransom. These it is for whom is a painful chastisement, and they shall have no helpers.

Part 4

SECTION 10:
Ever-living Testimony to the Truth of Islām

92 You cannot attain to righteousness unless you spend out of what you love. And what you spend, Allāh surely knows it.

93 All food was lawful to the Children of Israel, before the Torah was revealed, except that which Israel forbade himself. Say: Bring the Torah and read it, if you are truthful.

94 So whoever forges a lie against Allāh after this, these are the wrongdoers.

95 Say: Allāh speaks the truth; so follow the religion of Abraham, the upright one. And he was not one of the polytheists.

96 Certainly the first house appointed for men is the one at Bakkah, blessed and a guidance for the nations.

97 In it are clear signs: (It is) the Place of Abraham; and whoever enters it is safe; and pilgrimage to the House is a duty which men owe to Allāh — whoever can find a way to it. And whoever disbelieves, surely Allāh is above need of the worlds.

98 Say: O People of the Book, why do you disbelieve in the messages of Allāh? And Allāh is a witness of what you do.

99 Say: O People of the Book, why do you hinder those who believe from the way of Allāh, seeking (to make) it crooked, while you are witnesses? And Allāh is not heedless of what you do.

100 O you who believe, if you obey a party from among those who have been given the Book, they will turn you back as disbelievers after your belief.

101 And how can you disbelieve while to you are recited the messages of Allāh, and among you is His Messenger? And whoever holds fast to Allāh, he indeed is guided to a right path.

SECTION 11:
Muslims Exhorted to Remain United

102 O you who believe, keep your duty to Allāh, as it ought to be kept, and die

THE FAMILY OF AMRAN

not unless you are Muslims.

103 And hold fast by the covenant of Allāh all together and be not disunited. And remember Allāh's favour to you when you were enemies, then He united your hearts so by His favour you became brethren. And you were on the brink of a pit of fire, then He saved you from it. Thus Allāh makes clear to you His messages that you may be guided.

104 And from among you there should be a party who invite to good and enjoin the right and forbid the wrong. And these are they *who are successful*.

105 And be not like those who became divided and disagreed after clear arguments had come to them. And for them is a grievous chastisement.

106 On the day when (some) faces turn white and (some) faces turn black. Then as to those whose faces are black: Did you disbelieve after your belief? So taste the chastisement because you disbelieved.

107 And as to those whose faces are white, they shall be in Allāh's mercy. Therein they shall abide.

108 *These are the messages of Allāh which We recite to thee with truth*. And Allāh desires no injustice to (His) creatures.

109 And to Allāh belongs whatever is in the heavens and whatever is in the earth. And to Allāh are all affairs returned.

SECTION 12:
Relations of Jews with Muslims

110 You are the best nation raised up for men: you enjoin good and forbid evil and you believe in Allāh. And if the People of the Book had believed, it would have been better for them. Some of them are believers but most of them are transgressors.

111 They will not harm you save a slight hurt. And if they fight you, they will turn (their) backs to you. Then they will not be helped.

112 Abasement will be their lot wherever they are found, except under a covenant with Allāh and a covenant with men, and they shall incur the wrath of Allāh, and humiliation will be made to cling to them. This is because they disbelieved in the messages of Allāh and killed the prophets unjustly. This is because they disobeyed and exceeded the limits.

113 They are not all alike. Of the People of the Book there is an upright party who recite Allāh's messages in the night-time and they adore (Him).

114 They believe in Allāh and the Last Day, and they enjoin good and forbid evil and vie one with another in good deeds. And those are among the righteous.

115 And whatever good they do, they will not be denied it. And Allāh knows those who keep their duty.

116 Those who disbelieve, neither their wealth nor their children will avail them aught against Allāh. And these are the companions of the Fire; therein they abide.

117 The likeness of that which they spend in the life of this world is as the likeness of wind in which is intense cold; it smites the harvest of a people who are unjust to themselves and destroys it. And Allāh wronged them not but they wronged themselves.

118 O you who believe, take not for intimate friends others than your own people: they spare no pains to cause you loss. They love that which distresses you. Vehement hatred has already appeared from out of their mouths, and that which their hearts conceal is greater still. Indeed We have made the messages clear to you, if you understand.

119 Lo! you are they who will love them while they love you not, and you believe in the Book, (in) the whole of it. And when they meet you they say, We believe, and when they are alone, they bite (their) finger tips in rage against you. Say: Die in your rage. Surely Allāh is Knower of what is in the hearts.

120 If good befalls you, it grieves them, and if an evil afflicts you, they rejoice at it. And if you are patient and keep your duty, their struggle will not injure you in any way. Surely Allāh encompasses what they do.

SECTION 13:
The Battle of Uḥud

121 And when thou didst go forth early in the morning from thy family, to assign to the believers their positions for the battle. And Allāh is Hearing, Knowing.

122 When two parties from among you thought of showing cowardice, and Allāh was the Guardian of them both. And in Allāh should the believers trust.

123 And Allāh certainly helped you at Badr when you were weak. So keep your duty to Allāh that you may give thanks.

124 When thou didst say to the believers: Does it not suffice you that your Lord should help you with three thousand angels sent down?

125 Yea, if you are steadfast and keep your duty, and they come upon you in a headlong manner, your Lord will assist you with five thousand of havoc-making angels.

126 And Allāh made it only as good news for you, and that your hearts might be at ease thereby. And help comes only from Allāh, the Mighty, the Wise,

127 That He may cut off a part of those who disbelieve or abase them so that they should return in failure.

128 Thou hast no concern in the matter whether He turns to them (mercifully) or chastises them; surely they are wrongdoers.

129 And to Allāh belongs whatever is in the heavens and whatever is in the earth. He forgives whom He pleases and chastises whom He pleases. And Allāh is Forgiving, Merciful.

SECTION 14:
What Success meant for the Muslims

130 O you who believe, devour not usury, doubling and redoubling, and keep your duty to Allāh, that you may be successful.

131 And guard yourselves against the fire which has been prepared for the disbelievers.

132 And obey Allāh and the Messenger, that you may be shown mercy.

133 And hasten to forgiveness from your Lord and a Garden, as wide as the heavens and the earth; it is prepared for those who keep their duty:

134 Those who spend in ease as well as in adversity and those who restrain (their) anger and pardon men. And Allāh loves the doers of good (to others).

135 And those who, when they commit an indecency or wrong their souls, remember Allāh and ask forgiveness for their sins. And who forgives sins but Allāh? And they persist not knowingly in what they do.

136 Their reward is protection from their Lord, and Gardens wherein flow rivers, to abide in them. And excellent is the reward of the workers!

137 Indeed there have been examples before you; so travel in the earth and see what was the end of the deniers.

138 This is a clear statement for men, and a guidance and an admonition to those who would keep their duty.

139 And be not weakhearted, nor grieve, and you will have the upper hand if you are believers.

140 If a wound has afflicted you, a wound like it has also afflicted the (disbelieving) people. And We bring these days to men by turns, that Allāh may know those who believe and take witnesses from among you. And Allāh loves not the wrongdoers,

141 And that He may purge those who believe and deprive the disbelievers of blessings.

142 Do you think that you will enter the Garden while Allāh has not yet known those from among you who strive hard (nor) known the steadfast?

143 And certainly you desired death before you met it. So indeed you have seen it now while you look (at it).

SECTION 15:
Sufferings to be met with Perseverance

144 And Muḥammad is

but a messenger — messen-gers *have already passed away before him.* If then he dies or is killed, will you turn back upon your heels? And he who turns back upon his heels will do no harm at all to Allāh. And Allāh will reward the grateful.

145 And no soul can die but with Allāh's permission — the term is fixed. And whoever desires the reward of this world, We give him of it, and whoever desires the reward of the Hereafter, We give him of it. And We shall reward the grateful.

146 And how many a prophet has fought, with whom were many worshippers of the Lord. So they did not lose heart on account of that which befell them in Allāh's way, nor did they weaken, nor did they abase themselves. And Allāh loves the steadfast.

147 And their cry was only that they said: Our Lord, grant us protection from our sins and our extravagance in our affair, and make firm our feet and grant us victory over the disbelieving people.

148 So Allāh gave them *the reward of the world and* a good reward of the Hereafter. And Allāh loves the doers of good (to others).

SECTION 16:
Causes of Misfortune in Uḥud Battle

149 O you who believe, if you obey those who disbelieve, they will make you turn back upon your heels, so you will turn back losers.

150 Nay, Allāh is your Patron, and He is the Best of the helpers.

151 We will cast terror into the hearts of those who disbelieve because they set up with Allāh that for which He has sent down no authority, and their abode is the Fire. And evil is the abode of the wrongdoers.

152 And Allāh certainly made good His promise to you when you slew them by His permission, until you became weak-hearted and disputed about the affair and disobeyed after He had shown you that which you loved. Of you were some who desired this world, and of you were some who desired the Hereafter. Then He turned you away from them that He might try you; and He has indeed pardoned you. And Allāh is Gracious to the believers.

153 When you went away far, and paid no heed to anyone, and the Messenger was calling you in your rear. So He gave you (another) grief for (your) first grief that you might not grieve at what escaped you, nor (at) what befell you. And Allāh is Aware of what you do.

154 Then after grief He sent down security on you, slumber overcoming a party of you, while (there was) another party whom their own souls had rendered anxious — they entertained about Allāh thoughts of ignorance quite unjustly. They said: Have we any hand in the affair? Say: The affair is wholly (in the hands) of Allāh. They hide within their souls that which they would not reveal to thee. They say: Had we any hand in the affair, we would not have been slain here. Say: Had you remained in your houses, those for whom slaughter was ordained would have gone forth to the places where they would be slain. And (this happened) that Allāh might test what was in your breasts and that He might purge what was in your hearts. And Allāh is Knower of what is in the breasts.

155 Those of you who turned back on the day when the two armies met, only the devil sought to cause them to make a slip on account of some deeds they had done, and certainly Allāh has pardoned them. Surely Allāh is Forgiving, Forbearing.

SECTION 17:
Battle of Uḥud Afforded a Distinction

156 O you who believe, be not like those who disbelieve and say of their brethren when they travel in the earth or engage in fighting: Had they been with us, they would not have died, or been slain; that Allāh may make it to be a regret in their hearts. And Allāh gives life and causes death.

THE FAMILY OF AMRAN

And Allāh is Seer of what you do.

157 And if you are slain in Allāh's way or you die, surely Allāh's protection and (His) mercy are better than what they amass.

158 And if you die or you are slain, to Allāh you are gathered.

159 Thus it is by Allāh's mercy that thou art gentle to them. And hadst thou been rough, hard-hearted, they would certainly have dispersed from around thee. So pardon them and ask protection for them, and consult them in (important) matters. But when thou hast determined, put thy trust in Allāh. Surely Allāh loves those who trust (in Him).

160 If Allāh helps you, there is none that can overcome you; and if He forsakes you, who is there that can help you after Him? And in Allāh should the believers put their trust.

161 And it is not for a prophet to act dishonestly. And whoever acts dishonestly will bring his dishonesty on the day of Resurrection. Then shall every soul be paid back fully what it has earned, and they will not be wronged.

162 Is then he who follows the pleasure of Allāh like him who incurs Allāh's displeasure, and his abode is hell? And it is an evil destination.

163 There are grades with Allāh. And Allāh is Seer of what they do.

164 Certainly Allāh conferred a favour on the believers when He raised among them a Messenger from among themselves, reciting to them His messages and purifying them, and teaching them the Book and the Wisdom, although before that they were surely in manifest error.

165 What! When a misfortune befell you, and you had inflicted twice as much, you say: Whence is this? Say: It is from yourselves. Surely Allāh is Possessor of power over all things.

166 And that which befell you on the day when the two armies met was by Allāh's permission, that He might know the believers,

167 And that He might

know the hypocrites. And it was said to them: Come, fight in Allāh's way, or defend yourselves. They said: If we knew fighting, we would have followed you. They were on that day nearer to disbelief than to belief; they say with their mouths what is not in their hearts. And Allāh best knows what they conceal.

168 Those who said of their brethren whilst they (themselves) held back: Had they obeyed us, they would not have been killed. Say: Avert death from yourselves, if you are truthful.

169 And think not of those who are killed in Allāh's way as dead. Nay, they are alive being provided sustenance from their Lord,

170 Rejoicing in what Allāh has given them out of His grace, *and they rejoice* for the sake of those who, (being left) behind them, have not yet joined them, that they have no fear, nor shall they grieve.

171 They rejoice for Allāh's favour and (His) grace, and that Allāh wastes not the reward of the believers.

SECTION 18:
Uhud No Gain to the Enemy

172 Those who responded to the call of Allāh and the Messenger after the misfortune had befallen them — for such among them who do good and keep their duty is a great reward.

173 Those to whom men said: Surely people have gathered against you, so fear them; but this increased their faith, and they said: Allāh is sufficient for us and He is an excellent Guardian.

174 So they returned with favour from Allāh and (His) grace; no evil touched them, and they followed the pleasure of Allāh. And Allāh is the Lord of mighty grace.

175 It is the devil who only frightens his friends, but fear them not, and fear Me, if you are believers.

176 And let not those grieve thee who run into disbelief precipitately; surely they can do no harm to

THE FAMILY OF AMRAN

Allāh. Allāh intends not to assign them any portion in the Hereafter; and for them is a grievous chastisement.

177 Those who buy disbelief at the price of faith can do no harm to Allāh, and for them is a painful chastisement.

178 And let not those who disbelieve think that our granting them respite is good for themselves. We grant them respite only that they may add to their sins; and for them is a humiliating chastisement.

179 Allāh will not leave the believers in the condition in which you are until He separates the evil from the good. Nor is Allāh going to make you acquainted with the unseen, but Allāh chooses of His messengers whom He pleases. So believe in Allāh and His messengers. And if you believe and keep your duty, you will have a great reward.

180 And let not those who are niggardly in spending that which Allāh has granted them out of His grace, think that it is good for them. Nay, it is evil for them. They shall have a collar of their niggardliness on their necks on the Resurrection day. And Allāh's is the heritage of the heavens and the earth. And Allāh is Aware of what you do.

SECTION 19:
Carpings of People of the Book

181 Allāh has certainly heard the saying of those who said: Allāh is poor and we are rich. We shall record what they say, and their killing the prophets unjustly, and We shall say: Taste the chastisement of burning.

182 This is for that which your own hands have sent before, and because Allāh is not in the least unjust to the servants.

183 Those who say: Allāh has enjoined us that we should not believe in any messenger until he brings us an offering which is consumed by the fire. Say: Indeed there came to you messengers before me with clear arguments and with that which you demand. Why then did you try to kill them, if you are truthful?

184 But if they reject thee, so indeed were rejected before thee messengers who came with clear arguments and scriptures and the illuminating Book.

185 Every soul will taste of death. And you will be paid your reward fully only on the Resurrection day. Then whoever is removed far from the Fire and is made to enter the Garden, he indeed attains the object. And the life of this world is nothing but a provision of vanities.

186 You will certainly be tried in your property and your persons. And you will certainly hear from those who have been given the Book before you and from the idolaters much abuse. And if you are patient and keep your duty, surely this is an affair of great resolution.

187 And when Allāh took a covenant from those who were given the Book: You shall explain it to men and shall not hide it. But they cast it behind their backs and took a small price for it. So evil is that which they buy.

188 Think not that those who exult in what they have done, and love to be praised for what they have not done — think not them to be safe from the chastisement; and for them is a painful chastisement.

189 And Allāh's is the kingdom of the heavens and the earth. And Allāh is Possessor of power over all things.

SECTION 20:
Ultimate Triumph of the Faithful

190 In the creation of the heavens and the earth and the alternation of the night and the day, there are surely signs for men of understanding.

191 Those who remember Allāh standing and sitting and (lying) on their sides, and reflect on the creation of the heavens and the earth: Our Lord, Thou hast not created this in vain! Glory be to Thee! Save us from the chastisement of the Fire.

192 Our Lord, whomsoever Thou makest enter the Fire, him Thou indeed bringest to disgrace. And there will be no helpers for the wrongdoers.

193 Our Lord, surely we have heard a Crier calling to the faith, saying: Believe in your Lord. So we do believe. Our Lord, grant us protection from our sins and remove our evils and make us die with the righteous.

194 Our Lord, grant us what Thou hast promised us by Thy messengers and disgrace us not on the day of Resurrection. Surely Thou never failest in (Thy) promise!

195 So their Lord accepted their prayer, (saying): I will not suffer the work of any worker among you to be lost whether male or female, the one of you being from the other. So those who fled and were driven forth from their homes and persecuted in My way and who fought and were slain, I shall truly remove their evil and make them enter Gardens wherein flow rivers — a reward from Allāh. And with Allāh is the best reward.

196 Let not control in the land, of those who disbelieve, deceive thee.

197 A brief enjoyment! Then their abode is hell. And evil is the resting-place.

198 But those who keep their duty to their Lord, for them are Gardens wherein flow rivers, to abide therein; and entertainment from their Lord. And that which Allāh has in store for the righteous is best.

199 And of the People of the Book there are those who believe in Allāh and (in) that which has been revealed to you and (in) that which has been revealed to them, humbling themselves before Allāh — they take not a small price for the messages of Allāh. These it is that have their reward with their Lord. Surely Allāh is Swift to take account!

200 O you who believe, be steadfast and try to excel in steadfastness and guard (the frontiers). And keep your duty to Allāh that you may be successful.

Chapter 4
Al-Nisā': The Women

(Revealed at Madīnah: 24 *sections*; 176 *verses*)

SECTION 1:
Duties of Guardians to Orphan Wards

In the name of Allāh, the Beneficent, the Merciful.

1 O people, keep your duty to your Lord, Who created you from a single being and created its mate of the same (kind), and spread from these two many men and women. And keep your duty to Allāh, by Whom you demand one of another (your rights), and (to) the ties of relationship. Surely Allāh is ever a Watcher over you.

2 And give to the orphans *their property*, and substitute not worthless (things) for (their) good (ones), and devour not their property (adding) to your own property. This is surely a great sin.

3 And if you fear that you cannot do justice to orphans, marry such women as seem good to you, two, or three, or four; but if you fear that you will not do justice, then (marry) only one or that which your right hands possess. This is more proper that you may not do injustice.

4 And give women their dowries as a free gift. But if they of themselves be pleased to give you a portion thereof, consume it with enjoyment and pleasure.

5 And make not over your property, which Allāh has made a (means of) support for you, to the weak of understanding, and maintain them out of it, and clothe them and give them a good education.

6 And test the orphans until they reach the age of marriage. Then if you find

THE WOMEN

in them maturity of intellect, make over to them their property, and consume it not extravagantly and hastily against their growing up. And whoever is rich, let him abstain, and whoever is poor let him consume reasonably. And when you make over to them their property, call witnesses in their presence. And Allāh is enough as a Reckoner.

7 For men is a share of what the parents and the near relatives leave, and for women a share of what the parents and the near relatives leave, whether it be little or much — an appointed share.

8 And when relatives and the orphans and the needy are present at the division, give them out of it and speak to them kind words.

9 And let those fear who, should they leave behind them weakly offspring, would fear on their account; so let them observe their duty to Allāh and let them speak right words.

10 Those who swallow the property of the orphans unjustly, they swallow only fire into their bellies. And they will burn in blazing fire.

SECTION 2:
Law of Inheritance

11 Allāh enjoins you concerning your children: for the male is the equal of the portion of two females; but if there be more than two females, two-thirds of what the deceased leaves is theirs; and if there be one, for her is the half. And as for his parents, for each of them is the sixth of what he leaves, if he has a child; but if he has no child and (only) his two parents inherit him, for his mother is the third; but if he has brothers, for his mother is the sixth, after (payment of) a bequest he may have bequeathed or a debt. Your parents and your children, you know not which of them is the nearer to you in benefit. This is an ordinance from Allāh. Allāh is surely ever Knowing, Wise.

12 And yours is half of what your wives leave if they have no child; but if they have a child, your share is a fourth of what they leave after (payment of) any bequest they may have bequeathed or a debt; and theirs is the fourth of what you leave if you have no child, but if you have a child, their share is the eighth of what you leave after (payment of) a bequest you may have bequeathed or a debt. And if a man or a woman, having no children, leaves property to be inherited and he (or she) has a brother or a sister, then for each of them is the sixth; but if they are more than that, they shall be sharers in the third after (payment of) a bequest that may have been bequeathed or a debt not injuring (others). This is an ordinance from Allāh: and Allāh is Knowing, Forbearing.

13 These are Allāh's limits. And whoever obeys Allāh and His Messenger, He will admit him to Gardens wherein flow rivers, to abide in them. And this is the great achievement.

14 And whoever disobeys Allāh and His Messenger and goes beyond His limits, He will make him enter fire to abide in it, and for him is an abasing chastisement.

SECTION 3: Treatment of Women

15 And as for those of your women who are guilty of an indecency, call to witness against them four (witnesses) from among you; so if they bear witness, confine them to the houses until death takes them away or Allāh opens a way for them.

16 And as for the two of you who are guilty of it, give them both a slight punishment; then if they repent and amend, turn aside from them. Surely Allāh is ever Oft-returning (to mercy), the Merciful.

17 Repentance with Allāh is only for those who do evil in ignorance, then turn (to Allāh) soon, so these it is to whom Allāh turns (mercifully). And Allāh is ever Knowing, Wise.

18 And repentance is not for those who go on doing evil deeds, until when death comes to one of them, he says: Now I repent; nor (for) those who die while they are disbelievers. For such We have prepared a painful chastisement.

19 O you who believe, it

THE WOMEN

is not lawful for you to take women as heritage against (their) will. Nor should you straiten them by taking part of what you have given them, unless they are guilty of manifest indecency. And treat them kindly. Then if you hate them, it may be that you dislike a thing while Allāh has placed abundant good in it.

20 And if you wish to have (one) wife in the place of another and you have given one of them a heap of gold, take nothing from it. Would you take it by slandering (her) and (doing her) manifest wrong?

21 And how can you take it when one of you has already gone in to the other and they have taken from you a strong covenant?

22 And marry not women whom your fathers married, except what has already passed. This surely is indecent and hateful; and it is an evil way.

SECTION 4:
What Women may be taken in Marriage

23 Forbidden to you are your mothers, and your daughters, and your sisters, and your paternal aunts, and your maternal aunts, and brother's daughters and sister's daughters, and your mothers that have suckled you, and your foster-sisters, and mothers of your wives, and your stepdaughters who are in your guardianship (born) of your wives to whom you have gone in — but if you have not gone in to them, there is no blame on you — and the wives of your sons who are of your own loins; and that you should have two sisters together, except what has already passed. Surely Allāh is ever Forgiving, Merciful,

Part 5

24 And all married women except those whom your right hands possess (are forbidden); (this is) Allāh's ordinance to you. And lawful for you are (all women) besides those, provided that you seek (them) with your property, taking (them) in marriage, not committing fornication. Then as to those whom you profit by (by marrying), give them their dowries as appointed. And there is no blame on you about what you mutually agree after what is appointed (of dowry). Surely Allāh is ever Knowing, Wise.

25 And whoever among you cannot afford to marry free believing women, (let him marry) such of your believing maidens as your right hands possess. And Allāh knows best your faith — you are (sprung) the one from the other. So marry them with the permission of their masters, and give them their dowries justly, they being chaste, not fornicating, nor receiving paramours; then if they are guilty of adultery when they are taken in marriage, they shall suffer half the punishment for free married women. This is for him among you who fears falling into evil. And that you abstain is better for you. And Allāh is Forgiving, Merciful.

SECTION 5:
Women's Rights over their Earnings

26 Allāh desires to explain to you, and to guide you into the ways of those before you, and to turn to you (mercifully). And Allāh is Knowing, Wise.

27 And Allāh desires to turn to you (mercifully). And those who follow (their) lusts desire that you should deviate (with) a great deviation.

28 Allāh desires to make light your burdens, and man is created weak.

29 O you who believe, devour not your property among yourselves by illegal methods except that it be trading by your mutual consent. And kill not your people. Surely Allāh is ever Merciful to you.

30 And whoso does this aggressively and unjustly, We shall soon cast him into fire. And this is ever easy for Allāh.

31 If you shun the great things which you are forbidden, We shall do away with your evil (inclinations) and cause you to enter an honourable place of entering.

32 And covet not that by which Allāh has made some

of you excel others. For men is the benefit of what they earn. And for women is the benefit of what they earn. And ask Allāh of His grace. Surely Allāh is ever Knower of all things.

33 And to everyone We have appointed heirs of that which parents and near relatives leave. And as to those with whom your right hands have ratified agreements, give them their due. Surely Allāh is ever Witness over all things.

SECTION 6:
Disagreement between Husband and Wife

34 Men are the maintainers of women, with what Allāh has made some of them to excel others and with what they spend out of their wealth. So the good women are obedient, guarding the unseen as Allāh has guarded. And (as to) those on whose part you fear desertion, admonish them, and leave them alone in the beds and chastise them. So if they obey you, seek not a way against them. Surely Allāh is ever Exalted, Great.

35 And if you fear a breach between the two, appoint an arbiter from his people and an arbiter from her people. If they both desire agreement, Allāh will effect harmony between them. Surely Allāh is ever Knowing, Aware.

36 And serve Allāh, and associate naught with Him, and be good to the parents and to the near of kin and the orphans and the needy and the neighbour of (your) kin and the alien neighbour, and the companion in a journey and the wayfarer and those whom your right hands possess. Surely Allāh loves not such as are proud, boastful,

37 Who are niggardly and bid people to be niggardly and hide that which Allāh has given them out of His grace. And We have prepared for the disbelievers an abasing chastisement —

38 And those who spend their wealth to be seen of men and believe not in Allāh nor in the Last Day. And as for him whose companion is the devil, an evil companion is he!

39 And what (harm)

would it do them if they believe in Allāh and the Last Day and spend of that which Allāh has given them? And Allāh is ever Knower of them.

40 Surely Allāh wrongs not the weight of an atom; and if it is a good deed, He multiplies it and gives from Himself a great reward.

41 But how will it be when We bring from every people a witness and bring thee as a witness against these?

42 On that day will those who disbelieved and disobeyed the Messenger desire that the earth were levelled with them. And they can hide no fact from Allāh.

SECTION 7:
Purification of the Soul

43 O you who believe, go not near prayer when you are intoxicated till you know what you say, nor after sexual intercourse — except you are merely passing by — until you have bathed. And if you are sick, or on a journey, or one of you come from the privy, or you have touched the women, and you cannot find water, betake yourselves to pure earth, then wipe your faces and your hands. Surely Allāh is ever Pardoning, Forgiving.

44 Seest thou not those to whom a portion of the Book was given? They buy error and desire to make you err from the (right) way.

45 And Allāh best knows your enemies. And Allāh is sufficient as a Friend and Allāh is sufficient as a Helper.

46 Some of those who are Jews alter words from their places and say, We have heard and we disobey; and (say), Hear without being made to hear, and (say), *Rā'i-nā,* distorting with their tongues and slandering religion. And if they had said, We hear and we obey, and hearken, and *unẓur-nā,* it would have been better for them and more upright; but Allāh has cursed them on account of their disbelief, so they believe not but a little.

47 O you who have been given the Book, believe in what We have revealed, verifying that which you have, before We destroy the leaders and turn them on *their backs, or curse them as We cursed the Sabbath-breakers*. And the command of Allāh is ever executed.

48 Surely Allāh forgives not that a partner should be set up with Him, and forgives all besides that to whom He pleases. And whoever sets up a partner with Allāh, he devises indeed a great sin.

49 Hast thou not seen those who attribute purity to themselves? Nay, Allāh purifies whom He pleases, and they will not be wronged a whit.

50 See how they forge lies against Allāh! And sufficient is this as a manifest sin.

SECTION 8:
Kingdom granted to Abraham's Descendants

51 Hast thou not seen those to whom a portion of the Book was given? They believe in sorcery and diviners and say of those who disbelieve: These are better guided in the path than those who believe.

52 Those are they whom Allāh has cursed. And whomever Allāh curses, thou wilt not find a helper for him.

53 Or have they a share in the kingdom? But then they would not give to people even the speck on a date-stone.

54 Or do they envy the people for that which Allāh has given them of His grace? But indeed We have given to Abraham's children the Book and the Wisdom, and We have given them a grand kingdom.

55 So of them is he who believes in him, and of them is he who turns away from him. And Hell is sufficient to burn.

56 Those who disbelieve in Our Messages, We shall make them enter Fire. As often as their skins are burned, We shall change them for other skins, that they may taste the chastisement. Surely Allāh is ever Mighty, Wise.

57 And those who believe and do good deeds, We shall make them enter Gardens wherein flow rivers, to abide in them forever. For them therein are pure companions and We shall make them enter a pleasant shade.

58 Surely Allāh commands you to make over trusts to those worthy of them, and that when you judge between people, you judge with justice. Surely Allāh admonishes you with what is excellent. Surely Allāh is ever Hearing, Seeing.

59 O you who believe, obey Allāh and obey the Messenger and those in authority from among you; then if you quarrel about anything, refer it to Allāh and the Messenger, if you believe in Allāh and the Last Day. This is best and more suitable to (achieve) the end.

SECTION 9:
The Prophet must be Obeyed

60 Hast thou not seen those who assert that they believe in that which has been revealed to thee and that which was revealed before thee? They desire to seek the judgment of the devil, though they have been commanded to deny him. And the devil desires to lead them far astray.

61 And when it is said to them, Come to that which Allāh has revealed and to the Messenger, thou seest the hypocrites turning away from thee with aversion.

62 But how is it that when a misfortune befalls them on account of that which their hands have sent before, they come to thee swearing by Allāh: We desired naught but good and concord?

63 These are they, the secrets of whose hearts Allāh knows; so turn aside from them and admonish them and speak to them effective words concerning themselves.

64 And We sent no messenger but that he should be obeyed by Allāh's command. And had they, when they wronged themselves, come to thee and asked forgiveness of Allāh, and the Messenger had (also) asked forgiveness for them, they would have found Allāh Oft-returning (to mercy), merciful.

THE WOMEN

65 But no, by thy Lord! they believe not until they make thee a judge of what is in dispute between them, then find not any straitness in their hearts as to that which thou decidest and submit with full submission.

66 And if We had enjoined them, Lay down your lives or go forth from your homes, they would not have done it except a few of them. And if they had done what they are exhorted to do, it would certainly have been better for them and more strengthening:

67 And then We would certainly have given them from Ourselves a great reward,

68 And We would certainly have guided them in the right path.

69 And whoever obeys Allāh and the Messenger, they are with those upon whom Allāh has bestowed favours from among the prophets and the truthful and the faithful and the righteous, and a goodly company are they!

70 Such is the grace from Allāh, and Allāh is sufficient as Knower.

SECTION 10:
Believers must defend Themselves

71 O you who believe, take your precautions, then go forth in detachments or go forth in a body.

72 And among you is he who would hang back. Then if a misfortune befalls you he says: Allāh indeed bestowed a favour on me as I was not present with them.

73 And if bounty from Allāh comes to you, he would cry, as if there were no friendship between you and him: Would that I had been with them, then I should have achieved a mighty success!

74 So let those fight in the way of Allāh who sell this world's life for the Hereafter. And whoever fights in the way of Allāh, be he slain or be he victorious, We shall grant him a mighty reward.

75 And what reason have you not to fight in the way of Allāh, and of the weak among the men and the women and the children, who say: Our Lord, take us out of this town, whose people are oppressors, and grant us from Thee a friend, and grant us from Thee a helper!

76 Those who believe fight in the way of Allāh, and those who disbelieve fight in the way of the devil. So fight against the friends of the devil; surely the struggle of the devil is ever weak.

SECTION 11:
Attitude of the Hypocrites

77 Hast thou not seen those to whom it was said: Withhold your hands, and keep up prayer and pay the poor-rate. But when fighting is prescribed for them, lo! a party of them fear men as they ought to fear Allāh, or with a greater fear, and say: Our Lord, why hast Thou ordained fighting for us? Wouldst Thou not grant us respite to a near term? Say: The enjoyment of this world is short, and the Hereafter is better for him who keeps his duty. And you shall not be wronged a whit.

78 Wherever you are, death will overtake you, though you are in towers, raised high. And if good befalls them, they say: This is from Allāh; and if a misfortune befalls them, they say: This is from thee. Say: All is from Allāh. But what is the matter with these people that they make no effort to understand anything?

79 Whatever good befalls thee (O man), it is from Allāh, and whatever misfortune befalls thee, it is from thyself. And We have sent thee (O Prophet) to mankind as a Messenger. And Allāh is sufficient as a witness.

80 Whoever obeys the Messenger, he indeed obeys Allāh. And whoever turns away, We have not sent thee as a keeper over them.

81 And they say: Obedience. But when they go out from thy presence, a party of them plan by night doing otherwise than what thou sayest. And Allāh writes down what they plan by night, so turn aside from them and trust in Allāh. And Allāh is sufficient as having charge of affairs.

82 Will they not then meditate on the Qur'ān?

And if it were from any other than Allāh, they would have found in it many a discrepancy.

83 But if any news of security or fear comes to them, they spread it abroad. And if they had referred it to the Messenger and to those in authority among them, those of them who can search out knowledge of it would have known it. And were it not for the grace of Allāh upon you and His mercy, you would certainly have followed the devil save a few.

84 Fight then in Allāh's way — thou art not responsible except for thyself; and urge on the believers. It may be that Allāh will restrain the fighting of those who disbelieve. And Allāh is stronger in prowess and stronger to give exemplary punishment.

85 Whoever intercedes in a good cause has a share of it, and whoever intercedes in an evil cause has a portion of it. And Allāh is ever Keeper over all things.

86 And when you are greeted with a greeting, greet with one better than it, or return it. Surely Allāh ever takes account of all things.

87 Allāh, there is no god but He — He will certainly gather you together on the Resurrection day, there is no doubt in it. And who is more true in word than Allāh?

SECTION 12:
How to deal with the Hypocrites

88 Why should you, then, be two parties in relation to the hypocrites while Allāh has made them return (to disbelief) for what they have earned? Do you desire to guide him whom Allāh leaves in error? And whomsoever Allāh leaves in error thou canst not find a way for him.

89 They long that you should disbelieve as they have disbelieved so that you might be on the same level; so take not from among them friends until they flee (their homes) in Allāh's way. Then if they turn back (to hostility), seize them and kill them wherever you find them, and take no friend nor helper from among them,

90 Except those who join a people between whom and you there is an alliance, or who come to you, their hearts shrinking from fighting you or fighting their own people. And if Allāh had pleased, He would have given them power over you, so that they would have fought you. So if they withdraw from you and fight you not and offer you peace, then Allāh allows you no way against them.

91 You will find others who desire to be secure from you and secure from their own people. Whenever they are made to return to hostility, they are plunged into it. So if they withdraw not from you, nor offer you peace and restrain their hands, then seize them and kill them wherever you find them. And against these We have given you a clear authority.

SECTION 13:
Murderer of a Muslim

92 And a believer would not kill a believer except by mistake. And he who kills a believer by mistake should free a believing slave, and blood-money should be paid to his people unless they remit it as alms. But if he be from a tribe hostile to you and he is a believer, the freeing of a believing slave (suffices). And if he be from a tribe between whom and you there is a covenant, the blood-money should be paid to his people along with the freeing of a believing slave; but he who has not the means should fast for two months successively: a penance from Allāh. And Allāh is ever Knowing, Wise.

93 And whoever kills a believer intentionally, his punishment is hell, abiding therein; and Allāh is wroth with him and He has cursed him and prepared for him a grievous chastisement.

94 O you who believe, when you go forth (to fight) in Allāh's way, make investigation, and say not to any one who offers you salutation, Thou art not a believer, seeking the good of this world's life. But with Allāh there are abundant gains. You too were such before, then Allāh conferred a benefit on you; so make investigation. Surely Allāh is ever Aware of what you do.

95 The holders-back from among the believers, not disabled by injury, and those who strive hard in Allāh's way with their property and their persons, are not equal. Allāh has made the strivers with their property and their persons to excel the holders-back a (high) degree. And to each Allāh has promised good. And Allāh has granted to the strivers above the holders-back a mighty reward —

96 (High) degrees from Him and protection and mercy. And Allāh is ever Forgiving, Merciful.

SECTION 14:
Muslims who remained with the Enemy

97 (As for) those whom the angels cause to die while they are unjust to themselves, (the angels) will say: What were you doing? They will say: We were weak in the earth. (They will) say: Was not Allāh's earth spacious, so that you could have migrated therein? So these it is whose refuge is hell — and it is an evil resort.

98 Except the weak from among the men and the women and the children who have not the means, nor can they find a way (to escape);

99 So these, it may be that Allāh will pardon them. And Allāh is ever Pardoning, Forgiving.

100 And whoever flees in Allāh's way, he will find in the earth many a place of escape and abundant resources. And whoever goes forth from his home fleeing to Allāh and His Messenger, then death overtakes him, his reward is indeed with Allāh. And Allāh is ever Forgiving, Merciful.

SECTION 15:
Prayer when Fighting

101 And when you journey in the earth, there is no blame on you if you shorten the prayer, if you fear that those who disbelieve will give you trouble. Surely the disbelievers are an open enemy to you.

102 And when thou art among them and leadest the prayer for them, let a party of them stand up with thee, and let them take their arms. Then when they have performed their prostration, let them go to your rear, and let another party who have not prayed come forward and pray with thee, and let them take their precautions and their arms. Those who disbelieve long that you may neglect your arms and your baggage, that they may attack you with a sudden united attack. And there is no blame on you, if you are inconvenienced on account of rain or if you are sick, to put away your arms; and take your precautions. Surely Allāh has prepared abasing chastisement for the disbelievers.

103 So when you have finished the prayer, remember Allāh standing and sitting and reclining. But when you are secure (from danger) keep up (regular) prayer. Prayer indeed has been enjoined on the believers at fixed times.

104 And be not weak-hearted in pursuit of the enemy. If you suffer they (too) suffer as you suffer, and you hope from Allāh what they hope not. And Allāh is ever Knowing, Wise.

SECTION 16:
Hypocrites are Dishonest

105 Surely We have revealed the Book to thee with truth that thou mayest judge between people by means of what Allāh has taught thee. And be not one pleading the cause of the dishonest,

106 And ask the forgiveness of Allāh. Surely Allāh is ever Forgiving, Merciful.

107 And contend not on behalf of those who act unfaithfully to their souls. Surely Allāh loves not him who is treacherous, sinful:

108 They seek to hi͏̄ from men and they can͏̄ hide from Allāh, and H͏̄ with them when they ͏̄ sel by night matters please Him not. An͏̄ ever encompasse͏̄ they do.

109 Behold! Yo͏̄ who may conte͏̄

behalf in this world's life, but who will contend with Allāh on their behalf on the Resurrection day, or who will have charge of their affairs?

110 And whoever does evil or wrongs his soul, then asks forgiveness of Allāh, will find Allāh Forgiving, Merciful.

111 And whoever commits a sin, commits it only against himself. And Allāh is ever Knowing, Wise.

112 And whoever commits a fault or a sin, then accuses of it one innocent, he indeed takes upon himself the burden of a calumny and a manifest sin.

SECTION 17:
Secret Counsels of the Hypocrites

113 And were it not for Allāh's grace upon thee and His mercy, a party of them had certainly designed to ruin thee. And they ruin only themselves, and they cannot harm thee in any way. And Allāh has revealed to thee the Book and the Wisdom, and taught thee what thou knewest not, and Allāh's grace on thee is very great.

114 There is no good in most of their secret counsels except (in) him who enjoins charity or goodness or reconciliation between people. And whoever does this, seeking Allāh's pleasure, We shall give him a mighty reward.

115 And whoever acts hostilely to the Messenger after guidance has become manifest to him and follows other than the way of the believers, We turn him to that to which he (himself) turns and make him enter hell; and it is an evil resort.

SECTION 18:
Idolatry condemned

116 Surely Allāh forgives not setting up partners with Him, and He forgives all besides this to whom He pleases. And whoever sets up a partner with Allāh, he indeed goes far astray.

117 Besides Him they call on nothing but female divinities and they call on nothing but a rebellious devil,

118 Whom Allāh has

cursed. And he said: Certainly I will take of Thy servants an appointed portion;

119 And certainly I will lead them astray and excite in them vain desires and bid them so that they will slit the ears of the cattle, and bid them so that they will alter Allāh's creation. And whoever takes the devil for a friend, forsaking Allāh, he indeed suffers a manifest loss.

120 He promises them and excites vain desires in them. And the devil promises them only to deceive.

121 These — their refuge is hell, and they will find no way of escape from it.

122 And those who believe and do good, We shall make them enter Gardens in which rivers flow, to abide therein for ever. It is Allāh's promise, in truth. And who is more truthful in word than Allāh?

123 It will not be in accordance with your vain desires nor the vain desires of the People of the Book. Whoever does evil, will be requited for it and will not find for himself besides Allāh a friend or a helper.

124 And whoever does good deeds, whether male or female, and he (or she) is a believer — these will enter the Garden, and they will not be dealt with a whit unjustly.

125 And who is better in religion than he who submits himself entirely to Allāh while doing good (to others) and follows the faith of Abraham, the upright one? And Allāh took Abraham for a friend.

126 And to Allāh belongs whatever is in the heavens and whatever is in the earth. And Allāh ever encompasses all things.

SECTION 19:
Equitable Dealings with Orphans and Women

127 And they ask thee a decision about women. Say: Allāh makes known to you His decision concerning them; and that which is recited to you in the Book is concerning widowed women, whom you give not what is appointed for them, while you are not inclined to marry them, nor to the weak among children, and that you should deal justly with orphans. And whatever good you do, Allāh is surely ever Knower of it.

128 And if a woman fears ill-usage from her husband or desertion no blame is on them if they effect a reconciliation between them. And reconciliation is better. And avarice is met with in (men's) minds. And if you do good (to others) and keep your duty, surely Allāh is ever Aware of what you do.

129 And you cannot do justice between wives, even though you wish (it), but be not disinclined (from one) with total disinclination, so that you leave her in suspense. And if you are reconciled and keep your duty, surely Allāh is ever Forgiving, Merciful.

130 And if they separate, Allāh will render them both free from want out of His ampleness. And Allāh is ever Ample-giving, Wise.

131 And to Allāh belongs whatever is in the heavens and whatever is in the earth. And certainly We enjoined those who were given the Book before you and (We enjoin) you too to keep your duty to Allāh. And if you disbelieve, surely to Allāh belongs whatever is in the heavens and whatever is in the earth. And Allāh is ever Self-sufficient, Praiseworthy.

132 And to Allāh belongs whatever is in the heavens and whatever is in the earth. And Allāh suffices as having charge of affairs.

133 If He please, He will take you away, O people, and bring others. And Allāh is ever Powerful to do that.

134 Whoever desires the reward of this world — then with Allāh is the reward of this world and the Hereafter. And Allāh is ever Hearing, Seeing.

SECTION 20:
Hypocrisy Condemned

135 O you who believe, be maintainers of justice, bearers of witness for Allāh, even though it be against your own selves or (your) parents or near relatives — whether he be rich or poor, Allāh has a better right over them both. So follow not (your) low desires, lest you deviate. And if you distort or turn away from (truth), surely Allāh is ever Aware of what you do.

136 O you who believe, believe in Allāh and His Messenger and the Book which He has revealed to His Messenger and the Book which He revealed before. And whoever disbelieves in Allāh and His angels and His Books and His messengers and the Last Day, he indeed strays far away.

137 Those who believe then disbelieve, again believe and again disbelieve, then increase in disbelief, Allāh will never forgive them nor guide them in the (right) way.

138 Give news to the hypocrites that for them is a *painful chastisement—*

139 Those who take disbelievers for friends rather than believers. Do they seek for might from them? Might surely belongs wholly to Allāh.

140 And indeed He has revealed to you in the Book that when you hear Allāh's messages disbelieved in and mocked at, sit not with them until they enter into some other discourse, for then indeed you would be like them. Surely Allāh will gather together the hypocrites and the disbelievers all in hell —

141 Those who wait (for misfortunes) for you. Then if you have a victory from Allāh they say: Were we not with you? And if there is a chance for the disbelievers, they say: Did we not prevail over you and defend you from the believers? So Allāh will judge between you on the day of Resurrection. And Allāh will by no means give the disbelievers a way against the believers.

SECTION 21:
End of the Hypocrites

142 The hypocrites seek to deceive Allāh, and He will requite their deceit to them. And when they stand up for prayer, they stand up sluggishly — they do it only to be seen of men and remember Allāh but little,

THE WOMEN

143 Wavering between that (and this) — (belonging) neither to these nor to those. And whomsoever Allāh leaves in error, thou wilt not find a way for him.

144 O you who believe, take not the disbelievers for friends rather than the believers. Do you desire to give Allāh a manifest proof against yourselves?

145 The hypocrites are surely in the lowest depths of the Fire, and thou wilt find no helper for them,

146 Save those who repent and amend and hold fast to Allāh and are sincere in their obedience to Allāh — these are with the believers. And Allāh will soon grant the believers a mighty reward.

147 Why should Allāh chastise you if you are grateful and believe? And Allāh is ever Multiplier of rewards, Knowing.

Part 6

148 Allāh loves not the public utterance of hurtful speech, except by one who has been wronged. And Allāh is ever Hearing, Knowing.

149 If you do good openly or keep it secret or pardon an evil, Allāh surely is ever Pardoning, Powerful.

150 Those who disbelieve in Allāh and His messengers and desire to make a distinction between Allāh and His messengers and say: We believe in some and disbelieve in others; and desire to take a course in between —

151 These are truly disbelievers; and We have prepared for the disbelievers an abasing chastisement.

152 And those who believe in Allāh and His messengers and make no distinction between any of them, to them He will grant their rewards. And Allāh is ever Forgiving, Merciful.

SECTION 22:
Transgressions of the Jews

153 The People of the Book ask thee to bring down to them a Book from heaven; indeed they demanded of Moses a greater thing than that, for they said: Show us Allāh manifestly. So destructive punishment overtook them on account of their wrong-doing. Then they took the calf (for a god), after clear signs had come to them, but We pardoned this. And We gave Moses clear authority.

154 And We raised the mountain above them at their covenant. And We said to them: Enter the door making obeisance. And We said to them: Violate not the Sabbath; and We took from them a firm covenant.

155 Then for their breaking their covenant and their disbelief in the messages of Allāh and their killing the prophets wrongfully and their saying, Our hearts are covered; nay, Allāh has sealed them owing to their disbelief, so they believe not but a little:

156 And for their disbelief *and for their uttering* against Mary a grievous calumny:

157 And for their saying: We have killed the Messiah, Jesus, son of Mary, the messenger of Allāh, and they killed him not, nor did they cause his death on the cross, but he was made to appear to them as such. And certainly those who differ therein are in doubt about it. They have no knowledge about it, but only follow a conjecture, and they killed him not for certain:

158 Nay, Allāh exalted him in His presence. And Allāh is ever Mighty, Wise.

159 And there is none of the People of the Book but will believe in this before his death; and on the day of Resurrection he will be a witness against them.

160 So for the iniquity of the Jews, We forbade them the good things which had been made lawful for them, and for their hindering many (people) from Allāh's way.

161 And for their taking usury — though indeed they were forbidden it — and their devouring the property of people falsely. And We have prepared for the disbelievers from among them a painful chastisement.

162 But the firm in knowledge among them and the believers believe in that which has been

THE WOMEN

revealed to thee and that which was revealed before thee, and those who keep up prayer and give the poor-rate and the believers in Allāh and the Last Day — these it is to whom We shall give a mighty reward.

SECTION 23:
Previous Revelation bears out Quranic Statements

163 Surely We have revealed to thee as We revealed to Noah and the prophets after him, and We revealed to Abraham and Ishmael and Isaac and Jacob and the tribes, and Jesus and Job and Jonah and Aaron and Solomon, and We gave to David a scripture.

164 And (We sent) messengers We have mentioned to thee before and messengers We have not mentioned to thee. And to Moses Allāh addressed His word, speaking (to him) —

165 Messengers, bearers of good news and warners, so that the people may have no plea against Allāh after the (coming of) messengers. And Allāh is ever Mighty, Wise.

166 But Allāh bears witness by that which He has revealed to thee that He has revealed it with His knowledge, and the angels (also) bear witness. And Allāh is sufficient as a witness.

167 Those who disbelieve and hinder (others) from Allāh's way, they indeed have erred, going far astray.

168 Those who disbelieve and act unjustly, Allāh will never forgive them, nor guide them to a path,

169 Except the path of hell, to abide in it for a long time. And that is easy to Allāh.

170 O mankind, the Messenger has indeed come to you with truth from your Lord, so believe, it is better for you. And if you disbelieve, then surely to Allāh belongs whatever is in the heavens and the earth. And Allāh is ever Knowing, Wise.

171 O People of the Book, exceed not the limits in your religion nor speak anything about Allāh, but the truth. The Messiah, Jesus, son of Mary, is only a messenger of Allāh and His word which He communicated to Mary and a mercy from Him. So believe in Allāh and His messengers. And say not, Three. Desist, it is better for you. Allāh is only one God. Far be it from His glory to have a son. To Him belongs whatever is in the heavens and whatever is in the earth. And sufficient is Allāh as having charge of affairs.

SECTION 24:
Prophethood of Jesus

172 The Messiah disdains not to be a servant of Allāh, nor do the angels who are near to Him. And whoever disdains His service and is proud, He will gather them all together to Himself.

173 Then as for those who believe and do good, He will pay them fully their rewards and give them more out of His grace. And as for those who disdain and are proud, He will chastise them with a painful chastisement, and they will find for themselves besides Allāh no friend nor helper.

174 O people, manifest proof has indeed come to you from your Lord and We have sent down to you a clear light.

175 Then as for those who believe in Allāh and hold fast by Him, He will admit them to His mercy and grace, and guide them to Himself on a right path.

176 They ask thee for a decision. Say: Allāh gives you a decision concerning the person who has neither parents nor children. If a man dies (and) he has no son and he has a sister, hers is half of what he leaves, and he shall be her heir if she has no son. But if there be two (sisters), they shall have two-thirds of what he leaves. And if there are brethren, men and women, then for the male is the like of the portion of two females. Allāh makes clear to you, lest you err. And Allāh is Knower of all things.

CHAPTER 5
Al-Mā'idah: **The Food**

(REVEALED AT MADĪNAH: 16 *sections*; 120 *verses*)

SECTION 1:
Perfection of Religion in Islām

In the name of Allāh, the Beneficent, the Merciful.

1 O you who believe, fulfil the obligations. The cattle quadrupeds are allowed to you except that which is recited to you, not violating the prohibition against game when you are on the pilgrimage. Surely Allāh orders what He pleases.

2 O you who believe, violate not the signs of Allāh, nor the Sacred Month, nor the offerings, nor the victims with garlands, nor those repairing to the Sacred House seeking the grace and pleasure of their Lord. And when you are free from pilgrimage obligations, then hunt. And let not hatred of a people — because they hindered you from the Sacred Mosque — incite you to transgress. And help one another in righteousness and piety, and help not one another in sin and aggression, and keep your duty to Allāh. Surely Allāh is Severe in requiting (evil).

3 Forbidden to you is that which dies of itself, and blood, and flesh of swine, and that on which any other name than that of Allāh has been invoked, and the strangled (animal), and that beaten to death, and that killed by a fall, and that killed by goring with the horn, and that which wild beasts have eaten — except what you slaughter; and that which is sacrificed on stones set up (for idols), and that you seek to divide by arrows; that is a transgression. This day have those who disbelieve despaired of your religion, so fear them not, and fear Me. This day have I perfected for you your religion and completed My favour to you and chosen for you Islām as a religion. But whoever is compelled by hunger, not inclining wilfully to sin, then surely Allāh is Forgiving, Merciful.

4 They ask thee as to what is allowed them. Say: The good things are allowed to you, and what you have taught the beasts and birds of prey, training them to hunt — you teach them of what Allāh has taught you; so eat of that which they catch for you and mention the name of Allāh over it; and keep your duty to Allāh. Surely Allāh is Swift in reckoning.

5 This day (all) good things are made lawful for you. And the food of those who have been given the Book is lawful for you and your food is lawful for them. And so are the chaste from among the believing women and the chaste from among those who have been given the Book before you, when you give them their dowries, taking (them) in marriage, not fornicating nor taking them for paramours in secret. And whoever denies faith, his work indeed is vain; and in the Hereafter he is of the losers.

SECTION 2:
Duty of Uprightness

6 O you who believe, when you rise up for prayer, wash your faces, and your hands up to the elbows, and wipe your heads, and (wash) your feet up to the ankles. And if you are under an obligation, then wash (yourselves). And if you are sick or on a journey, or one of you comes from the privy, or you have had contact with women and you cannot find water, betake yourselves to pure earth and wipe your faces and your hands therewith. Allāh desires not to place a burden on you but He wishes to purify you, and that He may complete His favour on you, so that you may give thanks.

7 And remember Allāh's favour on you and His covenant with which He bound you when you said: We have heard and we obey. And keep your duty to Allāh. Surely Allāh knows what is in the breasts.

8 O you who believe, be upright for Allāh, bearers of witness with justice; and let not hatred of a people incite you not to act equitably. Be just; that is nearer to observance of duty. And keep your duty to Allāh. Surely Allāh is Aware of what you do.

9 Allāh has promised to those who believe and do good deeds: For them is forgiveness and a mighty reward.

10 And those who disbelieve and reject Our messages, such are the companions of the flaming fire.

11 O you who believe, *remember* Allāh's favour on you when a people had determined to stretch out their hands against you, but He withheld their hands from you; and keep your duty to Allāh. And on Allāh let the believers rely.

SECTION 3:
Christian Violation of the Covenant

12 And certainly Allāh made a covenant with the Children of Israel, and We raised up among them twelve chieftains. And Allāh said: Surely I am with you. If you keep up prayer and pay the poor-rate and believe in My messengers and assist them and offer to Allāh a goodly gift, I will certainly cover your evil deeds, and cause you to enter Gardens wherein rivers flow. But whoever among you disbelieves after that, he indeed strays from the right way.

13 But on account of their breaking their covenant We cursed them and hardened their hearts. They alter the words from their places and neglect a portion of that whereof they were reminded. And thou wilt always discover treachery in them excepting a few of them — so pardon them and forgive. Surely Allāh loves those who do good (to others).

14 And with those who say, We are Christians, We made a covenant, but they neglected a portion of that whereof they were reminded so We stirred up enmity and hatred among them to the day of Resurrection. And Allāh will soon inform them of what they did.

15 O People of the Book, indeed Our Messenger has come to you, making clear to you much of that which you concealed of the Book and passing over much. Indeed, there has come to you from Allāh, a Light and a clear Book,

16 Whereby Allāh guides such as follow His pleasure into the ways of peace, and brings them out of darkness into light by His will, and guides them to the right path.

17 They indeed disbelieve who say: Surely, Allāh — He is the Messiah, son of Mary. Say: Who then could control anything as against Allāh when He wished to destroy the Messiah, son of Mary, and his mother and all those on the earth? And Allāh's is the kingdom of the heavens and the earth and what is between them. He creates what He pleases. And Allāh is Possessor of power over all things.

18 And the Jews and the Christians say: We are the sons of Allāh and His beloved ones. Say: Why does He then chastise you for your sins? Nay, you are mortals from among those whom He has created. He forgives whom He pleases and chastises whom He pleases. And Allāh's is the kingdom of the heavens and the earth and what is between them, and to Him is the eventual coming.

19 O People of the Book, indeed Our Messenger has come to you explaining to you after a cessation of the messengers, lest you say: There came not to us a bearer of good news nor a warner. So indeed a bearer of good news and a warner has come to you. And Allāh is Possessor of power over all things.

SECTION 4:
Israelites' Violation of the Covenant

20 And when Moses said to his people: O my people, remember the favour of Allāh to you when He raised prophets among you and made you kings and gave you what He gave not to any other of the nations.

21 O my people, enter the Holy Land which Allāh has

ordained for you and turn not your backs, for then you will turn back losers.

22 They said: O Moses, therein are a powerful people, and we shall not enter it until they go out from it; if they go out from it, then surely we will enter.

23 Two men of those who feared, on whom Allāh had bestowed a favour, said: Enter upon them by the gate, for when you enter it you will surely be victorious; and put your trust in Allāh, if you are believers.

24 They said: O Moses, we will never enter it so long as they are in it; go therefore thou and thy Lord, and fight; surely here we sit.

25 He said: My Lord, I have control of none but my own self and my brother; so distinguish between us and the transgressing people.

26 He said: It will surely be forbidden to them for forty years — they will wander about in the land. So grieve not for the transgressing people.

SECTION 5: Cain and Abel – murderous plots against the Prophet

27 And relate to them with truth the story of the two sons of Adam, when they offered an offering, but it was accepted from one of them and was not accepted from the other. He said: I will certainly kill thee. (The other) said: Allāh accepts only from the dutiful.

28 If thou stretch out thy hand against me to kill me I shall not stretch out my hand against thee to kill thee. Surely I fear Allāh, the Lord of the worlds:

29 I would rather that thou shouldst bear the sin against me and thine own sin, thus thou wouldst be of the companions of the Fire; and that is the recompense of the unjust.

30 At length his mind made it easy for him to kill his brother, so he killed him; so he became one of the losers.

31 Then Allāh sent a crow scratching the ground to show him how to cover the dead body of his brother. He said: Woe is me! Am I not able to be as this crow and cover the dead body of my brother? So he became of those who regret.

32 For this reason We prescribed for the Children of Israel that whoever kills a person, unless it be for manslaughter or for mischief in the land, it is as though he had killed all men. And whoever saves a life, it is as though he had saved the lives of all men. And certainly Our messengers came to them with clear arguments, but even after that many of them commit excesses in the land.

33 The only punishment of those who wage war against Allāh and His Messenger and strive to make mischief in the land is that they should be murdered, or crucified, or their hands and *their feet should* be cut off on opposite sides, or they should be imprisoned. This shall be a disgrace for them in this world, and in the Hereafter they shall have a grievous chastisement.

34 Except those who repent before you overpower them; so know that Allāh is Forgiving, Merciful.

SECTION 6:
Punishment of Offenders

35 O you who believe, keep your duty to Allāh, and seek means of nearness to Him, and strive hard in His way that you may be successful.

36 Those who disbelieve, even if they had all that is in the earth, and the like of it with it, to ransom themselves therewith from the chastisement of the day of Resurrection, it would not be accepted from them; and theirs is a painful chastisement.

37 They would desire to come forth from the Fire, and they will not come forth from it, and theirs is a lasting chastisement.

38 And (as for) the man and the woman addicted to theft, cut off their hands as a punishment for what they have earned, an exemplary punishment from Allāh. And Allāh is Mighty, Wise.

39 But whoever repents after his wrongdoing and reforms, Allāh will turn to him (mercifully). Surely Allāh is Forgiving, Merciful.

40 Knowest thou not that Allāh is He to Whom belongs the kingdom of the heavens and the earth? He chastises whom He pleases, and forgives whom He pleases. And Allāh is Possessor of power over all things.

41 O Messenger, let not those grieve thee who hasten to disbelieve, from among those who say with their mouths, We believe, and their hearts believe not, and from among those who are Jews — they are listeners for the sake of a lie, listeners for another people who have not come to thee. They alter the words after they are put in their (proper) places, saying: If you are given this, take it, and if you are not given this, be cautious. And he for whom Allāh intends temptation, thou controllest naught for him against Allāh. Those are they whose hearts Allāh intends not to purify. For them is disgrace in this world, and for them a grievous chastisement in the Hereafter.

42 Listeners for the sake of a lie, devourers of forbidden things, so if they come to thee, judge between them or turn away from them. And if thou turn away from them, they cannot harm thee at all. And if thou judge, judge between them with equity. Surely Allāh loves the equitable.

43 And how do they make thee a judge and they have the Torah wherein is Allāh's judgment? Yet they turn away after that! And these are not believers.

SECTION 7:
The Qur'ān and Previous Scriptures

44 Surely We revealed the Torah, having guidance and light. By it did the prophets who submitted themselves (to Allāh) judge for the Jews, and the rabbis and the doctors of law, because they were required to guard the Book of Allāh, and they were witnesses thereof. So fear not the people and fear Me, and take not a small price for My messages. And whoever judges not by what

Allāh has revealed, those are the disbelievers.

45 And We prescribed to them in it that life is for life, and eye for eye, and nose for nose, and ear for ear, and tooth for tooth, and for wounds retaliation. But whoso forgoes it, it shall be an expiation for him. And whoever judges not by what Allāh has revealed, those are the wrongdoers.

46 And We sent after them in their footsteps Jesus, son of Mary, verifying that which was before him of the Torah; and We gave him the Gospel containing guidance and light, and verifying that which was before it of the Torah, and a guidance and an admonition for the dutiful.

47 And let the People of the Gospel judge by that which Allāh has revealed in it. And whoever judges not by what Allāh has revealed, those are the transgressors.

48 And We have revealed to thee the Book with the truth, verifying that which is before it of the Book and a guardian over it, so judge between them by what Allāh has revealed, and follow not their low desires, (turning away) from the truth that has come to thee. For everyone of you We appointed a law and a way. And if Allāh had pleased He would have made you a single people, but that He might try you in what He gave you. So vie one with another in virtuous deeds. To Allāh you will all return, so He will inform you of that wherein you differed;

49 And that thou shouldst judge between them by what Allāh has revealed, and follow not their low desires, and be cautious of them lest they seduce thee from part of what Allāh has revealed to thee. Then if they turn away, know that Allāh desires to afflict them for some of their sins. And surely many of the people are transgressors.

50 Is it then the judgment of ignorance that they desire? And who is better than Allāh to judge for a people who are sure?

SECTION 8:
Relations of Muslims with Enemies

51 O you who believe, take not the Jews and the Christians for friends. They are friends of each other. And whoever amongst you takes them for friends he is indeed one of them. Surely Allāh guides not the unjust people.

52 But thou seest those in whose hearts is a disease, hastening towards them, saying: We fear lest a calamity should befall us. Maybe Allāh will bring the victory or a commandment from Himself, so they will regret what they hid in their souls.

53 And those who believe will say: Are these they who swore by Allāh with their most forcible oaths that they were surely with you? Their deeds will bear no fruit, so they will be losers.

54 O you who believe, should anyone of you turn back from his religion, then Allāh will bring a people, whom He loves and who love Him, humble towards the believers, mighty against the disbelievers, striving hard in Allāh's way and not fearing the censure of any censurer. This is Allāh's grace — He gives it to whom He pleases. And Allāh is Ample-giving, Knowing.

55 Only Allāh is your Friend and His Messenger and those who believe, those who keep up prayer and pay the poor-rate, and they bow down.

56 And whoever takes Allāh and His Messenger and those who believe for friend — surely the party of Allāh, they shall triumph.

SECTION 9:
The Mockers

57 O you who believe, take not for friends those who take your religion as a mockery and a sport, from among those who were given the Book before you and the disbelievers; and keep your duty to Allāh if you are believers.

58 And when you call to prayer they take it as a mockery and a sport. That is because they are a people who understand not.

59 Say: O People of the Book, do you find fault with

us for aught except that we believe in Allāh and in that which has been revealed to us and that which was revealed before, while most of you are transgressors?

60 Say: Shall I inform you of those worse than this in retribution from Allāh? They are those whom Allāh has cursed and upon whom He brought His wrath and of whom He made apes and swine, and who serve the devil. These are in a worse plight and further astray from the straight path.

61 And when they come to you, they say, We believe, and surely they come in unbelief and they go forth in it. And Allāh knows best what they conceal.

62 And thou seest many of them vying one with another in sin and transgression, and their devouring *illegal gain.* Certainly evil is that which they do.

63 Why do not the rabbis and the doctors of law prohibit them from their sinful utterances and their devouring unlawful gain? Certainly evil are the works they do.

64 And the Jews say: The hand of Allāh is tied up. Their own hands are shackled and they are cursed for what they say. Nay, both His hands are spread out. He disburses as He pleases. And that which has been revealed to thee from thy Lord will certainly make many of them increase in inordinacy and disbelief. And We have cast among them enmity and hatred till the day of Resurrection. Whenever they kindle a fire for war Allāh puts it out, and they strive to make mischief in the land. And Allāh loves not the mischief-makers.

65 And if the People of the Book had believed and kept their duty We would certainly have removed from them their evils, and made them enter gardens of bliss.

66 And if they had observed the Torah and the Gospel and that which is revealed to them from their Lord, they would certainly have eaten from above them and from beneath their feet. There is a party of them keeping to the moderate course; and most of them — evil is that which they do.

SECTION 10:
Christian Deviation from the Truth

67 O Messenger, deliver that which has been revealed to thee from thy Lord; and if thou do (it) not, thou hast not delivered His message. And Allāh will protect thee from men. Surely Allāh guides not the disbelieving people.

68 Say: O People of the Book, you follow no good till you observe the Torah and the Gospel and that which is revealed to you from your Lord. And surely that which has been revealed to thee from thy Lord will make many of them increase in inordinacy and disbelief; so grieve not for the disbelieving people.

69 Surely those who believe and those who are Jews and the Sabians and the Christians — whoever believes in Allāh and the Last Day and does good — they shall have no fear nor shall they grieve.

70 Certainly We made a covenant with the Children of Israel and We sent to them messengers. Whenever a messenger came to them with that which their souls desired not, some (of them) they called liars and some they (even) sought to kill.

71 And they thought that there would be no affliction, so they became blind and deaf; then Allāh turned to them (mercifully) but many of them (again) became blind and deaf. And Allāh is Seer of what they do.

72 Certainly they disbelieve who say: Allāh, He is the Messiah, son of Mary. And the Messiah said: O Children of Israel, serve Allāh, my Lord and your Lord. Surely whoever associates (others) with Allāh, Allāh has forbidden to him the Garden and his abode is the Fire. And for the wrongdoers there will be no helpers.

73 Certainly they disbelieve who say: Allāh is the third of the three. And there is no God but One God. And if they desist not from what they say, a painful chastisement will surely befall such of them as disbelieve.

74 Will they not then turn to Allāh and ask His forgiveness? And Allāh is Forgiving, Merciful.

75 The Messiah, son of Mary, was only a messenger; messengers before him had indeed passed away. And his mother was a truthful woman. They both used to eat food. See how We make the messages clear to them! then behold, how they are turned away!

76 Say: Do you serve besides Allāh that which controls for you neither harm nor good? And Allāh — He is the Hearing, the Knowing.

77 Say: O People of the Book, exaggerate not in the matter of your religion unjustly, and follow not the low desires of people who went astray before and led many astray, and went astray from the right path.

SECTION 11:
Christian Nearness to Islām

78 Those who disbelieved from among the Children of Israel were cursed by the tongue of David and Jesus, son of Mary. This was because they disobeyed and exceeded the limits.

79 They forbade not one another the hateful things they did. Evil indeed was what they did.

80 Thou seest many of them befriending those who disbelieve. Certainly evil is that which their souls send before for them, so that Allāh is displeased with them, and in chastisement will they abide.

81 And if they believed in Allāh and the Prophet and that which is revealed to him, they would not take them for friends, but most of them are transgressors.

82 Thou wilt certainly find the most violent of people in enmity against the believers to be the Jews and the idolators; and thou wilt find the nearest in friendship to the believers to be those who say, We are Christians. That is because *there* are priests and monks among them and because they are not proud.

Part 7

83 And when they hear that which has been revealed to the Messenger thou seest their eyes overflow with tears because of the truth they recognize. They say: Our Lord, we believe, so write us down with the witnesses.

84 And what (reason) have we that we should not believe in Allāh and in the Truth that has come to us, while we earnestly desire that our Lord should cause us to enter with the righteous people?

85 So Allāh rewarded them for what they said, with Gardens wherein rivers flow to abide in them. And that is the reward of the doers of good.

86 And those who disbelieve and reject Our messages, such are the companions of the flaming fire.

SECTION 12:
A Warning – Besetting Sins of Previous People

87 O you who believe, forbid not the good things which Allāh has made lawful for you and exceed not the limits. Surely Allāh loves not those who exceed the limits.

88 And eat of the lawful and good (things) that Allāh has given you, and keep your duty to Allāh, in Whom you believe.

89 Allāh will not call you to account for that which is vain in your oaths, but He will call you to account for the making of deliberate oaths; so its expiation is the feeding of ten poor men with the average (food) you feed your families with, or their clothing, or the freeing of a neck. But whoso finds not (means) should fast for three days. This is the expiation of your oaths when you swear. And keep your oaths. Thus does Allāh make clear to you His messages that you may give thanks.

90 O you who believe, intoxicants and games of chance and (sacrificing to) stones set up and (dividing by) arrows are only an uncleanness, the devil's work; so shun it that you may succeed.

91 The devil desires only to create enmity and hatred among you by means of intoxicants and games of chance, and to keep you back from the remembrance of Allāh and from prayer.

Will you then keep back?

92 And obey Allāh and obey the Messenger and be cautious. But if you turn back then know that the duty of Our Messenger is only a clear deliverance of the message.

93 On those who believe and do good there is no blame for what they eat, when they keep their duty and believe and do good deeds, then keep their duty and believe, then keep their duty and do good (to others). And Allāh loves the doers of good.

SECTION 13:
Inviolability of the Ka'bah

94 O you who believe, Allāh will certainly try you in respect of some game which your hands and your lances can reach, that Allāh may know who fears Him in secret. Whoever exceeds the limit after this, for him is a painful chastisement.

95 O you who believe, kill not game while you are on pilgrimage. And whoever among you kills it intentionally, the compensation thereof is the like of what he killed, from the cattle, as two just persons among you judge, as an offering to be brought to the Ka'bah, or the expiation thereof is the feeding of the poor or equivalent of it in fasting, that he may taste the unwholesome result of his deed. Allāh pardons what happened in the past. And whoever returns (to it), Allāh will punish him. And Allāh is Mighty, Lord of Retribution.

96 Lawful to you is the game of the sea and its food, a provision for you and for the travellers, and the game of the land is forbidden to you so long as you are on pilgrimage, and keep your duty to Allāh, to Whom you shall be gathered.

97 Allāh has made the Ka'bah, the Sacred House, a means of support for the people, and the sacred month and the offerings and the victims with garlands. That is that you may know that Allāh knows whatever is in the heavens and whatever is in the earth, and that Allāh is Knower of all things.

98 Know that Allāh is Severe in requiting (evil)

THE FOOD

and that Allāh is Forgiving, Merciful.

99 The duty of the Messenger is only to deliver (the message). And Allāh knows what you do openly and what you hide.

100 Say: The bad and the good are not equal, though the abundance of the bad may please thee. So keep your duty to Allāh, O men of understanding, that you may succeed.

SECTION 14:
Some Directions for Muslims

101 O you who believe, ask not about things which if made known to you would give you trouble; and if you ask about them when the Qur'ān is being revealed, they will be made known to you. Allāh pardons this; and Allāh is Forgiving, Forbearing.

102 A people before you indeed asked such questions, then became disbelievers therein.

103 Allāh has not ordained a *baḥīrah* or a *sā'ibah* or a *waṣīlah* or a *ḥāmī*, but those who disbelieve fabricate a lie against Allāh. And most of them understand not.

104 And when it is said to them, Come to that which Allāh has revealed and to the Messenger, they say: Sufficient for us is that wherein we found our fathers. What! even though their fathers knew nothing and had no guidance!

105 O you who believe, take care of your souls — he who errs cannot harm you when you are on the right way. To Allāh you will all return, so He will inform you of what you did.

106 O you who believe, call to witness between you, when death draws nigh to one of you, at the time of making the will, two just persons from among you, or two others from among others than you, if you are travelling in the land and the calamity of death befalls you. You should detain them after the prayer. Then if you doubt (them), they shall both swear by Allāh (saying): We will not take for it a price, though there be a relative nor will we hide the testimony of Allāh, for then certainly we shall be sinners.

107 If it be discovered that they are guilty of a sin, two others shall stand up in their place from among those against whom the first two have been guilty of a sin; so they shall swear by Allāh: Certainly our testimony is truer than the testimony of those two, and we have not exceeded the limit, for then surely we should be unjust.

108 Thus it is more probable that they will give true testimony or fear that other oaths will be taken after their oaths. And keep your duty to Allāh and hearken. And Allāh guides not the transgressing people.

SECTION 15:
Christian Love of this Life

109 On the day when Allāh will gather together the messengers and say: What was the response you received? They will say: We have no knowledge. Surely Thou art the great Knower of the unseen.

110 When Allāh will say: O Jesus, son of Mary, remember My favour to thee and to thy mother, when I strengthened thee with the Holy Spirit; thou spokest to people in the cradle and in old age, and when I taught thee the Book and the Wisdom and the Torah and the Gospel, and when thou didst determine out of clay a thing like the form of a bird by My permission, then thou didst breathe into it and it became a bird by My permission; and thou didst heal the blind and the leprous by My permission; and when thou didst raise the dead by My permission; and when I withheld the Children of Israel from thee when thou camest to them with clear arguments — but those of them who disbelieved said: This is nothing but clear enchantment.

111 And when I revealed to the disciples, saying, Believe in Me and My messenger, they said: We believe and bear witness that we submit.

112 When the disciples said: O Jesus, son of Mary, is thy Lord able to send down food to us from heaven? He said: Keep your duty to Allāh if you are believers.

113 They said: We desire to eat of it, and that our hearts should be at rest, and that we may know that thou hast indeed spoken truth to us, and that we may be witnesses thereof.

114 Jesus, son of Mary, said: O Allāh, our Lord, send down to us food from heaven which should be to us an ever-recurring happiness to the first of us and the last of us, and a sign from Thee, and give us sustenance and Thou art the Best of the sustainers.

115 Allāh said: Surely I will send it down to you, but whoever disbelieves afterwards from among you, I will chastise him with a chastisement with which I will not chastise anyone among the nations.

SECTION 16:
False Doctrines introduced after Jesus' Death

116 And when Allāh will say: O Jesus, son of Mary, didst thou say to men, Take me and my mother for two gods besides Allāh? He will say: Glory be to Thee! it was not for me to say what I had no right to (say). If I had said it, Thou wouldst indeed have known it. Thou knowest what is in my mind, and I know not what is in Thy mind. Surely Thou art the great Knower of the unseen.

117 I said to them naught save as Thou didst command me: Serve Allāh, my Lord and your Lord; and I was a witness of them so long as I was among them, but when Thou didst cause me to die Thou wast the Watcher over them. And Thou art Witness of all things.

118 If Thou chastise them, surely they are Thy servants; and if Thou protect them, surely Thou art the Mighty, the Wise.

119 Allāh will say: This is a day when their truth will profit the truthful ones. For them are Gardens wherein flow rivers abiding therein forever. Allāh is well pleased with them and they are well pleased with Allāh. That is the mighty achievement.

120 Allāh's is the kingdom of the heavens and the earth and whatever is in them; and He is Possessor of power over all things.

CHAPTER 6
Al-An'ām: **The Cattle**

(REVEALED AT MAKKAH: 20 *sections*; 165 *verses*)

SECTION 1:
Ultimate Triumph of Divine Unity

In the name of Allāh, the Beneficent, the Merciful.

1 Praise be to Allāh, Who created the heavens and the earth, and made darkness and light. Yet those who disbelieve set up equals to their Lord.

2 He it is Who created you from clay, then He decreed a term. And there is a term named with Him; still you doubt.

3 And He is Allāh in the heavens and in the earth. He knows your secret (thoughts) and your open (words), and He knows what you earn.

4 And there comes not to them any message of the messages of their Lord but they turn away from it.

5 So they rejected the truth when it came to them, but soon will come to them the news of that which they mocked.

6 See they not how many a generation We destroyed before them, whom We had established in the earth as We have not established you, and We sent the clouds pouring abundant rain on them, and We made the rivers flow beneath them? Then We destroyed them for their sins, and raised up after them another generation.

7 And if We had sent down to thee a writing on paper, then they had touched it with their hands, those who disbelieve would have said: This is nothing but clear enchantment.

8 And they say: Why has not an angel been sent down to him? And if We send down an angel, the matter would be decided and then they would not be respited.

9 And if We had made him an angel, We would certainly have made him a man, and (thus) made confused to them what they confuse.

10 And certainly messengers before thee were derided, but that which they derided encompassed those of them who scoffed.

SECTION 2:
Greatness of Divine Mercy

11 Say: Travel in the land, then see what was the end of the rejectors.

12 Say: To whom belongs whatever is in the heavens and the earth? Say: To Allāh. He has ordained mercy on Himself. He will certainly gather you on the Resurrection day — there is no doubt about it. Those who have lost their souls will not believe.

13 And to Him belongs whatever dwells in the night and the day. And He is the Hearing, the Knowing.

14 Say: Shall I take for a friend other than Allāh, the Originator of the heavens and the earth, and He feeds and is not fed? Say: I am commanded to be the first of those who submit. And be thou not of the polytheists.

15 Say: Surely I fear, if I disobey my Lord, the chastisement of a grievous day.

16 He from whom it is averted on that day, Allāh indeed has had mercy on him. And this is a manifest achievement.

17 And if Allāh touch thee with affliction, there is none to remove it but He. And if He touch thee with good, He is Possessor of power over all things.

18 And He is the Supreme, above His servants. And He is the Wise, the Aware.

19 Say: What thing is the weightiest in testimony? Say: Allāh is witness between you and me. And this Qur'ān has been revealed to me that with it I may warn you and whomsoever it reaches. Do you really bear witness that there are other gods with Allāh? Say: I bear not witness. Say: He is only One God, and surely I am inno-

THE CATTLE

cent of that which you set up (with Him).

20 Those whom We have given the Book recognize him as they recognize their sons. Those who have lost their souls — they will not believe.

SECTION 3:
Polytheists' Witness against Themselves

21 And who is more unjust than he who forges a lie against Allāh or gives the lie to His messages? Surely the wrongdoers will not be successful.

22 And on the day We gather them all together, then We shall say to those who set up gods (with Allāh): Where are your associate-gods whom you asserted?

23 Then their excuse would be nothing but that they would say: By Allāh, our Lord! we were not polytheists.

24 See how they lie against their own souls, and that which they forged shall fail them!

25 And of them is he who hearkens to thee and We have cast veils over their hearts so that they understand it not and a deafness into their ears. And (even) if they see every sign they will not believe in it. So much so that when they come to thee they only dispute with thee — those who disbelieve say: This is naught but stories of the ancients.

26 And they forbid (others) from it, and they keep away from it; and they ruin none but their own souls while they perceive not.

27 And if thou couldst see when they are made to stand before the Fire, and say: Would that we were sent back! We would not reject the messages of our Lord but would be of the believers.

28 Nay, that which they concealed before will become manifest to them. And if they were sent back, they would certainly go back to that which they are forbidden, and surely they are liars.

29 And they say: There is nothing but our life of this world and we shall not be raised again.

30 And if thou couldst see when they are made to stand before their Lord! He will say: Is not this the truth? They will say: Yea, by our Lord! He will say: Taste then the chastisement because you disbelieved.

SECTION 4:
Rejection of the Truth

31 They are losers indeed who reject the meeting with Allāh, until when the hour comes upon them suddenly, they will say: O our grief for our neglecting it! And they bear their burdens on their backs. Now surely evil is that which they bear!

32 And this world's life is naught but a play and an idle sport. And certainly the abode of the Hereafter is better for those who keep their duty. Do you not then understand?

33 We know indeed that what they say grieves thee, for surely they give not thee the lie, but the wrongdoers give the lie to Allāh's messages.

34 And messengers indeed were rejected before thee, but they were patient when rejected and persecuted, until Our help came to them. And there is none to change the words of Allāh. And there has already come to thee some information about the messengers.

35 And if their turning away is hard on thee, then, if thou canst, seek an opening into the earth or a ladder to heaven, to bring them a sign! And if Allāh pleased, He would certainly have gathered them all to guidance, so be not of the ignorant.

36 Only those accept who listen. And (as for) the dead, Allāh will raise them, then to Him they will be returned.

37 And they say: Why has not a sign been sent down to him from his Lord? Say: Surely Allāh is Able to send down a sign, but most of them know not.

38 And there is no animal in the earth, nor a bird that flies on its two wings, but (they are) communities like yourselves. We have not neglected anything in the Book. Then to their Lord will they be gathered.

THE CATTLE

39 And those who reject Our messages are deaf and dumb, in darkness. Whom Allāh pleases He leaves in error. And whom He pleases He places on the right way.

40 Say: See, if the chastisement of Allāh overtake you or the hour come upon you, will you call on others than Allāh, if you are truthful?

41 Nay, Him you call upon, so He removes that for which you pray, if He pleases, and you forget what you set up (with Him).

SECTION 5:
Consequences of Rejection

42 And indeed We sent (messengers) to nations before thee then We seized them with distress and affliction that they might humble themselves.

43 Yet why did they not, when Our punishment came to them, humble themselves? But their hearts hardened and the devil made all that they did seem fair to them.

44 Then, when they neglected that with which they had been admonished, We opened for them the gates of all things. Until, when they rejoiced in that which they were given, We seized them suddenly; then lo! they were in utter despair.

45 So the roots of the people who did wrong were cut off. And praise be to Allāh, the Lord of the worlds.

46 Say: Have you considered that if Allāh should take away your hearing and your sight and seal your hearts, who is the god besides Allāh that can bring it to you? See how We repeat the messages yet they turn away!

47 Say: See, if the chastisement of Allāh should overtake you suddenly or openly, will any be destroyed but the wrongdoing people?

48 And We send not messengers but as bearers of good news and warners; then whoever believes and acts aright, they shall have no fear, nor shall they grieve.

49 And as for those who reject Our messages, chastisement will afflict them because they transgressed.

50 Say: I say not to you, I have with me the treasures of Allāh, nor do I know the unseen, nor do I say to you that I am an angel; I follow only that which is revealed to me. Say: Are the blind and the seeing alike? Do you not then reflect?

SECTION 6:
Reward of Believers

51 And warn with it those who fear that they will be gathered to their Lord — there is no protector for them, nor any intercessor besides Him — so that they may keep their duty.

52 And drive not away those who call upon their Lord, morning and evening, desiring only His pleasure. Neither art thou accountable for them in aught, nor are they accountable for thee in aught, that thou shouldst drive them away and thus be of the wrongdoers.

53 And thus do We try some of them by others so that they say: Are these they upon whom Allāh has conferred benefit from among us? Does not Allāh best know the grateful?

54 And when those who believe in Our messages come to thee, say: Peace be to you, your Lord has ordained mercy on Himself, (so) that if anyone of you does evil in ignorance, then turns after that and acts aright, then He is Forgiving, Merciful.

55 And thus do We make distinct the messages and so that the way of the guilty may become clear.

SECTION 7:
Divine Judgment

56 Say: I am forbidden to serve those whom you call upon besides Allāh. Say: I follow not your low desires, for then indeed I should go astray and should not be of the guided ones.

57 Say: Surely I have manifest proof from my Lord and you call it a lie. I have not with me that which you would hasten. The judgment is only Allāh's. He relates the truth and He is the Best of deciders.

THE CATTLE

58 Say: If that which you would hasten were with me, the matter would certainly been decided between you and me. And Allāh best knows the wrongdoers.

59 And with Him are the treasures of the unseen — none knows them but He. And He knows what is in the land and the sea. And there falls not a leaf but He knows it, nor is there a grain in the darkness of the earth, nor anything green or dry, but (it is all) in a clear book.

60 And He it is Who takes your souls at night, and He knows what you earn by day, then He raises you up therein that an appointed term may be fulfilled. Then to Him is your return, then He will inform you of what you did.

SECTION 8:
Divine Judgment

61 And He is the Supreme above His servants, and He sends keepers over you; until when death comes to one of you, Our messengers cause him to die, and they are not remiss.

62 Then are they sent back to Allāh, their Master, the True one. Now surely His is the judgment and He is Swiftest in taking account.

63 Say: Who is it that delivers you from the calamities of the land and the sea? (when) you call upon Him, in humility and in secret: If He deliver us from this, we will certainly be of the grateful ones.

64 Say: Allāh delivers you from this and from every distress, yet you set up others (with Him).

65 Say: He has the power to send on you a chastisement from above you or from beneath your feet, or to throw you into confusion, (making you) of different parties, and make some of you taste the violence of others. See how We repeat the messages that they may understand!

66 And thy people call it a lie and it is the Truth. Say: I am not put in charge of you.

67 For every prophecy is a term, and you will soon come to know (it).

68 And when thou seest those who talk nonsense about Our messages, withdraw from them until they enter into some other discourse. And if the devil cause thee to forget, then sit not after recollection with the unjust people.

69 And those who keep their duty are not accountable for them in aught but (theirs) is only to remind; haply they may guard against evil.

70 And leave those who take their religion for a play and an idle sport, and whom this world's life has deceived, and remind (men) hereby lest a soul be destroyed for what it has earned. It has besides Allāh no friend nor intercessor, and though it offer every compensation, it will not be accepted from it. Those are *they who are destroyed* for what they earn. For them is a drink of boiling water and a painful chastisement, because they disbelieved.

SECTION 9:
Abraham's Argument for Divine Unity

71 Say: Shall we call, besides Allāh, on that which profits us not nor harms us, and shall we be turned back on our heels after Allāh has guided us? Like one whom the devils cause to follow his low desires, in bewilderment in the earth — he has companions who call him to the right way (saying), Come to us. Say: Surely the guidance of Allāh, that is the (true) guidance. And we are commanded to submit to the Lord of the worlds:

72 And that you should keep up prayer and keep your duty to Him. And He it is to Whom you shall be gathered.

73 And He it is Who created the heavens and the earth with truth. And when He says, Be, it is. His word is the truth and His is the kingdom on the day when the trumpet is blown. The Knower of the unseen and the seen; and He is the Wise, the Aware.

74 And when Abraham said to his sire, Āzar: Tak-

THE CATTLE

est thou idols for gods? Surely I see thee and thy people in manifest error.

75 And thus did We show Abraham the kingdom of the heavens and the earth and that he might be of those having certainty.

76 So when the night overshadowed him, he saw a star. He said: Is this my Lord? So when it set, he said: I love not the setting ones.

77 Then when he saw the moon rising, he said: Is this my Lord? So when it set, he said: If my Lord had not guided me, I should certainly be of the erring people.

78 Then when he saw the sun rising, he said: Is this my Lord? Is this the greatest? So when it set, he said: O my people, I am clear of what you set up (with Allāh).

79 Surely I have turned myself, being upright, wholly to Him Who originated the heavens and the earth, and I am not of the polytheists.

80 And his people disputed with him. He said: Do you dispute with me respecting Allāh and He has guided me indeed? And I fear not in any way those that you set up with Him, unless my Lord please. My Lord comprehends all things in His knowledge. Will you not then mind?

81 And how should I fear what you have set up (with Him), while you fear not to set up with Allāh that for which He has sent down to you no authority? Which then of the two parties is surer of security, if you know?

82 Those who believe and mix not up their faith with iniquity — for them is security and they go aright.

SECTION 10:
Prophets among Abraham's Descendants

83 And this was Our argument which We gave to Abraham against his people. We exalt in degrees whom We please. Surely thy Lord is Wise, Knowing.

84 And We gave him Isaac and Jacob. Each did We guide; and Noah did We guide before, and of his descendants, David and

Solomon and Job and Joseph and Moses and Aaron. And thus do We reward those who do good (to others).

85 And Zacharias and John and Jesus and Elias; each one (of them) was of the righteous,

86 And Ishmael and Elisha and Jonah and Lot; and each one (of them) We made to excel the people;

87 And some of their fathers and their descendants and their brethren. And We chose them and guided them to the right way.

88 This is Allāh's guidance wherewith He guides whom He pleases of His servants. And if they had associated others (with Him), all that they did would have been vain.

89 *These are they to whom We gave the Book and authority and prophecy. Therefore if these disbelieve in it, We have indeed entrusted it to a people who are not disbelievers in it.*

90 These are they whom Allāh guided, so follow their guidance. Say: I ask you not for any reward for it. It is naught but a Reminder to the nations.

SECTION 11:
Truth of Divine Revelation

91 And they honour not Allāh with the honour due to Him, when they say: Allāh has not revealed anything to a mortal. Say: Who revealed the Book which Moses brought, a light and a guidance to men — you make it into (scattered) papers, which you show and you conceal much? And you are taught that which neither you nor your fathers knew. Say: Allāh. Then leave them sporting in their idle talk.

92 And this is a Blessed Book We have revealed, verifying that which is before it, and that thou *mayest* warn the mother of the towns and those around her. And those who believe in the Hereafter believe in it, and they keep a watch over their prayers.

93 And who is more unjust than he who forges a lie against Allāh, or says, Revelation has been grant-

THE CATTLE

ed to me; while nothing has been revealed to him; and he who says: I can reveal the like of that which Allāh has revealed? And if thou couldst see when the wrongdoers are in the agonies of death and the angels stretch forth their hands, (saying): Yield up your souls. This day you are awarded a chastisement of disgrace because you spoke against Allāh other than truth, and (because) you scorned His messages.

94 And certainly you have come to Us one by one as We created you at first, and you have left behind your backs what We gave you. And We see not with you your intercessors about whom you asserted that they were (Allāh's) associates in respect to you. Certainly the ties between you are now cut off and that which you asserted has failed you.

SECTION 12:
Ultimate Triumph of the Truth

95 Surely Allāh causes the grain and the date-stone to germinate. He brings forth the living from the dead and He is the bringer forth of the dead from the living. That is Allāh. How are you then turned away!

96 He is the Cleaver of the daybreak; and He has made the night for rest, and the sun and the moon for reckoning. That is the measuring of the Mighty, the Knowing.

97 And He it is Who has made the stars for you that you might follow the right way thereby in the darkness of the land and the sea. Indeed We have made plain the signs for a people who know.

98 And He it is Who has brought you into being from a single soul, then there is (for you) a resting-place and a repository. Indeed We have made plain the signs for a people who understand.

99 And He it is Who sends down water from the clouds, then We bring forth with it buds of all (plants), then We bring forth from it green (foliage), from which We produce clustered grain; and of the date-palm, of the sheaths of it, come forth clusters (of dates) within reach; and gardens of grapes and the olive and the pomegranate, alike and unlike. Look at the fruit of it when it bears fruit and the ripening of it. Surely there are signs in this for a people who believe!

100 And they regard the jinn to be partners with Allāh, and He created them, and they falsely attribute to Him sons and daughters without knowledge. Glory be to Him, and highly exalted is He above what they ascribe (to Him)!

SECTION 13:
Gradual Progress

101 Wonderful Originator of the heavens and the earth! How could He have a son when He has no consort? And He created everything, and He is the Knower of all things.

102 That is Allāh, your Lord. There is no god but He; the Creator of all things; therefore serve Him, and He has charge of all things.

103 Vision comprehends Him not, and He comprehends (all) vision; and He is the Subtle, the Aware.

104 Clear proofs have indeed come to you from your Lord; so whoever sees, it is for his own good; and whoever is blind, it is to his own harm. And I am not a keeper over you.

105 And thus do We repeat the messages, and that they may say, Thou hast studied; and that We may make it clear to a people who know.

106 Follow that which is revealed to thee from thy Lord — there is no god but He; and turn away from the polytheists.

107 And if Allāh had pleased, they would not have set up others (with Him). And We have not appointed thee a keeper over them, and thou art not placed in charge of them.

108 And abuse not those whom they call upon besides Allāh, lest, exceeding the limits, they abuse Allāh through ignorance. Thus to every people have We made their deeds fair-seeming; then to their Lord is their return so He will inform them of what they did.

109 And they swear their strongest oaths by Allāh that if a sign come to them they would certainly believe in it. Say: Signs are with Allāh. And what should make you know that when they come they believe not?

110 And We turn their hearts and their sights, even as they did not believe in it the first time; and We leave them in their inordinacy, blindly wandering on.

Part 8
SECTION 14:
Polytheists' Opposition

111 And even if We send down to them the angels and the dead speak to them and We bring together all things before them, they would not believe unless Allāh please, but most of them are ignorant.

112 And thus did We make for every prophet an enemy, the devils from among men and jinn, some of them inspiring others with gilded speech to deceive (them). And if thy Lord pleased, they would not do it, so leave them alone with what they forge —

113 And that the hearts of those who believe not in the Hereafter may incline thereto, and that they may be pleased with it, and that they may earn what they are earning.

114 Shall I then seek a judge other than Allāh, when He it is Who has sent down to you the Book fully explained. And those whom We have given the Book know that it is revealed by thy Lord with truth, so be not thou of the disputers.

115 And the word of thy Lord has been accomplished truly and justly. There is none who can change His words; and He is the Hearer, the Knower.

116 And if thou obey most of those in the earth, they will lead thee astray from Allāh's way. They follow naught but conjecture, and they only lie.

117 Surely thy Lord — He knows best who goes astray from His way, and He knows best the guided ones.

118 Eat, then, of that on which Allāh's name has been mentioned, if you are believers in His messages.

119 And what reason have you that you should not eat of that on which Allāh's name is mentioned, when He has already made plain to you what He has forbidden to you — excepting that which you are compelled to. And surely many lead (people) astray by their low desires through ignorance. Surely thy Lord — He best knows the transgressors.

120 And avoid open sins and secret ones. Surely they who earn sin will be rewarded for what they have earned.

121 And eat not of that on which Allāh's name has not been mentioned, and that is surely a transgression. And certainly the devils inspire their friends to contend with you; and if you obey them, you will surely be polytheists.

SECTION 15:
The Chief Opponents

122 Is he who was dead, then We raised him to life and made for him a light by which he walks among the people, like him whose likeness is that of one in darkness whence he cannot come forth? Thus their doings are made fair-seeming to the disbelievers.

123 And thus have We made in every town the leaders of its guilty ones, that they may make plans therein. And they plan not but against themselves, and they perceive not.

124 And when a message comes to them they say: We will not believe till we are given the like of that which Allāh's messengers are given. Allāh best knows where to place His message. Humiliation from Allāh and severe chastisement will surely befall the guilty for their planning.

125 So whomsoever Allāh intends to guide, He expands his breast for Islām, and whomsoever He intends to leave in error, He makes his breast strait (and) narrow as though he were ascending upwards. Thus does Allāh lay uncleanness on those who believe not.

THE CATTLE

126 And this is the path of thy Lord, (a) straight (path). Indeed We have made the messages clear for a people who mind.

127 Theirs is the abode of peace with their Lord, and He is their Friend because of what they do.

128 And on the day when He will gather them all together: O assembly of jinn, you took away a great part of men. And their friends from among men will say: Our Lord, some of us profited by others and we have reached our appointed term which Thou didst appoint for us. He will say: The Fire is your abode — you *shall abide therein*, except as Allāh please. Surely thy Lord is Wise, Knowing.

129 And thus do We make some of the iniquitous to befriend others on account of what they earn.

SECTION 16:
Evils of Idolatry

130 O community of jinn and men, did there not come to you messengers from among you, relating to you My messages and warning you of the meeting of this day of yours? They will say: We bear witness against ourselves. And this world's life deceived them, and they will bear witness against themselves that they were disbelievers.

131 This is because thy Lord would not destroy towns unjustly while their people are negligent.

132 And for all are degrees according to their doings. And thy Lord is not heedless of what they do.

133 And thy Lord is the Self-sufficient One, the Lord of mercy. If He please, He may remove you, and make whom He pleases successors after you, even as He raised you up from the seed of other people.

134 Surely that which you are promised will come to pass, and you cannot escape (it).

135 Say: O my people, act according to your ability, I too am acting; so you will soon come to know for whom is the (good) end of the abode. Surely the wrongdoers will not succeed.

136 And they set apart a portion for Allāh out of what He has created of tilth and cattle, and say: This is for Allāh — so they assert — and this for our associate-gods. Then that which is for their associate-gods reaches not Allāh, and that which is for Allāh reaches their associate-gods. Evil is what they judge.

137 And thus their associate-gods have made fair-seeming to many polytheists the killing of their children, that they may cause them to perish and obscure for them their religion. And if Allāh had pleased, they would not have done it, so leave them alone with that which they forge.

138 And they say: Such and such cattle and crops *are prohibited* — none shall eat them except such as we please — so they assert — and cattle whose backs are forbidden, and cattle on which they would not mention Allāh's name — forging a lie against Him. He will requite them for what they forge.

139 And they say: That which is in the wombs of such and such cattle is reserved for our males, and forbidden to our wives, and if it be stillborn, they are partners in it. He will reward them for their (false) attribution. Surely He is Wise, Knowing.

140 They are losers indeed who kill their children foolishly without knowledge, and forbid that which Allāh has provided for them, forging a lie against Allāh. They indeed go astray, and are not guided.

SECTION 17:
Idolaters' Self-imposed Prohibitions

141 And He it is Who produces gardens, trellised and untrellised, and palms and seed-produce of which the fruits are of various sorts, and olives and pomegranates like and unlike. Eat of its fruit when it bears fruit, and pay the due of it on the day of its reaping, and be not prodigal. Surely He loves not the prodigals;

142 And of the cattle (He

has created) some for burden and some for slaughter. Eat of that which Allāh has given you and follow not the footsteps of the devil. Surely he is your open enemy —

143 Eight in pairs — of the sheep two and of the goats two. Say: Has He forbidden the two males or the two females or that which the wombs of the two females contain? Inform me with knowledge, if you are truthful;

144 And of the camels two and of the cows two. Say: Has He forbidden the two males or the two females or that which the wombs of the two females contain? Or were you witnesses when Allāh enjoined you this? Who is then more unjust than he who forges a lie against Allāh to lead men astray without knowledge? Surely Allāh guides not the iniquitous people.

SECTION 18:
Prohibited Foods

145 Say: I find not in that which is revealed to me aught forbidden for an eater to eat thereof, except that it be what dies of itself, or blood poured forth, or flesh of swine — for that surely is unclean — or what is a transgression, other than (the name of) Allāh having been invoked on it. But whoever is driven to necessity, not desiring nor exceeding the limit, then surely thy Lord is Forgiving, Merciful.

146 And to those who are Jews We forbade every animal having claws, and of oxen and sheep We forbade them the fat thereof, except such as was on their backs or the entrails or what was mixed with bones. This was a punishment We gave them on account of their rebellion, and We are surely Truthful.

147 But if they give thee the lie, then say: Your Lord is the Lord of all-encompassing mercy; and His punishment cannot be averted from the guilty people.

148 Those who are polytheists say: If Allāh pleased we would not have set up (aught with Him) nor our fathers, nor would we have made anything unlawful. Thus did those before them reject (the truth) until they tasted Our punishment. Say: Have you any knowledge so you would bring it forth to us? You only follow a conjecture and you only tell lies.

149 Say: Then Allāh's is the conclusive argument; so if He had pleased, He would have guided you all.

150 Say: Bring your witnesses who bear witness that Allāh forbade this. If they bear witness, then do not thou bear witness with them. And follow not the low desires of those who reject Our messages and those who believe not in the Hereafter, and they make (others) equal with their Lord.

SECTION 19:
Guiding Rules of Life

151 Say: Come! I will recite what your Lord has forbidden to you: Associate naught with Him and do good to parents and slay not your children (for fear of) poverty — We provide for you and for them — and draw not nigh to indecencies, open or secret, and kill not the soul which Allāh has made sacred except in the course of justice. This He enjoins upon you that you may understand.

152 And approach not the property of the orphan except in the best manner, until he attains his maturity. And give full measure and weight with equity — We impose not on any soul a duty except to the extent of its ability. And when you speak, be just, though it be (against) a relative. And fulfil Allāh's covenant. This He enjoins on you that you may be mindful;

153 And (know) that this is My path, the right one, so follow it, and follow not (other) ways, for they will lead you away from His way. This He enjoins on you that you may keep your duty.

154 Again, We gave the Book to Moses to complete (Our blessings) on him who would do good, and making plain all things and a guidance and a mercy, so that they might believe in the meeting with their Lord.

SECTION 20:
The Goal for the Faithful

155 And this is a Book We have revealed, full of blessings; so follow it and keep your duty that mercy may be shown to you,

156 Lest you should say that the Book was revealed only to two parties before us and we were truly unaware of what they read,

157 Or, lest you should say: If the Book had been revealed to us, we would have been better guided than they. So indeed there has come to you clear proof from your Lord, and guidance and mercy. Who is *then more* unjust than he who rejects Allāh's messages and turns away from them? We reward those who turn away from Our messages with an evil chastisement because they turned away.

158 They wait not aught but that the angels should come to them, or that thy Lord should come, or that some of the signs of thy Lord should come. On the day when some of the signs of thy Lord come, its faith will not profit a soul which believed not before, nor earned good through its faith. Say: Wait; we too are waiting.

159 As for those who split up their religion and became sects, thou hast no concern with them. Their affair is only with Allāh, then He will inform them of what they did.

160 Whoever brings a good deed will have tenfold like it, and whoever brings an evil deed, will be recompensed only with the like of it, and they shall not be wronged.

161 Say: As for me, my Lord has guided me to the right path — a right religion, the faith of Abraham, the upright one, and he was not of the polytheists.

162 Say: My prayer and my sacrifice and my life and my death are surely for Allāh, the Lord of the worlds—

163 No associate has He. And this am I commanded, and I am the first of those who submit.

164 Say: Shall I seek a Lord other than Allāh, while He is the Lord of all things? And no soul earns (evil) but against itself. Nor does a bearer of burden bear another's burden. Then to your Lord is your return, so He will inform you of that in which you differed.

165 And He it is Who has made you successors in the land and exalted some of you in rank above others, that He may try you by what He has given you. Surely thy Lord is Quick in requiting (evil), *and He is* surely the Forgiving, the Merciful.

CHAPTER 7
Al-A'rāf: **The Elevated Places**

(REVEALED AT MAKKAH: 24 *sections*; 206 *verses*)

SECTION 1:
Opponents' Doom

In the name of Allāh, the Beneficent, the Merciful.

1 I, Allāh, am the best Knower, the Truthful.

2 A Book revealed to thee — so let there be no straitness in thy breast concerning it — that thou mayest warn thereby, and a Reminder to the believers.

3 Follow what has been revealed to you from your Lord and follow not besides Him any guardians; little do you mind!

4 And how many a town have We destroyed! So Our punishment came to it by night or while they slept at midday.

5 Yet their cry, when Our punishment came to them, was nothing but that they said: Surely we were wrong-doers.

6 Then certainly We shall question those to whom messengers were sent, and We shall question the messengers,

7 Then surely We shall relate to them with knowledge, and We are never absent.

8 And the judging on that day will be just; so as for those whose good deeds are heavy, they are the successful.

9 And as for those whose good deeds are light, those are they who ruined their souls because they disbelieved in Our messages.

10 And certainly We established you in the earth and made therein means of livelihood for you; little it is that you give thanks!

SECTION 2:
The Devil's Opposition to Man

11 And We indeed creat-

ed you, then We fashioned you, then We said to the angels: Make submission to Adam. So they submitted, except Iblīs; he was not of those who submitted.

12 He said: What hindered thee that thou didst not submit when I commanded thee? He said: I am better than he; Thou hast created me of fire, while him Thou didst create of dust.

13 He said: Then get forth from this (state), for it is not for thee to behave proudly therein. Go forth, therefore, surely thou art of the abject ones.

14 He said: Respite me till the day when they are raised.

15 He said: Thou art surely of the respited ones.

16 He said: As Thou hast adjudged me to be erring, I will certainly lie in wait for them in Thy straight path,

17 Then I shall certainly come upon them from before them and from behind them, and from their right and from their left; and Thou wilt not find most of them thankful.

18 He said: Get out of it, despised, driven away. Whoever of them will follow thee, I will certainly fill hell with you all.

19 And (We said): O Adam, dwell thou and thy wife in the garden, so eat from whence you desire, but go not near this tree, lest you become of the unjust.

20 But the devil made an evil suggestion to them that he might make manifest to them that which had been hidden from them of their shame, and he said: Your Lord has forbidden you this tree, lest you become angels or become of the immortals.

21 And he swore to them both: Surely I am a sincere adviser to you —

22 Thus he caused them to fall by deceit. So when they had tasted of the tree, their shame became manifest to them, and they both began to cover themselves with the leaves of the garden. And their Lord called to them: Did I not forbid you that tree, and say to you that the devil is surely your open enemy?

23 They said: Our Lord, we have wronged our-

THE ELEVATED PLACES

selves; and if Thou forgive us not, and have (not) mercy on us, we shall certainly be of the losers.

24 He said: Go forth — some of you, the enemies of others. And there is for you in the earth an abode and a provision for a time.

25 He said: Therein shall you live, and therein shall you die, and therefrom shall you be raised.

SECTION 3:
Warning against the Devil's Insinuations

26 O children of Adam, We have indeed sent down to you clothing to cover your shame, and (clothing) for beauty; and clothing that guards against evil — that is the best. This is of the messages of Allāh that they may be mindful.

27 O children of Adam, let not the devil seduce you, as he expelled your parents from the garden, pulling off from them their clothing that he might show them their shame. He surely sees you, he as well as his host, from whence you see him not. Surely We have made the devils to be the friends of those who believe not.

28 And when they commit an indecency they say: We found our fathers doing this, and Allāh has enjoined it on us. Say: Surely Allāh enjoins not indecency. Do you say of Allāh what you know not?

29 Say: My Lord enjoins justice. And set upright your faces at every time of prayer and call on Him, being sincere to Him in obedience. As He brought you into being, so shall you return.

30 A party has He guided, and another party — perdition is justly their due. Surely they took the devils for friends instead of Allāh, and they think that they are rightly guided.

31 O children of Adam, attend to your adornment at every time of prayer, and eat and drink and be not prodigal; surely He loves not the prodigals.

SECTION 4:
Messengers sent for Uplift of Humanity

32 Say: Who has forbidden the adornment of Allāh, which He has brought forth for His servants, and the good provisions? Say: These are for the believers in the life of this world, purely (theirs) on the Resurrection day. Thus do We make the messages clear for a people who know.

33 Say: My Lord forbids only indecencies, such of them as are apparent and such as are concealed, and sin and unjust rebellion, and that you associate with Allāh that for which He has sent down no authority, and that you say of Allāh what you know not.

34 And every nation has a term; so when its term comes, they cannot remain behind the least while, nor can they precede (it).

35 O children of Adam, if messengers come to you *from among you relating to* you My messages, then whosoever guards against evil and acts aright — they shall have no fear, nor shall they grieve.

36 And those who reject Our messages and turn away from them haughtily — these are the companions of the Fire; they shall abide in it.

37 Who is then more unjust than he who forges a lie against Allāh or rejects His messages? These — their portion of the Book shall reach them; until when Our messengers come to them causing them to die, they say: Where is that which you used to call upon besides Allāh? They would say: They are gone away from us. And they shall bear witness against themselves that they were disbelivers.

38 He will say: Enter into the Fire among the nations that have passed away before you from among the jinn and men. Every time a nation enters, it curses its sister; until when they all follow one another into it, the last of them will say *with regard* to the first of them. Our Lord, these led us astray, so give them a double chastisement of the Fire. He will say: Each one has double but you know not.

39 And the first of them will say to the last of them: You have no preference over us, so taste the chastisement for what you earned.

SECTION 5:
Those who accept the Message

40 Those who reject Our messages and turn away from them haughtily, the doors of heaven will not be opened for them, nor will they enter the Garden until the camel pass through the eye of the needle. And thus do We reward the guilty.

41 They shall have a bed of hell and over them coverings (of it). And thus do We requite the wrongdoers.

42 And as for those who believe and do good — We impose not on any soul a duty beyond its scope — they are the owners of the Garden; therein they abide.

43 And We shall remove whatever of ill-feeling is in their hearts — rivers flow beneath them. And they say: All praise is due to Allāh, Who guided us to this! And we would not have found the way if Allāh had not guided us. Certainly the messengers of our Lord brought the truth. And it will be cried out to them: This is the Garden which you are made to inherit for what you did.

44 And the owners of the Garden call out to the companions of the Fire: We have found that which our Lord promised us to be true; have you, too, found that which your Lord promised to be true? They will say: Yes. Then a crier will cry out among them: The curse of Allāh is on the wrongdoers,

45 Who hinder (men) from Allāh's way and seek to make it crooked, and they are disbelievers in the Hereafter.

46 And between them is a veil. And on the Elevated Places are men who know all by their marks. And they call out to the owners of the Garden: Peace be to you! They have not yet entered it, though they hope.

47 And when their eyes are turned towards the companions of the Fire, they say: Our Lord, place us not with the unjust people.

SECTION 6:
Helplessness of Opponents

48 And the owners of the Elevated Places call out to men whom they recognize by their marks, saying: Of no avail were to you your amassings and your arrogance.

49 Are these they about whom you swore that Allāh would not bestow mercy on them? Enter the Garden; you have no fear, nor shall you grieve.

50 And the companions of the Fire call out to the owners of the Garden: Pour on us some water or some of that which Allāh has provided for you. They say: Surely Allāh has forbidden them both to the disbelievers,

51 Who take their religion for an idle sport and a play, and this world's life deceives *them. So this day* We shall forsake them, as they neglected the meeting of this day of theirs, and as they denied Our messages.

52 And certainly We have brought them a Book which We make clear with knowledge, a guidance and a mercy for a people who believe.

53 Do they wait for aught but its final sequel? On the day when its final sequel comes, those who neglected it before will say: Indeed the messengers of our Lord brought the truth. Are there any intercessors on our behalf so that they should intercede for us? Or could we be sent back so that we should do (deeds) other than those which we did? Indeed they have lost their souls, and that which they forged has failed them.

SECTION 7:
The Righteous will prosper

54 Surely your Lord is Allāh, Who created the heavens and the earth in six periods, and He is established on the Throne of Power. He makes the night cover the day, which it pursues incessantly. And (He created) the sun and the moon and the stars, made subservient by His command. Surely His is the creation and the command. Blessed is Allāh, the Lord of the Worlds!

THE ELEVATED PLACES

55 Call on your Lord humbly and in secret. Surely He loves not the transgressors.

56 And make not mischief in the earth after its reformation, and call on Him, fearing and hoping. Surely the mercy of Allāh is nigh to the doers of good.

57 And He it is Who sends forth the winds bearing good news before His mercy; till, when they bear a laden cloud, We drive it to a dead land, then We send down water on it, then bring forth thereby fruits of all kinds. Thus do We bring forth the dead that you may be mindful.

58 And the good land — its vegetation comes forth (abundantly) by the permission of its Lord. And that which is inferior — (its herbage) comes forth but scantily. Thus do We repeat the messages for a people who give thanks.

SECTION 8: Noah

59 Certainly We sent Noah to his people, so he said: O my people, serve Allāh, you have no god other than Him. Indeed I fear for you the chastisement of a grievous day.

60 The chiefs of his people said: Surely we see thee in clear error.

61 He said: O my people, there is no error in me, but I am a messenger from the Lord of the worlds.

62 I deliver to you the messages of my Lord, and I offer you good advice, and I know from Allāh what you know not.

63 Do you wonder that a reminder has come to you from your Lord through a man from among you, that he may warn you and that you may guard against evil, and that mercy may be shown to you?

64 But they called him a liar, so We delivered him and those with him in the ark, and We drowned those who rejected Our messages. Surely they were a blind people!

SECTION 9: Hūd

65 And to 'Ād (We sent) their brother Hūd. He said: O my people, serve Allāh, you have no god other than

Him. Will you not then guard against evil?

66 The chiefs of those who disbelieved from among his people said: Certainly we see thee in folly, and we certainly think thee to be of the liars.

67 He said: O my people, there is no folly in me, but I am a messenger of the Lord of the worlds.

68 I deliver to you the messages of my Lord and I am a faithful adviser to you.

69 Do you wonder that a reminder has come to you from your Lord through a man from among you that he may warn you? And remember when He made you successors after Noah's people and increased you in excellence of make. So remember the bounties of Allāh, that you may be successful.

70 They said: Hast thou come to us that we may serve Allāh alone, and give up that which our fathers used to serve? Then bring to us what thou threatenest us with, if thou art of the truthful.

71 He said: Indeed uncleanness and wrath from your Lord have lighted upon you. Do you dispute with me about names which you and your fathers have named? Allāh has not sent any authority for them. Wait, then; I too with you am of those who wait.

72 So We delivered him and those with him by mercy from Us, and We cut off the roots of those who rejected Our messages and were not believers.

SECTION 10:
Ṣāliḥ and Lot

73 And to Thamūd (We sent) their brother Ṣāliḥ. He said: O my people, serve Allāh, you have no god other than Him. Clear proof has indeed come to you from your Lord. This is Allāh's she-camel — a sign for you — so leave her alone to pasture in Allāh's earth, and do her no harm, lest painful chastisement overtake you.

74 And remember when He made you successors after 'Ād and settled you in the land — you make mansions on its plains and hew out houses in the mountains. So remember Allāh's bounties and act not corruptly in the land, making mischief.

75 The arrogant chiefs of his people said to those who were weak, to those who believed from among them: Do you know that Ṣāliḥ is one sent by his Lord? They said: Surely we are believers in that wherewith he has been sent.

76 Those who were haughty said: Surely we are disbelievers in that which you believe.

77 Then they hamstrung the she-camel and revolted against their Lord's commandment, and said; O Ṣāliḥ, bring us that with which thou threatenest us, if thou art of the messengers.

78 So the earthquake seized them, and they were motionless bodies in their abodes.

79 So he turned away from them and said: O my people, I delivered to you the message of my Lord and gave you good advice, but you love not good advisers.

80 And (We sent) Lot, when he said to his people: Do you commit an abomination which no one in the world did before you?

81 Surely you come to males with lust instead of females. Nay, you are a people exceeding bounds.

82 And the answer of his people was no other than that they said: Turn them out of your town; surely they are a people who aspire to purity!

83 So We delivered him and his followers, except his wife — she was of those who remained behind.

84 And We rained upon them a rain. See, then, what was the end of the guilty!

SECTION 11: Shu'aib

85 And to Midian (We sent) their brother Shū'aib. He said: O my people, serve Allāh, you have no god other than Him. Clear proof indeed has come to you from your Lord, so give full measure and weight and diminish not to men their things, and make not mischief in the land after its reform. This is better for you, if you are believers.

86 And lie not in wait on every road, threatening and turning away from Allāh's way him who believes in Him and seeking to make it crooked. And remember when you were few, then He multiplied you, and see what was the end of the mischief-makers!

87 And if there is a party of you who believe in that wherewith I am sent and another party who believe not, then wait patiently till Allāh judges between us; and He is the Best of Judges.

Part 9

88 The arrogant chiefs of his people said: We will certainly *turn thee out*, O Shu'aib, and those who believe with thee from our town, or you shall come back to our religion. He said: Even though we dislike (it)?

89 Indeed we should have forged a lie against Allāh, if we go back to your religion after Allāh has delivered us from it. And it is not for us to go back to it, unless Allāh our Lord please. Our Lord comprehends all things in His knowledge. In Allāh do we trust. Our Lord, decide between us and our people with truth, and Thou art the Best of Deciders.

90 And the chiefs of his people, who disbelieved, said: If you follow Shu'aib, you are surely losers.

91 So the earthquake overtook them, and they were motionless bodies in their abode —

92 Those who called Shu'aib a liar were as though they had never dwelt therein — those who called Shu'aib a liar, they were the losers.

93 So he turned away from them and said: O my people, indeed I delivered to you the messages of my Lord and I gave you good advice; how, then, should I be sorry for a disbelieving people?

SECTION 12:
Makkans warned of Punishment

94 And We did not send a prophet to a town but We seized its people with distress and affliction that they might humble themselves.

95 Then We changed the evil for good, till they became affluent and said: Distress and happiness did indeed touch our fathers. So We took them by surprise while they perceived not.

96 And if the people of the towns had believed and kept their duty, We would certainly have opened for them blessings from the heavens and the earth. But they rejected, so We seized them for what they earned.

97 Are the people of the towns, then, secure from Our punishment coming to them by night while they sleep?

98 Or, are the people of the towns secure from Our punishment coming to them in the morning while they play?

99 Are they secure from Allāh's plan? But none feels secure from Allāh's plan except the people who perish.

SECTION 13:
Moses sent to Pharaoh with signs

100 Is it not clear to those who inherit the earth after its (former) residents that, if We please, We would afflict them for their sins, and seal their hearts so they would not hear?

101 Such were the towns some of whose news We have related to thee. And certainly their messengers came to them with clear arguments, but they would not believe what they had rejected before. Thus does Allāh seal the hearts of the disbelievers.

102 And We found not in most of them (faithfulness to) covenant; and We found most of them to be transgressors.

103 Then, after them, We sent Moses with Our messages to Pharaoh and his chiefs, but they disbelieved them. See, then, what was the end of the mischief-makers!

104 And Moses said: O

Pharaoh, surely I am a messenger from the Lord of the worlds,

105 Worthy of not saying anything about Allāh except the truth. I have come to you indeed with clear proof from your Lord, so let the Children of Israel go with me.

106 He said: If thou hast come with a sign, produce it, if thou art truthful.

107 So he threw his rod, then lo! it was a serpent manifest.

108 And he drew forth his hand, and lo! it was white to the beholders.

SECTION 14:
Pharaoh summons Enchanters

109 The chiefs of Pharaoh's people said: Surely this is a skilful *enchanter!*

110 He intends to turn you out of your land. What do you advise?

111 They said: Put him off and his brother, and send summoners into the cities,

112 To bring to thee every skilful enchanter.

113 And the enchanters came to Pharaoh, saying: We must surely have a reward if we prevail.

114 He said: Yes, and you shall certainly be of those who are near (to me).

115 They said: O Moses, wilt thou cast, or shall we (be the first to) cast?

116 He said: Cast. So when they cast, they deceived the people's eyes and overawed them, and they produced a mighty enchantment.

117 And We revealed to Moses: Cast thy rod. Then lo! it swallowed up their lies.

118 So the truth was established, and that which they did became null.

119 There they were vanquished, and they went back abased.

120 And the enchanters fell down prostrate —

121 They said: We believe in the Lord of the worlds,

122 The Lord of Moses and Aaron.

123 Pharaoh said: You believe in Him before I give

you permission! Surely this is a plot which you have plotted in the city, *to turn out of it its people*, but you shall know!

124 I shall certainly cut off your hands and your feet on opposite sides, then I shall crucify you all together!

125 They said: Surely to our Lord do we return.

126 And thou takest revenge on us only because we believed in the messages of our Lord when they came to us. Our Lord, pour out on us patience and cause us to die in submission (to Thee)!

SECTION 15:
Israelites' Persecution continues

127 And the chiefs of Pharaoh's people said: Wilt thou leave Moses and his people to make mischief in the land and forsake thee and thy gods? He said: We will slay their sons and spare their women, and surely we are dominant over them.

128 Moses said to his people: Ask help from Allah and be patient. Surely the land is Allāh's — He gives it for an inheritance to *such of His servants as He* pleases. And the end is for those who keep their duty.

129 They said: We were persecuted before thou camest to us and since thou hast come to us. He said: It may be that your Lord will destroy your enemy and make you rulers in the land, then He will see how you act.

SECTION 16:
Moses shows more Signs

130 And certainly We overtook Pharaoh's people with droughts and diminution of fruits that they might be mindful.

131 But when good befell them they said: This is due to us. And when evil afflicted them, they attributed it to the ill-luck of Moses and those with him. Surely their evil fortune is only from Allāh, but most of them know not.

132 And they said: Whatever sign thou mayest bring to us to charm us therewith — we shall not believe in thee.

133 So We sent upon them widespread death, and the locusts and the lice and the frogs and the blood — clear signs. But they behaved haughtily and they were a guilty people.

134 And when the plague fell upon them, they said: O Moses, pray for us to thy Lord as He has made promise with thee. If thou remove the plague from us, we will certainly believe in thee and will let the Children of Israel go with thee.

135 But when We removed the plague from them till a term which they should attain, lo! they broke (their promise).

136 So We exacted retribution from them and drowned them in the sea, because they rejected Our signs and were heedless of them.

137 And We made the people who were deemed weak to inherit the eastern lands and the western ones which We had blessed. And the good word of thy Lord was fulfilled in the Children of Israel — because of their patience. And We destroyed what Pharaoh and his people had wrought and what they had built.

138 And We took the Children of Israel across the sea. Then they came to a people who were devoted to their idols. They said: O Moses, make for us a god as they have gods. He said: Surely you are an ignorant people!

139 (As to) these, that wherein they are engaged shall be destroyed and that which they do is vain.

140 He said: Shall I seek for you a god other than Allāh, while He has made you excel (all) created things?

141 And when We delivered you from Pharaoh's people, who subjected you to severe torment, killing your sons and sparing your women. And therein was a great trial from your Lord.

SECTION 17:
Moses receives the Law

142 And We appointed for Moses thirty nights, and completed them with ten, so the appointed time of his Lord was complete forty nights. And Moses said to his brother Aaron: Take my place among my people, and act well and follow not the way of the mischief-makers.

143 And when Moses came at Our appointed time and his Lord spoke to him, he said: My Lord, show me (Thyself) so that I may look at Thee. He said: Thou canst not see Me; but look at the mountain; if it remains firm in its place, then wilt thou see Me. So when his Lord manifested His glory to the mountain, He made it crumble and Moses fell down in a swoon. Then when he recovered, he said: Glory be to Thee! I turn to Thee, and I am the first of the believers.

144 He said: O Moses, surely I have chosen thee above the people by My messages and My words. So take hold of what I give thee and be of the grateful.

145 And We ordained for him in the tablets admonition of every kind and clear explanation of all things. So take hold of them with firmness and enjoin thy people to take hold of what is best thereof. I shall show you the abode of the transgressors.

146 I shall turn away from My messages those who are unjustly proud in the earth. And if they see every sign, they will not believe in it; and if they see the way of rectitude, they take it not for a way; and if they see the way of error, they take it for a way. This is because they reject Our messages and are heedless of them.

147 And those who reject Our messages and the meeting of the Hereafter — their deeds are fruitless. Can they be rewarded except for what they do?

SECTION 18:
Israelites worship a calf

148 And Moses' people made of their ornaments a calf after him — a (lifeless) body, having a lowing sound. Could they not see that it spoke not to them, nor guided them in the way? They took it (for worship) and they were unjust.

149 And when they repented and saw that they

had gone astray, they said: If our Lord have not mercy on us and forgive us, we shall certainly be of the losers.

150 And when Moses returned to his people, wrathful, grieved, he said: Evil is that which you have done after me! Did you hasten on the judgment of your Lord? And he threw down the tablets and seized his brother by the head, dragging him towards him. He said: Son of my mother, the people reckoned me weak and had well-nigh slain me. So make not the enemies to rejoice over me and count me not among the unjust people.

151 He said: My Lord, forgive me and my brother, and admit us to Thy mercy, and Thou art the Most Merciful of those who show mercy.

SECTION 19:
The Torah and the Prophet's Advent

152 Those who took the calf (for a god) — wrath from their Lord, and disgrace in this world's life, will surely overtake them. And thus do We recompense those who invent lies.

153 And those who do evil deeds, then repent after that and believe — thy Lord after that is surely Forgiving, Merciful.

154 And when Moses' anger calmed down, he took up the tablets; and in the writing thereof was guidance and mercy for those who fear their Lord.

155 And Moses chose of his people seventy men for Our appointment. So when the earthquake overtook them, he said: My Lord, if Thou hadst pleased, Thou hadst destroyed them before and myself (too). Wilt Thou destroy us for that which the foolish among us have done? It is naught but Thy trial. Thou causest to perish whom Thou pleasest and guidest whom Thou pleasest. Thou art our Protector, so forgive us and have mercy on us, and Thou art the Best of those who forgive.

156 And ordain for us good in this world's life and in the Hereafter, for surely we turn to Thee. He said: I afflict with My chastisement whom I please, and My mercy encompasses all things. So I ordain it for those who keep their duty and pay the poor-rate, and those who believe in Our messages;

157 Those who follow the Messenger-Prophet, the *Ummī*, whom they find mentioned in the Torah and the Gospel. He enjoins them good and forbids them evil, and makes lawful to them the good things and prohibits for them impure things, and removes from them their burden and the shackles which were on *them*. So those who believe in him and honour him and help him, and follow the light which has been sent down with him — these are the successful.

SECTION 20:
Divine Favours on Israelites

158 Say: O mankind, surely I am the Messenger of Allāh to you all, of Him, Whose is the kingdom of the heavens and the earth. There is no god but He; He gives life and causes death. So believe in Allāh and His Messenger, the *Ummī* Prophet who believes in Allāh and His words, and follow him so that you may be guided aright.

159 And of Moses' people is a party who guide with truth, and therewith they do justice.

160 And We divided them into twelve tribes, as nations. And We revealed to Moses when his people asked him for water: Strike the rock with thy staff; so out flowed from it twelve springs. Each tribe knew its drinking-place. And We *made the clouds to give shade over them* and We sent to them manna and quails. Eat of the good things We have given you. And they did not do Us any harm, but they wronged themselves.

161 And when it was said to them: Dwell in this town and eat from it whence you wish, and make petition for forgiveness, and enter the gate submissively, We shall forgive you your wrongs. We shall give more

162 But those who were unjust among them changed it for a word other than that which they were told, so We sent upon them a pestilence from heaven for their wrongdoing.

SECTION 21:
Israelites' Transgressions

163 And ask them about the town which stood by the sea. When they violated the Sabbath, when their fish came to them on their Sabbath day on the surface, and when it was not their Sabbath they came not to them. Thus did We try them because they transgressed.

164 And when a party of them said: Why preach you to a people whom Allāh would destroy or whom He would chastise with a severe chastisement? They said: To be free from blame before your Lord, and that haply they may guard against evil.

165 So when they neglected that whereof they had been reminded, We delivered those who forbade evil and We overtook those who were iniquitous with an evil chastisement because they transgressed.

166 So when they revoltingly persisted in that which they had been forbidden, We said to them: Be (as) apes, despised and hated.

167 And when thy Lord declared that He would send against them to the day of Resurrection those who would subject them to severe torment. Surely thy Lord is Quick in requiting; and surely He is Forgiving, Merciful.

168 And We divided them in the earth into parties — some of them are righteous and some of them are otherwise. And We tried them with blessings and misfortunes that they might turn.

169 Then after them came *an evil posterity who inherited the Book, taking the frail goods of this low life and saying: It will be forgiven us. And if the like good came to them, they would take it (too). Was not a promise taken from them in the Book that they would not speak anything about

THE ELEVATED PLACES

Allāh but the truth? And they study what is in it. And the abode of the Hereafter is better for those who keep their duty. Do you not then understand?

170 And as for those who hold fast by the Book and keep up prayer — surely We waste not the reward of the reformers.

171 And when We shook the mountain over them as if it were a covering, and they thought that it was going to fall down upon them: Hold on firmly that which We have given you, and be mindful of that which is in it, so that you may guard against evil.

SECTION 22:
Evidence of Divine Impress on Man's Nature

172 And when thy Lord brought forth from the children of Adam, from their loins, their descendants, and made them bear witness about themselves: Am I not your Lord? They said: Yes; we bear witness. Lest you should say on the day of Resurrection: We were unaware of this,

173 Or (lest) you should say: Only our fathers ascribed partners (to Allāh) before (us), and we were (their) descendants after them. Wilt Thou destroy us for what liars did?

174 And thus do We make the messages clear, and that haply they may return.

175 And recite to them the news of him to whom We give Our messages, but he withdraws himself from them, so the devil follows him up, and he is of those who perish.

176 And if We had pleased, We would have exalted him thereby; but he clings to the earth and follows his low desire. His parable is as the parable of the dog — if thou drive him away, he lolls out his tongue, and if thou leave him alone, he lolls out his tongue. Such is the parable of the people who reject Our messages. So relate the narrative that they may reflect.

177 Evil is the likeness of the people who reject Our messages and wrong their own souls.

178 He whom Allāh guides is on the right way; and he whom He leaves in error — they are the losers.

179 And certainly We have created for hell many of the jinn and the men — they have hearts wherewith they understand not, and they have eyes wherewith they see not, and they have ears wherewith they hear not. They are as cattle; nay, they are more astray. These are the heedless ones.

180 And Allāh's are the best names, so call on Him thereby and leave alone those who violate the sanctity of His names. They will be recompensed for what they do.

181 And of those whom We have created is a community who guide with the truth and therewith do justice.

SECTION 23:
The Coming of the Doom

182 And those who reject Our messages — We lead them (to destruction) step by step from whence they know not.

183 And I grant them respite. Surely My scheme is effective.

184 Do they not reflect (that) there is no madness in their companion? He is only a plain warner.

185 Do they not consider the kingdom of the heavens and the earth and what things Allāh has created, and that it may be that their doom has drawn nigh? In what announcement after this will they then believe?

186 Whomsoever Allāh leaves in error, there is no guide for him. And He leaves them alone in their inordinacy, blindly wandering on.

187 They ask thee about the Hour, when will it come to pass? Say: The knowledge thereof is with my Lord only. None but He will manifest it at its time. It is momentous in the heavens and the earth. It will not come to you but of a sudden. They ask thee as if thou wert solicitous about it. Say: Its knowledge is with Allāh only, but most people know not.

188 Say: I control not benefit or harm for myself

THE ELEVATED PLACES

except as Allāh please. And had I known the unseen, I should have much of good, and no evil would touch me. I am but a warner and the giver of good news to a people who believe.

SECTION 24:
The Final Word

189 He it is Who created you from a single soul, and of the same did He make his mate, that he might find comfort in her. So when he covers her she bears a light burden, then moves about with it. Then when it grows heavy, they both call upon Allāh, their Lord: If Thou givest us a good one, we shall certainly be of the grateful.

190 But when He gives them a good one, they set up with Him associates in that which He has given them. High is Allāh above what they associate (with Him).

191 Do they associate (with Him) that which has created naught, while they are themselves created?

192 And they cannot give them help, nor can they help themselves.

193 And if you invite them to guidance, they will not follow you. It is the same to you whether you invite them or you are silent.

194 Those whom you call on besides Allāh are slaves like yourselves; so call on them, then let them answer you, if you are truthful.

195 Have they feet with which they walk, or have they hands with which they hold, or have they eyes with which they see, or have they ears with which they hear? Say: Call upon your associate-gods then plot against me and give me no respite.

196 Surely my Friend is Allāh, Who revealed the Book, and He befriends the righteous.

197 And those whom you call upon besides Him are not able to help you, nor can they help themselves.

198 And if you invite them to guidance, they hear not; and thou seest them looking towards thee, yet they see not.

199 Take to forgiveness

and enjoin good and turn away from the ignorant.

200 And if a false imputation from the devil afflict thee, seek refuge in Allāh. Surely He is Hearing, Knowing.

201 Those who guard against evil, when a visitation from the devil afflicts them, they become mindful, then lo! they see.

202 And their brethren increase them in error, then they cease not.

203 And when thou bringest them not a sign, they say: Why dost thou not demand it? Say: I follow only that which is revealed to me from my Lord. These are clear proofs from your Lord and a guidance and a mercy for a people who believe.

204 And when the Qur'ān is recited, listen to it and remain silent, that mercy may be shown to you.

205 And remember thy Lord within thyself humbly and fearing, and in a voice not loud, in the morning and the evening, and be not of the heedless.

206 Surely those who are with thy Lord are not too proud to serve Him, and they glorify Him and prostrate themselves before Him.

CHAPTER 8
Al-Anfāl: **Voluntary Gifts**

(REVEALED AT MADĪNAH: 10 *sections*; 75 *verses*)

SECTION 1:
The Battle of Badr

In the name of Allāh, the Beneficent, the Merciful.

1 They ask thee about voluntary gifts. Say: Voluntary gifts are for Allāh and the Messenger. So keep your duty to Allāh and set aright your differences, and obey Allāh and His Messenger, if you are believers.

2 They only are believers whose hearts are full of fear when Allāh is mentioned, and when His messages are recited to them they increase them in faith, and in their Lord do they trust,

3 Those who keep up prayer and spend out of what We have given them.

4 These are the believers in truth. For them are with their Lord exalted grades and protection and an honourable sustenance.

5 Even as thy Lord caused thee to go forth from thy house with truth, though a party of the believers were surely averse,

6 Disputing with thee about the truth after it had become clear — as if they were being driven to death while they saw (it).

7 And when Allāh promised you one of the two parties that it should be yours, and you loved that the one not armed should be yours, and Allāh desired to establish the Truth by His words, and to cut off the root of the disbelievers —

8 That He might cause the Truth to triumph and bring the falsehood to naught, though the guilty disliked.

9 When you sought the aid of your Lord, so He answered you: I will assist you with a thousand of the angels following one another.

10 And Allāh gave it only as good news, and that your hearts might be at ease thereby. And victory is only from Allāh; surely Allāh is Mighty, Wise.

SECTION 2:
The Battle of Badr

11 When He made slumber fall on you as a security from Him, and sent down upon you water from the clouds that He might thereby purify you, and take away from you the uncleanness of the devil, and that He might fortify your hearts and make firm (your) feet thereby.

12 When thy Lord revealed to the angels: I am with you, so make firm those who believe. I will cast terror into the hearts of those who disbelieve. So smite above the necks and smite every finger-tip of them.

13 This is because they opposed Allāh and His Messenger. And whoever opposes Allāh and His Messenger — then surely Allāh is Severe in requiting.

14 This — taste it, and (know) that for the disbelievers is the chastisement of the Fire.

15 O you who believe, when you meet those who disbelieve marching for war, turn not your backs to them.

16 And whoso turns his back to them on that day — unless manoeuvring for battle or turning to join a company — he, indeed, incurs Allāh's wrath and his refuge is hell. And an evil destination it is.

17 So you slew them not but Allāh slew them, and thou smotest not when thou didst smite (the enemy), but Allāh smote (him), and that He might confer upon the believers a benefit from Himself. Surely Allāh is Hearing, Knowing.

18 This — and (know) that Allāh will weaken the struggle of the disbelievers.

19 If you sought a judgment, the judgment has indeed come to you; and if you desist, it is better for you. And if you return (to fight), We (too) shall return and your forces will avail you nothing, though they may be many; and (know) that Allāh is with the believers.

SECTION 3:
The Way to Success

20 O you who believe, obey Allāh and His Messenger and turn not away from Him while you hear.

21 And be not like those who say, We hear; and they hear not.

22 Surely the vilest of beasts, in Allāh's sight, are the deaf, the dumb, who understand not.

23 And if Allāh had known any good in them, He would have made them hear. *And if* He makes them hear, they would turn away while they are averse.

24 O you who believe, respond to Allāh and His Messenger, when he calls you to that which gives you life. And know that Allāh comes in between a man and his heart, and that to Him you will be gathered.

25 And guard yourselves against an affliction which may not smite those of you exclusively who are unjust; and know that Allāh is Severe in requiting.

26 And remember when you were few, deemed weak *in the land*, fearing lest people should carry you off by force, He sheltered you and strengthened you with His help, and gave you of the good things that you might give thanks.

27 O you who believe, be not unfaithful to Allāh and the Messenger, nor be unfaithful to your trusts, while you know.

28 And know that your wealth and your children are a temptation, and that Allāh is He with Whom there is a mighty reward.

SECTION 4:
Muslims to be Guardians of the Sacred Mosque

29 O you who believe, if you keep your duty to Allāh, He will grant you a distinction and do away with your evils and protect you. And Allāh is the Lord of mighty grace.

30 And when those who disbelieved devised plans against thee that they might confine thee or slay thee or drive thee away — and they

devised plans and Allāh, too, had arranged a plan; and Allāh is the best of planners.

31 And when Our messages are recited to them, they say: We have heard. If we wished, we could say the like of it; this is nothing but the stories of the ancients.

32 And when they said: O Allāh, if this is indeed the truth from Thee, then rain down on us stones from heaven or inflict on us a painful chastisement.

33 And Allāh would not chastise them while thou wast among them; nor would Allāh chastise them while they seek forgiveness.

34 And what excuse have they that Allāh should not chastise them while they hinder (men) from the Sacred Mosque and they are not its (true) guardians? Its guardians are only those who keep their duty, but most of them know not.

35 And their prayer at the House is nothing but whistling and clapping of hands. Taste, then, the chastisement, because you disbelieved.

36 Surely those who disbelieve spend their wealth to hinder (people) from the way of Allāh. So they will go on spending it, then it will be to them a regret, then they will be overcome. And those who disbelieve will be gathered together to hell,

37 That Allāh may separate the wicked from the good, and put the wicked one upon another, then heap them together, then cast them into hell. These indeed are the losers.

SECTION 5:
Badr as a Sign of the Prophet's Truth

38 Say to those who disbelieve, if they desist, that which is past will be forgiven them; and if they return, then the example of those of old has already gone.

39 And fight with them until there is no more persecution, and all religions are for Allāh. But if they desist, then surely Allāh is Seer of what they do.

40 And if they turn back, then know that Allāh is your Patron. Most excellent the Patron and most excellent the Helper!

Part 10

41 And know that whatever you acquire in war, a fifth of it is for Allāh and for the Messenger and for the near of kin and the orphans and the needy and the wayfarer, if you believe in Allāh and in that which We revealed to Our servant, on the day of Discrimination, the day on which the two parties met. And Allāh is Possessor of power over all things.

42 When you were on the nearer side (of the valley) *and they were on the farther* side, while the caravan was in a lower place than you. And if you had tried to make a mutual appointment, you would certainly have broken away from the appointment, but — in order that Allāh might bring about a matter which had to be done; that he who perished by clear argument might perish, and he who lived by clear argument might live. And surely Allāh is Hearing, Knowing:

43 When Allāh showed them to thee in thy dream as few — and if He had shown them to thee as many, you would certainly have become weak-hearted and you would have disputed about the matter, but Allāh saved (you). Surely He is Knower of what is in the breasts.

44 And when He showed them to you, when you met, as few in your eyes, and He made you to appear few in their eyes, in order that Allāh might bring about a matter which had to be done. And to Allāh are all affairs returned.

SECTION 6:
Success does not depend on Numbers

45 O you who believe, when you meet an army, be firm, and remember Allāh much, that you may be successful.

46 And obey Allāh and His Messenger and dispute not one with another, lest you get weak-hearted and your power depart; and be steadfast. Surely Allāh is with the steadfast.

47 And be not like those who came forth from their homes exultingly and to be seen of men, and they hinder (people) from the way of Allāh. And Allāh encompasses what they do.

48 And when the devil made their works fair-seeming to them, and said: None among men can overcome you this day, and I am your protector. But when the two armies came in sight of one another, he turned upon his heels, and said: Surely I am clear of you, I see what you see not; surely I fear Allāh. And Allāh is Severe in requiting.

SECTION 7:
Enemy's Strength weakened

49 And when the hypocrites and those in whose hearts is a disease said: *Their religion* has deluded them. And whoever trusts in Allāh, then surely Allāh is Mighty, Wise.

50 And if thou couldst see when the angels cause to die those who disbelieve, smiting their faces and their backs, and (saying): Taste the punishment of burning.

51 This is for that which your own hands have sent on before, and because Allāh is not in the least unjust to the servants —

52 In the manner of the people of Pharaoh and those before them, they disbelieved in Allāh's messages, so Allāh punished them for their sins. Surely Allāh is Strong, Severe in requiting.

53 This is because Allāh never changes a favour which He has conferred upon a people until they change their own condition — and because Allāh is Hearing, Knowing —

54 In the manner of the people of Pharaoh, and those before them. They rejected the messages of their Lord, so We destroyed them for their sins. And We drowned Pharaoh's people and they were all wrongdoers.

55 Surely the vilest of beasts in Allāh's sight are those who disbelieve, then they would not believe.

56 Those with whom thou makest an agreement, then

they break their agreement every time, and they keep not their duty.

57 So if thou overtake them in war, scatter by them those who are behind them, that they may be mindful.

58 And if thou fear treachery on the part of a people, throw back to them (their treaty) on terms of equality. Surely Allāh loves not the treacherous.

SECTION 8:
Peace to be secured by Strength

59 And let not those who disbelieve think that they can outstrip (Us). Surely they cannot escape.

60 And make ready for them whatever force you can and horses tied at the frontier, to frighten thereby the enemy of Allāh and your enemy and others besides them, whom you know not — Allāh knows them. And whatever you spend in Allāh's way, it will be paid back to you fully and you will not be wronged.

61 And if they incline to peace, incline thou also to it, and trust in Allāh. Surely He is the Hearer, the Knower.

62 And if they intend to deceive thee, then surely Allāh is sufficient for thee. He it is Who strengthened thee with His help and with the believers,

63 And He has united their hearts. If thou hadst spent all that is in the earth, thou couldst not have united their hearts, but Allāh united them. Surely He is Mighty, Wise.

64 O Prophet, Allāh is sufficient for thee and those who follow thee of the believers.

SECTION 9:
Muslims to meet Overwhelming Numbers

65 O Prophet, urge the believers to fight. If there be of you twenty steadfast, they shall overcome two hundred; and if there be of you a hundred, they shall overcome a thousand of those who disbelieve, because they are a people who do not understand.

66 Now Allāh has lightened your burden and He

knows that there is weakness in you. So if there be of you a hundred steadfast, they shall overcome two hundred; and if there be of you a thousand, they shall overcome two thousand by Allāh's permission. And Allāh is with the steadfast.

67 It is not fit for a prophet to take captives unless he has fought and triumphed in the land. *You desire the frail goods of this world, while Allāh desires (for you) the Hereafter. And Allāh is Mighty, Wise.*

68 Were it not for an ordinance from Allāh that had gone before, surely there would have befallen you a great chastisement for what you were going to do.

69 Eat then of the lawful and good (things) which you have acquired in war, *and keep your duty to* Allāh. Surely Allāh is Forgiving, Merciful.

SECTION 10:
Relations of Muslim State with others

70 O Prophet, say to those of the captives who are in your hands: If Allāh knows anything good in your hearts, He will give you better than that which has been taken from you, and will forgive you. And Allāh is Forgiving, Merciful.

71 And if they intend to be treacherous to thee, so *indeed they have been* treacherous to Allāh before, but He gave (you) mastery over them. And Allāh is Knowing, Wise.

72 Surely those who believed and fled (their homes) and struggled hard in Allāh's way with their wealth and their lives, and those who gave shelter and helped — these are friends one of another. And those who believed and did not flee, you are not responsible for their protection until they flee. And if they seek help from you in the matter of religion, it is your duty to help (them) except against a people between whom and you there is a treaty. And Allāh is Seer of what you do.

73 And those who disbelieve are friends one of another. If you do it not, there will be persecution in *the land and great mischief.*

74 And those who believed and fled and struggled hard in Allāh's way, and those who gave shelter and helped — these are the believers truly. For them is forgiveness and an honourable provision.

75 And those who believed afterwards and *fled and struggled hard* along with you, they are of you. And the relatives are nearer one to another in the ordinance of Allāh. Surely Allāh is Knower of all things.

CHAPTER 9
Al-Barā'at: **The Immunity**

(REVEALED AT MADĪNAH: 16 *sections*; 129 *verses*)

SECTION 1:
Declaration of Immunity

1 A declaration of immunity from Allāh and His Messenger to those of the idolaters with whom you made an agreement.

2 So go about in the land for four months and know that you cannot escape Allāh and that Allāh will disgrace the disbelievers.

3 And an announcement from Allāh and His Messenger to the people on the day of the greater pilgrimage that Allāh is free from liability to the idolaters, and so is His Messenger. So if you repent, it will be better for you; and if you turn away, then know that you will not escape Allāh. And announce painful chastisement to those who disbelieve —

4 Except those of the idolaters with whom you made an agreement, then they have not failed you in anything and have not backed up anyone against you; so fulfil their agreement to the end of their term. Surely Allāh loves those who keep their duty.

5 So when the sacred months have passed, slay the idolaters, wherever you find them, and take them captive and besiege them and lie in wait for them in every ambush. But if they repent and keep up prayer and pay the poor-rate, leave their way free. Surely Allāh is Forgiving, Merciful.

6 And if anyone of the idolaters seek thy protection, protect him till he hears the word of Allāh, then convey him to his place of safety. This is because they are a people who know not.

SECTION 2:
Reasons for the Immunity

7 How can there be an

agreement for the idolaters with Allāh and with His Messenger, except those with whom you made an agreement at the Sacred Mosque? So as long as they are true to you, be true to them. Surely Allāh loves those who keep their duty.

8 How (can it be)? And if they prevail against you, they respect neither ties of relationship nor covenant in your case. They would please you with their mouths while their hearts refuse; and most of them are transgressors.

9 They have taken a small price for the messages of Allāh, so they hinder (men) from His way. Surely evil is that which they do.

10 They respect neither ties of relationship nor covenant, in the case of a believer. And these are they who go beyond the limits.

11 But if they repent and keep up prayer and pay the poor-rate, they are your brethren in faith. And We make the messages clear for a people who know.

12 And if they break their oaths after their agreement and revile your religion, then fight the leaders of disbelief — surely their oaths are nothing — so that they may desist.

13 Will you not fight a people who broke their oaths and aimed at the expulsion of the Messenger, and they attacked you first? Do you fear them? But Allāh has more right that you should fear Him, if you are believers.

14 Fight them; Allāh will chastise them at your hands and bring them to disgrace, and assist you against them and relieve the hearts of a believing people,

15 And remove the rage of their hearts. And Allāh turns (mercifully) to whom He pleases. And Allāh is Knowing, Wise.

16 Do you think that you would be left alone while Allāh has not yet known those of you who struggle hard and take not anyone as an intimate friend besides Allāh and His Messenger and the believers? And Allāh is Aware of what you do.

SECTION 3: Idolaters' Service of the Sacred House

17 The idolaters have no right to maintain the mosques of Allāh, while bearing witness to disbelief against themselves. These it is whose works are vain; and in the Fire will they abide.

18 Only he can maintain the mosques of Allāh who believes in Allāh and the Last Day, and keeps up prayer and pays the poor-rate and fears none but Allāh. So these it is who may be of the guided ones.

19 Do you hold the giving of drink to the pilgrims and the maintenance of the Sacred Mosque equal to (the service of) one who believes in Allāh and the Last Day and strives hard in Allāh's way? They are not equal in the sight of Allāh. And Allāh guides not the iniquitous people.

20 Those who believed and fled (their homes), and strove hard in Allāh's way with their wealth and their lives, are much higher in rank with Allāh. And it is these that shall triumph.

21 Their Lord gives them good news of mercy and pleasure, from Himself, and Gardens wherein lasting blessings will be theirs,

22 Abiding therein for ever. Surely Allāh has a mighty reward with Him.

23 O you who believe, take not your fathers and your brothers for friends if they love disbelief above faith. And whoever of you takes them for friends, such are the wrongdoers.

24 Say: If your fathers and your sons and your brethren and your wives and your kinsfolk and the wealth you have acquired, and trade whose dullness you fear, and dwellings you love, are dearer to you than Allāh and His Messenger and striving in His way, then wait till Allāh brings His command to pass. And Allāh guides not the transgressing people.

SECTION 4: Islām made Triumphant in Arabia

25 Certainly Allāh helped you in many battlefields, and on the day of Ḥunain, when your great numbers made you proud, but they

THE IMMUNITY

availed you nothing, and the earth with all its spaciousness was straitened for you, then you turned back retreating.

26 Then Allāh sent down His calm upon His Messenger and upon the believers, and sent hosts which you saw not, and chastised those who disbelieved. And such is the reward of the disbelievers.

27 Then will Allāh after this turn mercifully to whom He pleases. And Allāh is Forgiving, Merciful.

28 O you who believe, the idolaters are surely unclean, so they shall not approach the Sacred Mosque after this year of theirs. And if you fear poverty, then Allāh will enrich you out of His grace, if He please. Surely Allāh is Knowing, Wise.

29 Fight those who believe not in Allāh, nor in the Last Day, nor forbid that which Allāh and His Messenger have forbidden, nor follow the Religion of Truth, out of those who have been given the Book, until they pay the tax in acknowledgement of superiority and they are in a state of subjection.

SECTION 5:
Islām will Triumph in the World

30 And the Jews say: Ezra is the son of Allāh; and the Christians say: The Messiah is the son of Allāh. These are the words of their mouths. They imitate the saying of those who disbelieved before. Allāh's curse be on them! How they are turned away!

31 They take their doctors of law and their monks for Lords besides Allāh, and (also) the Messiah, son of Mary. And they were enjoined that they should serve one God only — there is no god but He. Be He glorified from what they set up (with Him)!

32 They desire to put out the light of Allāh with their mouths, and Allāh will allow nothing save the perfection of His light, though the disbelievers are averse.

33 He it is Who has sent His Messenger with the guidance and the Religion of Truth that He may make it prevail over all religions, though the polytheists are averse.

34 O you who believe, surely many of the doctors of law and the monks eat away the property of men falsely, and hinder (them) from Allāh's way. And those who hoard up gold and silver and spend it not in Allāh's way — announce to them a painful chastisement,

35 On the day when it will be heated in the Fire of hell, then their foreheads and their sides and their backs will be branded with it: This is what you hoarded up for yourselves, so taste what you used to hoard.

36 Surely the number of months with Allāh is twelve months by Allāh's ordinance, since the day when He created the heavens and the earth — of these four are sacred. That is the right religion; so wrong not yourselves therein. And fight the polytheists all together as they fight you all together. And know that Allāh is with those who keep their duty.

37 Postponing (of the sacred month) is only an addition in disbelief, whereby those who disbelieve are led astray. They allow it one year and forbid it (another) year, that they may agree in the number (of months) which Allāh has made sacred, and thus make lawful what Allāh has forbidden. The evil of their doings is made fair-seeming to them. And Allāh guides not the disbelieving people.

SECTION 6:
The Tabūk Expedition

38 O you who believe, what (excuse) have you that when it is said to you, Go forth in Allāh's way, you should incline heavily to earth? Are you contented with this world's life instead of the Hereafter? The provision of this world's life is but little as compared with the Hereafter.

39 If you go not forth, He will chastise you with a painful chastisement, and bring in your place a people other than you, and you can do Him no harm. And Allāh is Possessor of power over

THE IMMUNITY

40 If you help him not, Allāh certainly helped him when those who disbelieved expelled him — he being the second of the two; when they were both in the cave, when he said to his companion: Grieve not, surely Allāh is with us. So Allāh sent down His tranquillity on him and strengthened him with hosts which you saw not, and made lowest the word of those who disbelieved. And the word of Allāh, that is the uppermost. And Allāh is Mighty, Wise.

41 Go forth, light and heavy, and strive hard in Allāh's way with your wealth and your lives. This is better for you, if you know.

42 Had it been a near gain and a short journey, they would certainly have followed thee, but the hard journey was too long for them. And they will swear by Allāh: If we had been able, we would have gone forth with you. They cause their own souls to perish; and Allāh knows that they are liars.

SECTION 7:
The Hypocrites

43 Allāh pardon thee! Why didst thou permit them until those who spoke the truth had become manifest to thee and thou hadst known the liars?

44 Those who believe in Allāh and the Last Day ask not leave of thee (to stay away) from striving hard with their wealth and their persons. And Allāh is Knower of those who keep their duty.

45 They alone ask leave of thee who believe not in Allāh and the Last Day, and their hearts are in doubt, so in their doubt they waver.

46 And if they had intended to go forth, they would certainly have provided equipment for it; but Allāh did not like their going forth. So He withheld them, and it was said: Hold back with those who hold back.

47 Had they gone forth with you, they would have added to you naught but trouble, and would have hurried to and fro among you seeking (to sow) dissension among you. And among you there are those who would listen to them. And Allāh well knows the wrongdoers.

48 Certainly they sought (to sow) dissension before, and they devised plots against thee till the Truth came, and Allāh's command prevailed, though they did not like (it).

49 And among them is he who says: Excuse me and try me not. Surely into trial have they already fallen, and truly hell encompasses the disbelievers.

50 If good befalls thee, it grieves them; and if hardship afflicts thee, they say: Indeed we had taken care of our affair before. And they turn away rejoicing.

51 Say: Nothing will afflict us save that which Allāh has ordained for us. He is our Patron; and on Allāh let the believers rely.

52 Say: Do you await for us but one of two most excellent things? And we await for you that Allāh will afflict you with chastisement from Himself or by our hands. So wait; we too are waiting with you.

53 Say: Spend willingly or unwillingly, it will not be accepted from you. Surely you are a transgressing people.

54 And nothing hinders their contributions being accepted from them, except that they disbelieve in Allāh and in His Messenger and they come not to prayer except as lazy people, and they spend not but while they are reluctant.

55 Let not then their wealth nor their children excite thine admiration. Allāh only wishes to chastise them therewith in this world's life and (that) their souls may depart while they are disbelievers.

56 And they swear by Allāh that they are truly of you. And they are not of you, but they are a people who are afraid.

57 If they could find a refuge or caves or a place to enter, they would certainly have turned thereto, running away in all haste.

58 And of them are those who blame thee in the matter of the alms. So if they are given thereof, they are pleased, and if they are not given thereof, lo! they are enraged.

59 And if they were content with that which Allāh and His Messenger gave them, and had said: Allāh is sufficient for us; Allāh will soon give us (more) out of His grace and His Messenger too: surely to Allāh we make petition.

SECTION 8:
The Hypocrites

60 (Zakāt) charity is only for the poor and the needy, and those employed to administer it, and those whose hearts are made to incline (to truth), and (to free) the captives, and those in debt, and in the way of Allāh and for the wayfarer — an ordinance from Allāh. And Allāh is Knowing, Wise.

61 And of them are those who molest the Prophet and say, He is (all) ear. Say: A hearer of good for you — he believes in Allāh and believes the faithful, and is a mercy for those of you who believe. And those who molest the Messenger of Allāh, for them is a painful chastisement.

62 They swear by Allāh to you to please you; and Allāh — as well as His Messenger — has a greater right that they should please Him, if they are believers.

63 Know they not that whoever opposes Allāh and His Messenger, for him is the Fire of hell to abide in it? That is the grievous abasement.

64 The hypocrites fear lest a chapter should be sent down concerning them, telling them plainly of what is in their hearts. Say: Go on mocking, surely Allāh will bring to light what you fear.

65 And if thou ask them, they would certainly say: We were only talking idly and sporting. Say: Was it Allāh and His messages and His Messenger that you mocked?

66 Make no excuse, you disbelieved after your believing. If We pardon a party of you, We shall chastise a party, because they are guilty.

SECTION 9:
The Hypocrites

67 The hypocrites, men and women, are all alike. They enjoin evil and forbid good and withhold their hands. They have forsaken Allāh, so He has forsaken them. Surely the hypocrites are the transgressors.

68 Allāh promises the hypocrites, men and women, and the disbelievers the Fire of hell to abide therein. It is enough for them. And Allāh curses them, and for them is a lasting chastisement.

69 Like those before you — they were stronger than you in power and had more wealth and children. So they enjoyed their portion; thus have you enjoyed your portion as those before you enjoyed their portion, and you indulge in idle talk as they did. These are they whose works are null in this world and the Hereafter, and these are they who are the losers.

70 Has not the story reached them of those before them — of the people of Noah and 'Ād and Thamūd, and the people of Abraham and the dwellers of Midian and the overthrown cities? Their messengers came to them with clear arguments. So Allāh wronged them not but they wronged themselves.

71 And the believers, men and women, are friends one of another. They enjoin good and forbid evil and keep up prayer and pay the poor-rate, and obey Allāh and His Messenger. As for these, Allāh will have mercy on them. Surely Allāh is Mighty, Wise.

72 Allāh has promised to the believers, men and women, Gardens, wherein flow rivers, to abide therein, and goodly dwellings in Gardens of perpetual abode. And greatest of all is Allāh's goodly pleasure. That is the grand achievement.

SECTION 10:
The Hypocrites

73 O Prophet, strive hard against the disbelievers and the hypocrites and be firm against them. And their

THE IMMUNITY

abode is hell, and evil is the destination.

74 They swear by Allāh that they said nothing. And certainly they did speak the word of disbelief, and disbelieved after their Islām, and they purposed that which they could not attain. And they sought revenge only because Allāh — as well as His Messenger — had enriched them out of His grace. So if they repent, it will be good for them; and if they turn away, Allāh will chastise them with a painful chastisement in this world and the Hereafter; and they shall have in the earth neither a friend nor a helper.

75 And of them are those who made a covenant with Allāh: If He give us out of His grace, we will certainly give alms and be of the righteous.

76 But when He gave them out of His grace, they became niggardly of it and they turned away and they are averse.

77 So He requited them with hypocrisy in their hearts till the day when they meet Him, because they broke their promise with Allāh and because they lied.

78 Know they not that Allāh knows their hidden thoughts and their secret counsels, and that Allāh is the great Knower of the unseen things?

79 Those who taunt the free givers of alms among the believers as well as those who cannot find anything (to give) but with their hard labour — they scoff at them. Allāh will pay them back their mockery; and for them is a painful chastisement.

80 Ask forgiveness for them or ask not forgiveness for them. Even if thou ask forgiveness for them seventy times, Allāh will not forgive them. This is because they disbelieve in Allāh and His Messenger. And Allāh guides not the transgressing people.

SECTION 11:
The Hypocrites

81 Those who were left behind were glad on account of their sitting behind Allāh's Messenger, and they were averse to striving in Allāh's way with their property and their persons, and said: Go not forth in the heat. Say: The Fire of hell is fiercer in heat. If only they could understand!

82 Then let them laugh a little and weep much — a recompense for what they earned.

83 So if Allāh bring thee back to a party of them, then they ask thy permission to go forth, say: Never shall you go forth with me and never shall you fight an enemy with me. You chose to sit (at home) the first time; so sit (now) with those who remain behind.

84 And never offer prayer for anyone of them who dies, nor stand by his grave. Surely they disbelieved in Allāh and His Messenger and they died in transgression.

85 And let not their wealth and their children excite thy admiration. Allāh only intends to chastise them thereby in this world, and (that) their souls may depart while they are disbelievers.

86 And when a chapter is revealed, saying, Believe in Allāh and strive hard along with His Messenger, the wealthy among them ask permission of thee and say: Leave us (behind), that we may be with those who sit (at home).

87 They prefer to be with those who remain behind, and their hearts are sealed so they understand not.

88 But the Messenger and those who believe with him strive hard with their property and their persons. And these it is for whom are the good things and these it is who are successful.

89 Allāh has prepared for them Gardens wherein flow rivers, to abide therein. That is the great achievement.

SECTION 12:
The Hypocrites

90 And the defaulters from among the dwellers of the desert came that permission might be given to them, and they sat (at home) who lied to Allāh and His Messenger. A painful chastisement will afflict those of them who disbelieve.

91 No blame lies on the weak, nor on the sick, nor on those who can find nothing to spend, if they are sincere to Allāh and His Messenger. There is no way (to blame) against the doers of good. And Allāh is Forgiving, Merciful —

92 Nor on those to whom, when they came to thee that thou shouldst mount them, thou didst say: I cannot find that on which to mount you. They went back while their eyes overflowed with tears of grief that they could not find aught to spend.

93 The way (to blame) is only against those who ask permission of thee, though they are rich. They have chosen to be with those who remained behind; and Allāh has sealed their hearts, so they know not.

Part 11

94 They will make excuses to you when you return to them. Say: Make no excuse, we shall not believe you; Allāh has informed us of matters relating to you. And Allāh and His Messenger will now see your actions, then you will be brought back to the Knower of the unseen and the seen, then He will inform you of what you did.

95 They will swear by Allāh to you, when you return to them, so that you may leave them alone. So leave them alone. Surely they are unclean and their refuge is hell — a recompense for what they earned.

96 They will swear to you that you may be pleased with them. But if you are pleased with them, yet surely Allāh is not pleased with the transgressing people.

97 The dwellers of the desert are hardest in disbelief and hypocrisy, and most disposed not to know the limits of what Allāh has revealed to His Messenger. And Allāh is Knowing, Wise.

98 And of the dwellers of the desert are those who take what they spend to be a fine, and they wait for an evil turn of fortune for you. On them is the evil turn. And Allāh is Hearing, Knowing.

99 And of the desert

Arabs are those who believe in Allāh and the Last Day, and consider what they spend and the prayers of the Messenger, as bringing them nearer to Allāh. Surely they bring them nearer (to Allāh); Allāh will bring them into His mercy. Surely Allāh is Forgiving, Merciful.

SECTION 13:
The Hypocrites

100 And the foremost, the first of the Emigrants and the Helpers, and those who followed them in goodness — Allāh is well pleased with them and they are well pleased with Him, and He has prepared for them Gardens wherein flow rivers, abiding therein for ever. That is the mighty achievement.

101 And of those around you of the desert Arabs, there are hypocrites; and of the people of Madīnah (also) — they persist in hypocrisy. Thou knowest them not; We know them. We will chastise them twice, then they will be turned back to a grievous chastisement.

102 And others have acknowledged their faults — they mixed a good deed with another that was evil. It may be that Allāh will turn to them (mercifully). Surely Allāh is Forgiving, Merciful.

103 Take alms out of their property — thou wouldst cleanse them and purify them thereby — and pray for them. Surely thy prayer is a relief to them. And Allāh is Hearing, Knowing.

104 Know they not that Allāh is He Who accepts repentance from His servants and takes the alms, and that Allāh — He is the Oft-returning (to mercy), the Merciful?

105 And say, Work; so Allāh will see your work and (so will) His Messenger and the believers. And you *will* be brought back to the Knower of the unseen and the seen, then He will inform you of what you did.

106 And others are made to await Allāh's command, whether He chastise them or turn to them (mercifully). And Allāh is Knowing, Wise.

THE IMMUNITY

107 And those who built a mosque to cause harm (to Islām) and (to help) disbelief, and to cause disunion among the believers, and a refuge for him who made war against Allāh and His Messenger before. And they will certainly swear: We desired naught but good. And Allāh bears witness that they are certainly liars.

108 Never stand in it. Certainly a mosque founded on observance of duty from the first day is more deserving that thou shouldst stand in it. In it are men who love to purify themselves. And Allāh loves those who purify themselves.

109 Is he, then, who lays his foundation on duty to Allāh and (His) good pleasure better, or he who lays his foundation on the edge of a cracking hollowed bank, so it broke down with him into the Fire of hell? And Allāh guides not the unjust people.

110 The building which they have built will ever continue to be a source of disquiet in their hearts, unless their hearts be torn to pieces. And Allāh is Knowing, Wise.

SECTION 14:
The Faithful

111 Surely Allāh has bought from the believers their persons and their property — theirs (in return) is the Garden. They fight in Allāh's way, so they slay and are slain. It is a promise which is binding on Him in the Torah and the Gospel and the Qur'ān. And who is more faithful to his promise than Allāh? Rejoice therefore in your bargain which you have made. And that is the mighty achievement.

112 They who turn (to Allāh), who serve (Him), who praise (Him), who fast, who bow down, who prostrate themselves, who enjoin what is good and forbid what is evil, and who keep the limits of Allāh — and give good news to the believers.

113 It is not for the Prophet and those who believe to ask forgiveness for the polytheists, even though they should be near relatives, after it has become clear to them that they are companions of the flaming fire.

114 And Abraham's asking forgiveness for his sire was only owing to a promise which he had made to him; but when it became clear to him that he was an enemy of Allāh, he dissociated himself from him. Surely Abraham was tender-hearted, forbearing.

115 And it is not (attributable) to Allāh that He should lead a people astray after He has guided them, so far so that He makes clear to them what they should guard against. Surely Allāh is Knower of all things.

116 Surely Allāh's is the kingdom of the heavens and the earth. He gives life and causes death. And besides *Allāh you have no friend* nor helper.

117 Certainly Allāh has turned in mercy to the Prophet and the Emigrants and the Helpers who followed him in the hour of hardship, after the hearts of a part of them were about to deviate; then He turned to them in mercy. Surely to them He is Compassionate, Merciful;

118 And (He turned in mercy) to the three who were left behind; until the earth, vast as it is, became strait to them and their souls were also straitened to them; and they knew that there was no refuge from Allāh but in Him. Then He turned to them in mercy that they might turn (to Him). Surely Allāh — He is the Oft-returning to mercy, the Merciful.

SECTION 15:
What the Faithful should Do

119 O you who believe, keep your duty to Allāh and be with the truthful.

120 It was not proper for the people of Madīnah and those round about them of the desert Arabs to remain behind the Messenger of Allāh, nor to prefer their own lives to his life. That is because there afflicts them neither thirst nor fatigue nor hunger in Allāh's way, nor tread they a path which enrages the disbelievers, nor cause they any harm to an enemy, but a good work is written down for them on account of it. Surely Allāh wastes not the reward of the doers of good;

121 Nor spend they anything, small or great, nor do they traverse a valley but it is written down for them, that Allāh may reward them for the best of what they did.

122 And the believers should not go forth all together. Why, then, does not a company from every party from among them go forth that they may apply themselves to obtain understanding in religion, and that they may warn their people, when they come back to them, that they may be cautious?

SECTION 16:
The Prophet's Great Anxiety

123 O you who believe, fight those of the disbelievers who are near to you and let them find firmness in you. And know that Allāh is with those who keep their duty.

124 And whenever a chapter is revealed, there are some of them who say: Which of you has it strengthened in faith? So as for those who believe, it strengthens them in faith and they rejoice.

125 And as for those in whose hearts is a disease, it adds uncleanness to their uncleanness, and they die while they are disbelievers.

126 See they not that they are tried once or twice in every year, yet they repent not, nor do they mind.

127 And whenever a chapter is revealed, they look one at another: Does anyone see you? Then they turn away. Allāh has turned away their hearts because they are a people who understand not.

128 Certainly a Messenger has come to you from among yourselves; grievous to him is your falling into distress, most solicitous for you, to the believers (he is) compassionate, merciful.

129 But if they turn away, say: Allāh is sufficient for me — there is no god but He. On Him do I rely, and He is the Lord of the mighty Throne.

CHAPTER 10
Yūnus: **Jonah**

(REVEALED AT MAKKAH: 11 *sections*; 109 *verses*)

SECTION 1:
Truth of Revelation

In the name of Allāh, the Beneficent, the Merciful.

1 I, Allāh, am the Seer. These are the verses of the Book, full of wisdom.

2 Is it a wonder to the people that We have revealed to a man from among themselves: Warn the people and give good news to those who believe that for them is advancement in excellence with their Lord? The disbelievers say: This is surely a manifest enchanter.

3 Surely your Lord is Allāh, Who created the heavens and the earth in six *periods, and He is* established on the Throne of Power regulating the Affair. There is no intercessor except after His permission. This is Allāh, your Lord, therefore serve Him. Will you not mind?

4 To Him is your return, of all (of you). It is the promise of Allāh (made) in truth. Surely He produces the first creation, then He reproduces it, that He may reward with equity those who believe and do good. And as for those who disbelieve, for them is a drink of hot water and a painful chastisement because they disbelieved.

5 He it is Who made the sun a shining brightness, and the moon a light, and ordained for it stages that you might know the computation of years and the reckoning. Allāh created not this but with truth. He makes the signs manifest for a people who know.

6 Surely in the variation of the night and the day, and that which Allāh has created in the heavens and the earth, there are signs for a people who keep their duty.

7 Those who expect not the meeting with Us, and are pleased with this world's life and are satisfied with it, and those who are heedless of Our messages —

8 These, their abode is the Fire because of what they earned.

9 Those who believe and do good, their Lord guides them by their faith; rivers will flow beneath them in Gardens of bliss.

10 Their cry therein will be, Glory to Thee, O Allāh! and their greeting, Peace! And the last of their cry will be: Praise be to Allāh, the Lord of the worlds!

SECTION 2:
Punishment of Rejection

11 And if Allāh were to hasten for men the (consequences) of evil, as they would hasten on the good, their doom would certainly have been decreed for them. But We leave those alone, who have no hope of meeting with Us, in their inordinacy, blindly wandering on.

12 And when affliction touches a man, he calls on Us, whether lying on his side or sitting or standing; but, when We remove his affliction from him, he passes on as though he had never called on Us on account of an affliction that touched him. Thus is what they do, made fair-seeming to the extravagant.

13 And certainly We destroyed generations before you when they did wrong, and their messengers came to them with clear arguments, yet they would not believe. Thus do We recompense the guilty people.

14 Then We made you rulers in the land after them, so that We might see how you act.

15 And when Our clear messages are recited to them, those who have no hope of meeting with Us say: Bring a Qur'ān other than this or change it. Say: It is not for me to change it of my own accord. I follow naught but what is revealed to me. Indeed I fear, if I disobey my Lord, the chastisement of a grievous day.

16 Say: If Allāh had

desired, I would not have recited it to you, nor would He have made it known to you. I have lived among you a lifetime before it. Do you not understand?

17 Who is then more unjust than he who forges a lie against Allāh or gives the lie to His messages? Surely the guilty never succeed.

18 And they serve besides Allāh that which can neither harm them nor profit them, and they say: These are our intercessors with Allāh. Say: Would you inform Allāh of what He knows not in the heavens and the earth? Glory be to Him, and supremely exalted is He above what they set up (with Him)!

19 And (all) people are but a single nation, then they disagree. And had not a word already gone forth from thy Lord, the matter would have certainly been decided between them in respect of that wherein they disagree.

20 And they say: Why is not a sign sent to him from his Lord? Say: The unseen is only for Allāh, so wait; surely I too with you am of those who wait.

SECTION 3:
Merciful Dealing

21 And when We make people taste of mercy after an affliction touches them, lo! they devise plans against Our messages. Say: Allāh is quicker to plan. Surely Our messengers write down what you plan.

22 He it is Who makes you travel by land and sea; until, when you are in the ships, and they sail on with them in a pleasant breeze, and they rejoice at it, a violent wind overtakes them and the billows surge in on them from all sides, and they deem that they are encompassed about. Then they pray to Allāh, being sincere to Him in obedience: If Thou deliver us from this, we will certainly be of the grateful ones.

23 But when He delivers them, lo! they are unjustly rebellious in the earth. O men, your rebellion is against yourselves — a provision (only) of this world's life. Then to Us is your return, so We shall inform you of what you did.

24 The likeness of this world's life is only as water which We send down from the clouds, then the herbage of the earth, of which men and cattle eat, grows luxuriantly thereby; until when the earth puts on its golden raiment and it becomes adorned, and its people think that they are masters of it, Our command comes to it, by night or by day, so We render it as reaped seed-produce, as though it had not flourished yesterday. Thus do We make clear the messages for a people who reflect.

25 And Allāh invites to the abode of peace, and guides whom He pleases to the right path.

26 For those who do good is good (reward) and more (than this). Neither blackness nor ignominy will cover their faces. These are the owners of the Garden; therein they will abide.

27 And those who earn evil, the punishment of an evil is the like thereof, and abasement will cover them — they will have none to protect them from Allāh — as if their faces had been covered with slices of the dense darkness of night. These are the companions of the Fire; therein they will abide.

28 And on the day when We gather them all together, then We shall say to those who associated others (with Allāh): Keep where you are, you and your associate-gods. Then We shall separate them one from another, and their associates will say: It was not us that you served.

29 So Allāh suffices as a witness between us and you that we were quite unaware of your serving (us).

30 There will every soul become acquainted with what it sent before, and they will be brought back to Allāh, their true Patron, and that which they devised will escape from them.

SECTION 4:
Uniqueness of Divine Gifts

31 Say: Who gives you sustenance from the heaven and the earth, or who controls the hearing and the sight, and who brings forth the living from the dead, and brings forth the dead from the living? And who regulates the affair? They will say: Allāh. Say then: Will you not then guard against evil?

32 Such then is Allāh, your true Lord. And what is there after the truth but error? How then are you turned away!

33 Thus does the word of thy Lord prove true against those who transgress that they believe not.

34 Say: Is there anyone among your associate-gods who produces the first creation, then reproduces it? Say: Allāh produces the first creation, then He reproduces it. How are you then turned away!

35 Say: Is there any of your associate-gods who guides to the Truth? Say: Allāh guides to the Truth. Is He then Who guides to the Truth more worthy to be followed, or he who finds not the way unless he is guided? What is the matter with you? How do you judge?

36 And most of them follow naught but conjecture. Surely conjecture will not avail aught against the Truth. Truly Allāh is Knower of what they do.

37 And this Qur'ān is not such as could be forged by those besides Allāh, but it is a verification of that which is before it and a clear explanation of the Book, there is no doubt in it, from the Lord of the worlds.

38 Or say they: He has forged it? Say: Then bring a chapter like it, and invite whom you can besides Allāh, if you are truthful.

39 Nay, they reject that, whose knowledge thay cannot compass and whose final sequel has not yet come to them. Even thus did those before them reject; then see what was the end of the wrongdoers.

40 And of them is he who believes in it, and of them is he who believes not in it. And thy Lord best knows the mischief-makers.

SECTION 5:
The Reprobate and their Punishment

41 And if they reject thee, say: My work is for me and your work for you. You are clear of what I do and I am clear of what you do.

42 And of them are some who listen to thee. But canst thou make the deaf to hear, though they will not understand?

43 And of them are some who look at thee. But canst thou show the way to the blind, though they will not see?

44 Surely Allāh wrongs not men in aught, but men wrong themselves.

45 And on the day when He will gather them, as though they had not stayed but an hour of the day, they will recognize one another. They perish indeed who reject the meeting with Allāh, and they follow not the right way.

46 And if We show thee something of that which We promise them, or cause thee to die, yet to Us is their return, and Allāh is Witness to what they do.

47 And for every nation there is a messenger. So when their messenger comes, the matter is decided between them with justice, and they are not wronged.

48 And they say: When will this promise be fulfilled, if you are truthful?

49 Say: I control not for myself any harm, or any benefit, except what Allāh pleases. Every nation has a term. When their term comes, they cannot put it off an hour, nor can they bring it before (its time).

50 Say: Do you see if His chastisement overtakes you by night or by day? What then is there of it that the guilty would hasten?

51 And when it comes to pass, will you believe in it? What! now! and you hastened it on.

52 Then will it be said to those who were unjust: Taste abiding chastisement; you are not requited except for what you earned.

53 And they ask thee: Is that true? Say: Aye, by my Lord! it is surely the Truth, and you will not escape.

SECTION 6:
Mercy takes Precedence of Punishment

54 And if every soul that has done injustice had all that is in the earth, it would offer it for ransom. And they will manifest regret when they see the chastisement. And it will be decided between them with justice, and they will not be wronged.

55 Now surely whatever is in the heavens and the earth is Allāh's. Now surely Allāh's promise is true, but most of them know not.

56 He gives life and causes death, and to Him you will be returned.

57 O men, there has come to you indeed an admonition from your Lord and a healing for what is in the breasts; and a guidance and a mercy for the believers.

58 Say: In the grace of Allāh and in His mercy, in that they should rejoice. It is better than that which they hoard.

59 Say: See you what Allāh has sent down for you of sustenance, then you make (a part) of it unlawful and (a part) lawful. Say: Has Allāh commanded you or do you forge a lie against Allāh?

60 And what think those who forge lies against Allāh of the day of Resurrection? Surely Allāh is Bountiful to men, but most of them give not thanks.

SECTION 7:
Good News for the Faithful

61 And thou art not (engaged) in any affair and thou recitest not concerning it any portion of the Qur'ān, and you do no work, but We are Witness of you when you are engaged therein. And not the weight of an atom in the earth or in the heaven is hidden from thy Lord, nor anything less than that nor greater, but it is (all) in a clear book.

62 Now surely the friends of Allāh, they have no fear nor do they grieve —

63 Those who believe and keep their duty.

64 For them is good news in this world's life and in the Hereafter. There is no changing the words of

Allāh. That is the mighty achievement.

65 And let not their speech grieve thee. Surely might belongs wholly to Allāh. He is the Hearer, the Knower.

66 Now, surely, whatever is in the heavens and whatever is in the earth is Allāh's. And what do follow those who call on associates besides Allāh? They follow naught but conjecture, and they only lie.

67 He it is Who made for you the night that you might rest therein and the day giving light. Surely in this are signs for a people who hear.

68 They say: Allāh has taken a son (to Himself). Glory be to Him! He is the Self-sufficient. His is what is in the heavens and what is in the earth. You have no authority for this. Say you against Allāh what you know not?

69 Say: Those who forge a lie against Allāh will not succeed.

70 A little enjoyment in this world, then to Us is their return, then We shall make them taste severe chastisement because they disbelieved.

SECTION 8:
Noah and Moses

71 And recite to them the story of Noah, when he said to his people: O my people, if my staying (here) and my reminding (you) by the messages of Allāh is hard on you, on Allāh do I rely; so decide your course of action and (gather) your associates. Then let not your course of action be dubious to you, so have it executed against me and give me no respite.

72 But if you turn back, I ask for no reward from you. My reward is only with Allāh, and I am commanded to be of those who submit.

73 But they rejected him, so We delivered him and those with him in the ark, and We made them rulers and drowned those who rejected Our messages. See, then, what was the end of those who were warned.

74 Then, after him We sent messengers to their

people. They came to them with clear arguments, but they would not believe what they had rejected before. Thus do We seal the hearts of those who exceed the limits.

75 Then after them We sent Moses and Aaron to Pharaoh and his chiefs with Our signs, but they were arrogant, and they were a guilty people.

76 So when the truth came to them from Us, they said: This is surely clear enchantment!

77 Moses said: Say you (this) of the truth when it has come to you? Is it enchantment? And the enchanters never succeed.

78 They said: Hast thou come to us to turn us away from that which we found our fathers following, and (that) greatness in the land may be for you two? And we are not going to believe in you.

79 And Pharaoh said: Bring to me every skilful enchanter.

80 So when the enchanters came, Moses said to them: Cast what you are going to cast.

81 So when they had cast down, Moses said: What you have brought is deception. Surely Allāh will make it naught. Surely Allāh allows not the work of mischief-makers to thrive.

82 And Allāh will establish the truth by His words, though the guilty be averse.

SECTION 9:
End of Opposition to Moses

83 But, on account of the fear of Pharaoh and their chiefs persecuting them, none believed in Moses except a few of his people. And Pharaoh was truly high-handed in the land; and surely he was extravagant.

84 And Moses said: O my people, if you believe in Allāh, then rely on Him if you submit (to Him).

85 They said: On Allāh we rely; our Lord, make us not a trial for the unjust people.

86 And deliver us by Thy mercy from the disbelieving people.

JONAH

87 And We revealed to Moses and his brother: Take for your people houses to abide in Egypt and make your houses places of worship and keep up prayer. And give good news to the believers.

88 And Moses said: Our Lord, surely Thou hast given Pharaoh and his chiefs finery and riches in this world's life, our Lord, that they may lead (people) astray from Thy way. Our Lord, destroy their riches and harden their hearts, so that they believe not till they see the painful chastisement.

89 He said: Your prayer *is accepted; so continue in the right way and follow* not the path of those who know not.

90 And We brought the Children of Israel across the sea. Then Pharaoh and his hosts followed them for oppression and tyranny, till, when drowning overtook him, he said: I believe that there is no god but He in Whom the Children of Israel believe, and I am of those who submit.

91 What! Now! And indeed before (this) thou didst disobey and thou wast *of the mischief-makers!*

92 But this day We shall save thee in thy body that thou mayest be a sign to those after thee. And surely most of the people are heedless of Our signs.

SECTION 10:
Those who heed Warning will benefit

93 And certainly We lodged the Children of Israel in a goodly abode and provided them with good things. Then they differed not till the knowledge came to them. Surely thy Lord will judge between them on the day of Resurrection concerning that in which they differed.

94 But if thou art in doubt as to that which We have revealed to thee, ask those who read the Book before thee. Certainly the Truth has come to thee from thy Lord, so be not thou of the doubters.

95 And be not of those who reject the messages of Allāh, (for) then thou wilt be of the losers.

96 Surely those against whom the word of thy Lord has proved true will not believe,

97 Though every sign should come to them, till they see the painful chastisement.

98 And why was there not a town which believed, so that their belief should have profited them, but the people of Jonah? When they believed, We removed from them the chastisement of disgrace in this world's life, and We gave them provision for a while.

99 And if thy Lord had pleased, all those who are in the earth would have believed, all of them. Wilt thou then force men till they are believers?

100 And it is not for any soul to believe except by Allāh's permission. And He casts *uncleanness* on those who will not understand.

101 Say: Behold what is in the heavens and the earth! And signs and warners avail not a people who believe not.

102 What do they wait for, then, but the like of the days of those who passed away before them? Say: Wait then; I, too, am with you of those who wait.

103 Then We deliver Our messengers and those who believe — even so (now); it is binding on Us to deliver the believers.

SECTION 11:
Divine Judgment

104 Say: O people, if you are in doubt as to my religion, (know that) I serve not those whom you serve besides Allāh, but I serve Allāh, Who causes you to die; and I am commanded to be of the believers,

105 And that thou set thy purpose towards the Religion uprightly; and be not of the polytheists.

106 And call not besides Allāh that which can *neither benefit thee nor harm thee*; for if thou dost, thou shalt then be of the unjust.

107 And if Allāh afflicts thee with harm, there is none to remove it but He; and if He intends good to thee, there is none to repel His grace. He brings it to whom He pleases of His servants. And He is the Forgiving, the Merciful.

108 Say: O people, the Truth has indeed come to you from your Lord; so whoever goes aright, goes aright only for the good of his own soul; and whoever errs, errs only against it. And I am not a custodian over you.

109 And follow what is revealed to thee and be patient till Allāh give judgment, and He is the Best of the judges.

CHAPTER 11

Hūd

(REVEALED AT MAKKAH: 10 *sections*; 123 *verses*)

SECTION 1:
A Warning

In the name of Allāh, the Beneficent, the Merciful.

1 I, Allāh, am the Seer. A Book, whose verses are characterized by wisdom, then they are made plain, from One Wise, Aware:

2 That you should serve none but Allāh. Surely I am to you from Him a warner and a giver of good news.

3 And ask forgiveness of your Lord, then turn to Him. He will provide you with a goodly provision to an appointed term, and will bestow His grace on every one endowed with grace. *And if* you turn away, I fear for you the chastisement of a great day.

4 To Allāh is your return, and He is Possessor of power over all things.

5 Now surely they cover up their breasts to conceal (their enmity) from Him. Now surely, *when they put* their garments as a covering, He knows what they hide and what they make public. Surely He is Knower of what is in the breasts.

Part 12

6 And there is no animal in the earth but on Allāh is the sustenance of it, and He knows its resting-place and its depository. All is in a clear record.

7 And He it is Who created the heavens and the earth in six periods; and His Throne of Power is ever on water that He might manifest (the good qualities in) you, whoever of you is best in deeds. And if thou sayest, You shall surely be raised up after death, those who disbelieve say: This is nothing but clear deceit.

HŪD

8 And if We delay for them the chastisement for a stated period, they will certainly say: What prevents it? Now surely on the day when it will come to them, it will not be averted from them, and that which they scoffed at will beset them.

SECTION 2:
Truth of Revelation

9 And if We make man taste mercy from Us, then withdraw it from him, he is surely despairing, ungrateful.

10 And if We make him taste a favour after distress has afflicted him, he says: The evils are gone away from me. Certainly he is exultant, boastful,

11 Except those who are patient and do good. For them is forgiveness and a great reward.

12 Then, may it be that thou wilt give up part of what is revealed to thee and thy breast will be straitened by it, because they say: Why has not a treasure been sent down for him or an angel come with him? Thou art only a warner. And Allāh is in charge of all things.

13 Or, say they: He has forged it. Say: Then bring ten forged chapters like it, and call upon whom you can besides Allāh, if you are truthful.

14 But if they answer you not, then know that it is revealed by Allāh's knowledge, and that there is no God but He. Will you then submit?

15 Whoever desires this world's life and its finery — We repay them their deeds therein, and they are not made to suffer loss in it.

16 These are they for whom there is nothing but Fire in the Hereafter. And what they work therein is fruitless and their deeds are vain.

17 Is he then (like these) who has with him clear proof from his Lord, and a witness from Him recites it, and before it (is) the Book of Moses, a guide and a mercy? These believe in it. And whoever of the parties disbelieves in it, the Fire is his promised place. So be not in doubt about it. Surely it is the truth from thy Lord, but most men believe not.

18 And who is more unjust than he who forges a lie against Allāh? These will be brought before their Lord, and the witnesses will say: These are they who lied against their Lord. Now surely the curse of Allāh is on the wrongdoers,

19 Who hinder (men) from the path of Allāh and desire to make it crooked. And they are disbelievers in the Hereafter.

20 These will not escape in the earth, nor have they guardians besides Allāh. The chastisement will be doubled for them. They could not bear to hear, and they did not see.

21 These are they who have lost their souls, and that which they forged is gone from them.

22 Truly in the Hereafter they are the greatest losers.

23 Surely those who believe and do good and humble themselves before their Lord, these are the owners of the Garden; therein they will abide.

24 The likeness of the two parties is as the blind and the deaf, and the seer and the hearer. Are they equal in condition? Will you not then mind?

SECTION 3:
History of Noah

25 And certainly We sent Noah to his people: Surely I am a plain warner to you,

26 To serve none but Allāh. Verily I fear for you the chastisement of a painful day.

27 But the chiefs of his people who disbelieved said: We see thee not but a mortal like us, and we see not that any follow thee but those who are the meanest of us at first thought. Nor do we see in you any superiority over us; nay, we deem you liars.

28 He said: O my people, *see you if I* have with me clear proof from my Lord, and He has granted me mercy from Himself and it has been made obscure to you. Can we compel you to (accept) it while you are averse to it?

29 And, O my people, I ask you not for wealth (in

return) for it. My reward is only with Allāh, and I am not going to drive away those who believe. Surely they will meet their Lord, but I see you a people who are ignorant.

30 And, O my people, who will help me against Allāh, if I drive them away? Will you not then mind?

31 And I say not to you that I have the treasures of Allāh; and I know not the unseen; nor do I say that I am an angel. Nor do I say about those whom your eyes scorn that Allāh will not grant them (any) good — Allāh knows best what is in their souls — for then indeed I should be of the wrongdoers.

32 They said: O Noah, indeed thou hast disputed with us and prolonged dispute with us, so bring upon us that which thou threatenest us with, if thou art truthful.

33 He said: Only Allāh will bring it on you, if He please, and you will not escape:

34 And my advice will not profit you, if I intend to give you good advice, if Allāh intends to destroy you. He is your Lord; and to Him you will be brought back.

35 Or say they: He has forged it? Say: If I have forged it, on me is my guilt; and I am free of that of which you are guilty.

SECTION 4:
History of Noah

36 And it was revealed to Noah: None of thy people will believe except those who have already believed, so grieve not at what they do:

37 And make the ark under Our eyes and Our revelation, and speak not to Me on behalf of those who are unjust. Surely they will be drowned.

38 And he began to make the ark. And whenever the chiefs of his people passed by him, they laughed at him. He said: If you laugh at us, surely we, too, laugh at you as you laugh (at us).

39 So you shall know who it is on whom will come a chastisement which will disgrace him, and on whom a lasting chastisement will fall.

40 At length when Our command came and water gushed forth from the valley, We said: Carry in it two of all things, a pair, and thine own family — except those against whom the word has already gone forth — and those who believe. And there believed not with him but a few.

41 And he said: Embark in it, in the name of Allāh be its sailing and its anchoring. Surely my Lord is Forgiving, Merciful.

42 And it moved on with them amid waves like mountains. And Noah called out to his son, and he was aloof: O my son, embark with us and be not with the disbelievers.

43 He said: I will betake myself for refuge to a mountain that will save me from the water. He said: There is none safe today from Allāh's command, but he on whom He has mercy. And a wave intervened between them, so he was among the drowned.

44 And it was said: O earth, swallow thy water, and O cloud, clear away. And the water was made to abate, and the affair was decided, and it rested on the Jūdī, and it was said: Away with the iniquitous people!

45 And Noah cried to his Lord and said: My Lord, surely my son is of my family, and Thy promise is true, and Thou art the Justest of the judges.

46 He said: O Noah, he is not of thy family; he is (an embodiment of) unrighteous conduct. So ask not of Me that of which thou hast no knowledge. I admonish thee lest thou be of the ignorant.

47 He said: My Lord, I seek refuge in Thee from asking of Thee that of which I have no knowledge. And unless thou forgive me and have mercy on *me, I* shall be of the losers.

48 It was said: O Noah, descend with peace from Us and blessing on thee and on nations (springing) from those with thee. And there are nations whom We afford provisions, then a painful punishment from Us afflicts them.

49 These are announcements relating to the unseen which We reveal to thee; thou didst not know them —(neither) thou nor thy people — before this. So be patient. Surely, the (good) end is for the dutiful.

SECTION 5:
History of Hūd

50 And to 'Ād (We sent) their brother Hūd. He said: O my people, serve Allāh, you have no god save Him. You are only fabricators.

51 O my people, I ask of you no reward for it. My reward is only with Him Who created me. Do you not then understand?

52 And, O my people, ask forgiveness of your Lord, then turn to Him, He will send on you clouds pouring down abundance of rain and add strength to your strength, and turn not back, guilty.

53 They said: O Hūd, thou hast brought us no clear argument, and we are not going to desert our gods for thy word, and we are not believers in thee.

54 We say naught but that some of our gods have smitten thee with evil. He said: Surely I call Allāh to witness, and do you, too, bear witness that I am innocent of what you associate (with Allāh)

55 Besides Him. So scheme against me all together, then give me no respite.

56 Surely I put my trust in Allāh, my Lord and your Lord. There is no living creature but He grasps it by its forelock. Surely my Lord is on the right path.

57 But if you turn away, then indeed I have delivered to you that with which I am sent to you. And my Lord will bring another people in your place, and you cannot do Him any harm. Surely my Lord is the Preserver of all things.

58 And when Our commandment came to pass, We delivered Hūd and those who believed with him with mercy from Us; and We delivered them from a hard chastisement.

59 And such were 'Ād. They denied the messages of their Lord, and disobeyed His messengers and followed the bidding of every insolent opposer (of truth).

60 And they were overtaken by a curse in this world and on the day of Resurrection. Now surely 'Ād disbelieved in their Lord. Now surely, away with 'Ād, the people of Hūd!

SECTION 6:
History of Ṣāliḥ

61 And to Thamūd (We sent) their brother Ṣāliḥ. He said: O my people, serve Allāh, you have no god other than Him. He brought you forth from the earth and made you dwell in it, so ask forgiveness of Him, then turn to Him. Surely my Lord is Nigh, Answering.

62 They said: O Ṣāliḥ, thou wast *among us a centre* of (our) hopes before this. Dost thou forbid us to worship what our fathers worshipped? And surely we are in grave doubt about that to which thou callest us.

63 He said: O my people, see you if I have clear proof from my Lord and He has granted me mercy from Himself — who will then help me against Allāh, if I disobey Him? So you would add to me naught but perdition.

64 And, O my people, this is Allāh's she-camel, a sign for you, so leave her to pasture on Allāh's earth and touch her not with evil, lest a near chastisement overtake you.

65 But they hamstrung her, so he said: Enjoy yourselves in your houses for three days. That is a promise not to be belied.

66 So when Our commandment came to pass, We saved Ṣāliḥ and those who believed with him by mercy from Us from the disgrace of that day. Surely thy Lord — He is the Strong, the Mighty.

67 And the cry overtook those who did wrong, so they were motionless bodies in their abodes.

68 As though they had never dwelt therein. Now surely Thamūd disbelieved in their Lord. So away with Thamūd!

SECTION 7:
Abraham and Lot

69 And certainly Our messengers came to Abraham with good news. They said: Peace! Peace! said he. And he made no delay in bringing a roasted calf.

70 But when he saw that their hands reached not to it, he mistrusted them and conceived fear of them. They said: Fear not; we have been sent to Lot's people.

71 And his wife was standing (by), so she wondered. Then We gave her the good news of Isaac, and beyond Isaac, of Jacob.

72 She said: O wonder! Shall I bear a son when I am an extremely old woman, and this my husband an extremely old man? This is a wonderful thing indeed!

73 They said: Wonderest thou at Allāh's commandment? The mercy of Allāh and His blessings on you, O people of the house! Surely He is Praised, Glorious.

74 So when fear departed from Abraham and good news came to him, he began to plead with Us for Lot's people.

75 Surely Abraham was forbearing, tender-hearted, oft-returning (to Allāh).

76 O Abraham, cease from this. Surely the decree of thy Lord has gone forth and there must come to them a chastisement that cannot be averted.

77 And when Our messengers came to Lot, he was grieved for them, and he was unable to protect them, and said: This is a distressful day!

78 And his people came to him, (as if) driven on towards him, and they were used to the doing of evil deeds before. He said: O my people, these are my daughters — they are purer for you; so guard against (the punishment of) Allāh and disgrace me not about my guests. Is there not among you any right-minded man?

79 They said: Certainly thou knowest that we have no claim on thy daughters, and thou knowest what we desire.

80 He said: Would that I had the power to repel you! — rather I shall have recourse to a strong support.

81 They said: O Lot, we are the messengers of thy Lord. They shall not reach thee. So travel with thy people for a part of the night — and let none of you turn back — except thy wife. Surely whatsoever befalls them shall befall her. Surely their appointed time is the morning. Is not the morning nigh?

82 So when Our decree came to pass, We turned them upside down, and rained on them stones, as decreed, one after another,

83 Marked (for punishment) with thy Lord. And it is not far off from the wrongdoers.

SECTION 8:
History of Shu'aib

84 *And to Midian (We sent) their brother* Shu'aib. He said: O my people, serve Allāh, you have no other god save Him. And give not short measure and weight. I see you in prosperity, and I fear for you the chastisement of an all-encompassing day:

85 And, O my people, give full measure and weight justly, and defraud not men of their things, and act not corruptly in the land, making mischief:

86 What remains with Allāh is better for you, if you are believers. And I am not a keeper over you.

87 They said: O Shu'aib, does thy prayer enjoin thee that we should forsake what our fathers worshipped or that we should not do what we please with regard to our property? Forsooth thou art the forbearing, the right-directing one!

88 He said: O my people, see you if I have a clear proof from my Lord and He has given me a goodly sustenance from Himself. And I desire not to act in opposition to you, in that which I forbid you. I desire nothing but reform, so far as I am able. And with none but Allāh is the direction of my affair to a right issue. In Him I trust and to Him I turn.

89 And, O my people, let not opposition to me make you guilty so that there may befall you the like of that *which befell the people of Noah, or the people of Hūd, or the people of Ṣāliḥ. Nor are the people of Lot far off from you.*

90 And ask forgiveness of your Lord, then turn to Him. Surely my Lord is Merciful, Loving-kind.

91 They said: O Shu'aib, we understand not much of what thou sayest and surely we see thee to be weak among us. And were it not for thy family, we would surely stone thee, and thou art not mighty against us.

92 He said: O my people, is my family more esteemed by you than Allāh? And you neglect Him as a thing cast behind your backs! Surely my Lord encompasses what you do.

93 And, O my people, act according to your ability, I too am acting. You will come to know who it is on whom will light the punishment that will disgrace him, and who it is that is a liar. And watch, surely I too am watching with you.

94 And when Our decree came to pass, We delivered Shu'aib and those who believed with him by mercy from Us. And the cry overtook those who were iniquitous, so they were motionless bodies in their abodes,

95 As though they had never dwelt in them. So away with Midian, just as Thamūd perished!

SECTION 9:
The Iniquitous and the Righteous

96 And certainly We sent Moses with Our signs and a clear authority,

97 To Pharaoh and his chiefs, but they followed the bidding of Pharaoh; and Pharaoh's bidding was not right-directing.

98 He will lead his people on the day of Resurrection, and bring them down to the Fire. And evil the place to which they are brought!

99 And they are overtaken by a curse in this (world), and on the day of Resurrection. Evil the gift which shall be given!

100 This is an account of the towns which We relate to thee. Of them are some that stand and (others) mown down.

101 And We wronged them not but they wronged themselves. And their gods whom they called upon besides Allāh availed them naught when the decree of thy Lord came to pass. And they added to them naught but ruin.

102 And such is the punishment of thy Lord, when He punishes the towns while they are iniquitous. Surely His punishment is painful, severe.

103 Surely there is a sign in this for him who fears the chastisement of the Hereafter. That is a day on which people will be gathered together, and that is a day to be witnessed.

104 And We delay it not but for an appointed term.

105 On the day when it comes, no soul will speak except by His permission; so (some) of them will be unhappy and (others) happy.

106 Then as for those who are unhappy, they will be in the Fire; for them therein will be sighing and groaning —

107 Abiding therein so long as the heavens and the earth endure, except as thy Lord please. Surely thy Lord is Doer of what He intends.

108 And as for those who are made happy, they will be in the Garden abiding therein so long as the heavens and the earth endure, except as thy Lord please — a gift never to be cut off.

109 So be not thou in doubt as to that which these worship. They worship only as their fathers worshipped before. And surely We shall pay them in full their due undiminished.

SECTION 10:
Believers Comforted

110 And We certainly gave the Book to Moses, but differences arose therein. And had not a word gone forth from thy Lord, the matter would have been decided between them. And they are surely in a disquieting doubt about it.

111 And thy Lord will surely pay back to all their deeds in full. He indeed is Aware of what they do.

112 Continue then in the

right way as thou art commanded, as also (should) those who turn (to Allāh) with thee. And be not inordinate, (O men). Surely He is Seer of what you do.

113 And incline not to those who do wrong, lest the fire touch you; and you have no protectors besides Allāh, then you would not be helped.

114 And keep up prayer at the two ends of the day and in the first hours of the night. Surely good deeds take away evil deeds. This is a reminder for the mindful.

115 And be patient, for surely Allāh wastes not the reward of the doers of good.

116 Why were there not then among the generations before you those possessing understanding, forbidding mischief in the earth, except a few among them whom We delivered? And the unjust pursued the enjoyment of plenty, and they were guilty.

117 And thy Lord would not destroy the towns unjustly, while their people acted well.

118 And if thy Lord had pleased, He would have made people a single nation. And they cease not to differ,

119 Except those on whom thy Lord has mercy; and for this did He create them. And the word of thy Lord is fulfilled: I shall fill hell with jinn and men, all together.

120 And all We relate to thee of the account of the messengers is to strengthen thy heart therewith. And in this has come to thee the truth and an admonition and a reminder for the believers.

121 And say to those who believe not: Act according to your power, surely we too are acting;

122 And wait, surely we are waiting (also).

123 And Allāh's is the unseen in the heavens and the earth, and to Him the whole affair will be returned. So serve Him and put thy trust in Him. And thy Lord is not heedless of what you do.

CHAPTER 12
Yūsuf: **Joseph**

(REVEALED AT MAKKAH: 12 *sections*; 111 *verses*)

SECTION 1:
Joseph's Vision

In the name of Allāh, the Beneficent, the Merciful.

1 I, Allāh, am the Seer. These are the verses of the Book that makes manifest.

2 Surely We have revealed it — an Arabic Qur'ān — that you may understand.

3 We narrate to thee the best of narratives, in that We have revealed to thee this Qur'ān, though before this thou wast of those unaware.

4 When Joseph said to his father: O my father, I saw eleven stars and the sun and *the moon* — *I saw* them making obeisance to me.

5 He said: O my son, relate not thy dream to thy brethren, lest they devise a plan against thee. The devil indeed is an open enemy to man.

6 And thus will thy Lord choose thee and teach thee the interpretation of sayings, and make His favour complete to thee and to the Children of Jacob, as He made it complete before to thy fathers, Abraham and Isaac. Surely thy Lord is Knowing, Wise.

SECTION 2:
Plot against Joseph by his Brothers

7 Verily in Joseph and his brethren there are signs for the inquirers.

8 When they said: Certainly Joseph and his brother are dearer to our father than we, though we are a (strong) company. Surely our father is in manifest error —

9 Slay Joseph or banish him to some (other) land, so that your father's regard may be exclusively for you,

10 A speaker among *them* said: Slay not Joseph, but, if you are going to do anything, cast him down to the bottom of the well. Some of the travellers may pick him up.

11 They said: O our father, why dost thou not trust us with Joseph, and surely we are his sincere well-wishers?

12 Send him with us tomorrow that he may enjoy himself and play, and we shall surely guard him well.

13 He said: Indeed it grieves *me* that you should take him away and I fear lest the wolf devour him, while you are heedless of him.

14 They said: If the wolf should devour him, while we are a (strong) company, we should then certainly be losers.

15 So when they took him away and agreed to put him down at the bottom of the pit, We revealed to him: Thou wilt certainly inform them of this affair of theirs while they perceive not.

16 And they came to their *father at nightfall, weeping.*

17 They said: O our father, we went off racing one with another and left Joseph by our goods, so the wolf devoured him. And thou wilt not believe us, though we are truthful.

18 And they came with false blood on his shirt. He said: Nay, your souls have made a matter light for you. So patience is goodly. And Allāh is He Whose help is sought against what you describe.

19 And there came travellers, and they sent their water-drawer and he let down *his bucket. He* said: O good news! This is a youth. And they concealed him as an article of merchandise, and Allāh was Cognizant of what they did.

20 And they sold him for a small price, a few pieces of silver, and they showed no desire for him.

SECTION 3:
Joseph's Firmness under Temptation

21 And the Egyptian who

bought him said to his wife: Make his stay honourable. Maybe he will be useful to us, or we may adopt him as a son. And thus We established Joseph in the land, and that We might teach him the interpretation of sayings. And Allāh has full control over His affair, but most people know not.

22 And when he attained his maturity, We gave him wisdom and knowledge. And thus do We reward the doers of good.

23 And she in whose house he was, sought to seduce him, and made fast the doors and said: Come. He said: Allāh forbid! Surely my Lord made good my abode. The wrongdoers never prosper.

24 And certainly she desired him, and he would have desired her, were it not *that he had seen* the manifest evidence of his Lord. Thus (it was) that We might turn away from him evil and indecency. Surely he was one of Our chosen servants.

25 And they raced with one another to the door, and she rent his shirt from behind, and they met her husband at the door. She said: What is the punishment for one who intends evil to thy wife, except imprisonment or a painful chastisement?

26 He said: She sought to seduce me. And a witness of her own family bore witness: If his shirt is rent in front, she speaks the truth and he is of the liars.

27 And if his shirt is rent behind, she tells a lie and he is of the truthful.

28 So when he saw his shirt rent behind, he said: Surely it is a device of you women. Your device is indeed great!

29 O Joseph, turn aside from this. And (O my wife), ask forgiveness for thy sin. Surely thou art one of the sinful.

SECTION 4:
Joseph is Imprisoned

30 And women in the city said: The chief's wife seeks to seduce her slave. He has indeed affected her deeply with (his) love. Truly we see her in manifest error.

31 So when she heard of

their device, she sent for them and prepared for them a repast, and gave each of them a knife, and said (to Joseph): Come out to them. So when they saw him, they deemed him great, and cut their hands (in amazement), and said: Holy Allāh! This is not a mortal! This is but a noble angel.

32 She said: This is he about whom you blamed me. And certainly I sought to seduce him, but he was firm in continence. And if he do not what I bid him, he shall certainly be imprisoned, and he shall certainly be of the abject.

33 He said: My Lord, the prison is dearer to me than that to which they invite me. And if Thou turn not away their device from me, I shall yearn towards them and be of the ignorant.

34 So his Lord accepted his prayer and turned away their device from him. Surely He is the Hearer, the Knower.

35 Then it occurred to them after they had seen the signs that they should imprison him till a time.

SECTION 5:
Joseph's Preaching in the Prison

36 And two youths entered the prison with him. One of them said: I saw myself pressing wine. And the other said: I saw myself carrrying bread on my head, of which birds were eating. Inform us of its interpretation; surely we see thee to be of the doers of good.

37 He said: The food with which you are fed shall not come to you, but I shall inform you of its interpretation before it comes to you. This is of what my Lord has taught me. Surely I have forsaken the religion of a people who believe not in Allāh, and are deniers of the Hereafter.

38 And I follow the religion of my fathers, Abraham and Isaac and Jacob. It beseems us not to associate aught with Allāh. This is by Allāh's grace upon us and on mankind, but most people give not thanks.

39 O my two fellow-prisoners, are sundry lords better or Allāh the One, the Supreme?

40 You serve not besides Him but names which you have named, you and your fathers — Allāh has sent down no authority for them. Judgment is only Allāh's. He has commanded that you serve none but Him. This is the right religion, but most people know not.

41 O my two fellow-prisoners, as for one of you, he will serve wine for his lord to drink; and as for the other, he will be crucified, so that the birds will eat from his head. The matter is decreed concerning which you inquired.

42 And he said to him whom he knew would be delivered of the two: Remember me with thy lord. But the devil caused him to forget mentioning (it) to his lord, so he remained in the prison a *few years*.

SECTION 6:
The King's Vision Interpreted by Joseph

43 And the king said: I have seen seven fat kine which seven lean ones devoured; and seven green ears and (seven) others dry. O chiefs, explain to me my dream, if you can interpret the dream.

44 They said: Confused dreams, and we know not the interpretation of dreams.

45 And of the two, he who had found deliverance and remembered after a long time said: I will inform you of its interpretation, so send me.

46 Joseph, O truthful one, explain to us seven fat kine which seven lean ones devoured, and seven green ears and (seven) others dry, that I may go back to the people so that they may know.

47 He said: You shall sow for seven years as usual, then that which you reap, leave it in its ear, except a little which you eat.

48 *Then after that will come seven years of hardship, which will eat away all you have beforehand stored for them, except a little which you have preserved.*

49 *Then after that will come a year in which people will have rain and in* which they will press (grapes).

SECTION 7:
Joseph Cleared of the Charges

50 And the king said: Bring him to me. So when the messenger came to him, he said: Go back to thy lord and ask him, what is the case of the women who cut their hands. Surely my Lord knows their device.

51 (The king) said: What was your affair when you sought to seduce Joseph? They said: Holy Allāh! We knew of no evil on his part. The chief's wife said: Now has the truth become manifest. I sought to seduce him and he is surely of the truthful.

52 This is that he might know that I have not been unfaithful to him in secret, and that Allāh guides not the device of the unfaithful.

Part 13

53 And I call not myself sinless; surely (man's) self is wont to command evil, except those on whom my Lord has mercy. Surely my Lord is Forgiving, Merciful.

54 And the king said: Bring him to me, I will choose him for myself. So when he talked with him, he said: Surely thou art in our presence today dignified, trusted.

55 He said: Place me (in authority) over the treasures of the land; surely I am a good keeper, knowing well.

56 And thus did We give to Joseph power in the land — he had mastery in it wherever he liked. We bestow Our mercy on whom We please, and We waste not the reward of the doers of good.

57 And certainly the reward of the Hereafter is better for those who believe and guard against evil.

SECTION 8:
Joseph helps his Brothers

58 And Joseph's brethren came and went in to him, and he knew them, while they recognized him not.

59 And when he furnished them with their provision, he said: Bring to me a brother of yours from your father. See you not that I give full measure and that I am the best of hosts?

60 But if you bring him not to me, you shall have no measure (of corn) from me, nor shall you come near me.

61 They said: We shall strive to make his father yield about him, and we are sure to do (it).

62 And he said to his servants: Put their money into their bags that they may recognize it when they go back to their family, so that they may come back.

63 So when they returned to their father, they said: O our father, the measure is withheld from us, so send with us our brother that we may get the measure, and we will surely guard him.

64 He said: Can I trust you with him, except as I trusted you with his brother before. So Allāh is the Best Keeper, and He is the most Merciful of those who show mercy.

65 And when they opened their goods, they found their money returned to them. They said: O our father, what (more) can we desire? This is our property returned to us, and we shall bring corn for our family and guard our brother, and have in addition the measure of a camel-load. This is an easy measure.

66 He said: I will by no means send him with you, until you give me a firm covenant in Allāh's name that you will bring him back to me, unless you are completely surrounded. And when they gave him their covenant, he said: Allāh is Guardian over what we say.

67 And he said: O my sons, enter not by one gate but enter by different gates. And I can avail you naught against Allāh. Judgment is only Allāh's. On Him I rely, and on Him let the reliant rely.

68 And when they entered as their father had bidden them, it availed them naught against Allāh, but (it was only) a desire in the soul of Jacob, which he satisfied. And surely he was possessed of knowledge, because We had given him knowledge, but most people know not.

SECTION 9:
The Youngest Brother

69 And when they went in to Joseph, he lodged his brother with himself, saying: I am thy brother, so grieve not at what they do.

70 Then when he furnished them with their provision, (someone) placed the drinking-cup in his brother's bag. Then a crier cried out: O caravan, you are surely thieves!

71 They said, while they turned towards them: What is it that you miss?

72 They said: We miss the king's drinking-cup, and he who brings it shall have a camel-load, and I am responsible for it.

73 They said: By Allāh! You know for certain that we have not come to make mischief in the land, and we are not thieves.

74 They said: But what is the penalty for this, if you are liars?

75 They said: The penalty for this — the person in whose bag it is found, he himself is the penalty for it. Thus do we punish the wrongdoers.

76 So he began with their sacks before the sack of his brother, then he brought it out from his brother's sack. Thus did We plan for the sake of Joseph. He could not take his brother under the king's law, unless Allāh pleased. We raise in degree whom We please. And above everyone possessed of knowledge is the All-Knowing One.

77 They said: If he steal, a brother of his did indeed steal before. But Joseph kept it secret in his soul, and disclosed it not to them. He said: You are in an evil condition, and Allāh knows best what you state.

78 They said: O chief, he has a father, a very old man, so take one of us in his place. Surely we see thee to be of the doers of good.

79 He said: Allāh forbid that we should seize other than him with whom we found our property, for then surely we should be unjust!

SECTION 10:
Joseph Discloses his Identity

80 So when they de-

spaired of him, they conferred together privately. The eldest of them said: Know you not that your father took from you a covenant in Allāh's name, and how you fell short of your duty about Joseph before? So I shall not leave this land, until my father permits me or Allāh decides for me; and He is the Best of the judges.

81 Go back to your father and say: O our father, thy son committed theft. And we bear witness only to what we know, and we could not keep watch over the unseen.

82 And ask the town where we were, and the caravan with which we proceeded. And surely we are truthful.

83 He said: Nay, your souls have contrived an affair for you, so patience is good. Maybe Allāh will bring them together to me. Surely He is the Knowing, the Wise.

84 And he turned away from them, and said: O my sorrow for Joseph! And his eyes were filled (with tears) on account of the grief, then he repressed (grief).

85 They said: By Allāh! Thou wilt not cease remembering Joseph till thou art a prey to disease or thou art of those who perish.

86 He said: I complain of my grief and sorrow only to Allāh, and I know from Allāh what you know not.

87 O my sons, go and inquire about Joseph and his brother, and despair not of Allāh's mercy. Surely none despairs of Allāh's mercy except the disbelieving people.

88 So when they came to him, they said: O chief, distress has afflicted us and our family, and we have brought scanty money, so give us full measure and be charitable to us. Surely Allāh rewards the charitable.

89 He said: Do you know how you treated Joseph and his brother, when you were ignorant?

90 They said: Art thou indeed Joseph? He said: I am Joseph and this is my brother; Allāh has indeed been gracious to us. Surely he who keeps his duty and is patient — Allāh never

JOSEPH

wastes the reward of the doers of good.

91 They said: By Allāh! Allāh has indeed chosen thee over us, and we were certainly sinners.

92 He said: No reproof be against you this day. Allāh may forgive you, and He is the most Merciful of those who show mercy.

93 Take this my shirt and cast it before my father's face — he will come to know. And come to me with all your family.

SECTION 11:
Israel goes to Egypt

94 And when the caravan left (Egypt), their father said: Surely I scent (the power of) Joseph, if you call me not a dotard.

95 They said: By Allāh! thou art surely in thy old error.

96 Then when the bearer of good news came, he cast it before his face so he became certain. He said: Did I not say to you that I know from Allāh what you know not?

97 They said: O our father, ask forgiveness of our sins for us, surely we are sinners.

98 He said: I shall ask forgiveness for you of my Lord. Surely He is the Forgiving, the Merciful.

99 Then when they went in to Joseph, he lodged his parents with himself and said: Enter Egypt in safety, if Allāh please.

100 And he raised his parents on the throne, and they fell prostrate for his sake. And he said: O my father, this is the significance of my vision of old — my Lord has made it true. And He was indeed kind to me, when He brought me forth from the prison, and brought you from the desert after the devil had sown dissensions between me and my brethren. Surely my Lord is Benignant to whom He pleases. Truly He is the Knowing, the Wise.

101 My Lord, Thou hast given me of the kingdom and taught me of the interpretation of sayings. Originator of the heavens and the earth, Thou art my Friend in this world and the Hereafter. Make me die in submission and join me with the righteous.

102 This is of the announcements relating to the unseen (which) We reveal to thee, and thou wast not with them when they resolved upon their affair, and they were devising plans.

103 And most men believe not, though thou desirest it eagerly.

104 And thou askest them no reward for it. It is nothing but a reminder for all mankind.

SECTION 12:
A Lesson for the Prophet's Opponents

105 And how many a sign in the heavens and the earth do they pass by! yet they turn away from it.

106 *And most of them* believe not in Allāh without associating others (with Him).

107 Do they then feel secure from the coming to them of an all-encompassing chastisement from Allāh or from the coming to them of the hour suddenly, while they perceive not?

108 Say: This is my way: I call to Allāh, with certain knowledge — I and those who follow me. And glory be to Allāh! and I am not of the polytheists.

109 And We sent not before thee any but men, from the people of the towns, to whom We sent revelation. Have they not then travelled in the land and seen what was the end of those before them? And certainly the abode of the Hereafter is best for those who keep their duty. Do you not then understand?

110 Until, when the messengers despaired and (the people) thought that they were told a lie, Our help came to them, and whom We pleased was delivered. And Our punishment is not averted from the guilty people.

111 *In* their histories there is certainly a lesson for men of understanding. It is not a narrative which could be forged, but a verification of what is before it, and a distinct explanation of all things, and a guide and a mercy to a people who believe.

Chapter 13
Al-Ra'd: The Thunder

(REVEALED AT MAKKAH: *6 sections*; *43 verses*)

SECTION 1:
Truth of Revelation

In the name of Allāh, the Beneficent, the Merciful.

1 I, Allāh, am the Best Knower, the Seer. These are verses of the Book. And that which is revealed to thee from thy Lord is the Truth, but most people believe not.

2 Allāh is He Who raised the heavens without any pillars that you can see, and He is established on the Throne of Power, and He made the sun and the moon subservient (to you). Each one runs to an appointed term. He regulates the affair, making clear the messages that you may be certain of the meeting with your Lord.

3 And He it is Who spread the earth, and made in it firm mountains and rivers. And of all fruits He has made in it pairs, two (of every kind). He makes the night cover the day. Surely there are signs in this for a people who reflect.

4 And in the earth are tracts side by side, and gardens of vines, and corn, and palm-trees growing from one root and distinct roots — they are watered with one water; and We make some of them to excel others in fruit. Surely there are signs in this for a people who understand.

5 *And if thou wonderest, then wondrous is their saying:* When we are dust, shall we then be raised in a new creation? These are they who disbelieve in their Lord, and these have chains on their necks, and they are the companions of the Fire; in it they will abide.

6 And they ask thee to hasten on the evil before the good, and indeed there have been exemplary punishments before them. And surely thy Lord is full of forgiveness for mankind notwithstanding their iniquity. And surely thy Lord is Severe in requiting.

7 And those who disbelieve say: Why has not a sign been sent down to him from his Lord? Thou art only a warner and for every people a guide.

SECTION 2:
Fall and Rise of Nations

8 Allāh knows what every female bears, and that of which the wombs fall short of completion and that which they grow. And everything with Him has a measure.

9 The Knower of the unseen and the seen, the Great, the Most High.

10 Alike (to Him) among you is he *who conceals* (the) word and he who speaks openly, and he who hides himself by night and (who) goes forth by day.

11 For him are (angels) guarding the consequences (of his deeds), before him and behind him, who guard him by Allāh's command. Surely Allāh changes not the condition of a people, until they change their own condition. And when Allāh intends evil to a people, there is no averting it, and besides Him they have no protector.

12 He it is Who shows you the lightning causing fear and hope and (Who) brings up the heavy cloud.

13 And the thunder celebrates His praise, and the angels too for awe of Him. And He sends the thunderbolts and smites with them whom He pleases, yet they dispute concerning Allāh, and He is Mighty in prowess.

14 To Him is due the true prayer. And those to whom they pray besides Him give them no answer, but (they are) like one who stretches forth his two hands towards water that it may reach his mouth, but it will not reach it. And the prayer of the disbelievers is only wasted.

15 And whoever is in the heavens and the earth makes obeisance to Allāh only, willingly and unwillingly, and their shadows, too, at morn and eve.

THE THUNDER

16 Say: Who is the Lord of the heavens and the earth? Say: Allāh. Say: Do you then take besides Him, guardians who control no benefit or harm even for themselves? Say: Are the blind and the seeing alike? Or, are darkness and light equal? Or, have they set up with Allāh associates who have created creation like His, so that what is created became confused to them? Say: Allāh is the Creator of all things, and He is the One, the Supreme.

17 He sends down water from the clouds, then watercourses flow according to their measure, and the torrent bears along the swelling foam. And from that which they melt in the fire for the sake of making ornaments or apparatus arises a scum like it. Thus does Allāh compare truth and falsehood. Then as for the scum, it passes away as a worthless thing; and as for that which does good to men, it tarries in the earth. Thus does Allāh set forth parables.

18 For those who respond to their Lord is good. And as for those who respond not to Him, even if they had all that is in the earth and the like thereof with it, they would certainly offer it for a ransom. As for those, theirs is an evil reckoning and their abode is hell; and evil is the resting-place.

SECTION 3:
Good and Evil bring their own Reward

19 Is he who knows that what is revealed to thee from thy Lord is the truth like him who is blind? Only men of understanding mind —

20 Those who fulfil the pact of Allāh, and break not the covenant,

21 And those who join that which Allāh has bidden to be joined and have awe of their Lord, and fear the evil reckoning.

22 And those who are steadfast seeking the pleasure of their Lord, and keep up prayer and spend of that which We have given them, secretly and openly, and repel evil with good; for such is the (happy) issue of the abode —

23 Gardens of perpetuity, which they will enter along with those who do good from among their fathers and their spouses and their offspring; and the angels will enter in upon them from every gate.

24 Peace be to you, because you were constant — how excellent is then the final Abode!

25 And those who break the covenant of Allāh after its confirmation, and cut asunder that which Allāh has ordered to be joined, and make mischief in the land, for them is the curse, and theirs is the evil end of the Abode.

26 Allāh amplifies and straitens provision for whom He pleases. And they rejoice in this world's life. And this world's life, compared with the Hereafter, is *only a temporary enjoyment*.

SECTION 4:
Revolution to be brought about by Qur'ān

27 And those who disbelieve say: Why is not a sign sent down to him by his Lord? Say: Allāh leaves in error whom He pleases, and guides to Himself those who turn (to Him) —

28 Those who believe and whose hearts find rest in the remembrance of Allāh. Now surely in Allāh's remembrance do hearts find rest.

29 Those who believe and do good, a good final state is theirs and a goodly return.

30 Thus We have sent thee among a nation before which other nations have passed away, that thou mightest recite to them what We have revealed to thee, and (still) they deny the Beneficent. Say: He is my Lord, there is no god but He; in Him do I trust and to Him is my return.

31 And if there could be a Qur'ān with which the *mountains* were made to pass away, or the earth were cloven asunder, or the dead were made to speak — nay, the commandment is wholly Allāh's. Do not those who believe know that, if Allāh please, He would certainly guide all the people? And as for those who disbelieve, disaster will not cease to afflict them because of what they do, or it will alight close by their abodes, until the promise of Allāh come to pass. Surely Allāh will not fail in (His) promise.

SECTION 5:
Opposition will fail

32 And messengers before thee were certainly mocked, but I gave respite to those who disbelieved, then I seized them. How (awful) was then My requital!

33 Is, then, He Who watches every soul as to *what it earns* —? And yet they ascribe partners to Allāh! Say: Name them. Would you inform Him of that which He knows not in the earth, or of an outward saying? Rather, their plan is made fair-seeming to those who disbelieve, and they are kept back from the path. And whom Allāh leaves in error, he has no guide.

34 For them is chastisement in this world's life, and the chastisement of the Hereafter is certainly more grievous. And they have no protector against Allāh.

35 A parable of the Garden which is promised to those who keep their duty: Therein flow rivers. Its fruits are perpetual and its plenty. Such is the end for those who keep their duty; and the end for the disbelievers is the Fire.

36 And those to whom We have given the Book rejoice in that which has been revealed to thee, and of the confederates are some who deny a part of it. Say: I am commanded only to serve Allāh and not associate anything with Him. To Him do I invite (you), *and to Him* is my return.

37 And thus have We revealed it, a true judgment, in Arabic. And if thou follow their low desires after that which has come to thee of knowledge, thou wouldst have against Allāh no guardian nor protector.

SECTION 6:
Steady Progress of Truth

38 And certainly We sent messengers before thee and appointed for them wives and children. And it is not in (the power of) a messenger to bring a sign except by Allāh's permission. For every term there is an appointment.

39 Allāh effaces what He pleases and establishes (what He pleases), and with Him is the basis of the Book.

40 Whether We let thee see part of that which We promise them, or cause thee to die, thine is but the delivery of the message, and Ours to call (them) to account.

41 See they not that We are visiting the land, curtailing it of its sides? And Allāh pronounces a doom — there is no repeller of His decree. And He is Swift in calling to account.

42 And those before them planned indeed, but all planning is Allāh's. He knows what every soul earns. And the disbelievers will come to know for whom is the (good) end of the Abode.

43 And those who disbelieve say: Thou art not a messenger. Say: Allāh is sufficient for a witness between me and you, and whoever has knowledge of the Book.

CHAPTER 14

Ibrāhīm: **Abraham**

(REVEALED AT MAKKAH: 7 *sections*; 52 *verses*)

SECTION 1:
Revelation dispels Darkness

In the name of Allāh, the Beneficent, the Merciful.

1 I, Allāh, am the Seer. A Book which We have revealed to thee that thou mayest bring forth men, by their Lord's permission, from darkness into light, to the way of the Mighty, the Praised One,

2 Of Allāh, Whose is whatever is in the heavens *and whatever is* in the earth. And woe to the disbelievers for the severe chastisement!

3 Those who love this world's life more than the Hereafter, and turn away from Allāh's path, and would have it crooked. Those are far astray.

4 And We sent no messenger but with the language of his people, so that he might explain to them clearly. Then Allāh leaves in error whom He pleases and He guides whom He pleases. And He is the Mighty, the Wise.

5 And certainly We sent Moses with Our messages, saying: Bring forth thy people from darkness into light and remind them of the days of Allāh. In this are surely signs for every steadfast, grateful one.

6 And when Moses said to his people: Call to mind Allāh's favour to you, when He delivered you from Pharaoh's people, who subjected you to severe torment, and slew your sons and spared your women. And therein was a great trial from your Lord.

SECTION 2:
Truth is rejected first

7 And when your Lord made it known: If you are grateful, I will give you more, and if you are ungrateful, My chastisement is truly severe.

8 And Moses said: If you are ungrateful, you and all those on earth, then Allāh is surely Self-sufficient, Praised.

9 Has not the account reached you of those before you, of the people of Noah and 'Ād and Thamūd — and those after them? None knows them but Allāh. Their messengers came to them with clear arguments, but they thrust their hands into their mouths and said: We deny that with which you are sent, and surely we are in serious doubt as to that to which you invite us.

10 Their messengers said: Is there doubt about Allāh, the Maker of the heavens and the earth? He invites you to forgive you your faults and to respite you till an appointed term. They said: You are nothing but mortals like us; you wish to turn us away from that which our fathers used to worship; so bring us clear authority.

11 Their messengers said to them: We are nothing but mortals like yourselves, but Allāh bestows (His) favours on whom He pleases of His servants. And it is not for us to bring you an authority, except by Allāh's permission. And on Allāh let the believers rely.

12 And why should we not rely on Allāh? and He has indeed guided us in our ways. And we would certainly bear with patience your persecution of us. And on Allāh should the reliant rely.

SECTION 3:
Opposition is at last destroyed

13 And those who disbelieved said to their messengers: We will certainly drive you out of our land, unless you come back into our religion. So their Lord revealed to them: We shall certainly destroy the wrongdoers,

14 And We shall certainly settle you in the land after them. This is for him who fears standing in My presence and fears My threat.

15 And they sought judgment, and every insolent opposer was disappointed:

ABRAHAM

16 Hell is before him and he is given to drink of boiling water;

17 He drinks it little by little and is not able to swallow it; and death comes to him from every quarter, yet he dies not. And before him is vehement chastisement.

18 The parable of those who disbelieve in their Lord: Their works are as ashes on which the wind blows hard on a stormy day. They have no power over aught they have earned. That is straying far away.

19 Seest thou not that Allāh created the heavens and the earth with truth? If He please, He will take you away and bring a new creation,

20 And that is not difficult for Allāh.

21 And they will all come forth to Allāh, then the weak will say to those who were proud: We were your followers, can you then avert from us aught of the chastisement of Allāh? They will say: If Allāh had guided us, we would have guided you. It is the same to us whether we cry or bear patiently; there is no escape for us.

SECTION 4:
Truth is confirmed

22 And the devil will say, when the matter is decided: Surely Allāh promised you a promise of truth, and I promised you, then failed you. And I had no authority over you, except that I called you and you obeyed me; so blame me not but blame yourselves. I cannot come to your help, nor can you come to my help. I deny your associating me with Allāh before. Surely for the unjust is a painful chastisement.

23 *And those who believe* and do good are made to enter Gardens, wherein flow rivers, abiding therein by their Lord's permission. Their greeting therein is, Peace!

24 Seest thou not how Allāh sets forth a parable of a good word as a good tree, whose root is firm and whose branches are high,

25 Yielding its fruit in every season by the permission of its Lord? And Allāh sets forth parables for men that they may be mindful.

26 And the parable of an evil word is as an evil tree pulled up from the earth's surface; it has no stability.

27 Allāh confirms those who believe with the sure word in this world's life and in the Hereafter; and Allāh leaves the wrongdoers in error; and Allāh does what He pleases.

SECTION 5:
Man's Injustice in rejecting Truth

28 Seest thou not those who change Allāh's favour for disbelief and make their people to alight in the abode of perdition —

29 Hell. They will burn in it. And an evil place it is to settle in!

30 And they set up equals with Allāh to lead astray from His path. Say: Enjoy yourselves, for surely your return is to the Fire.

31 Tell My servants who believe to keep up prayer and spend out of what We have given them, secretly and openly, before the coming of the day in which there is no bartering, nor befriending.

32 Allāh is He Who created the heavens and the earth and sent down water from the clouds, then brought forth with it fruits as a sustenance for you, and He has made the ships subservient to you to run their course in the sea by His command, and He has made the rivers subservient to you.

33 And He has made subservient to you the sun and the moon, pursuing their courses; and He has made subservient to you the night and the day.

34 And He gives you of all you ask of Him. And if you count Allāh's favours, you will not be able to number them. Surely man is very unjust, very ungrateful.

SECTION 6:
Abraham's Prayer

35 And when Abraham said: My Lord, make this city secure, and save me and my sons from worshipping idols.

36 My Lord, surely they have led many men astray.

So whoever follows me, he is surely of me; and whoever disobeys me, Thou surely art Forgiving, Merciful.

37 Our Lord, I have settled a part of my offspring in a valley unproductive of fruit near Thy Sacred House, our Lord, that they may keep up prayer; so make the hearts of some people yearn towards them, and provide them with fruits; haply they may be grateful.

38 Our Lord, surely Thou knowest what we hide and what we proclaim. And nothing is hidden from Allāh, either in the earth, or in the heaven.

39 Praise be to Allāh, Who has given me, in old age, Ishmael and Isaac! Surely my Lord is the Hearer of prayer.

40 My Lord, make me keep up prayer and from my offspring (too), our Lord, and accept my prayer.

41 Our Lord, grant me protection and my parents and the believers on the day when the reckoning comes to pass.

SECTION 7:
The End of Opposition

42 And think not Allāh to be *heedless of what the unjust do*. He only respites them to a day when the eyes will stare (in terror),

43 Hastening forward, their heads upraised, their gaze not returning to them, and their hearts vacant.

44 And warn people of a day when the chastisement will come to them, then the wrongdoers will say: Our Lord, respite us to a near term, we will respond to Thy call and follow the messengers. Did you not swear before that there will be no passing away for you?

45 And you dwell in the abodes of those who wronged themselves, and it is clear to you how We dealt with them and We made (them) examples for you.

46 And they have indeed planned their plan, and their plan is with Allāh, though their plan is such that the mountains should be moved thereby.

47 So think not that Allāh will fail in His promise to

His messengers. Surely Allāh is Mighty, the Lord of retribution.

48 On the day when the earth will be changed into a different earth, and the heavens (as well), and they will come forth to Allāh, the One, the Supreme.

49 And thou wilt see the guilty on that day linked together in chains —

50 Their shirts made of pitch, and fire covering their faces,

51 That Allāh may repay each soul what it has earned. Surely Allāh is Swift in reckoning.

52 This is a message for the people and that they may be warned thereby, and that they may know that He is One God, and that men of understanding may mind.

Chapter 15
Al-Ḥijr: **The Rock**

(Revealed at Makkah: 6 *sections*; 99 verses)

SECTION 1:
The Qur'ān is guarded

In the name of Allāh, the Beneficent, the Merciful.

1 I, Allāh, am the Seer. These are the verses of the Book and (of) a Qur'ān that makes manifest.

Part 14

2 Often will those who disbelieve wish that they were Muslims.

3 Leave them to eat and enjoy themselves, and let (false) hope beguile them, for they will soon know.

4 And never did We destroy a town but it had a decree made known.

5 No people can hasten on their doom, nor can they postpone (it).

6 And they say: O thou to whom the Reminder is revealed, thou art indeed mad.

7 Why bringest thou not the angels to us, if thou art of the truthful?

8 We send not angels but with truth, and then they would not be respited.

9 Surely We have revealed the Reminder, and surely We are its Guardian.

10 And certainly We sent (messengers) before thee among the sects of yore.

11 And there never came a messenger to them but they mocked him.

12 Thus do We make it enter the hearts of the guilty —

13 They believe not in it; and the example of the ancients has gone before.

14 And even if We open to them a gate of heaven, and they keep on ascending into it,

15 They would say: Only our eyes have been covered over, rather we are an enchanted people.

SECTION 2:
Forces of Evil will be destroyed

16 And certainly We have made strongholds in the heaven, and We have made it fair-seeming to the beholders,

17 And We guard it against every accursed devil,

18 But he who steals a hearing; so there follows him a visible flame.

19 And the earth — We have spread it out and made in it firm mountains and caused to grow in it of every suitable thing.

20 And We have made in it means of subsistence for you and for him for whom you provide not.

21 And there is not a thing but with Us are the treasures of it, and We send it not down but in a known measure.

22 And We send the winds fertilizing, then send down water from the clouds, so We give it to you to drink; nor is it you who store it up.

23 And surely it is We, Who give life and cause death, and We are the Inheritors.

24 And certainly We know those among you who go forward and We certainly know those who lag behind.

25 And surely thy Lord will gather them together. He indeed is Wise, Knowing.

SECTION 3:
The Devil's Opposition to the Righteous

26 And surely We created man of sounding clay, of black mud fashioned into shape.

27 And the jinn, We created before of intensely hot fire.

28 And when thy Lord said to the angels: I am going to create a mortal of sounding clay, of black mud fashioned into shape.

29 So when I have made him complete and breathed into him of My spirit, fall down making obeisance to him.

30 So the angels made

THE ROCK

obeisance, all of them together —

31 But Iblīs (did it not). He refused to be with those who made obeisance.

32 He said: O Iblīs, what is the reason that thou art not with those who make obeisance?

33 He said: I am not going to make obeisance to a mortal, whom Thou hast created of sounding clay, of black mud fashioned into shape.

34 He said: Then go forth, for surely thou art driven away,

35 And surely on thee is a curse till the day of Judgment.

36 He said: My Lord, respite me till the time when they are raised.

37 He said: Surely thou art of the respited ones,

38 Till the period of the time made known.

39 He said: My Lord, as Thou hast judged me erring, I shall certainly make (evil) fair-seeming to them on earth, and I shall cause them all to deviate,

40 Except Thy servants from among them, the purified ones.

41 He said: This is a right way with Me.

42 As regards My servants, thou hast no authority over them except such of the deviators as follow thee.

43 And surely hell is the promised place for them all —

44 It has seven gates. For each gate is an appointed portion of them.

SECTION 4:
Mercy for the Righteous — Abraham

45 Surely those who keep their duty are in Gardens and fountains.

46 Enter them in peace, secure.

47 And We shall root out whatever of rancour is in their breasts — as brethren, on raised couches, face to face.

48 Toil afflicts them not therein, nor will they be ejected therefrom.

49 Inform My servants that I am the Forgiving, the Merciful,

50 And that My chastisement —that is the painful chastisement.

51 And inform them of the guests of Abraham.

52 When they entered upon him, they said, Peace! He said: We are afraid of you.

53 They said: Be not afraid, we give thee good news of a boy, possessing knowledge.

54 He said: Do you give me good news when old age has come upon me? Of what then do you give me good news?

55 They said: We give thee good news with truth, so be not thou of the despairing ones.

56 He said: And who despairs of the mercy of his Lord but the erring ones?

57 He said: What is your *business, then, O messengers?*

58 They said: We have been sent to a guilty people,

59 Except Lot's followers. We shall deliver them all,

60 Except his wife: We ordained that she shall surely be of those who remain behind.

SECTION 5:
Lot and Shu'aib

61 So when the messengers came to Lot's followers,

62 He said: Surely you are an unknown people.

63 They said: Nay, we have come to thee with that about which they disputed.

64 And we have come to thee with the truth, and we are surely truthful.

65 So travel with thy followers for a part of the night and thyself follow their rear; and let not anyone of you turn round, and go whither you are commanded.

66 And We made known to him this decree, that the roots of these should be cut off in the morning.

67 And the people of the town came rejoicing.

68 He said: These are my guests, so disgrace me not,

69 And keep your duty to Allāh and shame me not.

70 They said: Did we not

forbid thee from (entertaining) people?

71 He said: These are my daughters, if you will do (aught).

72 By thy life! they blindly wandered on in their frenzy.

73 So the cry overtook them at sunrise;

74 Thus We turned it upside down, and rained upon them hard stones.

75 Surely in this are signs for those who take a lesson.

76 And it is on a road that still abides.

77 Verily therein is a sign for the believers.

78 And the dwellers of the grove were indeed iniquitous:

79 So We inflicted retribution on them. And they are both on an open high road.

SECTION 6:
Dwellers of the Rock and a Warning

80 And the dwellers of the Rock indeed rejected the messengers;

81 And We gave them Our messages, but they turned away from them;

82 *And they hewed houses in the mountains, in security.*

83 So the cry overtook them in the morning;

84 And what they earned availed them not.

85 And We created not the heavens and the earth and what is between them but with truth. And the Hour is surely coming, so turn away with kindly forgiveness.

86 Surely thy Lord — He is the Creator, the Knower.

87 And certainly We have given thee seven oft-repeated (verses) and the grand Qur'ān.

88 Strain not thine eyes at what We have given certain classes of them to enjoy, and grieve not for them, and make thyself gentle to the believers.

89 And say: I am indeed the plain warner.

90 Like as We sent down on them who took oaths,

91 Those who divided the Qur'ān into parts.

92 So, by thy Lord! We

shall question them all,

93 As to what they did.

94 Therefore declare openly what thou art commanded, and turn away from the polytheists.

95 Surely We are sufficient for thee against the scoffers —

96 Those who set up another god with Allāh; so they will come to know.

97 And We know indeed that thy breast straitens at what they say;

98 So celebrate the praise of thy Lord, and be of those who make obeisance.

99 And serve thy Lord, until there comes to thee that which is certain.

CHAPTER 16
Al-Naḥl: **The Bee**

(REVEALED AT MAKKAH: 16 *sections*; 128 *verses*)

SECTION 1:
Revelation testified to by Nature

In the name of Allāh, the Beneficent, the Merciful.

1 Allāh's commandment will come to pass, so seek not to hasten it. Glory be to Him, and highly exalted be He above what they associate (with Him)!

2 He sends down angels with revelation by His command on whom He pleases of His servants, saying: Give the warning that there is no God but Me, so keep your duty to Me.

3 He created the heavens and the earth with truth. Highly exalted be He above what they associate (with Him)!

4 He created man from a small life-germ, and lo! he is an open contender.

5 And the cattle, He has created them for you. You have in them warm clothing and (other) advantages, and of them you eat.

6 And therein is beauty for you, when you drive them back (home) and when you send them out (to pasture).

7 And they carry your heavy loads to regions which you could not reach but with distress to yourselves. Surely your Lord is Compassionate, Merciful.

8 And (He made) horses and mules and asses that you might ride upon them and as an ornament. And He creates what you know not.

9 And upon Allāh it rests to show the right way, and there are some deviating (ways). And if He please, He would guide you all aright.

SECTION 2: **Nature upholds Unity**

10 He it is Who sends

down water from the clouds for you; it gives drink, and by it (grow) the trees on which you feed.

11 He causes to grow for you thereby herbage, and the olives, and the date-palms, and the grapes, and all the fruits. Surely there is a sign in this for a people who reflect.

12 And He has made subservient for you the night and the day and the sun and the moon. And the stars are made subservient by His command. Surely there are signs in this for a people who understand.

13 And what He has created for you in the earth is of varied hues. Surely there is a sign in this for a people who are mindful.

14 And He it is Who has made the sea subservient that you may eat fresh flesh from it and bring forth from it ornaments which you wear. And thou seest the ships cleaving through it, so that you seek of His bounty and that you may give thanks.

15 And He has cast firm mountains in the earth lest it quake with you, and rivers and roads that you may go aright,

16 And landmarks. And by the stars they find the right way.

17 Is He then Who creates like him who creates not? Do you not then mind?

18 And if you would count Allāh's favours, you would not be able to number them. Surely Allāh is Forgiving, Merciful.

19 And Allāh knows what you conceal and what you do openly.

20 And those whom they call on besides Allāh created naught, while they are themselves created.

21 Dead (are they), not living. And they know not when they will be raised.

SECTION 3:
Denial due to Ignorance

22 Your God is one God: so those who believe not in the Hereafter, their hearts refuse to know and they are proud.

23 Undoubtedly Allāh knows what they hide and what they manifest. Surely

He loves not the proud.

24 And when it is said to them, What is it that your Lord has revealed? they say, Stories of the ancients!

25 That they may bear their burdens in full on the day of Resurrection, and also of the burdens of those whom they lead astray without knowledge. Ah! evil is what they bear.

SECTION 4:
The Wicked will come to Disgrace

26 Those before them plotted, so Allāh demolished their building from the foundations, so the roof fell down on them from above them, and the chastisement came to them from whence they perceived not.

27 Then on the Resurrection day He will bring them to disgrace and say: Where are My partners, for whose sake you became hostile? Those who are given the knowledge will say: Surely disgrace this day and evil are upon the disbelievers,

28 Whom the angels cause to die, while they are unjust to themselves. Then would they offer submission: We did not do any evil. Nay! Surely Allāh knows what you did.

29 So enter the gates of hell, to abide therein. Evil indeed is the dwelling-place of the proud.

30 And it is said to those who guard against evil: What has your Lord revealed? They say, Good. For those who do good in this world is good. And certainly the abode of the Hereafter is better. And excellent indeed is the abode of those who keep their duty —

31 Gardens of perpetuity which they enter, wherein flow rivers: they have therein what they please. Thus does Allāh reward those who keep their duty,

32 Whom the angels cause to die in purity, saying: Peace be to you! enter the Garden for what you did.

33 Await they aught but that the angels should come to them or that thy Lord's command should come to pass. Thus did those before them. And Allāh wronged them not, but they wronged themselves.

34 So the evil of what they did afflicted them, and that which they mocked encompassed them.

SECTION 5:
Prophets are raised to explain

35 And the idolaters say: If Allāh pleased we would not have served aught but Him, (neither) we nor our fathers, nor would we have prohibited aught without (order from) Him. Thus did those before them. But have the messengers any duty except a plain delivery (of the message)?

36 And certainly We raised in every nation a messenger, saying: Serve Allāh and shun the devil. Then of them was he whom Allāh guided, and of them was he whose remaining in error was justly due. So travel in the land, then see what was the end of the rejectors.

37 If thou desirest their guidance, yet Allāh will not guide him who leads astray, nor have they any helpers.

38 And they swear by Allāh their most energetic oaths: Allāh will not raise up him who dies. Yea! it is a promise binding on Him, quite true, but most people know not:

39 So that He might make manifest to them that about which they differ, and that those who disbelieve might know that they were liars.

40 Our word for a thing, when We intend it, is only that We say to it, Be; and it is.

SECTION 6:
Doom of Opponents is coming

41 And those who flee for Allāh's sake after they are oppressed, We shall certainly give them a good abode in the world; and the reward of the Hereafter is much greater. Did they but know!

42 Those who are steadfast and on their Lord they rely.

43 And We sent not before thee any but men to whom We sent revelation — so ask the followers of the Reminder if you know not —

44 With clear arguments and Scriptures. And We have revealed to thee the Reminder that thou mayest make clear to men that which has been revealed to them, and that haply they may reflect.

45 Are they, then, who plan evil (plans), secure that Allāh will not abase them in the earth, or that chastisement will not overtake them from whence they perceive not?

46 Or that He will not seize them in their going to and fro, then they will not be able to escape?

47 Or that He will not seize them with a gradual diminution? Your Lord is surely Compassionate, Merciful.

48 See they not everything that Allāh has created? Its (very) shadows return from right and left, making obeisance to Allāh, while they are in utter abasement.

49 And to Allāh makes obeisance every living creature that is in the heavens and that is in the earth, and the angels (too) and they are not proud.

50 They fear their Lord above them and do what they are commanded.

SECTION 7:
Human Nature revolts against Polytheism

51 And Allāh has said: Take not two gods. He is only one God: So Me alone should you fear.

52 And whatever is in the heavens and the earth is His, and to Him is obedience due always. Will you then fear other than Allāh?

53 And whatever good you have, it is from Allāh; then, when evil afflicts you, to Him do you cry for aid.

54 Then when He removes the evil from you, lo! some of you associate others with their Lord,

55 So as to deny what We have given them. Then enjoy yourselves, for soon will you know.

56 And they set apart for what they know not, a portion of what We have given them. By Allāh! you shall certainly be questioned about that which you forged.

57 And they ascribe daughters to Allāh. Glory be to Him! And for themselves is what they desire!

58 And when the birth of a daughter is announced to one of them, his face becomes black and he is full of wrath.

59 He hides himself from the people because of the evil of what is announced to him. Shall he keep it with disgrace or bury it (alive) in the dust? Now surely evil is what they judge!

60 For those who believe not in the Hereafter are evil attributes and Allāh's are the sublime attributes. And He is the Mighty, the Wise.

SECTION 8:
Iniquity of Deniers

61 And if Allāh were to destroy men for their iniquity, He would not leave therein a single creature, but He respites them till an appointed time. So when their doom comes, they are not able to delay (it) an hour, nor can they advance (it).

62 And they ascribe to Allāh what they (themselves) hate, and their tongues relate the lie that for them is good. Assuredly for them is the Fire, and they will be (therein) abandoned.

63 By Allāh! We certainly sent (messengers) to nations before thee, but the devil made their deeds fair-seeming to them. So he is their patron today, and for them is a painful chastisement.

64 And We have not revealed to thee the Book except that thou mayest make clear to them that wherein they differ, and (as) a guidance and a mercy for a people who believe.

65 And Allāh sends down water from above, and therewith gives life to the earth after its death. Surely there is a sign in this for a people who listen.

SECTION 9:
Parables showing the Truth of Revelation

66 And surely there is a lesson for you in the cattle: We give you to drink of what is in their bellies — from betwixt the faeces and

THE BEE

the blood — pure milk, agreeable to the drinkers.

67 And of the fruits of the palms and the grapes, you obtain from them intoxicants and goodly provision. There is surely a sign in this for a people who ponder.

68 And thy Lord revealed to the bee: Make hives in the mountains and in the trees and in what they build,

69 Then eat of all the fruits and walk in the ways of thy Lord submissively. There comes forth from their bellies a beverage of many hues, in which there is healing for men. Therein is surely a sign for a people who reflect.

70 And Allāh creates you, then He causes you to die; and of you is he who is brought back to the worst part of life, so that he knows nothing after having knowledge. Surely Allāh is Knowing, Powerful.

SECTION 10:
The Recipient of Revelation

71 And Allāh has made some of you excel others in the means of subsistence; so those who are made to excel give not away their sustenance to those whom their right hands possess, so that they may be equal therein. Will they then deny the favour of Allāh?

72 And Allāh has made wives for you from among yourselves, and has given you sons and daughters from your wives, and has provided you with good things. Will they then believe in falsehood and deny the favour of Allāh?

73 And they serve besides Allāh that which controls for them no sustenance at all from the heavens and the earth; nor have they any power.

74 So coin not similitudes for Allāh. Surely Allāh knows and you know not.

75 Allāh sets forth a parable: There is a slave, the property of another, controlling naught, and there is one to whom We have granted from Ourselves goodly provisions, so he spends from it secretly and openly. Are the two alike? Praise be to Allāh! Nay, most of them know not.

76 And Allāh sets forth a parable of two men: One of them dumb, controlling naught, and he is a burden to his master; wherever he sends him, he brings no good. Is he equal with him who enjoins justice, and he is on the right path?

SECTION 11:
Punishment withheld

77 And Allāh's is the unseen of the heavens and the earth. And the matter of the Hour is but as a twinkling of the eye or it is nigher still. Surely Allāh is Possessor of power over all things.

78 And Allāh brought you forth from the wombs of your mothers — you knew nothing — and He gave you hearing and sight and hearts that you might give thanks.

79 See they not the birds, constrained in the middle of the sky? None withholds them but Allāh. Surely in this are signs for a people who believe.

80 And Allāh has given you an abode in your houses, and He has given you houses of the skins of cattle, which you find light to carry on the day of your march and on the day of your halting, and of their wool and their fur and their hair, household stuff and a provision for a time.

81 And Allāh has made for you, of what He has created, shelters, and He has given you in the mountains, places of retreat, and He has given you garments to save you from the heat, and coats of mail to save you in your fighting. Thus does He complete His favour to you that you may submit.

82 Then if they turn away, thy duty is only clear deliverance (of the message).

83 They recognize the favour of Allāh, yet they deny it, and most of them are ungrateful.

SECTION 12:
Prophets testify

84 And on the day when We raise up a witness out of every nation, then permission (to offer excuse) will not be given to the disbelievers, nor will they be

THE BEE

allowed to make amends.

85 And when the wrongdoers see the chastisement, it will not be lightened for them, nor will they be respited.

86 And when those who ascribed partners (to Allāh) see their associate-gods, they will say: Our Lord, these are our associate-gods on whom we called besides Thee. But they will throw back at them the word: Surely you are liars.

87 And they will tender submission to Allāh on that day, and what they used to forge will fail them.

88 Those who disbelieve and hinder (men) from Allāh's way, We will add chastisement to their chastisement because they made mischief.

89 And on the day when We raise up in every people a witness against them from among themselves, and bring thee as a witness against these. And We have revealed the Book to thee explaining all things, and a guidance and mercy and good news for those who submit.

SECTION 13:
Revelation enjoins Good

90 Surely Allāh enjoins justice and the doing of good (to others) and the giving to the kindred, and He forbids indecency and evil and rebellion. He admonishes you that you may be mindful.

91 And fulfill the covenant of Allāh, when you have made a covenant, and break not the oaths after making them fast, and you have indeed made Allāh your surety. Surely Allāh knows what you do.

92 And be not like her who unravels her yarn, disintegrating it into pieces, after she has spun it strongly. You make your oaths to be means of deceit between you because (one) nation is more numerous than (another) nation. Allāh only tries you by this. And He will certainly make clear to you on the day of Resurrection that wherein you differed.

93 And if Allāh please, He would make you a single nation, but He leaves in error whom He pleases and guides whom He pleases. And certainly you will be

94 And make not your oaths a means of deceit between you, lest a foot should slip after its stability, and you should taste evil because you hinder (men) from Allāh's way and grievous chastisement be your (lot).

95 And take not a small price for Allāh's covenant. Surely what is with Allāh is better for you, did you but know!

96 What is with you passes away and what is with Allāh is enduring. And We shall certainly give to those who are patient their reward for the best of what they did.

97 Whoever does good, whether male or female, and is a believer, We shall certainly make *him live a good life*, and We shall certainly give them their reward for the best of what they did.

98 So when thou recitest the Qur'ān, seek refuge in Allāh from the accursed devil.

99 Surely he has no authority over those who believe and rely on their Lord.

100 His authority is only over those who befriend him and those who associate others with Him.

SECTION 14:
The Qur'ān is not a Forgery

101 And, when We change a message for a message — and Allāh knows best what He reveals — they say: Thou art only a forger. Nay, most of them know not.

102 Say: The Holy Spirit has revealed it from thy Lord with truth, that it may establish those who believe, and as a guidance and good news for those who submit.

103 And indeed We know that they say: Only a mortal *teaches* him. The tongue of him whom they hint at is foreign, and this is clear Arabic language.

104 Those who believe not in Allāh's messages, Allāh guides them not, and for them is a painful chastisement.

105 Only they forge lies

who believe not in Allāh's messages, and they are the liars.

106 Whoso disbelieves in Allāh after his belief — not he who is compelled while his heart is content with faith, but he who opens (his) breast for disbelief — on them is the wrath of Allāh, and for them is a grievous chastisement.

107 That is because they love this world's life more than the Hereafter, and because Allāh guides not the disbelieving people.

108 These are they whose hearts and ears and eyes Allāh has sealed and these are the heedless ones.

109 No doubt that in the Hereafter they are the losers.

110 Then surely thy Lord, to those who flee after they are persecuted, then struggle hard and are patient, surely thy Lord after that is Protecting, Merciful.

SECTION 15:
Fate of the Opponents

111 On the day when every soul will come pleading for itself, and every soul will be paid in full what it has done, and they will not be dealt with unjustly.

112 And Allāh sets forth a parable: A town safe and secure, to which its means of subsistence came in abundance from every quarter; but it disbelieved in Allāh's favours, so Allāh made it taste a pall of hunger and fear because of what they wrought.

113 And certainly there came to them a Messenger from among them, but they rejected him, so the chastisement overtook them, while they were wrongdoers.

114 So eat of what Allāh has given you, lawful and good (things), and give thanks for Allāh's favour, if He it is you serve.

115 He has forbidden you only what dies of itself and blood and the flesh of swine and that over which any other name than that of Allāh has been invoked; but whoever is driven to (it), not desiring nor exceeding the limit, then surely Allāh is Forgiving, Merciful.

116 And utter not, for what your tongues describe, the lie: This is lawful and this unlawful; so that you forge a lie against Allāh. Surely those who forge a lie against Allāh will not prosper.

117 A little enjoyment — and for them is a painful chastisement.

118 And to those who are Jews We prohibited what We have related to thee already, and We did them no wrong, but they wronged themselves.

119 And surely thy Lord, for those who do evil in ignorance, then turn after that and make amends, surely thy Lord after that is Forgiving, Merciful.

SECTION 16:
The Way to Greatness

120 Surely Abraham was a model (of virtue), obedient to Allāh, upright, and he *was not of the* polytheists,

121 Grateful for His favours. He chose him and guided him on the right path.

122 And We gave him good in this world; and in the Hereafter he is surely among the righteous.

123 Then We revealed to thee: Follow the faith of Abraham, the upright one; and he was not of the polytheists.

124 The Sabbath was ordained only against those who differed about it. And surely thy Lord will judge between them on the day of Resurrection concerning that wherein they differed.

125 Call to the way of thy Lord with wisdom and goodly exhortation, and argue with them in the best manner. Surely thy Lord knows best him who strays from His path, and He knows best those who go aright.

126 And if you take your turn, then punish with the like of that with which you were afflicted. But if you show patience, it is certainly best for the patient.

127 And be patient and thy patience is not but by (the help of) Allāh, and grieve not for them, nor be in distress for what they plan.

128 Surely Allāh is with those who keep their duty and those who do good (to others).

Part 15

CHAPTER 17
Banī Isrā'īl: The Israelites
(REVEALED AT MAKKAH: 12 *sections*; 111 *verses*)

SECTION 1:
Israelites punished Twice

In the name of Allāh, the Beneficent, the Merciful.

1 Glory to Him Who carried His servant by night from the Sacred Mosque to the Remote Mosque, whose precincts We blessed, that We might show him of Our signs! Surely He is the Hearing, the Seeing.

2 And We gave Moses the Book and made it a guidance to the Children of Israel (saying): Take no guardian beside Me —

3 The offspring of those whom We bore with Noah. Surely he was a grateful servant.

4 And We made known to the Children of Israel in the Book: Certainly you will make mischief in the land twice, and behave insolently with mighty arrogance.

5 So when of the two, the first warning came to pass, We raised against you Our servants, of mighty prowess, so they made havoc in (your) houses. And it was an accomplished threat.

6 Then We gave you back the turn against them, and aided you with wealth and children and made you a numerous band.

7 If you do good, you do good for your own souls. And if you do evil, it is for them. So when the second warning came, (We raised another people) that they might bring you to grief and that they might enter the Mosque as they entered it the first time, and that they might destroy, whatever they conquered, with utter destruction.

8 It may be that your Lord will have mercy on you. And if you return (to mischief), We will return (to punishment). And We have made hell a prison for the disbelievers.

9 Surely this Qur'ān guides to that which is most upright, and gives good news to the believers who do good that theirs is a great reward,

10 And that those who believe not in the Hereafter, We have prepared for them a painful chastisement.

SECTION 2:
Every Deed has a Consequence

11 And man prays for evil as he ought to pray for good; and man is ever hasty.

12 And We made the night and the day two signs, then We have made the sign of the night to pass away and We have made the sign of the day manifest, so that you may seek grace from your Lord, and that you may know the numbering of years and the reckoning. And We have explained everything with distinctness.

13 And We have made every man's actions to cling to his neck, and We shall bring forth to him on the day of Resurrection a book which he will find wide open.

14 Read thy book. Thine own soul is sufficient as a reckoner against thee this day.

15 Whoever goes aright, for his own soul does he go aright; and whoever goes astray, to its detriment only does he go astray. And no bearer of a burden can bear the burden of another. Nor do We chastise until We raise a messenger.

16 And when We wish to destroy a town, We send commandments to its people who lead easy lives, but they transgress therein; thus the word proves true against it, so We destroy it with utter destruction.

17 And how many generations did We destroy after Noah! And thy Lord suffices as being Aware and Seer of His servants' sins.

18 Whoso desires this transitory life, We hasten to him therein what We please for whomsoever We desire,

THE ISRAELITES

then We assign to him the hell; he will enter it despised, driven away.

19 And whoso desires the Hereafter and strives for it as he ought to strive and he is a believer — those are they whose striving is amply rewarded.

20 All do We aid — these as well as those — out of the bounty of thy Lord, and the bounty of thy Lord is not limited.

21 See how We have made some of them to excel others. And certainly the Hereafter is greater in degrees and greater in excellence.

22 Associate not any other god with Allāh, lest thou sit down despised, forsaken.

SECTION 3:
Moral Precepts

23 And thy Lord has decreed that you serve none but Him, and do good to parents. If either or both of them reach old age with thee, say not "Fie" to them, nor chide them, and speak to them a generous word.

24 And lower to them the wing of humility out of mercy, and say: My Lord, have mercy on them, as they brought me up (when I was) little.

25 Your Lord knows best what is in your minds. If you are righteous, He is surely Forgiving to those who turn (to Him).

26 And give to the near of kin his due and (to) the needy and the wayfarer, and squander not wastefully.

27 Surely the squanderers are the devil's brethren. And the devil is ever ungrateful to his Lord.

28 And if thou turn away from them to seek mercy from thy Lord, which thou hopest for, speak to them a gentle word.

29 And make not thy hand to be shackled to thy neck, nor stretch it forth to the utmost (limit) of its stretching forth, lest thou sit down blamed, stripped off.

30 Surely thy Lord makes plentiful the means of subsistence for whom He pleases, and He straitens. Surely He is ever Aware, Seer, of His servants.

SECTION 4:
Moral Precepts

31 And kill not your children for fear of poverty — We provide for them and for you. Surely the killing of them is a great wrong.

32 And go not nigh to fornication: surely it is an obscenity. And evil is the way.

33 And kill not the soul which Allāh has forbidden except for a just cause. And whoever is slain unjustly, We have indeed given to his heir authority — but let him not exceed the limit in slaying. Surely he will be helped.

34 And draw not nigh to the orphan's property, except in a goodly way, till he attains his maturity. And fulfil the promise; surely, the promise will be enquired into.

35 And give full measure when you measure out, and weigh with a true balance. This is fair and better in the end.

36 And follow not that of which thou hast no knowledge. Surely the hearing and the sight and the heart, of all of these it will be asked.

37 And go not about in the land exultingly, for thou canst not rend the earth, nor reach the mountains in height.

38 All this, the evil thereof, is hateful in the sight of thy Lord.

39 This is of the wisdom which thy Lord has revealed to thee. And associate not any other god with Allāh lest thou be thrown into hell, blamed, cast away.

40 Has then your Lord preferred to give you sons, and (for Himself) taken daughters from among the angels? Surely you utter a grievous saying.

SECTION 5:
Disbelievers grow harder

41 And certainly We have repeated (warnings) in this Qur'ān that they may be mindful. And it adds not save to their aversion.

42 Say: If there were with Him gods, as they say, then certainly they would have been able to seek a way to the Lord of the Throne.

THE ISRAELITES

43 Glory to Him! and He is highly exalted above what they say!

44 The seven heavens and the earth and those in them declare His glory. And there is not a single thing but glorifies Him with His praise, but you do not understand their glorification. Surely He is Forbearing, Forgiving.

45 And when thou recitest the Qur'ān, We place between thee and those who believe not in the Hereafter a hidden barrier;

46 And We put coverings on their hearts and a deafness in their ears lest they understand it; and when thou makest mention of thy Lord alone in the Qur'ān, they turn their backs in aversion.

47 We know best what they listen to when they listen to thee, and when they take counsel secretly, when the wrongdoers say: You follow only a man deprived of reason.

48 See, what they liken thee to! So they have gone astray, and cannot find the way.

49 And they say: When we are bones and decayed particles, shall we then be raised up as a new creation?

50 Say: Be stones or iron,

51 Or some other creature of those which are too hard (to receive life) in your minds! But they will say: Who will return us? Say: He Who created you at first. Still they will shake their heads at thee and say: When will it be? Say: Maybe it has drawn nigh.

52 On the day when He will call you forth, then will you obey Him, giving Him praise, and you will think that you tarried but a little (while).

SECTION 6:
Punishment must follow

53 And say to My servants that they speak what is best. Surely the devil sows dissensions among them. The devil is surely an open enemy to man.

54 Your Lord knows you best. He will have mercy on you, if He please, or He will chastise you, if He please. And We have not sent thee as being in charge of them.

55 And thy Lord best knows those who are in the heavens and the earth. And certainly We made some of the prophets to excel others, and to David We gave the Zabūr.

56 Say: Call on those whom you assert besides Him; they have no power to remove distress from you nor to change.

57 Those whom they call upon, themselves seek the means of access to their Lord — whoever of them is nearest — and they hope for His mercy and fear His chastisement. Surely the chastisement of thy Lord is a thing to be cautious of.

58 And there is not a town but We will destroy it before the day of Resurrection or chastise it with a severe chastisement. That is written in the Book.

59 *And* nothing hindered Us from sending signs, but the ancients rejected them. And We gave to Thamūd the she-camel, a manifest sign, but they did her wrong, and We send not signs but to warn.

60 And when We said to thee: Surely thy Lord encompasses men. And We made not the vision which We showed thee but a trial for men, as also the tree cursed in the Qur'ān. And We warn them, but it only adds to their great inordinacy.

SECTION 7:
The Devil's Opposition to the Righteous

61 And when We said to the angels: Be submissive to Adam; they submitted, except Iblīs. He said: Shall I submit to him whom Thou hast created of dust?

62 He said: Seest Thou? This is he whom Thou hast honoured above me! If Thou respite me to the day of Resurrection, I will certainly cause his progeny to perish except a few.

63 *He said: Begone!* whoever of them follows thee surely hell is your recompense, a full recompense.

64 And incite whom thou canst of them with thy voice, and collect against them thy horse and thy foot, and share with them in wealth and children, and promise them. And the devil promises them only to deceive.

65 My servants — thou hast surely no authority over them. And thy Lord suffices as having charge of affairs.

66 Your Lord is He Who speeds the ships for you in the sea that you may seek of His grace. Surely He is ever Merciful to you.

67 And when distress afflicts you in the sea, away go those whom you call on except He; but when He brings you safe to the land, you turn away. And man is ever ungrateful.

68 Do you then feel secure that He will not bring you low on a tract of land, or send on you a violent wind? Then you will not find a protector for yourselves;

69 Or, do you feel secure that He will not take you back into it another time, then send on you a fierce gale and thus overwhelm you for your ungratefulness? Then you will not find any aider against Us in the matter.

70 And surely We have honoured the children of Adam, and We carry them in the land and the sea, and We provide them with good things, and We have made them to excel highly most of those whom We have created.

SECTION 8:
Opposition to the Prophet

71 On the day when We shall call every people with their leader: then whoever is given his book in his right hand, these will read their book; and they will not be dealt with a whit unjustly.

72 And whoever is blind in this (world) he will be blind in the Hereafter, and further away from the path.

73 And surely they had purposed to turn thee away from that which We have revealed to thee, that thou shouldst forge against Us other than that, and then they would have taken thee for a friend.

74 And if We had not made thee firm, thou mightest have indeed inclined to them a little;

75 Then We would have made thee taste a double (punishment) in life and a double (punishment) after death, and then thou wouldst not have found any helper against Us.

76 And surely they purposed to unsettle thee from the land that they might expel thee from it, and then they will not tarry after thee but a little.

77 (This is Our) way with Our messengers whom We sent before thee, and thou wilt not find a change in Our course.

SECTION 9:
Truth will prevail

78 Keep up prayer from the declining of the sun till the darkness of the night, and the recital of the Qur'ān at dawn. *Surely the recital of the Qur'ān at dawn is witnessed.*

79 And during a part of the night, keep awake by it, beyond what is incumbent on thee; maybe thy Lord will raise thee to a position of great glory.

80 And say: My Lord, make me enter a truthful entering, and make me go forth a truthful going forth, and grant me from Thy presence an authority to help (me).

81 And say: The Truth has come and falsehood vanished. Surely falsehood is ever bound to vanish.

82 And We reveal of the Qur'ān that which is a healing and a mercy to the believers, and it adds only to the perdition of the wrongdoers.

83 And when We bestow favours on man, he turns away and behaves proudly; and when evil afflicts him, he is in despair.

84 Say: Everyone acts according to his manner. But your Lord best knows who is best guided on the path.

SECTION 10:
The Qur'ān — a Unique Guidance

85 And they ask thee about the revelation. Say: The revelation is by the commandment of my Lord, and of knowledge you are given but a little.

THE ISRAELITES

86 And if We please, We could certainly take away that which We have revealed to thee, then thou wouldst find none to plead (thy cause) against Us —

87 But it is a mercy from thy Lord. Surely His bounty to thee is abundant.

88 Say: If men and jinn should combine together to bring the like of this Qur'ān, they could not bring the like of it, though some of them were aiders of others.

89 And certainly We have made clear for men in this Qur'ān every kind of description, but most men consent to naught save denying.

90 And they say: We will by no means believe in thee, till thou cause a spring to gush forth from the earth for us,

91 Or thou have a garden of palms and grapes in the midst of which thou cause rivers to flow forth abundantly,

92 Or thou cause the heaven to come down upon us in pieces, as thou thinkest, or bring Allāh and the angels face to face (with us),

93 Or thou have a house of gold, or thou ascend into heaven. And we will not believe in thy ascending till thou bring down to us a book we can read. Say: Glory to my Lord! am I aught but a mortal messenger?

SECTION 11:
Justice of Retribution

94 And nothing prevents people from believing, when the guidance comes to them, except that they say: Has Allāh raised up a mortal to be a messenger?

95 Say: Had there been in the earth angels walking about secure, We would have sent down to them from the heaven an angel as messenger.

96 Say: Allāh suffices for a witness between me and you. Surely He is ever Aware of His servants, Seeing.

97 And he whom Allāh guides, he is on the right way; and he whom He leaves in error, for them thou wilt find no guardians besides Him. And We shall gather them together on the day of Resurrection on their faces, blind and dumb and deaf. Their abode is hell. Whenever it abates, We make them burn the more.

98 This is their retribution because they disbelieve in Our messages and say: When we are bones and decayed particles, shall we then be raised up into a new creation?

99 See they not that Allāh, Who created the heavens and the earth, is able to create the like of them? And He has appointed for them a term, whereof there is no doubt. But the wrongdoers consent to naught but denying.

100 Say: If you control the treasures of the mercy of my Lord, then you would withhold (them) for fear of spending. And man is ever niggardly.

SECTION 12:
Comparison with Moses

101 And certainly We gave Moses nine clear signs; so ask the Children of Israel. When he came to them, Pharaoh said to him: Surely I deem thee, O Moses, to be one bewitched.

102 He said: Truly thou knowest that none but the Lord of the heavens and the earth has sent these as clear proofs; and surely I believe thee, O Pharaoh, to be lost.

103 So he desired to scare them from the land, but We drowned him and those with him, all together;

104 And We said to the Children of Israel after him: Abide in the land. But when the latter promise came, We brought you all rolled up.

105 And with truth have We revealed it, and with truth did it come. And We have not sent thee but as a giver of good news and as a warner.

106 And it is a Qur'ān *We have* made distinct, so that thou mayest read it to the people by slow degrees, and We have revealed it in portions.

107 Say: Believe in it or believe not. Surely those who are given the knowledge before it, fall down prostrate on their faces, when it is recited to them,

108 And say: Glory to our Lord! Surely the promise of our Lord was to be fulfilled.

109 And they fall down on their faces, weeping, and it adds to their humility.

110 Say: Call on Allāh or call on the Beneficent. By whatever (name) you call on Him, He has the best names. And utter not thy prayer loudly nor be silent in it, and seek a way between these.

111 And say: Praise be to Allāh! Who has not taken to Himself a son, and Who has not a partner in the kingdom, and Who has not a helper because of weakness; and proclaim His greatness, magnifying (Him).

Chapter 18
Al-Kahf: The Cave

(Revealed at Makkah: 12 *sections*; 110 *verses*)

SECTION 1:
A Warning to the Christians

In the name of Allāh, the Beneficent, the Merciful.

1 Praise be to Allāh! Who revealed the Book to His servant, and allowed not therein any crookedness,

2 Rightly directing, to give warning of severe punishment from Him and to give good news to the believers who do good that theirs is a goodly reward,

3 Staying in it for ever;

4 And to warn those who say: Allāh has taken to Himself a son.

5 They have no knowledge of it, nor had their fathers. Grievous is the word that comes out of their mouths. They speak nothing but a lie.

6 Then maybe thou wilt kill thyself with grief, sorrowing after them, if they believe not in this announcement.

7 Surely We have made whatever is on the earth an embellishment for it, so that We may try which of them is best in works.

8 And We shall surely make what is on it dust, without herbage.

9 Or, thinkest thou that the companions of the Cave and the Inscription were of Our wonderful signs?

10 When the youths sought refuge in the Cave, they said: Our Lord, grant us mercy from Thyself, and provide for us a right course in our affair.

11 So We prevented them from hearing in the Cave for a number of years,

12 Then We raised them up that We might know which of the two parties was best able to calculate

the time for which they remained.

SECTION 2: The Dwellers in the Cave

13 We relate to thee their story with truth. Surely they were youths who believed in their Lord and We increased them in guidance.

14 And We strengthened their hearts when they stood up and said: Our Lord is the Lord of the heavens and the earth; we call upon no god beside Him, for then indeed we should utter an enormity.

15 These our people have taken gods beside Him. Why do they not bring clear *authority for them?* Who is then more unjust than he who forges a lie against Allāh?

16 And when you withdraw from them and what they worship save Allāh, take refuge in the Cave; your Lord will spread for you of His mercy, and provide for you a profitable course in your affair.

17 And thou mightest see the sun, when it rose, decline from their Cave to the right, and when it set leave them behind on the left, while they were in a wide space thereof. This is of the signs of Allāh. He whom Allāh guides, he is on the right way; and whom He leaves in error, thou wilt not find for him a friend to guide aright.

SECTION 3: The Dwellers in the Cave

18 And thou mightest think them awake while they were asleep, and We turned them about to the right and to the left, with their dog outstretching its paws at the entrance. If thou didst look at them, thou wouldst turn back from *them* in flight, and thou wouldst be filled with awe because of them.

19 And thus did We rouse them that they might question each other. A speaker from among them said: How long have you tarried? They said: We have tarried for a day or a part of a day. (Others) said: Your Lord knows best how long you have tarried. Now send one of you with this silver (coin) of yours to the city, then let him see what food is purest, and bring you provision from it, and let him behave with gentleness, and not make your case known to anyone.

20 For if they prevail against you, they would stone you to death or force you back to their religion, and then you would never succeed.

21 And thus did We make (men) to get knowledge of them, that they might know that Allāh's promise is true and that the Hour — there is no doubt about it. When they disputed among themselves about their affair and said: Erect an edifice over them. Their Lord knows best about them. Those who prevailed in their affair said: We shall certainly build a place of worship over them.

22 (Some) say: (They were) three, the fourth of them their dog; and (others) say: Five, the sixth of them their dog, making conjectures about the unseen. And (others) say: Seven, and the eighth of them their dog. Say: My Lord best knows their number — none knows them but a few. So contend not in their matter but with an outward contention, and question not any of them concerning them.

SECTION 4:
The Qur'ān as a Guidance

23 And say not of anything: I will do that tomorrow,

24 Unless Allāh please. And remember thy Lord when thou forgettest and say: Maybe my Lord will guide me to a nearer course to the right than this.

25 And they remained in their cave three hundred years, and they add nine.

26 Say: Allāh knows best how long they remained. His is the unseen of the heavens and the earth. How clear His sight and His hearing! There is no guardian for them beside Him, and He associates none in His judgment.

27 And recite that which has been revealed to thee of the Book of thy Lord. There is none who can alter His words. And thou wilt find no refuge beside Him.

THE CAVE

28 And keep thyself with those who call on their Lord morning and evening desiring His goodwill, and let not thine eyes pass from them, desiring the beauties of this world's life. And follow not him whose heart We have made unmindful of Our remembrance, and he follows his low desires and his case exceeds due bounds.

29 And say: The Truth is from your Lord; so let him who please believe, and let him who please disbelieve. Surely We have prepared for the iniquitous a Fire, an enclosure of which will encompass them. And if they cry for water, they are given water like molten brass, scalding their faces. Evil the drink! And ill the resting-place!

30 As for those who believe and do good, We waste not the reward of him who does a good work.

31 These it is for whom are Gardens of perpetuity wherein flow rivers; they are adorned therein with bracelets of gold, and they wear green robes of fine silk and thick brocade, reclining therein on raised couches. Excellent the recompense! And goodly the resting-place!

SECTION 5:
A Parable

32 And set forth to them the parable of two men — for one of them We made two gardens of grape-vines, and We surrounded them with date-palms, and between them We made corn-fields.

33 Both these gardens yielded their fruits, and failed not in aught thereof, and We caused a river to gush forth in their midst,

34 And he had fruit. So *he* said to his companion, while he argued with him: *I* have greater wealth than thou, and am mightier in followers.

35 And he went into his garden, while he was unjust to himself. He said: I think not that this will ever perish,

36 And I think not the Hour will come; and even if I am returned to my Lord, I will certainly find a returning-place better than this.

37 His companion said to him, while arguing with him: Disbelievest thou in Him Who created thee of dust, then of a small life-germ, then He made thee a perfect man?

38 But as for me, He, Allāh, is my Lord, and I associate none with my Lord.

39 And wherefore didst thou not say, when thou enteredst thy garden: It is as Allāh has pleased — there is no power save in Allāh? If thou consider me as less than thee in wealth and children —

40 Then maybe my Lord will give me better than thy garden, and will send on (thine) a reckoning from heaven so that it is dust without plant:

41 Or its water will sink down into the ground, so *that thou art* unable to find it.

42 And his fruit was destroyed; so he began to wring his hands for what he had spent on it, while it lay waste, its roofs fallen down, and he said: Ah me! would that I had ascribed no partners to my Lord!

43 And he had no host to help him against Allāh, nor could he defend himself.

44 Thus protection is only Allāh's, the True One. He is Best to reward and Best in requiting.

SECTION 6:
The Guilty are brought to Judgment

45 And set forth to them the parable of the life of this world as water which We send down from the cloud, so the herbage of the earth becomes luxuriant thereby, then it becomes dry, broken into pieces which the winds scatter. And Allāh is the Holder of power over all things.

46 Wealth and children are an adornment of the life of this world; but the ever-abiding, the good works, are *better* with thy Lord in reward and better in hope.

47 And the day when We cause the mountains to pass away, and thou seest the earth a levelled plain and We gather them together and leave none of them behind.

48 And they are brought

before thy Lord in ranks. Now certainly you have come to Us as We created you at first. Nay, you thought that We had not made an appointment for you.

49 And the book is placed, and thou seest the guilty fearing for what is in it, and they say: O woe to us! what a book is this! It leaves out neither a small thing nor a great one, but numbers them (all), and they find what they did confronting them. And thy Lord wrongs not anyone.

SECTION 7:
Their Helplessness

50 And when We said to the angels: Make submission to Adam, they submitted except Iblis. He was of the jinn, so he transgressed the commandment of his Lord. Will you then take him and his offspring for friends rather than Me, and they are your enemies? Evil is the exchange for the unjust.

51 I made them not to witness the creation of the heavens and the earth, nor their own creation. Nor could I take those who mislead for aiders.

52 And one day He will say: Call on those whom you considered to be My partners. So they will call on them, but they will not answer them, and We shall cause a separation between them.

53 And the guilty will see the Fire, and know that they are about to fall into it, and they will find no escape from it.

SECTION 8:
Warning is disregarded

54 And certainly We have made distinct in this Qur'ān for mankind every kind of description; and man is in most things contentious.

55 And nothing prevents men from believing when the guidance comes to them, and from asking forgiveness of their Lord, but that (they wait) for the way of the ancients to overtake them, or that the chastisement should confront them.

56 And We send not messengers but as givers of good news and warning, and those who disbelieve contend with falsehood to weaken thereby the Truth, and they take My messages and the warning for a mockery.

57 And who is more unjust than he who is reminded of the messages of his Lord, then he turns away from them and forgets what *his hands have sent before*? Surely We have placed veils over their hearts, lest they understand it, and a deafness in their ears. And if thou call them to the guidance, they will even then never follow the right course.

58 And thy Lord is Forgiving, Full of mercy. Were He to punish them for what they earn, He would certainly hasten the chastisement for them. But for them there is an appointed time from which they will find *no refuge*.

59 And these towns — We destroyed them when they did wrong. And We have appointed a time for their destruction.

SECTION 9:
Moses travels in Search of Knowledge

60 And when Moses said to his servant: I will not cease until I reach the junction of the two rivers, otherwise I will go on for years.

61 So when they reached *the junction of the two* (rivers), they forgot their fish, and it took its way into the river, being free.

62 But when they had gone further, he said to this servant: Bring to us our morning meal, certainly we have found fatigue in this our journey.

63 He said: Sawest thou when we took refuge on the rock, I forgot the fish, and none but the devil made me forget to speak of it, and it took its way into the river; what a wonder!

64 He said: This is what *we sought for.* So they returned retracing their footsteps.

65 Then they found one of Our servants whom We had granted mercy from Us and whom We had taught knowledge from Ourselves.

66 Moses said to him:

May I follow thee that thou *mayest teach* me of the good thou hast been taught?

67 He said: Thou canst not have patience with me.

68 And how canst thou have patience in that whereof thou hast not a comprehensive knowledge?

69 He said: If Allāh please, thou wilt find me patient, nor shall I disobey thee in aught.

70 He said: If thou wouldst follow me, question me not about aught until I myself speak to thee about it.

SECTION 10:
Moses travels in Search of Knowledge

71 So they set out until, when they embarked in a boat, he made a hole in it. (Moses) said: Hast thou made a hole in it to drown its occupants? Thou hast surely done a grievous thing.

72 He said: Did I not say that thou couldst not have patience with me?

73 He said: Blame me not for what I forgot, and be not hard upon me for what I did.

74 So they went on, until, when they met a boy, he slew him. (Moses) said: Hast thou slain an innocent person, not guilty of slaying another? Thou hast indeed done a horrible thing.

Part 16

75 He said: Did I not say to thee that thou couldst not have patience with me?

76 He said: If I ask thee about anything after this, keep not company with me. Thou wilt then indeed have found an excuse in my case.

77 So they went on, until, when they came to the people of a town, they asked its people for food, but they refused to entertain them as guests. Then they found in it a wall which was on the point of falling, so he put it into a right state. (Moses) said: If thou hadst wished, thou couldst have taken a recompense for it.

78 He said: This is the parting between me and thee. Now I will inform thee of the significance of that with which thou couldst not have patience.

79 As for the boat, it belonged to poor people working on the river, and I intended to damage it, for there was behind them a king who seized every boat by force.

80 And as for the boy, his parents were believers and we feared lest he should involve them in wrongdoing and disbelief.

81 So we intended that their Lord might give them in his place one better in purity and nearer to mercy.

82 And as for the wall, it belonged to two orphan boys in the city, and there was beneath it a treasure belonging to them, and their father had been a righteous man. So thy Lord intended that they should attain their maturity and take out their treasure — a mercy from thy Lord — and I did not do it of my own accord. This is the significance of that with which thou couldst not have patience.

SECTION 11:
Dhu-l-qarnain and Gog and Magog

83 And they ask thee about Dhu-l-qarnain. Say: I will recite to you an account of him.

84 Truly We established him in the land and granted him means of access to everything;

85 So he followed a course.

86 Until, when he reached the setting-place of the sun, he found it going down into a black sea, and found by it a people. We said: O Dhu-l-qarnain, either punish them or do them a benefit.

87 He said: As for him who is unjust, we shall chastise him, then he will be returned to his Lord, and He will chastise him with an exemplary chastisement.

88 And as for him who believes and does good, for him is a good reward, and We shall speak to him an easy word of Our command.

89 Then he followed a course.

90 Until, when he reached

THE CAVE

(the land of) the rising sun, he found it rising on a people to whom We had given no shelter from it—

91 So it was. And We had full knowledge of what he had.

92 Then he followed a course.

93 Until, when he reached (a place) between the two mountains, he found on that side of them a people who could hardly understand a word.

94 They said: O Dhu-l-qarnain, Gog and Magog do mischief in the land. May we then pay thee tribute on condition that thou raise a barrier between us and them?

95 He said: That wherein my Lord has established me is better, so if only you help me with strength (of men), I will make a fortified barrier between you and them:

96 Bring me blocks of iron. At length, when he had filled up the space between the two mountain sides, he said, Blow. Till, when he had made it (as) fire, he said: Bring me molten brass to pour over it.

97 So they were not able to scale it, nor could they make a hole in it.

98 He said: This is a mercy from my Lord, but when the promise of my Lord comes to pass He will crumble it, and the promise of my Lord is ever true.

99 And on that day We shall let some of them surge against others and the trumpet will be blown, then We shall gather them all together,

100 And on that day We shall bring forth hell, exposed to view, on that day before the disbelievers,

101 Whose eyes were under a cover from My Reminder, and they could not bear to hear.

SECTION 12:
Christian Nations

102 Do those who disbelieve think that they can take My servants to be friends besides Me? Surely We have prepared hell as an entertainment for the disbelievers.

103 Say: Shall We inform you who are the greatest

losers in respect of deeds?

104 Those whose effort goes astray in this world's life, and they think that they are making good manufactures.

105 Those are they who disbelieve in the messages of their Lord and meeting with Him, so their works are vain. Nor shall We set up a balance for them on the day of Resurrection.

106 That is their reward — hell, because they disbelieved and held My messages and My messengers in mockery.

107 As for those who believe and do good deeds, for them are Gardens of Paradise, an entertainment,

108 To abide therein; they will not desire removal therefrom.

109 Say: If the sea were ink for the words of my Lord, the sea would surely be exhausted before the words of my Lord were exhausted, though We brought the like of it to add (thereto).

110 Say: I am only a mortal like you — it is revealed to me that your God is one God. So whoever hopes to meet his Lord, he should do good deeds, and join no one in the service of his Lord.

CHAPTER 19
Maryam: **Mary**

(REVEALED AT MAKKAH: 6 *sections*; 98 *verses*)

SECTION 1:
Zacharias and John

In the name of Allāh, the Beneficent, the Merciful.

1 Sufficient, Guide, Blessed, Knowing, Truthful God.

2 A mention of the mercy of thy Lord to His servant Zacharias —

3 When he called upon his Lord, crying in secret.

4 He said: My Lord, my bones are weakened, and my head flares with hoariness, and I have never been unsuccessful in my prayer to Thee, my Lord.

5 And I fear my kinsfolk after me, and my wife is barren, so grant me from Thyself an heir

6 Who should inherit me and inherit of the Children of Jacob, and make him, my Lord, acceptable (to Thee).

7 O Zacharias, We give thee good news of a boy, whose name is John: We have not made before anyone his equal.

8 He said: My Lord, how shall I have a son, and my wife is barren, and I have reached extreme old age?

9 He said: So (it will be). Thy Lord says: It is easy to Me, and indeed I created thee before, when thou wast nothing.

10 He said: My Lord, give me a sign. He said: Thy sign is that thou speak not to people three nights, being in sound health.

11 So he went forth to his people from the sanctuary and proclaimed to them: Glorify (Allāh) morning and evening.

12 O John, take hold of the Book with strength. And We granted him wisdom when a child,

13 And kind-heartedness from Us and purity. And he

was dutiful,

14 And kindly to his parents, and he was not insolent, disobedient.

15 And peace on him the day he was born and the day he died, and the day he is raised to life!

SECTION 2:
Mary and Jesus

16 And mention Mary in the Book. When she drew aside from her family to an eastern place;

17 So she screened herself from them. Then We sent to her Our spirit and it appeared to her as a well-made man.

18 She said: I flee for refuge from thee to the Beneficent, if thou art one guarding against evil.

19 He said: I am only bearer of a *message of thy* Lord: That I will give thee a pure boy.

20 She said: How can I have a son and no mortal has yet touched me, nor have I been unchaste?

21 He said: So (it will be). Thy Lord says: It is easy to Me; and that We may make him a sign to men and a mercy from Us. And it is a matter decided.

22 Then she conceived him; and withdrew with him to a remote place.

23 And the throes of childbirth drove her to the trunk of a palm-tree. She said: Oh, would that I had died before this, and had been a thing quite forgotten!

24 So a voice came to her from beneath her: Grieve not, surely thy Lord has provided a stream beneath thee.

25 And shake towards thee the trunk of the palm-tree, it will drop on thee fresh ripe dates.

26 So eat and drink and cool the eye. Then if thou seest any mortal, say: Surely I have vowed a fast to the Beneficent, so I will not speak to any man today.

27 Then she came to her people with him, carrying him. They said: O Mary, thou hast indeed brought a strange thing!

28 O sister of Aaron, thy father was not a wicked man, nor was thy mother an unchaste woman!

29 But she pointed to him. They said: How should we speak to one who is a child in the cradle?

30 He said: I am indeed a servant of Allāh. He has given me the Book and made me a prophet:

31 And He has made me blessed wherever I may be, and He has enjoined on me prayer and poor-rate so long as I live:

32 And to be kind to my mother; and He has not made me insolent, unblessed.

33 And peace on me the day I was born, and the day I die, and the day I am raised to life.

34 Such is Jesus son of Mary — a statement of truth about which they dispute.

35 It beseems not Allāh that He should take to Himself a son. Glory be to Him! when He decrees a matter He only says to it, Be, and it is.

36 And surely Allāh is my Lord and your Lord, so serve Him. This is the right path.

37 But parties from among them differed; so woe to those who disbelieve, because of their presence on a grievous day!

38 How clearly will they hear and see on the day when they come to Us; but the wrongdoers are today in manifest error.

39 And warn them of the day of Regret, when the matter is decided. And they are (now) in negligence and they believe not.

40 Surely We inherit the earth and those thereon, and to Us they are returned.

SECTION 3:
Abraham

41 And mention Abraham in the Book. Surely he was a truthful man, a prophet.

42 When he said to his sire: O my sire, why worshippest thou that which hears not, nor sees, nor can it avail thee aught?

43 O my sire, to me indeed has come the knowledge which has not come to thee; so follow me, I will guide thee on a right path.

44 O my sire, serve not the devil. Surely the devil is disobedient to the Beneficent.

45 O my sire, surely I fear lest a punishment from the Beneficent should afflict thee, so that thou become a friend of the devil.

46 He said: Dislikest thou my gods, O Abraham? If thou desist not, I will certainly drive thee away. And leave me for a time.

47 He said: Peace be to thee! I shall pray my Lord to forgive thee. Surely He is ever Kind to me.

48 And I withdraw from you and that which you call on besides Allāh, and I call upon my Lord. Maybe I shall not remain unblessed in calling upon my Lord.

49 So, when he withdrew from them and that which they worshipped besides Allāh, We gave him Isaac and Jacob. And each (of them) We made a prophet.

50 And We gave them of Our mercy, and We granted them a truthful mention of eminence.

SECTION 4:
Other Prophets are raised

51 And mention Moses in the Book. Surely he was one purified, and was a messenger, a prophet.

52 And We called to him from the blessed side of the mountain, and We made him draw nigh in communion.

53 And We gave him out of Our mercy his brother Aaron, a prophet.

54 And mention Ishmael in the Book. Surely he was truthful in promise, and he was a messenger, a prophet.

55 And he enjoined on his people prayer and almsgiving, and was one in whom his Lord was well pleased.

56 And mention Idris in the Book. Surely he was a truthful man, a prophet,

57 And We raised him to an elevated state.

58 These are they on whom Allāh bestowed favours, from among the prophets, of the seed of Adam, and of those whom We carried with Noah, and of the seed of Abraham and Israel, and of those whom

We guided and chose. When the messages of the *Beneficent were recited to* them, they fell down in submission, weeping.

59 But there came after them an evil generation, who wasted prayers and followed lusts, so they will meet perdition,

60 Except those who repent and believe and do good — such will enter the Garden, and they will not be wronged in aught:

61 Gardens of perpetuity which the Beneficent has promised to His servants in the Unseen. Surely His promise ever comes to pass.

62 They will hear therein no vain discourse, but only, Peace! And they have their sustenance therein, morning and evening.

63 This is the Garden which We cause those of Our servants to inherit who keep their duty.

64 And we descend not but by the command of thy Lord. To Him belongs what is before us and what is behind us and what is between these, and thy Lord is never forgetful.

65 Lord of the heavens and the earth and what is *between them, so serve* Him and be patient in His service. Knowest thou any one equal to Him?

SECTION 5:
How the Opponents were Dealt with

66 And says man: When I am dead, shall I truly be brought forth alive?

67 Does not man remember that We created him before, when he was nothing?

68 So by thy Lord! We shall certainly gather them together and the devils, then shall We bring them around hell on their knees.

69 Then We shall draw forth from every sect those most rebellious against the Beneficent.

70 Again, We certainly know best those who deserve most to be burned therein.

71 And there is not one of you but shall come to it. This is an unavoidable decree of thy Lord.

72 And We shall deliver

those who guard against evil, and leave the wrongdoers therein on their knees.

73 And when Our clear messages are recited to them, those who disbelieve say to those who believe: Which of the two parties is better in position and better in assembly?

74 And how many a generation have We destroyed before them, who had better possessions and appearance!

75 Say: As for him who is in error, the Beneficent will prolong his length of days; until they see what they were threatened with, either the punishment or the Hour. Then they will know who is worse in position and weaker in forces.

76 And Allāh increases in guidance those who go aright. And deeds that *endure, the good deeds,* are, with thy Lord, better in recompense and yield better return.

77 Hast thou seen him who disbelieves in Our messages and says: I shall certainly be given wealth and children?

78 Has he gained knowledge of the unseen, or made a covenant with the Beneficent?

79 By no means! We write down what he says, and We shall lengthen to him the length of the chastisement,

80 And We shall inherit from him what he says, and he will come to Us alone.

81 And they have taken gods besides Allāh, that they should be to them a source of strength —

82 By no means! They will soon deny their worshipping them, and be their adversaries.

SECTION 6:
False Doctrine of Sonship

83 Seest thou not that We send the devils against the disbelievers, inciting them incitingly?

84 So make no haste against them. We only number out to them a number (of days).

85 The day when We gather the dutiful to the Beneficent to receive honours,

86 And drive the guilty to hell, as thirsty beasts.

87 They have no power of intercession, save him who has made a covenant with the Beneficent.

88 And they say: The Beneficent has taken to Himself a son.

89 Certainly you make an abominable assertion!

90 The heavens may almost be rent thereat, and the earth cleave asunder, and the mountains fall down in pieces,

91 That they ascribe a son to the Beneficent!

92 And it is not worthy of the Beneficent that He should take to Himself a son.

93 There is none in the heavens and the earth but comes to the Beneficent as a servant.

94 Certainly He comprehends them, and has numbered them all.

95 And everyone of them will come to Him on the day of Resurrection, alone.

96 Those who believe and do good deeds, for them the Beneficent will surely bring about love.

97 So We have made it easy in thy tongue only that thou shouldst give good news thereby to those who guard against evil, and shouldst warn thereby a contentious people.

98 And how many a generation before them have We destroyed! Canst thou see anyone of them or hear a sound of them?

CHAPTER 20
Ṭā Hā

(REVEALED AT MAKKAH: 8 *sections*; 135 *verses*)

SECTION 1:
Moses is Called

In the name of Allāh, the Beneficent, the Merciful.

1 O man,

2 We have not revealed the Qur'ān to thee that thou mayest be unsuccessful;

3 But it is a reminder to him who fears:

4 A revelation from Him Who created the earth and the high heavens.

5 The Beneficent is established on the Throne of Power.

6 To Him belongs whatever is in the heavens and whatever is in the earth and whatever is between them *and whatever is beneath* the soil.

7 And if thou utter the saying aloud, surely He knows the secret, and what is yet more hidden.

8 Allāh — there is no God but He. His are the most beautiful names.

9 And has the story of Moses come to thee?

10 When he saw a fire, he said to his people: Stay, I see a fire; haply I may bring to you therefrom a live coal or find guidance at the fire.

11 So when he came to it, a voice came: O Moses,

12 Surely I am thy Lord, so take off thy shoes; surely thou art in the sacred valley Tuwā.

13 And I have chosen thee so listen to what is revealed:

14 Surely I am Allāh, there is no God but I, so serve Me, and keep up prayer for My remembrance,

15 Surely the Hour is coming — I am about to make it manifest — so that every soul may be rewarded as it strives.

16 So let not him, who

TĀ HĀ

believes not in it and follows his low desire, turn thee away from it, lest thou perish.

17 And what is this in thy right hand, O Moses?

18 He said: This is my staff — I lean on it, and I beat the leaves with it for my sheep, and I have other uses for it.

19 He said: Cast it down, O Moses.

20 So he cast it down, and lo! it was a serpent, gliding.

21 He said: Seize it and fear not. We shall return it to its former state.

22 And press thy hand to *thy side*, it will come out white without evil — another sign:

23 That We may show thee of Our greater signs.

24 Go to Pharaoh, surely he has exceeded the limits.

SECTION 2:
Moses and Aaron go to Pharaoh

25 He said: My Lord, expand my breast for me:

26 And ease my affair for me:

27 And loose the knot from my tongue,

28 (That) they may understand my word.

29 And give to me an aider from my family:

30 Aaron, my brother;

31 Add to my strength by him,

32 And make him share my task —

33 So that we may glorify Thee much,

34 And much remember Thee.

35 Surely, Thou art ever Seeing us.

36 He said: Thou art indeed granted thy petition, O Moses.

37 And indeed We bestowed on thee a favour at another time,

38 When We revealed to thy mother that which was revealed:

39 Put him into a chest, then cast it into the river, the river will cast it upon the shore — there an enemy to Me and an enemy to him shall take him up. And I shed on thee love from Me; and that thou mayest be brought up before My eyes.

40 When thy sister went and said: Shall I direct you to one who will take charge of him? So We brought thee back to thy mother that her eye might be cooled and she should not grieve. And thou didst kill a man, then We delivered thee from grief, and tried thee with (many) trials. Then thou didst stay for years among the people of Midian. Then thou camest hither as ordained, O Moses.

41 And I have chosen thee for Myself.

42 Go thou and thy brother with My messages and be not remiss in remembering Me.

43 Go both of you to Pharaoh, surely he is inordinate;

44 Then speak to him a gentle word, haply he may mind or fear.

45 They said: Our Lord, we fear lest he hasten to do evil to us or be inordinate.

46 He said: Fear not, surely I am with you — I do hear and see.

47 So go you to him and say: Surely we are two messengers of thy Lord; so send forth the Children of Israel with us; and torment them not. Indeed we have brought to thee a message from thy Lord, and peace to him who follows the guidance.

48 It has indeed been revealed to us that punishment will overtake him who rejects and turns away.

49 (Pharaoh) said: Who is your Lord, O Moses?

50 He said: Our Lord is He Who gives to everything its creation, then guides (it).

51 He said: What then is the state of the former generations?

52 He said: The knowledge thereof is with my Lord in a book; my Lord neither errs nor forgets —

53 Who made the earth for you an expanse and *made* for you therein paths and sent down water from the clouds. Then thereby We bring forth pairs of various herbs.

54 Eat and pasture your cattle. Surely there are signs in this for men of understanding.

SECTION 3:
Moses and the Enchanters

55 From it We created you, and into it We shall return you, and from it raise you a second time.

56 And truly We showed him all Our signs but he rejected and refused.

57 Said he: Hast thou come to us to turn us out of our land by thy enchantment, O Moses?

58 We too can bring to thee enchantment like it, so make an appointment between us and thee, which we break not, (neither) we nor thou, (in) a central place.

59 (Moses) said: Your appointment is the day of the Festival, and let the people be gathered in the early forenoon.

60 So Pharaoh went back and settled his plan, then came.

61 Moses said to them: Woe to you! Forge not a lie against Allāh, lest He destroy you by punishment, and he fails indeed who forges (a lie).

62 So they disputed one with another about their affair and kept the discourse secret.

63 They said: These are surely two enchanters who would drive you out from your land by their enchantment, and destroy your excellent institutions.

64 So settle your plan, then come in ranks, and he will succeed indeed this day who is uppermost.

65 They said: O Moses, wilt thou cast, or shall we be the first to cast down?

66 He said: Nay! Cast you down. Then lo! their cords and their rods — it appeared to him by their enchantment as if they ran.

67 So Moses conceived fear in his mind.

68 We said: Fear not, surely thou art the uppermost.

69 And cast down what is in thy right hand — it will eat up what they have wrought. What they have wrought is only the trick of an enchanter, and the enchanter succeeds not wheresoever he comes from.

70 So the enchanters fell

down prostrate, saying: We believe in the Lord of Aaron and Moses.

71 (Pharaoh) said: You believe in him before I give you leave! Surely he is your chief who taught you enchantment. So I shall cut off your hands and your feet on opposite sides and I shall crucify you on the trunks of palm-trees, and you shall certainly know which of us can give the severer and the more abiding chastisement.

72 They said: We cannot prefer thee to what has come to us of clear arguments and to Him Who made us, so decide as thou wilt decide. Thou canst only decide about this world's life.

73 Surely we believe in our Lord that He may forgive us our faults and the magic to which thou didst compel us. And Allāh is Best and ever Abiding.

74 Whoso comes guilty to his Lord, for him is surely hell. He will neither die therein, nor live.

75 And whoso comes to Him a believer, having done good deeds, for them are high ranks —

76 Gardens of perpetuity, wherein flow rivers, to abide therein. And such is the reward of him who purifies himself.

SECTION 4:
The Israelites worship the Calf

77 And certainly We revealed to Moses: Travel by night with My servants, then strike for them a dry path in the sea, not fearing to be overtaken, nor being afraid.

78 So Pharaoh followed them with his armies, then there covered them of the sea that which covered them.

79 And Pharaoh led his people astray and he guided not aright.

80 *O Children of Israel, We truly delivered you from your enemy, and made a covenant with you on the blessed side of the mountain, and sent to you the manna and the quails.*

81 Eat of the good things We have provided for you, and be not inordinate in

ṬĀ HĀ

respect thereof, lest My wrath come upon you; and he on whom My wrath comes, he perishes indeed.

82 And surely I am Forgiving toward him who repents and believes and does good, then walks aright.

83 And what made thee hasten from thy people, O Moses?

84 He said: They are here on my track, and I hastened on to Thee, my Lord, that Thou mightest be pleased.

85 He said: Surely We have tried thy people in thy absence, and the Sāmirī has led them astray.

86 So Moses returned to his people angry, sorrowing. He said: O my people, did not your Lord promise you a goodly promise? Did the promised time, then, seem long to you, or did you wish that displeasure from your Lord should come upon you, so that you broke (your) promise to me?

87 They said: We broke not the promise to thee of our own accord, but we were made to bear the burdens of the ornaments of the people, then we cast them away, and thus did the Sāmirī suggest.

88 Then he brought forth for them a calf, a body, which had a hollow sound, so they said: This is your god and the god of Moses; but he forgot.

89 Could they not see that it returned no reply to them, nor controlled any harm or benefit for them?

SECTION 5:
The End of Calf-worship

90 And Aaron indeed had said to them before: O my people, you are only tried by it, and surely your Lord is the Beneficent God, so follow me and obey my order.

91 They said: We shall not cease to keep to its worship until Moses returns to us.

92 (Moses) said: O Aaron, what hindered thee, when thou sawest them going astray,

93 That thou didst not follow me? Hast thou, then, disobeyed my order?

94 He said: O son of my mother, seize me not by my beard, nor by my head. Surely I was afraid lest thou shouldst say: Thou hast caused division among the Children of Israel and not waited for my word.

95 (Moses) said: What was thy object, O Sāmirī?

96 He said: I perceived what they perceived not, so I took a handful from the footprints of the messenger then I cast it away. Thus did my soul embellish (it) to me.

97 He said: Begone then! It is for thee in this life to say, Touch (me) not. And for thee is a promise which shall not fail. And look at thy god to whose worship thou hast kept. We will certainly burn it, then we will scatter it in the sea.

98 Your Lord is only Allāh, there is no God but *He*. *He* comprehends all things in (His) knowledge.

99 Thus relate We to thee of the news of what has gone before. And indeed We have given thee a Reminder from Ourselves.

100 Whoever turns away from it, he will surely bear a burden on the day of Resurrection,

101 Abiding therein. And evil will be their burden on the day of Resurrection —

102 The day when the trumpet is blown; and We shall gather the guilty, blue-eyed, on that day,

103 Consulting together secretly: You tarried but ten (days).

104 We know best what they say when the fairest of them in course would say: You tarried but a day.

SECTION 6:
The Prophet's Opponents

105 And they ask thee about the mountains. Say: My Lord will scatter them, as scattered dust,

106 Then leave it a plain, smooth, level,

107 Wherein thou seest no crookedness nor unevenness.

108 On that day they will follow the Inviter, in whom is no crookedness; and the voices are low before the Beneficent God, so that thou hearest naught but a soft sound.

ṬĀ HĀ

109 On that day no intercession avails except of him whom the Beneficent allows, and whose word He is pleased with.

110 He knows what is before them and what is behind them, while they cannot comprehend it in knowledge.

111 And faces shall be humbled before the Living, the Self-subsistent. And he who bears iniquity is indeed undone.

112 And whoever does good works and he is a believer, he has no fear of injustice, nor of the withholding of his due.

113 And thus have We sent it down an Arabic Qur'ān, and have distinctly set forth therein of threats that they may guard against evil, or that it may be a reminder for them.

114 Supremely exalted then is Allāh, the King, the Truth. And make not haste with the Qur'ān before its revelation is made complete to thee, and say: My Lord, increase me in knowledge.

115 And certainly We gave a commandment to Adam before, but he forgot; and We found in him no resolve (to disobey).

SECTION 7:
The Devil's misleading

116 And when We said to the angels: Be submissive to Adam, they submitted except Iblis; he refused.

117 We said: O Adam, this is an enemy to thee and to thy wife; so let him not drive you both out of the garden so that thou art unhappy.

118 Surely it is granted to thee therein that thou art not hungry, nor naked,

119 And that thou art not thirsty therein, nor exposed to the sun's heat.

120 But the devil made an evil suggestion to him; he said: O Adam, shall I lead thee to the tree of immortality and a kingdom which decays not?

121 So they both ate of it, then their evil inclinations became manifest to them, and they began to cover themselves with the leaves of the garden. And Adam disobeyed his Lord, and was disappointed.

122 Then his Lord chose him, so He turned to him and guided (him).

123 He said: Go forth herefrom both — all (of you) — one of you (is) enemy to another. So there will surely come to you guidance from Me; then whoever follows My guidance, he will not go astray nor be unhappy.

124 And whoever turns away from My Reminder, for him is surely a straitened life, and We shall raise him up blind on the day of Resurrection.

125 He will say: My Lord, why hast Thou raised me up blind, while I used to see?

126 He will say: Thus did Our messages come to thee, but thou didst neglect them. And thus art thou forsaken this day.

127 And thus do We recompense him who is extravagant and believes not in the messages of his Lord. And certainly the chastisement of the Hereafter is severer and more lasting.

128 Does it not manifest to them how many of the generations, in whose dwellings they go about, We destroyed before them? Surely there are signs in this for men of understanding.

SECTION 8:
Punishment is certain

129 And had not a word gone forth from thy Lord, and a term been fixed, it would surely have overtaken them.

130 So bear patiently what they say, and celebrate the praise of thy Lord before the rising of the sun and before its setting, and glorify (Him) during the hours of the night and parts of the day, that thou mayest be well pleased.

131 And strain not thine eyes toward that with which We have provided different *classes* of them, (of) the splendour of this world's life, that We may thereby try them. And the sustenance of thy Lord is better and more abiding.

132 And enjoin prayer on thy people, and steadily adhere to it. We ask not of thee a sustenance. We provide for thee. And the (good) end is for guarding against evil.

133 And they say: Why does he not bring us a sign from his Lord? Has not there come to them a clear evidence of what is in the previous Books?

134 And if We had destroyed them with chastisement before it, they would have said: Our Lord, *why didst Thou not send to us a messenger, so that we might have followed Thy messages before we met disgrace and shame?*

135 Say: Everyone (of us) is waiting, so wait. Soon you will come to know who is the follower of the even path and who goes aright.

Part 17

CHAPTER 21

Al-Anbiyā': The Prophets

(Revealed at Makkah: 7 *sections*; 112 *verses*)

SECTION 1:
Judgment approaches

In the name of Allāh, the Beneficent, the Merciful.

1 Their reckoning draws nigh to men, and they turn away in heedlessness.

2 There comes not to them a new Reminder from their Lord but they hear it while they sport,

3 Their hearts trifling. And they — the wrongdoers — counsel in secret: He is nothing but a mortal like yourselves; will you then yield to enchantment while you see?

4 He said: My Lord knows (every) utterance in the heaven and the earth, and He is *the Hearer, the Knower.*

5 Nay, say they: Medleys of dreams! nay, he has forged it! nay, he is a poet! so let him bring to us a sign such as the former (prophets) were sent (with).

6 Not a town believed before them which We destroyed: will they then believe?

7 And We sent not before thee any but men to whom We sent revelation; so ask the followers of the Reminder if you know not.

8 Nor did We give them bodies not eating food, nor did they abide.

9 Then We made Our promise good to them; so We delivered them and whom We pleased, and We destroyed the extravagant.

10 Certainly We have revealed to you a Book which will give you eminence. Do you not then understand?

SECTION 2:
Truth has always Triumphed

11 And how many a town

which was iniquitous did We demolish, and We *raised up after it another people!*

12 So when they felt Our might, lo! they began to flee from it.

13 Flee not and return to the easy lives which you led, and to your dwellings, that you may be questioned.

14 They said: O woe to us! Surely we were unjust.

15 And this cry of theirs ceased not till We made them cut off, extinct.

16 And We created not the heaven and the earth and what is between them for sport.

17 Had We wished to take a pastime, We would have taken it from before Ourselves; by no means would We do (so).

18 Nay, We hurl the Truth against falsehood, so it knocks out its brains, and lo! it vanishes. And woe to you for what you describe!

19 And to Him belongs whoever is in the heavens and the earth. And those who are with Him are not too proud to serve Him, nor are they weary.

20 They glorify (Him) night and day: they flag not.

21 Or have they taken gods from the earth who give life?

22 If there were in them gods besides Allāh, they would both have been in disorder. So glory be to Allāh, the Lord of the Throne, being above what they describe!

23 He cannot be questioned as to what He does, and they will be questioned.

24 Or, have they taken gods besides Him? Say: Bring your proof. This is the reminder of those with me and the reminder of those before me. Nay, most of them know not the Truth, so they turn away.

25 And We sent no messenger before thee but We revealed to him that there is no God but Me, so serve Me.

26 And they say: The Beneficent has taken to Himself a son. Glory be to Him! Nay, they are honoured servants—

27 They speak not before He speaks, and according to His command they act.

28 He knows what is before them and what is behind them, and they intercede not except for him whom He approves, and for fear of Him they tremble.

29 And whoever of them should say, I am a god besides Him, such a one We recompense with hell. Thus We reward the unjust.

SECTION 3:
Truth of Revelation

30 Do not those who disbelieve see that the heavens and the earth were closed up, so We rent them. And We made from water everything living. Will they not then believe?

31 And We made firm mountains in the earth lest it be convulsed with them, and We made in it wide ways that they might follow a right direction.

32 And We have made the heaven a guarded canopy; yet they turn away from its signs.

33 And He it is Who created the night and the day and the sun and the moon. All float in orbits.

34 And We granted abiding forever to no mortal before thee. If thou diest, will they abide?

35 Every soul must taste of death. And We test you by evil and good by way of trial. And to Us you are returned.

36 And when those who disbelieve see thee, they treat thee not but with mockery: Is this he who speaks of your gods? And they deny when the Beneficent God is mentioned.

37 Man is created of haste. Soon will I show you My signs, so ask Me not to hasten them.

38 And they say: When will this threat come to pass, if you are truthful?

39 If those who disbelieve but knew the time when they will not be able to ward off the fire from their faces, nor from their backs, and they will not be helped!

40 Nay, it will come to them all of a sudden and confound them, so they will not have the power to avert it, nor will they be respited.

41 And messengers before thee were indeed mocked, *so there befell those of them* who scoffed, that whereat they scoffed.

SECTION 4:
Allāh deals with Men mercifully

42 Say: Who guards you by night and by day from the Beneficent? Nay, they turn away at the mention of their Lord.

43 Or, have they gods who can defend them against Us? They cannot help themselves, nor can they be defended from Us.

44 Nay, We gave provision to these and their fathers, until life was prolonged to them. See they not then that We are visiting the land, curtailing it of its sides? Can they then prevail?

45 Say: I warn you only by revelation; and the deaf hear not the call when they are warned.

46 And if a blast of the chastisement of thy Lord were to touch them, they would say: O woe to us! Surely we were unjust.

47 And We will set up a just balance on the day of Resurrection, so no soul will be wronged in the least. And if there be the weight of a grain of mustard seed, We will bring it. And Sufficient are We to take account.

48 And certainly We gave Moses and Aaron the criterion and a light and a reminder for those who keep from evil,

49 Who fear their Lord in secret and they are fearful of the Hour.

50 And this is a blessed Reminder, which We have revealed. Will you then deny it?

SECTION 5:
Abraham is Delivered

51 And certainly We gave Abraham his rectitude before, and We knew him well.

52 When he said to his sire and his people: What are these images to whose worship you cleave?

53 They said: We found our fathers worshipping them.

54 He said: Certainly you have been, you and your fathers, in manifest error.

55 They said: Hast thou brought us the truth, or art thou of the jesters?

56 He said: Nay, your Lord is the Lord of the heavens and the earth, Who created them; and I am of those who bear witness to this.

57 And, by Allāh! I will certainly plan against your idols after you go away, turning your backs.

58 So he broke them into pieces, except the chief of them, that haply they might return to it.

59 They said: Who has done this to our gods? Surely he is one of the unjust.

60 They said: We heard a youth, who is called Abraham, speak of them.

61 They said: Then bring him before the people's eyes, perhaps they may bear witness.

62 They said: Hast thou done this to our gods, O Abraham?

63 He said: Surely (someone) has done it. The chief of them is this; so ask them, if they can speak.

64 Then they turned to themselves and said: Surely you yourselves are wrongdoers;

65 Then they were made to hang down their heads: Thou knowest indeed that they speak not.

66 He said: Serve you then besides Allāh what does you no good, nor harms you?

67 Fie on you and on what you serve besides Allāh! Have you no sense?

68 They said: Burn him, and help your gods, if you are going to do (anything).

69 We said: O fire, be coolness and peace for Abraham.

70 And they intended a plan against him, but We made them the greater losers.

71 And We delivered him and Lot (directing them) to the land which We had blessed for the nations.

72 And We gave him Isaac; and Jacob, a son's son. And We made (them) all good.

THE PROPHETS

73 And We made them leaders who guided (people) by Our command, and We revealed to them the doing of good and the keeping up of prayer and the giving of alms, and Us (alone) they served;

74 And to Lot We gave wisdom and knowledge, and We delivered him from the town which wrought abomination. Surely they were an evil people, transgressors;

75 And We admitted him to Our mercy; surely he was of the righteous.

SECTION 6:
Allāh always delivers Prophets

76 And Noah, when he cried aforetime, so We answered him, and delivered him and his people from the great calamity.

77 And We helped him against the people who rejected Our messages. Surely they were an evil people, so We drowned them all.

78 And David and Solomon, when they gave judgment concerning the field, when the people's sheep strayed therein by night, and We were bearers of witness to their judgment.

79 So We made Solomon to understand it. And to each (of them) We gave wisdom and knowledge. And We made the mountains, declaring (Our) glory, and the birds, subservient to David. And We were the Doers.

80 And We taught him the making of coats of mail for you, to protect you in your wars; will you then be grateful?

81 And to Solomon (We subdued) the wind blowing violent, pursuing its course by His command to the land which We had blessed, and We are ever Knower of all things.

82 And of the devils there were those who dived for him and did other work besides that; and We kept guard over them:

83 And Job, when he cried to his Lord: Distress has afflicted me! and Thou art the most Merciful of those who show mercy.

84 So We responded to him and removed the distress he had, and We gave him his people and the like of them with them: a mercy from Us and a reminder to the worshippers.

85 And Ishmael and Idrîs and Dhu-l-Kifl; all were of the patient ones;

86 And We admitted them to Our mercy; surely they were of the good ones.

87 And Dhu-l-Nūn, when he went away in wrath, and he thought that We would not straiten him, so he called out among afflictions: There is no God but Thou, glory be to Thee! Surely I am of the sufferers of loss.

88 So We responded to him and delivered him from grief. And thus do We deliver the believers.

89 And Zacharias, when *he cried to his Lord*: My Lord, leave me not alone! and Thou art the Best of inheritors.

90 So We responded to him and gave him John and made his wife fit for him. Surely they used to vie, one with another, in good deeds and called upon Us, hoping and fearing; and they were humble before Us.

91 And she who guarded her chastity, so We breathed into her of Our inspiration, and made her and her son a sign for the nations.

92 Surely this your community is a single community, and I am your Lord, so serve Me.

93 And they cut off their affair among them: to Us will all return.

SECTION 7:
The Righteous will inherit the Land

94 So whoever does good deeds and is a believer, there is no rejection of his effort, and We surely write (it) down for him.

95 And it is forbidden to a town which We destroy: they shall not return.

96 Even when Gog and Magog are let loose and they sally forth from every elevated place.

97 And the True Promise draws nigh, then lo! the eyes of those who disbelieve will be fixedly open: O woe to us! Surely we were heedless of this; nay, we were unjust.

98 Surely you and what you worship besides Allāh are fuel of hell; to it you will come.

99 Had these been gods, they would not have come to it. And all will abide therein.

100 For them therein is groaning and therein they hear not.

101 Those for whom the good has already gone forth from Us, they will be kept far off from it —

102 They will not hear the faintest sound of it and they will abide in that which their souls desire.

103 The great Terror will not grieve them, and the angels will meet them: This is your day which you were promised.

104 The day when We roll up heaven like the rolling up of the scroll of writings. As We began the first creation, We shall reproduce it. A promise (binding) on Us. We shall bring it about.

105 And certainly We wrote in the Book after the reminder that My righteous servants will inherit the land.

106 Surely in this is a message for a people who serve (Us).

107 And We have not sent thee but as a mercy to the nations.

108 Say: It is only revealed to me that your God is one God: will you then submit?

109 But if they turn back, say: I have warned you in fairness, and I know not whether that which you are promised is near or far.

110 Surely He knows what is spoken openly and He knows what you hide.

111 And I know not if this may be a trial for you and a provision till a time.

112 He said: My Lord, judge Thou with truth. And our Lord is the Beneficent, Whose help is sought against what you ascribe (to Him).

CHAPTER 22
Al-Ḥajj: The Pilgrimage
(REVEALED AT MAKKAH: 10 *sections*; 78 *verses*)

SECTION 1:
The Judgment

In the name of Allāh, the Beneficent, the Merciful.

1 O people, keep your duty to your Lord; surely the shock of the Hour is a grievous thing.

2 The day you see it, every woman giving suck will forget her suckling and every pregnant one will lay down her burden, and thou wilt see men as drunken, yet they will not be drunken, but the chastisement of Allāh will be severe.

3 And among men is he who disputes about Allāh without knowledge, and *follows every rebellious* devil —

4 For him it is written that whoever takes him for a friend, he will lead him astray and conduct him to the chastisement of the burning Fire.

5 O people, if you are in doubt about the Resurrection, then surely We created you from dust, then from a small life-germ, then from a clot, then from a lump of flesh, complete in make and incomplete, that We may make clear to you. And We cause what We please to remain in the wombs till an appointed time, then We bring you forth as babies, then that you may attain your maturity. And of you is he who is caused to die, and of you is he who is brought back to the worst part of life, so that after knowledge he knows nothing. And thou seest the earth barren, but when We send down thereon water, it stirs and swells and brings forth a beautiful (growth) of every kind.

6 That is because Allāh, He is the Truth, and He gives life to the dead, and He is Possessor of power

THE PILGRIMAGE

7 And the Hour is coming, there is no doubt about it; and Allāh will raise up those who are in the graves.

8 And among men is he who disputes about Allāh without knowledge, and without guidance, and without an illuminating Book.

9 Turning away haughtily to lead men astray from the way of Allāh. For him is disgrace in this world, and on the day of Resurrection We shall make him taste the punishment of burning.

10 This is for that which thy two hands have sent before, and Allāh is not in the least unjust to the servants.

SECTION 2:
Certainty of Divine Help

11 And among men is he who serves Allāh, (standing) on the verge, so that if good befalls him he is satisfied therewith, but if a trial afflicts him he turns back headlong. He loses this world and the Hereafter. That is a manifest loss.

12 He calls besides Allāh on that which harms him not, nor benefits him; that is straying far.

13 He calls on him whose harm is nearer than his benefit. Certainly an evil guardian and an evil associate!

14 Surely Allāh causes those who believe and do good deeds to enter Gardens wherein flow rivers. Allāh indeed does what He pleases.

15 Whoever thinks that Allāh will not assist him in this life and the Hereafter, let him raise (himself) by some means to the heaven, then let him cut (it) off, then let him see if his plan will take away that at which he is enraged.

16 And thus have We revealed it, clear arguments, and Allāh guides whom He will.

17 Those who believe and those who are Jews and the Sabians and the Christians and the Magians and the polytheists — surely Allāh will decide between them on the day of Resurrection. Surely Allāh is Witness over all things.

18 Seest thou not that to Allāh makes submission whoever is in the heavens and whoever is in the earth, and the sun and the moon and the stars, and the mountains and the trees, and the animals and many of the people? And many there are to whom chastisement is due. And he whom Allāh abases, none can give him honour. Surely Allāh does what He pleases.

19 These are two adversaries who dispute about their Lord. So those who disbelieve, for them are cut out garments of fire. Boiling water will be poured out over their heads.

20 With it will be melted what is in their bellies and (their) skins as well.

21 And for them are whips of iron.

22 Whenever they desire *to go forth from it*, from grief, they are turned back into it, and (it is said): Taste the chastisement of burning.

SECTION 3:
Believers are Triumphant

23 Surely Allāh will make those who believe and do good deeds enter Gardens wherein flow rivers — they are adorned therein with bracelets of gold and (with) pearls. And their garments therein are of silk.

24 And they are guided to pure words, and they are guided to the path of the Praised One.

25 Those who disbelieve and hinder (men) from Allāh's way and from the Sacred Mosque, which We have made equally for all men, (for) the dweller therein and the visitor. And whoever inclines therein to wrong, unjustly, We shall make him taste of painful chastisement.

SECTION 4:
Pilgrimage

26 And when We pointed *to Abraham the place of the House*, saying: Associate naught with Me, and purify My House for those who make circuits and stand to pray and bow and prostrate themselves.

27 And proclaim to men the Pilgrimage: they will come to thee on foot and on

THE PILGRIMAGE

every lean camel, coming from every remote path:

28 That they may witness benefits (provided) for them, and mention the name of Allāh on appointed days over what He has given them of the cattle quadrupeds; then eat of them and feed the distressed one, the needy.

29 Then let them accomplish their needful acts of cleansing, and let them fulfil their vows and go round the Ancient House.

30 That (shall be so). And whoever respects the sacred ordinances of Allāh, it is good for him with his Lord. And the cattle are made lawful for you, except that which is recited to you, so shun the filth of the idols and shun false words,

31 Being upright for Allāh, not associating aught with Him. And whoever associates (aught) with Allāh, it is as if he had fallen from on high, then the birds had snatched him away, or the wind had carried him off to a distant place.

32 That (shall be so). And whoever respects the ordinances of Allāh, this is *surely from the piety of hearts.*

33 Therein are benefits for you for a term appointed, then their place of sacrifice is the Ancient House.

SECTION 5:
Sacrifices

34 And for every nation We appointed acts of devotion that they might mention the name of Allāh on what He has given them of the cattle quadrupeds. So your God is One God, therefore to Him should you submit. And give good news to the humble,

35 Whose hearts tremble when Allāh is mentioned, and who are patient in their afflictions, and who keep up prayer, and spend of what We have given them.

36 And the camels, We have made them of the signs appointed by Allāh for you — for you therein is much good. So mention the name of Allāh on them standing in a row. Then when they fall down on their sides, eat of them and feed the contented one and the beggar. Thus have We made them subservient to you that you may be grateful.

37 Not their flesh, nor their blood, reaches Allāh, but to Him is acceptable observance of duty on your part. Thus has He made them subservient to you, that you may magnify Allāh for guiding you aright. And give good news to those who do good (to others).

38 Surely Allāh defends those who believe. Surely Allāh loves not anyone who is unfaithful, ungrateful.

SECTION 6:
Believers permitted to Fight

39 Permission (to fight) is given to those on whom war is made, because they are oppressed. And surely Allāh is Able to assist them —

40 Those who are driven from their homes without a just cause except that they say: Our Lord is Allāh. And if Allāh did not repel some people by others, cloisters, and churches, and synagogues, and mosques in which Allāh's name is much remembered, would have been pulled down. And surely Allāh will help him who helps Him. Surely Allāh is Strong, Mighty.

41 Those who, if We establish them in the land, will keep up prayer and pay the poor-rate and enjoin good and forbid evil. And Allāh's is the end of affairs.

42 And if they reject thee, already before them did the people of Noah and 'Ād and Thamūd reject (prophets),

43 And the people of Abraham and the people of Lot,

44 And the dwellers of Midian. And Moses (too) was rejected. But I gave respite to the disbelievers, then I seized them; so how (severe) was My disapproval!

45 How many a town We destroyed while it was iniquitous, so it is fallen down upon its roofs; and (how many) a deserted well and palace raised high!

46 Have they not trav-

47 And they ask thee to hasten on the chastisement, and Allāh by no means fails in His promise. And surely a day with thy Lord is as a thousand years of what you reckon.

48 And how many a town to which I gave respite while it was unjust, then I seized it! And to Me is the return.

SECTION 7:
Opposition to the Prophet

49 Say: O people, I am only a plain warner to you.

50 So those who believe and do good, for them is forgiveness and an honourable sustenance.

51 And those who strive to oppose Our messages, they are the inmates of the flaming Fire.

52 And We never sent a messenger or a prophet before thee but when he desired, the devil made a suggestion respecting his desire; but Allāh annuls that which the devil casts, then does Allāh establish His messages. And Allāh is Knowing, Wise —

53 That He may make what the devil casts a trial for those in whose hearts is a disease and the hard-hearted. And surely the wrongdoers are in severe opposition,

54 And that those who have been given knowledge may know that it is the Truth from thy Lord, so they should believe in it that their hearts may be lowly before Him. And surely Allāh is the Guide of those who believe, into a right path.

55 And those who disbelieve will not cease to be in doubt concerning it, until the Hour overtakes them suddenly, or there comes to them the chastisement of a destructive day.

56 The kingdom on that day is Allāh's. He will judge between them. So those who believe and do good will be in Gardens of bliss.

57 And those who disbelieve and reject Our messages, for them is an abasing chastisement.

SECTION 8:
The Faithful shall be Established

58 And those who flee in Allāh's way and are then slain or die, Allāh will certainly grant them a goodly sustenance. And surely Allāh is the Best of providers.

59 He will certainly cause them to enter a place which they are pleased with. And surely Allāh is Knowing, Forbearing.

60 That (is so). And whoever retaliates with the like of that with which he is afflicted and he is oppressed, Allāh will certainly help him. Surely Allāh is Pardoning, Forgiving.

61 That is because Allāh causes the night to enter into the day and causes the day to enter into the night, and because Allāh is Hearing, Seeing.

62 That is because Allāh is the Truth, and that which they call upon besides Him — that is the falsehood, and because Allāh — He is the High, the Great.

63 Seest thou not that Allāh sends down water from the cloud, then the earth becomes green? Surely Allāh is Knower of subtilities, Aware.

64 To Him belongs whatever is in the heavens and whatever is in the earth. And surely Allāh — He is the Self-Sufficient, the Praised.

SECTION 9:
Divine Mercy in dealing with Men

65 Seest thou not that Allāh has made subservient to you all that is in the earth, and the ships gliding in the sea by His command? And He withholds the heaven from falling on the earth except with His permission. Surely Allāh is Compassionate, Merciful to men.

66 And He it is Who brings you to life, then He causes you to die, then He will bring you to life. Surely man is ungrateful.

67 To every nation We appointed acts of devotion, which they observe, so let them not dispute with thee in the matter, and call to thy Lord. Surely thou art on a right guidance.

68 And if they contend with thee, say: Allāh best knows what you do.

69 Allāh will judge between you on the day of Resurrection respecting that in which you differ.

70 Knowest thou not that Allāh knows what is in the heaven and the earth? Surely this is in a book. That is surely easy to Allāh.

71 And they serve besides Allāh that for which He has not sent any authority, and of which they have no knowledge. And for the unjust there is no helper.

72 And when Our clear messages are recited to them, thou wilt notice a denial on the faces of those who disbelieve — they almost attack those who recite to them Our messages. Say: Shall I inform you of what is worse than this? The Fire. Allāh has promised it to those who disbelieve. And evil is the resort.

SECTION 10:
Polytheism will be uprooted

73 O people, a parable is set forth, so listen to it. Surely those whom you call upon besides Allāh cannot create a fly, though they should all gather for it. And if the fly carry off aught from them, they cannot take it back from it. Weak are (both) the invoker and the invoked.

74 They estimate not Allāh with His due estimation. Surely Allāh is Strong, Mighty.

75 Allāh chooses messengers from angels and from men. Surely Allāh is Hearing, Seeing.

76 He knows what is before them and what is behind them. And to Allāh are all affairs returned.

77 O you who believe, bow down and prostrate yourselves and serve your Lord, and do good that you may succeed.

78 And strive hard for Allāh with due striving. He has chosen you and has not laid upon you any hardship in religion — the faith of your father Abraham. He named you Muslims before and in this, that the Messenger may be a bearer of witness to you, and you may be bearers of witness to the people; so keep up prayer and pay the poor-rate and hold fast to Allāh. He is your Protector; excellent the Protector and excellent the Helper!

Part 18

CHAPTER 23

Al-Mu'minūn: The Believers

(REVEALED AT MAKKAH: 6 *sections*; 118 *verses*)

SECTION 1:
Success of the Faithful

In the name of Allāh, the Beneficent, the Merciful.

1 Successful indeed are the believers,

2 Who are humble in their prayers,

3 And who shun what is vain,

4 And who act for the sake of purity,

5 And who restrain their sexual passions —

6 Except in the presence of their mates or those whom their right hands possess, for such surely are not blameable,

7 But whoever seeks to go beyond that, such are transgressors,

8 And those who are keepers of their trusts and their covenant,

9 And those who keep a guard on their prayers.

10 These are the heirs,

11 Who inherit Paradise. Therein they will abide.

12 And certainly We create man of an extract of clay,

13 Then We make him a small life-germ in a firm resting-place,

14 Then We make the life-germ a clot, then We make the clot a lump of flesh, then We make (in) the lump of flesh bones, then We clothe the bones with flesh, then We cause it to grow into another creation. So blessed be Allāh, the Best of creators!

15 Then after that you certainly die.

16 Then on the day of Resurrection you will surely be raised up.

17 And indeed We have made above you seven

ways — and never are We heedless of creation.

18 And We send down water from the cloud according to a measure, then We cause it to settle in the earth, and We are indeed able to carry it away.

19 Then We cause to grow thereby gardens of palm-trees and grapes for you. You have therein many fruits and of them you eat;

20 And a tree that grows out of Mount Sinai, which produces oil and relish for the eaters.

21 And surely there is a lesson for you in the cattle. We make you to drink of what is in their bellies, and you have in them many advantages and of them you eat,

22 And on them and on the ships you are borne.

SECTION 2:
Noah

23 And certainly We sent Noah to his people, so he said: O my people, serve Allāh, you have no God other than Him. Will you not guard against evil?

24 But the chiefs of those who disbelieved from among his people said: He is nothing but a mortal like yourselves, who desires to have superiority over you. And if Allāh had pleased, He could have sent down angels. We have not heard of this among our fathers of yore.

25 He is only a madman, so bear with him for a time.

26 He said: My Lord, help me against their calling me a liar.

27 So We revealed to him: Make the ark under Our eyes and according to Our revelation; then when Our command comes, and water gushes forth from the valley, take into it of every kind a pair, two, and thy people, except those among them against whom the word has gone forth, and speak not to Me in respect of those who are unjust; surely they will be drowned.

28 Then when thou art firmly seated, thou and those with thee, in the ark, say: Praise be to Allāh, Who delivered us from the unjust people!

29 And say: My Lord, cause me to land a blessed landing and Thou art the Best of those who bring to land.

30 Surely there are signs in this, and surely We are ever trying (men).

31 Then We raised after them another generation.

32 So We sent among them a messenger from among them, saying: Serve Allāh — you have no God other than Him. Will you not guard against evil?

SECTION 3:
Prophets after Noah

33 And the chiefs of his people who disbelieved and called the meeting of the Hereafter a lie, and whom We had given plenty to enjoy in this world's life, said: This is only a mortal like you, eating of that whereof you eat and drinking of that you drink.

34 And if you obey a mortal like yourselves, then surely you are losers.

35 Does he promise you that, when you are dead and become dust and bones, you will then be brought forth?

36 Far, very far, is that which you are promised:

37 There is naught but our life in this world: we die and we live and we shall not be raised again:

38 He is naught but a man who has forged a lie against Allāh, and we are not going to believe in him.

39 He said: My Lord, help me against their calling me a liar.

40 He said: In a little while they will certainly be repenting.

41 So the punishment overtook them in justice, and We made them as rubbish; so away with the unjust people!

42 Then We raised after them other generations.

43 No people can hasten on their doom, nor can they postpone (it).

44 Then We sent Our messengers one after another. Whenever its messenger came to a people, they called him a liar, so We made them follow one another and We made them

45 Then We sent Moses and his brother Aaron with Our messages and a clear authority

46 To Pharaoh and his chiefs, but they behaved haughtily and they were an insolent people.

47 So they said: Shall we believe in two mortals like ourselves while their people serve us?

48 So they rejected them and became of those who were destroyed.

49 And certainly We gave Moses the Book that they might go aright.

50 And We made the son of Mary and his mother a sign, and We gave them refuge on a lofty ground having meadows and springs.

SECTION 4:
Higher Values of Life

51 O ye messengers, eat of the good things and do good. Surely I am Knower of what you do.

52 And surely this your community is one community, and I am your Lord, so keep your duty to Me.

53 But they became divided into sects, each party rejoicing in that which was with them.

54 So leave them in their ignorance till a time.

55 Think they that by the wealth and children wherewith We aid them,

56 We are hastening to them of good things? Nay, they perceive not.

57 Surely they who live in awe for fear of their Lord,

58 And those who believe in the messages of their Lord,

59 And those who associate naught with their Lord,

60 And those who give what they give while their hearts are full of fear that to their Lord they must return —

61 These hasten to good things and they are foremost in attaining them.

62 And We lay not on any soul a burden except to the extent of its ability, and with Us is a book which speaks the truth, and they are not wronged.

63 Nay, their hearts are in ignorance about it, and they have besides this other deeds which they do.

64 Until, when We seize those who lead easy lives among them with chastisement, lo! they cry for succour.

65 Cry not for succour this day. Surely you will not be helped by Us.

66 My messages were indeed recited to you, but you used to turn back on your heels

67 Haughtily, passing nights in talking nonsense about it.

68 Do they not then ponder the Word? Or has there come to them that which did not come to their fathers of old?

69 Or do they not recognize their Messenger, that they deny him?

70 Or say they: There is madness in him? Nay, he has brought them the Truth, and most of them hate the Truth.

71 And if the Truth follow their desires, the heavens and the earth and all those who are therein would perish. Nay, We have brought them their reminder, but they turn away from their reminder.

72 Or dost thou ask them a recompense? But the recompense of thy Lord is best, and He is the Best of providers.

73 And surely thou callest them to a right way.

74 And surely those who believe not in the Hereafter are deviating from the way.

75 And if We show mercy to them and remove the distress they have, they would persist in their inordinacy, blindly wandering on.

76 And already We seized them with chastisement, but they were not submissive to their Lord, nor did they humble themselves.

77 Until, when We open for them a door of severe chastisement, lo! they are in despair at it.

SECTION 5: **Polytheism is self-condemned**

78 And He it is Who made for you the ears and the eyes and the hearts. Little it is that you give thanks!

79 And He it is Who multiplied you in the earth, and to Him you will be gathered.

80 And He it is Who gives life and causes death, and His is the alternation of the night and the day. Do you not then understand?

81 Nay, they say the like of what the ancients said.

82 They say: When we die and become dust and bones, shall we then be raised up?

83 We are indeed promised this, and (so were) our fathers before. This is naught but stories of those of old!

84 Say: Whose is the earth, and whoever is therein, if you know?

85 They will say: Allāh's. Say: Will you not then mind?

86 Say: Who is the Lord of the seven heavens and the Lord of the mighty Throne of power?

87 They will say: (This is) Allāh's. Say: Will you not then guard against evil?

88 Say: Who is it in Whose hand is the kingdom of all things and He protects, and none is protected against Him, if you know?

89 They will say: (This is) Allāh's. Say: Whence are you then deceived?

90 Nay, We have brought them the Truth and surely they are liars.

91 Allāh has not taken to Himself a son, nor is there with Him any (other) god — in that case would each god have taken away what he created, and some of them would have overpowered others. Glory be to Allāh above what they describe —

92 The Knower of the unseen and the seen; so may He be exalted above what they associate (with Him)!

SECTION 6: **Regrets of the Wicked**

93 Say: My Lord, if Thou show me that which they

THE BELIEVERS

are promised —

94 My Lord, then place me not with the unjust people.

95 And surely We are well Able to show thee what We promise them.

96 Repel evil with that which is best. We know best what they describe.

97 And say: My Lord, I seek refuge in Thee from the evil suggestions of the devils,

98 And I seek refuge in Thee, my Lord, lest they come to me.

99 Until when death overtakes one of them, he says: My Lord, send me back,

100 That I may do good in that which I have left. By no means! It is but a word that he speaks. And before them is a barrier, until the day they are raised.

101 So when the trumpet is blown, there will be no ties of relationship among them that day, nor will they ask of one another.

102 Then those whose good deeds are heavy, those are the successful.

103 And those whose good deeds are light, those are they who have lost their souls, abiding in hell.

104 The Fire will scorch their faces, and they therein will be in severe affliction.

105 Were not My messages recited to you, but you used to reject them?

106 They will say: Our Lord, our adversity overcame us, and we were an erring people.

107 Our Lord, take us out of it; then if we return (to evil), we shall be unjust.

108 He will say: Begone therein, and speak not to Me.

109 Surely there was a party of My servants who said: Our Lord, we believe, so forgive us and have mercy on us, and Thou are the Best of those who show mercy.

110 But you ridiculed them, until they made you forget remembrance of Me, and you used to laugh at them.

111 Surely I have rewarded them this day because they were patient, that they are the achievers.

112 He will say: How many years did you tarry in the earth?

113 They will say: We tarried a day or part of a day, but ask those who keep account.

114 He will say: You tarried but a little — if you only knew!

115 Do you then think that We have created you in vain, and that you will not be returned to Us?

116 So exalted be Allāh, the True King! No God is there but He, the Lord of the Throne of Grace.

117 And whoever invokes, besides Allāh, another god — he has no proof of this — his reckoning is only with his Lord. Surely the disbelievers will not be successful.

118 And say: My Lord, forgive and have mercy, and Thou art the Best of those who show mercy.

Chapter 24
Al-Nūr: The Light

(Revealed at Madīnah: 9 *sections*; 64 *verses*)

SECTION 1:
Law relating to Adultery

In the name of Allāh, the Beneficent, the Merciful.

1 (This is) a chapter which We have revealed and made obligatory and wherein We have revealed clear messages that you may be mindful.

2 The adulteress and the adulterer, flog each of them (with) a hundred stripes, and let not pity for them detain you from obedience to Allāh, if you believe in Allāh and the Last Day, and let a party of believers witness their chastisement.

3 The adulterer cannot have sexual relations with any but an adulteress or an idolatress, and the adulteress, none can have sexual relations with her but an adulterer or an idolater; and it is forbidden to believers.

4 And those who accuse free women and bring not four witnesses, flog them (with) eighty stripes and never accept their evidence, and these are the transgressors—

5 Except those who afterwards repent and act aright; surely Allāh is Forgiving, Merciful.

6 And those who accuse their wives and have no witnesses except themselves, let one of them testify four times, bearing Allāh to witness, that he is of those who speak the truth.

7 And the fifth (time) that the curse of Allāh be on him, if he is of those who lie.

8 And it shall avert the chastisement from her, if she testify four times, bearing Allāh to witness, that he is of those who lie.

9 And the fifth (time) that the wrath of Allāh to be on her, if he is of those who speak the truth.

10 And were it not for Allāh's grace upon you and His mercy — and that Allāh is Oft-returning (to mercy) Wise!

SECTION 2:
'Ā'ishah's Slanderers

11 Surely they who concocted the lie are a party from among you. Deem it not an evil to you. Nay, it is good for you. For every man of them is what he has earned of sin; and as for him among them who took upon himself the main part thereof, he shall have a grievous punishment.

12 Why did not the believing men and the believing women, when you heard it, think well of their own people, and say: This is an evident falsehood?

13 Why *did they not* bring four witnesses of it? So, as they have not brought witnesses, they are liars in the sight of Allāh.

14 And were it not for Allāh's grace upon you and His mercy in this world and the Hereafter, a grievous chastisement would certainly have touched you on account of the talk you indulged in.

15 When you received it on your tongues and spoke with your mouths that of which you had no knowledge, and you deemed it a trifle, while with Allāh it was serious.

16 And why did you not, when you heard it, say: It beseems us not to talk of it. Glory be to Thee! This is a great calumny.

17 Allāh admonishes you that you return not to the like of it ever again, if you are believers.

18 And Allāh makes clear to you the messages; and Allāh is Knowing, Wise.

19 Those who love that scandal should circulate respecting those who believe, for them is a grievous chastisement in this world and the Hereafter. And Allāh knows, while you know not.

20 And were it not for Allāh's grace on you and His mercy — and that Allāh is Compassionate, Merciful.

SECTION 3:
Slanderers of Women

21 O you who believe, follow not the footsteps of the devil. And whoever follows the footsteps of the devil, surely he commands indecency and evil. And were it not for Allāh's grace on you and His mercy, not one of you would ever have been pure, but Allāh purifies whom He pleases. And Allāh is Hearing, Knowing.

22 And let not possessors of grace and abundance among you swear against giving to the near of kin and the poor and those who have fled in Allāh's way; and pardon and overlook. Do you not love that Allāh should forgive you? And Allāh is Forgiving, Merciful.

23 Surely those who accuse chaste believing women, unaware (of the evil), are cursed in this world and the Hereafter, and for them is a grievous chastisement,

24 On the day when their tongues and their hands and their feet bear witness against them as to what they did,

25 On that day Allāh will pay back to them in full their just reward, and they will know that Allāh, He is the Evident Truth.

26 Unclean things are for unclean ones and unclean ones are for unclean things, and good things are for good ones and good ones are for good things; these are free from what they say. For them is forgiveness and an honourable sustenance.

SECTION 4:
Preventive Measures

27 O you who believe, enter not houses other than your own houses, until you have asked permission and saluted their inmates. This is better for you that you may be mindful.

28 But if you find no one therein, enter them not, until permission is given to you; and if it is said to you, Go back, then go back; this is purer for you. And Allāh is Knower of what you do.

29 It is no sin for you to enter uninhabited houses wherein you have your necessaries. And Allāh knows what you do openly and what you hide.

30 Say to the believing men that they lower their gaze and restrain their sexual passions. That is purer for them. Surely Allāh is Aware of what they do.

31 And say to the believing women that they lower their gaze and restrain their sexual passions and do not display their adornment except what appears thereof. And let them wear their head-coverings over their bosoms. And they should not display their adornment except to their husbands, or their fathers, or the fathers of their husbands, or their sons, or the sons of their husbands, or their brothers, or their brothers' sons, or their sisters' sons, or their women, or those whom their right hands possess, or guileless male servants, or the children who know not women's nakedness. And let them not strike their feet so that the adornment that they hide may be known. And turn to Allāh all, O believers, so that you may be successful.

32 And marry those among you who are single, and those who are fit among your male slaves and your female slaves. If they are needy, Allāh will make them free from want out of His grace. And Allāh is Ample-giving, Knowing.

33 And let those who cannot find a match keep chaste, until Allāh makes them free from want out of His grace. And those of your slaves who ask for a writing (of freedom), give them the writing, if you know any good in them, and give them of the wealth of Allāh which He has given you. And compel not your slave-girls to prostitution when they desire to keep chaste, in order to seek the frail goods of this world's life. And whoever compels them, then surely after their compulsion Allāh is Forgiving, Merciful.

34 And certainly We have sent to you clear messages and a description of those who passed away before you, and an admonition to those who guard against evil.

SECTION 5: Manifestation of Divine Light

35 Allāh is the light of the heavens and the earth. A likeness of His light is as a pillar on which is a lamp — the lamp is in a glass, the glass is as it were a brightly shining star — lit from a blessed olive-tree, neither eastern nor western, the oil whereof gives light, though fire touch it not — light upon light. Allāh guides to His light whom He pleases. And Allāh sets forth parables for men, and Allāh is Knower of all things —

36 (It is) in houses which Allāh has permitted to be exalted and His name to be remembered therein. Therein do glorify Him, in the mornings and the evenings,

37 Men whom neither merchandise nor selling diverts from the remembrance of Allāh and the keeping up of prayer and the paying of the poor-rate — they fear a day in which the hearts and the eyes will turn about,

38 That Allāh may give them the best reward for what they did, and give them more out of His grace. And Allāh provides without measure for whom He pleases.

39 And those who disbelieve, their deeds are as a mirage in a desert, which the thirsty man deems to be water, until, when he comes to it, he finds it naught, and he finds Allāh with him, so He pays him his due. And Allāh is Swift at reckoning —

40 Or like darkness in the deep sea — there covers him a wave, above which is a wave, above which is a cloud — (layers of) darkness one above another — when he holds out his hand, he is almost unable to see it. And to whom Allāh gives not light, he has no light.

SECTION 6: Manifestation of Divine Power

41 Seest thou not that Allāh is He, Whom do glorify all those who are in the heavens and the earth, and the birds with wings outspread? Each one knows its prayer and its glorification. And Allāh is Knower of what they do.

42 And Allāh's is the kingdom of the heavens and the earth, and to Allāh is the eventual coming.

43 Seest thou not that Allāh drives along the clouds, then gathers them together, then piles them up, so that thou seest the rain coming forth from their midst? And He sends down from the heaven (clouds like) mountains, wherein is hail, afflicting therewith whom He pleases and turning it away from whom He pleases. The flash of His lightning almost takes away the sight.

44 Allāh causes the night and the day to succeed one another. Surely there is a lesson in this for those who have sight.

45 And Allāh has created every animal of water. So of them is that which crawls *upon its belly, and of them* is that which walks upon two feet, and of them is that which walks upon four. Allāh creates what He pleases. Surely Allāh is Possessor of power over all things.

46 We have indeed revealed clear messages. And Allāh guides whom He pleases to the right way.

47 And they say: We believe in Allāh and in the Messenger and we obey; then a party of them turn away after this, and these are not believers.

48 And when they are invited to Allāh and His Messenger that he may judge between them, lo! a party of them turn aside.

49 And if the right is on their side, they hasten to him in submission.

50 Is there in their hearts a disease, or are they in doubt, or fear they that Allāh and His Messenger will deal with them unjustly? Nay! they themselves are the wrongdoers.

SECTION 7:
Establishment of the Kingdom of Islām

51 The response of the believers, when they are invited to Allāh and His Messenger that he may judge between them, is only that they say: We hear and we obey. And these it is that are successful.

52 And he who obeys

Allāh and His Messenger, and fears Allāh and keeps duty to Him, these it is that are the achievers.

53 And they swear by Allāh with their strongest oaths that, if thou command them, they would certainly go forth. Say: Swear not; reasonable obedience (is desired). Surely Allāh is Aware of what you do.

54 Say: Obey Allāh and obey the Messenger. But if you turn away, he is responsible for the duty imposed on him, and you are responsible for the duty imposed on you. And if you obey him, you go aright. And the Messenger's duty is only to deliver (the message) plainly.

55 Allāh has promised to those of you who believe and do good that He will surely make them rulers in the earth as He made those before them rulers, and that He will surely establish for them their religion, which He has chosen for them, and that He will surely give them security in exchange after their fear. They will serve Me, not associating aught with Me. And whoever is ungrateful after this, they are the transgressors.

56 And keep up prayer and pay the poor-rate and obey the Messenger, so that mercy may be shown to you.

57 Think not that those who disbelieve will weaken (the Truth) in the earth; and their abode is the Fire. And it is indeed an evil resort!

SECTION 8:
Respect for Privacy

58 O you who believe, let those whom your right hands possess and those of you who have not attained to puberty ask permission of you three times: Before the morning prayer, and when you put off your clothes for the heat of noon, and after the prayer of night. These are three times of privacy for you; besides these it is no sin for you nor for them — some of you go round about (waiting) upon others. Thus does Allāh make clear to you the messages. And Allāh is Knowing, Wise.

59 And when the children among you attain to puberty, let them seek permission as those before them sought permission. Thus does Allāh make clear to you His messages. And Allāh is Knowing, Wise.

60 And (as for) women past childbearing, who hope not for marriage, it is no sin for them if they put off their clothes without displaying their adornment. And if they are modest, it is better for them. And Allāh is Hearing, Knowing.

61 There is no blame on the blind man, nor any blame on the lame, nor no blame on the sick, nor on yourselves that you eat in your own houses, or your fathers' houses, or your mothers' houses, or your brothers' houses, or your sisters' houses, or your paternal uncles' houses, or your paternal aunts' houses, *or your maternal uncles'* houses, or your maternal aunts' houses, or (houses) whereof you possess the keys, or your friends' (houses). It is no sin in you that you eat together or separately. So when you enter houses, greet your people with a salutation from Allāh, blessed (and) goodly. Thus does Allāh make clear to you the messages that you may understand.

SECTION 9:
Matters of State to take Precedence

62 Only those are believers who believe in Allāh and His Messenger, and when they are with him on a momentous affair, they go not away until they have asked leave of him. Surely they who ask leave of thee, are they who believe in Allāh and His Messenger; so when they ask leave of thee for some affair of theirs, give leave to whom thou wilt of them, and ask forgiveness for them from Allāh. Surely Allāh is Forgiving, Merciful.

63 Make not the calling among you of the Messenger as your calling one of another. Allāh indeed knows those who steal away from among you, concealing themselves. So let those who go against his order beware, lest a trial afflict them or there befall them a painful chastisement.

64 Now surely Allāh's is whatever is in the heavens and the earth. *He knows indeed your condition. And on the day when they are* returned to Him, He will inform them of what they *did. And Allāh is Knower* of all things.

Chapter 25
Al-Furqān: **The Discrimination**

(Revealed at Makkah: 6 *sections*; 77 verses)

SECTION 1:
A Warner for all Nations

In the name of Allāh, the Beneficent, the Merciful.

1 Blessed is He Who sent down the Discrimination upon His servant that he might be a warner to the nations —

2 He, Whose is the kingdom of the heavens and the earth, and Who did not take to Himself a son, and Who has no associate in the kingdom, and Who created everything, then ordained for it a measure.

3 And they take besides Him gods who create naught, while they are themselves created, and they control for themselves no harm nor profit, and they control not death, nor life, nor raising to life.

4 And those who disbelieve say: This is nothing but a lie, which he has forged, and other people have helped him at it. So indeed they have brought an iniquity and a falsehood.

5 And they say: Stories of the ancients, which he has got written, so they are read out to him morning and evening!

6 Say: He has revealed it, Who knows the secret of the heavens and the earth. Surely He is ever Forgiving, Merciful.

7 And they say: What a Messenger is this? He eats food and goes about in the markets. Why has not an angel been sent down to him to be a warner with him?

8 Or a treasure given to him, or a garden from which to eat? And the evildoers say: You follow but a man bewitched!

9 See what parables they set forth for thee — they have gone astray, so they cannot find a way.

SECTION 2:
Truth of the Warning

10 Blessed is He Who, if He please, will give thee what is better than this: Gardens wherein flow rivers. And He will give thee palaces.

11 But they deny the Hour, and We have prepared a burning Fire for him who denies the Hour.

12 When it sees them from a far-off place, they will hear its raging and roaring.

13 And when they are cast into a narrow place thereof in chains, they will there pray for destruction.

14 Pray not this day for destruction once but pray for destruction again and again.

15 Say: Is this better or the Garden of Perpetuity, which the dutiful are promised? That is a reward and a resort for them.

16 For them therein is what they desire, to abide. It is a promise to be prayed for from thy Lord.

17 And on the day when He will gather them, and that which they serve besides Allāh, He will say: Was it you who led astray these My servants, or did they themselves stray from the path?

18 They will say: Glory be to Thee! it was not beseeming for us that we should take for protectors others besides Thee, but Thou didst make them and their fathers to enjoy until they forgot the Reminder, and they became a lost people.

19 So they will give you the lie in what you say, then you can neither ward off (evil), nor (obtain) help. And whoever among you does wrong, We shall make him taste a great chastisement.

20 And We did not send before thee any messengers but they surely ate food and went about in the markets. And We make some of you a trial for others. Will you bear patiently? And thy Lord is ever Seeing.

Part 19
SECTION 3:
The Day of Discrimination

21 And those who look not for meeting with Us, say: Why have not angels been sent down to us, or (why) do we not see our Lord? Indeed they are too proud of themselves and revolt in great revolt.

22 On the day when they will see the angels, there will be no good news for the guilty, and they will say: Let there be a strong barrier!

23 And We shall turn to the work they have done, so We shall render it as scattered motes.

24 The owners of the Garden will on that day be in a better abiding-place and a fairer resting-place.

25 And on the day when the heaven bursts asunder with clouds, and the angels are sent down, as they are sent.

26 The kingdom on that day rightly belongs to the Beneficent, and it will be a hard day for the disbelievers.

27 And on the day when the wrongdoer will bite his hands, saying: Would that I had taken a way with the Messenger!

28 O woe is me! would that I had not taken such a one for a friend!

29 Certainly he led me astray from the Reminder after it had come to me. And the devil ever deserts man.

30 And the Messenger will say: My Lord, surely my people treat this Qur'ān as a forsaken thing.

31 And thus have We made for every prophet an enemy from among the guilty, and sufficient is thy Lord as a Guide and a Helper.

32 And those who disbelieve say: Why has not the Qur'ān been revealed to him all at once? Thus, that We may strengthen thy heart thereby and We have arranged it well in arranging.

33 And they cannot bring thee a question, but We have brought thee the truth and the best explanation.

34 Those who will be

gathered to hell on their faces — they are in an evil plight and straying farther away from the path.

SECTION 4:
A Lesson in the Fate of Former People

35 And certainly We gave Moses the Book and We appointed with him his brother Aaron, an aider.

36 Then We said: Go you both to the people who reject Our messages. So We destroyed them with utter destruction.

37 And the people of Noah, when they rejected the messengers, We *drowned them*, and made them a sign for men. And We have prepared a painful chastisement for the wrong-doers —

38 And 'Ād and Thamūd and the dwellers of Rass and many generations in between.

39 And to each We gave examples and each did We destroy with utter destruction.

40 And indeed they pass by the town wherein was rained an evil rain. Do they not see it? Nay, they hope not to be raised again.

41 And when they see thee, they take thee for naught but a jest: Is this he whom Allāh has raised to be a messenger?

42 He had well-nigh led us astray from our gods had we not adhered to them patiently! And they will know, when they see the chastisement, who is more astray from the path.

43 Hast thou seen him who takes his low desires for his god? Wilt thou be a guardian over him?

44 Or thinkest thou that most of them hear or understand? They are but as the cattle; nay, they are farther astray from the path.

SECTION 5:
A Lesson from Nature

45 Seest thou not how thy Lord extends the shade? And if He pleased, He would have made it stationary. Then We have made the sun an indication of it,

46 Then We take it to Ourselves, taking little by little.

47 And He it is Who made the night a covering for you, and sleep a rest, and He made the day to rise up again.

48 And He it is Who sends the winds as good news before His mercy; and We send down pure water from the clouds,

49 That We may give life thereby to a dead land, and give it for drink to cattle and many people that We have created.

50 And certainly We repeat this to them that they may be mindful, but most men consent to naught but denying.

51 And if We pleased, We could raise a warner in every town.

52 So obey not the disbelievers, and strive against them a mighty striving with it.

53 And He it is Who has made the two seas to flow freely, the one sweet, very sweet, and the other saltish, bitter. And between the two He has made a barrier and inviolable obstruction.

54 And He it is Who created man from water, then He has made for him blood-relationship and marriage-relationship. And thy Lord is ever Powerful.

55 And they serve besides Allāh that which can neither profit them, nor harm them. And the disbeliever is ever an aider against his Lord.

56 And We have not sent thee but as a giver of good news and as a warner.

57 Say: I ask of you naught in return for it except that he who will may take a way to his Lord.

58 And rely on the Ever-Living Who dies not, and celebrate His praise. And sufficient is He as being Aware of His servants' sins,

59 Who created the heavens and the earth and what is between them in six periods, and He is established on the Throne of Power, the Beneficent. So ask respecting Him one aware.

60 And when it is said to them: Make obeisance to the Beneficent, they say: And what is the Beneficent? Shall we make obeisance to what thou biddest us? And it adds to their aversion.

SECTION 6:
The Transformation wrought

61 Blessed is He Who made the stars in the heavens and made therein a sun and a moon giving light!

62 And He it is, Who made the night and the day to follow each other, for him who desires to be mindful or desires to be thankful.

63 And the servants of the Beneficent are they who walk on the earth in humility, and when the ignorant address them, they say, Peace!

64 And they who pass the night prostrating themselves before their Lord and standing.

65 And they who say: Our Lord, avert from us the chastisement of hell; surely the chastisement thereof is a lasting evil:

66 It is surely an evil abode and resting-place!

67 And they who, when they spend, are neither extravagant nor parsimonious, and the just mean is ever between these.

68 And they who call not upon another god with Allāh and slay not the soul which Allāh has forbidden, except in the cause of justice, nor commit fornication; and he who does this shall meet a requital of sin —

69 The chastisement will be doubled to him on the day of Resurrection, and he will abide therein in abasement —

70 Except him who repents and believes and does good deeds; for such Allāh changes their evil deeds to good ones. And Allāh is ever Forgiving, Merciful.

71 And whoever repents and does good, he surely turns to Allāh a (goodly) turning.

72 And they who witness no falsehood, and when they pass by what is vain, they pass by nobly.

73 And they who, when reminded of the messages of their Lord, fall not down thereat deaf and blind.

74 And they who say,

Our Lord, grant us in our wives and our offspring the joy of our eyes, and make us leaders for those who guard against evil.

75 These are rewarded with high places because they are patient, and are met therein with greetings and salutation,

76 Abiding therein. Goodly the abode and the resting-place!

77 Say: My Lord would not care for you, were it not for your prayer. Now indeed you have rejected, so the punishment will come.

CHAPTER 26
Al-Shu'arā': The Poets

(REVEALED AT MAKKAH: 11 *sections*; 227 *verses*)

SECTION 1:
The Prophet is consoled

In the name of Allāh, the Beneficent, the Merciful.

1 Benignant, Hearing, Knowing God.

2 These are the verses of the Book that makes manifest.

3 Perhaps thou wilt kill thyself with grief because they believe not.

4 If We please, We could send down on them a sign from heaven, so that their necks would bend before it.

5 And there comes not to them a new Reminder from the Beneficent but they turn away from it.

6 They indeed reject, so the news will soon come to them of that at which they mock.

7 See they not the earth, how many of every noble kind We cause to grow in it?

8 Surely in this is a sign; yet most of them believe not.

9 And surely thy Lord is the Mighty, the Merciful.

SECTION 2:
Moses is called and sent to Pharaoh

10 And when thy Lord called Moses, saying: Go to the iniquitous people —

11 The people of Pharaoh. Will they not guard against evil?

12 He said: My Lord, I fear that they will reject me.

13 And my breast straitens, and my tongue is not eloquent, so send for Aaron (too).

14 And they have a crime against me, so I fear that they will kill me.

15 He said: By no means; so go you both with Our signs; surely We are with you, Hearing.

16 Then come to Pharaoh, and say: We are bearers of a message of the Lord of the worlds:

17 Send with us the Children of Israel.

18 (Pharaoh) said: Did we not bring thee up as a child among us, and thou didst tarry (many) years of thy life among us?

19 And thou didst (that) deed of thine which thou didst and thou art of the ungrateful ones.

20 He said: I did it then when I was of those who err.

21 So I fled from you when I feared you, then my Lord granted me judgment and made me of the messengers.

22 And is it a favour of which thou remindest me *that thou hast enslaved* the Children of Israel?

23 Pharaoh said: And what is the Lord of the worlds?

24 He said: The Lord of the heavens and the earth and what is between them, if you would be sure.

25 (Pharaoh) said to those around him: Do you not hear?

26 He said: Your Lord and the Lord of your fathers of old.

27 (Pharaoh) said: Surely your messenger, who is sent to you, is mad.

28 He said: The Lord of the East and the West and what is between them, if you have any sense.

29 (Pharaoh) said: If thou takest a god besides me, I will certainly put thee in prison.

30 He said: Even if I show thee something plain?

31 (Pharaoh) said: Show it, then, if thou art of the truthful.

32 So he cast down his rod, and lo! it was an obvious serpent;

33 And he drew forth his hand, and lo! it appeared white to the beholders.

SECTION 3:
Moses and the Enchanters

34 (Pharaoh) said to the chiefs around him: Surely this is a skilful enchanter,

35 Who desires to turn you out of your land with *his enchantment. What is it* then that you counsel?

36 They said: Give him and his brother respite and send heralds into the cities

37 That they bring to thee every skilful enchanter.

38 So the enchanters were gathered together for the appointment of a well-known day,

39 And it was said to the people: Will you gather together?

40 Haply we may follow the enchanters, if they are the vanquishers.

41 So when the enchanters came, they said to Pharaoh: Will there be a reward for us, if we are the vanquishers?

42 He said: Yes, and surely you will then be of those who are nearest (to me).

43 Moses said to them: Cast what you are going to cast.

44 So they cast down their cords and their rods and said: By Pharaoh's power we shall most surely be victorious.

45 Then Moses cast down *his rod, and lo! it swallowed up their fabrication.*

46 And the enchanters were thrown down prostrate —

47 They said: We believe in the Lord of the worlds,

48 The Lord of Moses and Aaron.

49 (Pharaoh) said: You believe in him before I give you leave; surely he is the chief of you who taught you enchantment, so you shall know. Certainly I will cut off your hands and your feet on opposite sides, and I will crucify you all.

50 *They said: No harm;* surely to our Lord we return.

51 We hope that our Lord will forgive us our wrongs because we are the first of the believers.

SECTION 4:
Moses is delivered and Pharaoh drowned

52 And We revealed to Moses, saying: Travel by night with My servants — you will be pursued.

53 And Pharaoh sent heralds into the cities (proclaiming):

54 These are indeed a small band,

55 And they have surely enraged us:

56 And we are truly a vigilant multitude.

57 So We turned them out of gardens and springs,

58 And treasures and goodly dwellings —

59 Even so. And We gave them as a heritage to the Children of Israel.

60 Then they pursued them at sunrise.

61 So when the two hosts saw each other, the companions of Moses cried out: Surely we are overtaken.

62 He said: By no means; surely my Lord is with me — He will guide me.

63 Then We revealed to Moses: March on to the sea with thy staff. So it parted, and each party was like a huge mound.

64 And there We brought near the others.

65 And We saved Moses and those with him, all.

66 Then We drowned the others.

67 Surely there is a sign in this; yet most of them believe not.

68 And surely thy Lord is the Mighty, the Merciful.

SECTION 5:
History of Abraham

69 And recite to them the story of Abraham.

70 When he said to his sire and his people: What do you worship?

71 They said: We worship idols, so we shall remain devoted to them.

72 He said: Do they hear you when you call (on them),

73 Or do they benefit or harm you?

74 They said: Nay, we found our fathers doing so.

75 He said: Do you then see what you worship —

76 You and your ancient sires?

77 Surely they are an enemy to me, but not (so) the Lord of the worlds,

78 Who created me, then He shows me the way,

79 And Who gives me to eat and to drink,

80 And when I am sick, He heals me,

81 And Who will cause me to die, then give me life,

82 And Who, I hope, will forgive me my mistakes on the day of Judgment.

83 My Lord, grant me wisdom, and join me with the righteous,

84 And ordain for me a goodly mention in later generations,

85 And make me of the heirs of the Garden of bliss,

86 And forgive my sire, surely he is of the erring ones,

87 And disgrace me not on the day when they are raised —

88 The day when wealth will not avail, nor sons,

89 Save him who comes to Allāh with a sound heart.

90 And the Garden is brought near for the dutiful,

91 And hell is made manifest to the deviators,

92 And it is said to them: Where are those that you worshipped

93 Besides Allāh? Can they help you or help themselves?

94 So they are hurled into it, they and the deviators,

95 And the hosts of the devil, all.

96 They will say, while they quarrel therein:

97 By Allāh! We were certainly in manifest error,

98 When we made you equal with the Lord of the worlds.

99 And none but the guilty led us astray.

100 So we have no intercessors,

101 Nor a true friend.

102 Now, if we could but once return, we would be believers.

103 Surely there is a sign in this; yet most of them believe not.

104 And surely thy Lord is the Mighty, the Merciful.

SECTION 6:
History of Noah

105 The people of Noah rejected the messengers.

106 When their brother

Noah said to them: Will you not guard against evil?

107 Surely I am a faithful messenger to you:

108 So keep your duty to Allāh and obey me.

109 And I ask of you no reward for it: my reward is only with the Lord of the worlds.

110 So keep your duty to Allāh and obey me.

111 They said: Shall we believe in thee and the meanest follow thee?

112 He said: And what knowledge have I of what they did?

113 Their reckoning is only with my Lord, if you but perceive.

114 And I am not going to drive away the believers;

115 I am only a plain warner.

116 They said: If thou desist not, O Noah, thou wilt certainly be stoned to death.

117 He said: My Lord, my people give me the lie.

118 So judge Thou between me and them openly, and deliver me and the believers who are with me.

119 So We delivered him and those with him in the laden ark.

120 Then We drowned the rest afterwards.

121 Surely there is a sign in this, yet most of them believe not.

122 And surely thy Lord is the Mighty, the Merciful.

SECTION 7:
History of Hūd

123 'Ād gave the lie to the messengers.

124 When their brother Hūd said to them: Will you not guard against evil?

125 Surely I am a faithful messenger to you:

126 So keep your duty to Allāh and obey me.

127 And I ask of you no reward for it; surely my reward is only with the Lord of the worlds.

128 Do you build on every height a monument? You (only) sport.

129 And you make fortresses that you may abide.

130 And when you seize,

THE POETS

you seize as tyrants.

131 So keep your duty to Allāh and obey me.

132 And keep your duty to Him Who aids you with that which you know —

133 He aids you with cattle and children

134 And gardens and fountains.

135 Surely I fear for you the chastisement of a grievous day.

136 They said: It is the same to us whether thou admonish, or art not one of the admonishers:

137 This is naught but a fabrication of the ancients:

138 And we will not be chastised.

139 So they rejected him, then We destroyed them. Surely there is a sign in this; yet most of them believe not.

140 And surely thy Lord is the Mighty, the Merciful.

SECTION 8:
History of Ṣāliḥ

141 Thamūd gave the lie to the messengers.

142 When their brother Ṣāliḥ said to them: Will you not guard against evil?

143 Surely I am a faithful messenger to you:

144 So keep your duty to Allāh and obey me.

145 And I ask of you no reward for it; my reward is only with the Lord of the worlds.

146 Will you be left secure in what is here,

147 In gardens and fountains,

148 And corn-fields and palm-trees having fine flower-spikes?

149 And you hew houses out of the mountains exultingly.

150 So keep your duty to Allāh and obey me.

151 And obey not the bidding of the extravagant,

152 Who make mischief in the land and act not aright.

153 They said: Thou art only a deluded person.

154 Thou art naught but a mortal like ourselves — so bring a sign if thou art truthful.

155 He said: This is a

she-camel; she has her portion of water, and you have your portion of water at an appointed time.

156 And touch her not with evil, lest the chastisement of a grievous day overtake you.

157 But they hamstrung her, then regretted,

158 So the chastisement overtook them. Surely there is a sign in this; yet most of them believe not.

159 And surely thy Lord is the Mighty, the Merciful.

SECTION 9:
History of Lot

160 The people of Lot gave the lie to the messengers.

161 When their brother Lot said to them: Will you not guard against evil?

162 *Surely I am a faithful* messenger to you:

163 So keep your duty to Allāh and obey me.

164 And I ask of you no reward for it; my reward is only with the Lord of the worlds.

165 Do you come to the males from among the creatures,

166 And leave your wives whom your Lord has created for you? Nay, you are a people exceeding limits.

167 They said: If thou desist not, O Lot, thou wilt surely be banished.

168 He said: Surely I abhor what you do.

169 My Lord, deliver me and my followers from what they do.

170 So We delivered him and his followers all,

171 Except an old woman, among those who remained behind.

172 Then We destroyed the others.

173 And We rained on them a rain, and evil was the rain on those warned.

174 Surely there is a sign in this; yet most of them believe not.

175 And surely thy Lord is the Mighty, the Merciful.

SECTION 10:
History of Shu'aib

176 The dwellers of the grove gave the lie to the

messengers.

177 When Shu'aib said to them: Will you not guard against evil?

178 Surely I am a faithful messenger to you;

179 So keep your duty to Allāh and obey me.

180 And I ask of you no reward for it; my reward is only with the Lord of the worlds.

181 Give full measure and be not of those who diminish.

182 And weigh with a true balance.

183 And wrong not men of their dues, and act not corruptly in the earth, making mischief.

184 And keep your duty to Him Who created you and the former generations.

185 They said: Thou art only a deluded person,

186 And thou art naught but a mortal like ourselves, and we deem thee to be a liar.

187 So cause a portion of the heaven to fall on us, if thou art truthful.

188 He said: My Lord knows best what you do.

189 But they rejected him, so the chastisement of the day of Covering overtook them. Surely it was the chastisement of a grievous day!

190 Surely there is a sign in this; yet most of them believe not.

191 And surely thy Lord is the Mighty, the Merciful.

SECTION 11:
Prophet's opponents warned

192 And surely this is a revelation from the Lord of the worlds.

193 The Faithful Spirit has brought it,

194 On thy heart that thou mayest be a warner,

195 In plain Arabic language.

196 And surely the same is in the Scriptures of the ancients.

197 Is it not a sign to them that the learned men of the Children of Israel know it?

198 And if We had revealed it to any of the foreigners,

199 And he had read it to them, they would not have believed in it.

200 Thus do We cause it to enter into the hearts of the guilty.

201 They will not believe in it till they see the painful chastisement;

202 So it will come to them suddenly, while they perceive not;

203 Then they will say: Shall we be respited?

204 Do they still seek to hasten on Our chastisement?

205 Seest thou, if We let them enjoy themselves for years,

206 Then that which they are promised comes to them —

207 That which they were made to enjoy will not *avail them?*

208 And We destroyed no town but it had (its) warners —

209 To remind. And We are never unjust.

210 And the devils have not brought it.

211 And it behoves them not, nor have they the power to do (it).

212 Surely they are far removed from hearing it.

213 So call not upon another god with Allāh, lest thou be of those who are chastised.

214 And warn thy nearest relations,

215 And lower thy wing to the believers who follow thee.

216 But if they disobey thee, say: I am clear of what you do.

217 And rely on the Mighty, the Merciful,

218 Who sees thee when thou standest up,

219 And thy movements among those who prostrate themselves.

220 Surely He is the Hearing, the Knowing.

221 Shall I inform you upon whom the devils descend?

222 They descend upon every lying, sinful one —

223 They give ear, and most of them are liars.

224 And the poets — the

deviators follow them.

225 Seest thou not that they wander in every valley,

226 And that they say that which they do not?

227 Except those who believe and do good and remember Allāh much, and defend themselves after they are oppressed. And they who do wrong, will know to what final place of turning they will turn back.

Chapter 27
Al-Naml: The Naml

(Revealed at Makkah: 7 sections; 93 verses)

SECTION 1:
A Reference to Moses' History

In the name of Allāh, the Beneficent, the Merciful.

1 Benignant, Hearing God! These are the verses of the Qur'ān and the Book that makes manifest:

2 A guidance and good news for the believers,

3 Who keep up prayer and pay the poor-rate, and they are sure of the Hereafter.

4 Those who believe not in the Hereafter, We make their deeds fair-seeming to them, but they blindly wander on.

5 These are they for whom is an evil chastisement, and in the Hereafter they are the greatest losers.

6 And thou art surely made to receive the Qur'ān from the Wise, the Knowing.

7 When Moses said to his family: Surely I see a fire; I will bring you news thence, or bring you therefrom a burning brand, so that you may warm yourselves.

8 So when he came to it, a voice issued, saying: Blessed is he who is in search of fire and those around it. And glory be to Allāh, the Lord of the worlds!

9 O Moses, surely I am Allāh, the Mighty, the Wise:

10 And cast down thy rod. So when he saw it in motion as if it were a serpent, he turned back retreating and did not return. O Moses, fear not. Surely the messengers fear not in My presence —

11 Nor he who does wrong, then does good instead after evil; surely I am Forgiving, Merciful,

THE NAML

12 And put thy hand into thy bosom, it will come forth white without evil, among nine signs to Pharaoh and his people. Surely they are a transgressing people.

13 So when Our clear signs came to them, they said: This is clear enchantment.

14 And they denied them unjustly and proudly, while their souls were convinced of them. See, then, what was the end of the mischief-makers!

SECTION 2:
History of Solomon

15 And certainly We gave knowledge to David and Solomon. And they said: Praise be to Allāh, Who has made us excel many of His believing servants!

16 And Solomon was David's heir, and he said: O men, we have been taught the speech of birds, and we have been granted of all things. Surely this is manifest grace.

17 And his hosts of the jinn and the men and the birds were gathered to Solomon, and they were formed into groups.

18 Until when they came to the valley of the Naml, a Namlite said: O Naml, enter your houses, (lest) Solomon and his hosts crush you, while they know not.

19 So he smiled, wondering at her word, and said: My Lord, grant me that I may be grateful for Thy favour which Thou hast bestowed on me and on my parents, and that I may do good such as Thou art pleased with, and admit me, by Thy mercy, among Thy righteous servants.

20 And he reviewed the birds, then said: How is it I see not Hudhud, or is it that he is one of the absentees?

21 I will certainly punish him with a severe punishment, or kill him, or he shall bring me a clear excuse.

22 And he tarried not long, then said: I have compassed that which thou hast not compassed and I have come to thee from Saba' with sure information —

23 I found a woman ruling over them, and she has been given of everything and she has a mighty throne.

24 I found her and her people adoring the sun instead of Allāh, and the devil has made their deeds fair-seeming to them and turned them from the way, so they go not aright —

25 So that they worship not Allāh, Who brings forth what is hidden in the heavens and the earth and knows what you hide and what you proclaim.

26 Allāh, there is no God but He, the Lord of the mighty Throne.

27 He said: We shall see whether thou speakest the truth or whether thou art a liar.

28 Take this my letter and hand it over to them, then turn from them and see *what (answer) they return.*

29 She said: O chiefs, an honourable letter has been delivered to me.

30 It is from Solomon, and it is in the name of Allāh, the Beneficent, the Merciful:

31 Proclaiming, Exalt not yourselves against me and come to me in submission.

SECTION 3:
History of Solomon

32 She said: O chiefs, advise me respecting my affair; I never decide an affair until you are in my presence.

33 They said: We are possessors of strength and possessors of mighty prowess. And the command is thine, so consider what thou wilt command.

34 She said: Surely the kings, when they enter a town, ruin it and make the noblest of its people to be low; and thus they do.

35 And surely I am going to send them a present, and to see what (answer) the messengers bring back.

36 So when (the envoy) came to Solomon, he said: Will you help me with wealth? But what Allāh has given me is better than that which He has given you. Nay, you are exultant because of your present.

37 Go back to them, so we shall certainly come to them with hosts which they have no power to oppose, and we shall certainly expel them therefrom in disgrace, while they are abased.

38 He said: O chiefs, which of you can bring me her throne before they come to me in submission?

39 One audacious among the jinn said: I will bring it to thee before thou rise up from thy place; and surely I am strong, trusty for it.

40 One having knowledge of the Book said: I will bring it to thee in the twinkling of an eye. Then when he saw it settled beside him, he said: This is of the grace of my Lord, that He may try me whether I am grateful or ungrateful. And whoever is grateful, he is grateful only for his own soul, and whoever is ungrateful, then surely my Lord is Self-sufficient, Bountiful.

41 He said: Alter her throne for her; we may see whether she follows the right way or is of those who go not aright.

42 So when she came, it was said: Was thy throne like this? She said: It is as it were the same; and we were given the knowledge before about it, and we submitted.

43 And that which she worshipped besides Allāh prevented her; for she was of a disbelieving people.

44 It was said to her: Enter the palace. But when she saw it she deemed it to be a great expanse of water, and prepared herself to meet the difficulty. He said: Surely it is a palace made smooth with glass. She said: My Lord, surely I have wronged myself, and I submit with Solomon to Allāh, the Lord of the worlds.

SECTION 4:
Ṣāliḥ and Lot

45 And certainly We sent to Thamūd their brother Ṣāliḥ, saying: Serve Allāh. Then lo! they became two parties, contending.

46 He said: O my people, why do you hasten on the evil before the good? Why do you not ask forgiveness of Allāh so that you may have mercy?

47 They said: We augur evil of thee and those with

thee. He said: Your evil augury is with Allāh; nay, you are a people who are tried.

48 And there were in the city nine persons who made mischief in the land and did not aright.

49 They said: Swear one to another by Allāh that we shall attack him and his family by night, then we shall say to his heir: We witnessed not the destruction of his family, and we are surely truthful.

50 And they planned a plan, and We planned a plan, while they perceived not.

51 See, then, what was the end of their plan, that We destroyed them and their people, all (of them).

52 So those are their houses fallen down because they were iniquitous. Surely there is a sign in this for a people who know.

53 And We delivered those who believed and kept their duty.

54 And Lot, when he said to his people: Do you commit foul deeds, while you see?

55 Will you come to men lustfully rather than women? Nay, you are a people who act ignorantly.

56 But the answer of his people was naught except that they said: Drive out Lot's followers from your town; surely they are a people who would keep pure!

57 But We delivered him and his followers except his wife; We ordained her to be of those who remained behind.

58 And We rained on them a rain; so evil was the rain on those who had been warned.

SECTION 5:
The Faithful will be Exalted

59 Say: Praise be to Allāh and peace on His servants whom He has chosen! Is Allāh better, or what they associate (with Him)?

Part 20

60 Or, Who created the heavens and the earth, and sends down for you water from the cloud? Then We cause to grow thereby beautiful gardens — it is not possible for you to make the trees thereof to grow. Is there a god with Allāh? Nay, they are a people who deviate!

61 Or, Who made the earth a resting-place, and made in it rivers, and raised on it mountains, and placed between the two seas a barrier? Is there a god with Allāh? Nay, most of them know not!

62 Or, Who answers the distressed one when he calls upon Him and removes the evil, and will make you successors in the earth? Is there a god with Allāh? Little is it that you mind!

63 Or, Who guides you in the darkness of the land and the sea, and Who sends the winds as good news before His mercy? Is there a god with Allāh? Exalted be Allāh above what they associate (with Him)!

64 Or, Who originates the creation, then reproduces it, and Who gives you sustenance from the heaven and the earth? Is there a god with Allāh? Say: Bring your proof, if you are truthful.

65 Say: No one in the heavens and the earth knows the unseen but Allāh; and they know not when they will be raised.

66 Nay, their knowledge reaches not the Hereafter. Nay, they are in doubt about it. Nay, they are blind to it.

SECTION 6:
The Spiritual Resurrection

67 And those who disbelieve say: When we have become dust and our fathers (too), shall we indeed be brought forth?

68 We have certainly been promised this — we and our fathers before; these are naught but stories of the ancients!

69 Say: Travel in the earth, then see what was the end of the guilty!

70 And grieve not for them, nor be distressed because of what they plan.

71 And they say: When will this promise come to pass, if you are truthful?

72 Say: Maybe somewhat of that which you seek to

hasten has drawn nigh to you.

73 And surely thy Lord is Full of grace to men, but most of them do not give thanks.

74 And surely thy Lord knows what their breasts conceal and what they manifest.

75 And there is nothing concealed in the heaven and the earth but it is in a clear book.

76 Surely this Qur'ān declares to the Children of Israel most of that wherein they differ.

77 And surely it is a guidance and a mercy for the believers.

78 Truly thy Lord will judge between them by His judgment, and He is the Mighty, the Knowing.

79 So rely on Allāh. Surely thou art on the plain truth.

80 Certainly thou canst not make the dead to hear, nor canst thou make the deaf to hear the call, when they go back retreating.

81 Nor canst thou lead the blind out of their error. Thou canst make none to hear except those who believe in Our messages, so they submit.

82 And when the word comes to pass against them, We shall bring forth for them a creature from the earth that will speak to them, because people did not believe in Our messages.

SECTION 7:
Passing away of Opposition

83 And the day when We gather from every nation a party from among those who rejected Our messages, then they will be formed into groups.

84 Until, when they come, He will say: Did you reject My messages, while you did not comprehend them in knowledge? Or what was it that you did?

85 And the word will come to pass against them because they were unjust, so they will not speak.

86 See they not that We have made the night that they may rest therein, and the day to give light? Surely there are signs in this for a people who believe.

87 And the day when the trumpet is blown, then those in the heavens and those in the earth will be struck with terror, except such as Allāh please. And all shall come to Him abased.

88 And thou seest the mountains — thou thinkest them firmly fixed — passing away as the passing away of the cloud: the handiwork of Allāh, Who has made everything thoroughly. Surely He is Aware of what you do.

89 Whoever brings good, he will have better than it; and they will be secure from terror that day.

90 And whoever brings evil, these will be thrown down on their faces into the Fire. Are you rewarded aught except for what you did?

91 I am commanded only to serve the Lord of this city, Who has made it sacred, and His are all things, and I am commanded to be of those who submit,

92 And to recite the Qur'ān. So whoever goes aright, he goes aright for his own soul, and whoever goes astray — say: I am only one of the warners.

93 And say: Praise be to Allāh! He will show you His signs so that you shall recognize them. And thy Lord is not heedless of what you do.

CHAPTER 28
Al-Qaṣaṣ: **The Narrative**

(REVEALED AT MAKKAH: 9 *sections*; 88 *verses*)

SECTION 1:
History of Moses

In the name of Allāh, the Beneficent, the Merciful.

1 Benignant, Hearing, Knowing God!

2 These are the verses of the Book that makes manifest.

3 We recite to thee the story of Moses and Pharaoh with truth, for a people who believe.

4 Surely Pharaoh exalted himself in the land and made its people into parties, weakening one party from among them; he slaughtered their sons and let their women live. Surely he was one of the mischief-makers.

5 *And We desired to* bestow a favour upon those who were deemed weak in the land, and to make them the leaders, and to make them the heirs,

6 And to grant them power in the land, and to make Pharaoh and Hāmān and their hosts see from them what they feared.

7 And We revealed to Moses' mother, saying: Give him suck; then when thou fearest for him, cast him into the river and fear not, nor grieve; surely We shall bring him back to thee and make him one of the messengers.

8 So Pharaoh's people took him up that he might be an enemy and a grief for them. Surely Pharaoh and Hāmān and their hosts were wrongdoers.

9 And Pharaoh's wife said: A refreshment of the eye to me and to thee — slay him not; maybe he will be useful to us, or we may take him for a son. And they perceived not.

10 And the heart of Moses' mother was free (from anxiety). She would almost have disclosed it, had We not strengthened her heart, so that she might be of the believers.

11 And she said to his sister: Follow him up. So she watched him from a distance, while they perceived not.

12 And We did not allow him to suck before, so she said: Shall I point out to you the people of a house who will bring him up for you, and they will wish him well?

13 So We gave him back to his mother that her eye might be refreshed, and that she might not grieve, and that she might know that the promise of Allāh is true. But most of them know not.

SECTION 2:
History of Moses

14 And when he attained his maturity and became full-grown, We granted him wisdom and knowledge. And thus do We reward those who do good (to others).

15 And he went into the city at a time of carelessness on the part of its people, so he found therein two men fighting — one being of his party and the other of his foes; and he who was of his party cried out to him for help against him who was of his enemies, so Moses struck him with his fist and killed him. He said: This is on account of the devil's doing; surely he is an enemy, openly leading astray.

16 He said: My Lord, surely I have done harm to myself, so do Thou protect me; so He protected him. Surely He is the Forgiving, the Merciful.

17 He said: My Lord, because Thou hast bestowed a favour on me, I shall never be a backer of the guilty.

18 And he was in the city, fearing, awaiting, when lo, he who had asked his assistance the day before was crying out to him for help. Moses said to him: Thou art surely one erring manifestly.

19 So when he desired to seize him who was an enemy to them both, he said: O Moses, dost thou intend to kill me as thou didst kill a person yesterday? Thou only desirest to be a tyrant in the land, and thou desirest not to be of those who act aright.

20 And a man came running from the remotest part of the city. He said: O Moses, the chiefs are consulting together to slay thee, so depart (at once); surely I am of those who wish thee well.

21 So he went forth therefrom, fearing, awaiting. He said: My Lord, deliver me from the iniquitous people.

SECTION 3:
History of Moses

22 And when he turned his face towards Midian, he said: Maybe my Lord will guide me in the right path.

23 And when he came to the water of Midian, he found there a group of men watering, and he found besides them two women keeping back (their flocks). He said: What is the matter with you? They said: We cannot water until the shepherds take away (their sheep) from the water; and our father is a very old man.

24 So he watered (their sheep) for them, then went back to the shade, and said: My Lord, I stand in need of whatever good Thou mayest send to me.

25 Then one of the two women came to him walking bashfully. She said: My father invites thee that he may reward thee for having watered for us. So when he came to him and related to him the story, he said: Fear not, thou art secure from the iniquitous people.

26 One of them said: O my father, employ him; surely the best of those that thou canst employ is the strong, the faithful one.

27 He said: I desire to marry one of these two daughters of mine to thee on condition that thou serve me for eight years; but, if thou complete ten, it will be of thy own free will, and I wish not to be hard on thee. If Allāh please, thou wilt find me one of the righteous.

28 He said: That is (agreed) between me and thee; whichever of the two terms I fulfil, there will be no injustice to me; and

THE NARRATIVE

Allāh is surety over what we say.

SECTION 4:
History of Moses

29 Then when Moses had completed the term, and was travelling with his family, he perceived a fire on the side of the mountain. He said to his family: Wait, I see a fire; maybe I will bring to you from it some news or a brand of fire, so that you may warm yourselves.

30 And when he came to it, he was called from the right side of the valley in the blessed spot of the bush: O Moses, surely I am Allāh, the Lord of the worlds.

31 And cast down thy rod. So when he saw it in motion as if it were a serpent, he turned away retreating, and looked not back. O Moses, come forward and fear not; surely thou art of those who are secure.

32 Insert thy hand into thy bosom, it will come forth white without evil, and remain calm in fear. These two are two arguments from thy Lord to Pharaoh and his chiefs. Surely they are a transgressing people.

33 He said: My Lord, I killed one of them, so I fear lest they slay me.

34 And my brother, Aaron, he is more eloquent in speech than I, so send him with me as a helper to confirm me. Surely I fear that they would reject me.

35 He said: We will strengthen thine arm with thy brother, and We will give you both an authority, so that they shall not reach you. With Our signs, you two and those who follow you, will triumph.

36 So when Moses came to them with Our clear signs, they said: This is nothing but forged enchantment, and we never heard of it among our fathers of old!

37 And Moses said: My Lord knows best who comes with guidance from Him, and whose shall be the good end of the abode. Surely the wrongdoers will not be successful.

38 And Pharaoh said: O

chiefs, I know no god for you besides myself; so kindle a fire for me, O Hāmān, on (bricks of) clay, then prepare for me a lofty building, so that I may obtain knowledge of Moses' God, and surely I think him a liar.

39 And he was unjustly proud in the land, he and his hosts, and they deemed that they would not be brought back to Us.

40 So We caught hold of him and his hosts, then We cast them into the sea, and see what was the end of the iniquitous.

41 And We made them leaders who call to the Fire, and on the day of Resurrection they will not be helped.

42 And We made a curse to follow them in this world, and on the day of Resurrection they will be *hideous*.

SECTION 5:
A Prophet like Moses

43 And certainly We gave Moses the Book after We had destroyed the former generations — clear arguments for men and a guidance and a mercy, that they may be mindful.

44 And thou wast not on the western side when We revealed to Moses the commandment, nor wast thou among those present;

45 But We raised up generations, then life became prolonged to them. And thou wast not dwelling among the people of Midian, reciting to them Our messages, but We are the Sender (of messengers).

46 And thou wast not at the side of the mountain when We called, but a mercy from thy Lord that thou mayest warn a people to whom no warner came before thee, that they may be mindful.

47 And lest, if a disaster should befall them for what their hands have sent before, they should say: Our Lord, why didst Thou not send to us a messenger so that we might have followed Thy messages and been of the believers?

48 But (now) when the Truth has come to them from Us, they say: Why is he not given the like of what was given to Moses? Did they not disbelieve in that which was given to Moses before? They say: Two enchantments backing up each other! And they say: Surely we are disbelievers in both.

49 Say: Then bring some (other) Book from Allāh which is a better guide than these two, I will follow it — if you are truthful.

50 But if they answer thee not, know that they only follow their low desires. And who is more erring than he who follows his low desires without any guidance from Allāh? Surely Allāh guides not the iniquitous people.

SECTION 6:
The Truth of Revelation

51 And certainly We have made the Word to have many connections for their sake, so that they may be mindful.

52 Those to whom We gave the Book before it, they are believers in it.

53 And when it is recited to them they say: We believe in it; surely it is the Truth from our Lord; we were indeed before this submitting ones.

54 These will be granted their reward twice, because they are steadfast, and they repel evil with good and spend out of what We have given them.

55 And when they hear idle talk, they turn aside from it and say: For us are our deeds and for you your deeds. Peace be to you! We desire not the ignorant.

56 Surely thou canst not guide whom thou lovest, but Allāh guides whom He pleases; and He knows best those who walk aright.

57 And they say: If we follow the guidance with thee, we should be carried off from our country. Have We not settled them in a safe, sacred territory to which fruits of every kind are drawn? A sustenance from Us — but most of them know not.

58 And how many a town have We destroyed which exulted in its means of subsistence! So those are their abodes: they have not been dwelt in after them except a little. And We are ever the Inheritors.

59 And thy Lord never destroyed the towns, until He had raised in their metropolis a messenger, reciting to them Our messages, and We never destroyed the towns except when their people were iniquitous.

60 And whatever things you have been given are only a provision of this world's life and its adornment, and whatever is with Allāh is better and more lasting. Do you not then understand?

SECTION 7:
Opponents shall be brought low

61 Is he to whom We have promised a goodly promise, which he will meet with, like him whom We have provided with the provisions of this world's life, then on the day of Resurrection he will be of those brought up (for punishment)?

62 And the day when He will call them and say: Where are those whom you deemed to be My associates?

63 Those against whom the word has proved true will say: Our Lord, these are they whom we caused to deviate — we caused them to deviate as we ourselves deviated. We declare our innocence before Thee. Us they never worshipped.

64 And it will be said: Call your associate-gods. So they will call upon them, but they will not answer them, and they will see the chastisement. Would that they had followed the right way!

65 And the day He will call them, then say: What was the answer you gave to the messengers?

66 On that day excuses will become obscure to them, so they will not ask each other.

67 But as to him who repents and believes and does good, maybe he will be among the successful.

68 And thy Lord creates and chooses whom He pleases. To choose is not theirs. Glory be to Allāh and exalted be He above

THE NARRATIVE

what they associate (with Him)!

69 And thy Lord knows what their breasts conceal and what they proclaim.

70 And He is Allāh, there is no God but He! His is the praise in this (life) and the Hereafter; and His is the judgment, and to Him you will be brought back.

71 Say: Do you see if Allāh were to make the night to continue incessantly on you till the day of Resurrection, who is the god besides Allāh who could bring you light? Will you not then hear?

72 Say: Do you see if Allāh were to make the day to continue incessantly on you till the day of Resurrection, who is the god besides Allāh that could bring you the night in which you take rest? Do you not then see?

73 And out of His mercy He has made for you the night and the day, that you may rest therein, and that you may seek of His grace, and that you may give thanks.

74 And the day when He will call them and say: Where are My associates whom you pretended?

75 And We shall draw forth from among every nation a witness and say: Bring your proof. Then shall they know that the Truth is Allāh's and that which they forged will fail them.

SECTION 8:
Korah's Wealth leads him to Ruin

76 Korah was surely of the people of Moses, but he oppressed them, and We gave him treasures, so much so that his hoards of wealth would weigh down a body of strong men. When his people said to him: Exult not; surely Allāh loves not the exultant.

77 And seek the abode of the Hereafter by means of what Allāh has given thee, and neglect not thy portion of the world, and do good (to others) as Allāh has done good to thee, and seek not to make mischief in the land. Surely Allāh loves not the mischief-makers.

78 He said: I have been given this only on account

of the knowledge I have. Did he not know that Allāh had destroyed before him generations who were mightier in strength than he and greater in assemblage? And the guilty are not questioned about their sins.

79 So he went forth to his people in his finery. Those who desired this world's life said: O would that we had the like of what Korah is given! Surely he is possessed of mighty good fortune!

80 But those who were given the knowledge said: Woe to you! Allāh's reward is better for him who believes and does good, and none is made to receive this except the patient.

81 So We made the earth to swallow him up and his abode. He had no host to help him against Allāh, nor was he of those who can defend themselves.

82 And those who had yearned for his place the day before began to say: Ah! (know) that Allāh amplifies and straitens the means of subsistence for whom He pleases of His servants; had not Allāh been gracious to us, He would have abased us. Ah! (know) that the ungrateful are never successful.

SECTION 9:
The Prophet will return to Makkah

83 That abode of the Hereafter, We assign it to those who have no desire to exalt themselves in the earth nor to make mischief. And the good end is for those who keep their duty.

84 Whoever brings good, he will have better than it; and whoever brings evil, those who do evil will be requited only for what they did.

85 He Who has made the Qur'ān binding on thee will surely bring thee back to the Place of Return. Say: My Lord knows best him who has brought the guidance and him who is in manifest error.

86 And thou didst not expect that the Book would be inspired to thee, but it is a mercy from thy Lord, so be not a backer up of the disbelievers.

87 And let them not turn

thee aside from the messages of Allāh after they have been revealed to thee, and call (men) to thy Lord and be not of the polytheists.

88 And call not with Allāh any other god. There is no God but He. Everything will perish but He. His is the judgment, and to Him you will be brought back.

CHAPTER 29
Al-'Ankabūt: **The Spider**

(REVEALED AT MAKKAH: 7 *sections*; 69 verses)

SECTION 1:
Trials purify

In the name of Allāh, the Beneficent, the Merciful.

1 I, Allāh, am the best Knower.

2 Do men think that they will be left alone on saying, We believe, and will not be tried?

3 And indeed We tried those before them, so Allāh will certainly know those who are true and He will know the liars.

4 Or do they who work evil think that they will escape Us? Evil is it that they judge!

5 Whoever hopes to meet with Allāh, the term of Allāh is then surely coming. And He is the Hearing, the Knowing.

6 And whoever strives hard, strives for himself. Surely Allāh is Self-sufficient, above (need of) (His) creatures.

7 And those who believe and do good, We shall certainly do away with their afflictions and reward them for the best of what they did.

8 And We have enjoined on man goodness to his parents. But if they contend with thee to associate (others) with Me, of which thou hast no knowledge, obey them not. To Me is your return, so I will inform you of what you did.

9 And those who believe and do good, We shall surely make them enter among the righteous.

10 And among men is he who says: We believe in Allāh; but when he is persecuted for the sake of Allāh, he thinks the persecution of men to be as the chastisement of Allāh. And if there comes help from thy Lord, they will say: Surely we were with you. Is not Allāh the Best Knower of what is in the hearts of mankind?

11 And certainly Allāh will know those who believe, and He will know the hypocrites.

12 And those who disbelieve say to those who believe: Follow our path and we will bear your wrongs. And they can never bear aught of their wrongs. Surely they are liars.

13 And they will certainly bear their own burdens, and other burdens besides their own burdens; and they will certainly be questioned on the day of Resurrection as to what they forged.

SECTION 2:
Noah and Abraham

14 And We indeed sent Noah to his people, so he remained among them a thousand years save fifty years. And the deluge overtook them, and they were wrongdoers.

15 So We delivered him and the inmates of the ark, and made it a sign to the nations.

16 And (We sent) Abraham, when he said to his people: Serve Allāh and keep your duty to Him. That is better for you, if you did but know.

17 You only worship idols besides Allāh and you invent a lie. Surely they whom you serve besides Allāh control no sustenance for you; so seek sustenance from Allāh and serve Him and be grateful to Him. To Him you will be brought back.

18 And if you reject, nations before you did indeed reject (the Truth). And the duty of the Messenger is only to deliver (the message) plainly.

19 See they not how Allāh originates the creation, then reproduces it? Surely that is easy to Allāh.

20 Say: Travel in the earth then see how He makes the first creation, then Allāh creates the latter creation. Surely Allāh is Possessor of power over all things.

21 He chastises whom He pleases and has mercy on whom He pleases, and to Him you will be turned back.

22 And you cannot escape in the earth nor in the heaven, and you have no protector or helper besides Allāh.

SECTION 3:
Abraham and Lot

23 And those who disbelieve in the messages of Allāh and the meeting with Him, they despair of My mercy, and for them is a painful chastisement.

24 So naught was the answer of his people except that they said: Slay him or burn him! But Allāh delivered him from the fire. Surely therein are signs for a people who believe.

25 And he said: You have only taken idols besides Allāh by way of friendship between you in this world's life, then on the day of Resurrection some of you will *deny others, and some of* you will curse others; and your abode is the Fire, and you will have no helpers.

26 So Lot believed in him. And he said: I am fleeing to my Lord. Surely He is the Mighty, the Wise.

27 And We granted him Isaac and Jacob, and ordained prophethood and the Book among his seed. And We gave him his reward in this world, and in the Hereafter he will surely be among the righteous.

28 And (We sent) Lot, when he said to his people: Surely you are guilty of an abomination which none of the nations has done before you.

29 Do you come to males and commit robbery on the highway, and commit evil deeds in your assemblies? But the answer of his people was only that they said: Bring on us Allāh's chastisement, if thou art truthful.

30 He said: My Lord, help me against the mischievous people.

SECTION 4:
Opposition to Truth ever a Failure

31 And when Our messengers came to Abraham with good news, they said: We are going to destroy the people of this town, for its people are iniquitous.

32 He said: Surely in it is Lot. They said: We know

well who is in it; we shall certainly deliver him and his followers, except his wife; she is of those who remain behind.

33 And when Our messengers came to Lot, he was grieved on account of them, and he lacked strength to protect them. And they said: Fear not, nor grieve; surely we will deliver thee and thy followers, except thy wife — she is of those who remain behind.

34 Surely We are going to bring down upon the people of this town a punishment from heaven, because they transgressed.

35 And certainly We have left a clear sign of it for a people who understand.

36 And to Midian (We sent) their brother <u>Sh</u>u'aib, so he said: O my people, serve Allāh and fear the Latter day, and act not corruptly, making mischief, in the land.

37 But they rejected him, so a severe earthquake overtook them and they lay prostrate in their abodes.

38 And 'Ād and <u>Th</u>amūd! And some of their dwellings are indeed apparent to you. And the devil made their deeds fairseeming to them, so he kept them back from the path, and they could see clearly.

39 And Korah and Pharaoh and Hāmān! And certainly Moses came to them with clear arguments, but they behaved haughtily in the land; and they could not outstrip (Us).

40 So each one We punished for his sin. Of them was he on whom We sent a violent storm, and of them was he whom the rumbling overtook, and of them was he whom We caused the earth to swallow, and of them was he whom We drowned. And it was not Allāh, Who wronged them, but they wronged themselves.

41 The parable of those who take guardians besides Allāh is as the parable of the spider that makes for itself a house; and surely the frailest of the houses is the spider's house — if they but knew!

42 Surely Allāh knows whatever they call upon besides Him. And He is the

Mighty, the Wise.

43 And these parables, We set them forth for men, and none understand them but the learned.

44 Allāh created the heavens and the earth with truth. Surely there is a sign in this for the believers.

Part 21
SECTION 5:
The Qur'ān is a Purifier

45 Recite that which has been revealed to thee of the Book and keep up prayer. Surely prayer keeps (one) away from indecency and evil; and certainly the remembrance of Allāh is the greatest (force). And Allāh knows what you do.

46 And argue not with the People of the Book except by what is best, save such of them as act unjustly. But say: We believe in that which has been revealed to us and revealed to you, and our God and your God is One, and to Him we submit.

47 And thus have We revealed the Book to thee. So those whom We have given the Book believe in it, and of these there are those who believe in it; and none deny Our messages except the disbelievers.

48 And thou didst not recite before it any book, nor didst thou transcribe one with thy right hand, for then could the liars have doubted.

49 Nay, it is clear messages in the hearts of those who are granted knowledge. And none deny Our messages except the iniquitous.

50 And they say: Why are not signs sent down upon him from his Lord? Say: Signs are with Allāh only, and I am only a plain warner.

51 Is it not enough for them that We have revealed to thee the Book which is recited to them? Surely there is mercy in this and a reminder for a people who believe.

SECTION 6:
Warning and Consolation

52 Say: Allāh is sufficient as a witness between me and you — He knows what is in the heavens and the earth. And those who believe in falsehood and disbelieve in Allāh, these it is that are the losers.

53 And they ask thee to hasten on the chastisement. And had not a term been appointed, the chastisement would certainly have come to them. And certainly it will come to them all of a sudden, while they perceive not.

54 They ask thee to hasten on the chastisement, and surely hell encompasses the disbelievers—

55 The day when the chastisement will cover them from above them, and from beneath their feet! And He will say: Taste what you did.

56 O My servants who believe, surely My earth is vast, so serve Me only.

57 Every soul must taste of death; then to Us you will be returned.

58 And those who believe and do good, We shall certainly give them an abode in high places in the Garden wherein flow rivers, abiding therein. Excellent the reward of the workers,

59 Who are patient, and on their Lord they rely!

60 And how many a living creature carries not its sustenance! Allāh sustains it and yourselves. And He is the Hearing, the Knowing.

61 And if thou ask them, Who created the heavens and the earth and made the sun and the moon subservient? they would say, Allāh. Whence are they then turned away?

62 Allāh makes abundant the means of subsistence for whom He pleases of His servants, or straitens (them) for him. Surely Allāh is Knower of all things.

63 And if thou ask them, Who is it that sends down water from the clouds, then gives life to the earth with it after its death? they will say, Allāh. Say: Praise be to Allāh! Nay, most of them understand not.

SECTION 7:
Triumph of the Faithful

64 And the life of this world is but a sport and a play. And the home of the Hereafter, that surely is the Life, did they but know!

65 So when they ride in

the ships, they call upon Allāh, being sincerely obedient to Him; but when He brings them safe to the land, lo! they associate others (with Him),

66 That they may be ungrateful for what We have given them, and that they may enjoy. But they shall soon know.

67 See they not that We have made a sacred territory secure, while men are carried off by force from around them? Will they still believe in the falsehood and disbelieve in the favour of Allāh?

68 And who is more iniquitous than one who forges a lie against Allāh, or gives the lie to the Truth, when it has come to him? Is there not an abode in hell for the disbelievers?

69 And those who strive hard for Us, We shall certainly guide them in Our ways. And Allāh is surely with the doers of good.

CHAPTER 30
Al-Rūm: **The Romans**

(REVEALED AT MAKKAH: 6 *sections*; 60 verses)

SECTION 1:
A Great Prophecy

In the name of Allāh, the Beneficent, the Merciful.

1 I, Allāh, am the Best Knower.

2 The Romans are vanquished

3 In a near land, and they, after their defeat, will gain victory

4 Within nine years. Allāh's is the command before and after. And on that day the believers will rejoice

5 In Allāh's help. He helps whom He pleases, and He is the Mighty, the Merciful —

6 (It is) Allāh's promise! Allāh will not fail in His promise, but most people know not.

7 They know the outward of this world's life, but of the Hereafter they are heedless.

8 Do they not reflect within themselves? Allāh did not create the heavens and the earth and what is between them but with truth, and (for) an appointed term. And surely most of the people are deniers of the meeting with their Lord.

9 Have they not travelled in the earth and seen what was the end of those before them? They were stronger than these in prowess, and dug up the earth, and built on it more than these have built. *And their messengers* came to them with clear arguments. So it was not Allāh, Who wronged them, but they wronged themselves.

10 Then evil was the end of those who did evil, because they rejected the messages of Allāh and mocked at them.

SECTION 2: The two Parties

11 Allāh originates the creation, then reproduces it, then to Him you will be returned.

12 And the day when the Hour comes, the guilty will despair.

13 And they will have no intercessors from among their associate-gods, and they will deny their associate-gods.

14 And the day when the Hour comes, that day they will be separated one from the other.

15 Then as to those who believed and did good, they will be made happy in a garden.

16 And as for those who disbelieved and rejected Our messages and the meeting of the Hereafter, they will be *brought to chastisement*.

17 So glory be to Allāh when you enter the evening and when you enter the morning.

18 And to Him be praise in the heavens and the earth, and in the afternoon, and when the sun declines.

19 He brings forth the living from the dead and brings forth the dead from the living, and gives life to the earth after its death. And thus will you be brought forth.

SECTION 3: Manifestations of Divine Power in Nature

20 And of His signs is this, that He created you from dust, then lo! you are mortals (who) scatter.

21 And of His signs is this, that He created mates for you from yourselves that you might find quiet of mind in them, and He put between you love and compassion. Surely there are signs in this for a people who reflect.

22 And of His signs is the creation of the heavens and the earth and the diversity of your tongues and colours. Surely there are signs in this for the learned.

23 And of His signs is your sleep by night and by day and your seeking of His bounty. Surely there are signs in this for a people who would hear.

THE ROMANS

24 And of His signs is this, that He shows you the lightning for fear and for hope, and sends down water from the cloud, then gives life therewith to the earth after its death. Surely there are signs in this for a people who understand.

25 And of His signs is this, that the heaven and the earth subsist by His command. Then when He calls you — from the earth — lo! you come forth.

26 And His is whosoever is in the heavens and the earth. All are obedient to Him.

27 And He it is, Who originates the creation, then reproduces it, and it is very easy to Him. And His is the most exalted state in the heavens and the earth; and He is the Mighty, the Wise.

SECTION 4:
Appeal to Human Nature

28 He sets forth to you a parable relating to yourselves. Have you among those whom your right hands possess partners in that which We have provided you with, so that with respect to it you are alike — you fear them as you fear each other? Thus do We make the messages clear for a people who understand.

29 Nay, those who are unjust follow their low desires without any knowledge; so who can guide him whom Allāh leaves in error? And they shall have no helpers.

30 So set thy face for religion, being upright, the nature made by Allāh in which He has created men. There is no altering Allāh's creation. That is the right religion — but most people know not —

31 Turning to Him; and keep your duty to Him, and keep up prayer and be not of the polytheists,

32 Of those who split up their religion and become parties; every sect rejoicing in that which is with it.

33 And when harm afflicts men, they call upon their Lord, turning to Him, then when He makes them taste of mercy from Him, lo! some of them begin to associate (others) with their Lord,

34 So as to be ungrateful for that which We have given them. So enjoy yourselves a while — you will soon come to know.

35 Or, have We sent to them an authority so that it speaks of that which they associate with Him?

36 And when We make people taste of mercy they rejoice in it, and if an evil befall them for what their hands have already wrought, lo! they despair.

37 See they not that Allāh enlarges provision and straitens (it) for whom He pleases? Certainly there are signs in this for a people who believe.

38 So give to the near of kin his due, and to the needy and the wayfarer. This is best for those who desire Allāh's pleasure, and these it is who are successful.

39 And whatever you lay out at usury, so that it may increase in the property of men, it increases not with Allāh; and whatever you give in charity, desiring Allāh's pleasure — these will get manifold.

40 Allāh is He Who created you, then He sustains you, then He causes you to die, then brings you to life. Is there any of your associate-gods who does aught of it? Glory be to Him, and exalted be He above what they associate (with Him)!

SECTION 5:
A Transformation

41 Corruption has appeared in the land and the sea on account of that which men's hands have wrought, that He may make them taste a part of that which they have done, so that they may return.

42 Say: Travel in the land, then see what was the end of those before! Most of them were polytheists.

43 Then set thyself, being upright, to the right religion before there come from Allāh the day which cannot be averted: on that day they will be separated.

44 Whoever disbelieves will be responsible for his disbelief; and whoever does good, such prepare (good) for their own souls,

45 That He may reward

THE ROMANS

out of His grace those who believe and do good. Surely He loves not the disbelievers.

46 And of His signs is this, that He sends forth the winds bearing good news, and that He may make you taste of His mercy, and that the ships may glide by His command, and that you may seek of His grace, and that you may be grateful.

47 And certainly We sent before thee messengers to their people, so they came to them with clear arguments, then We punished those who were guilty. And to help believers is ever incumbent on Us.

48 Allāh is He Who sends forth the winds, so they raise a cloud, then He spreads it forth in the sky as He pleases, and He breaks it, so that you see the rain coming forth from inside it; then when He causes it to fall upon whom He pleases of His servants, lo! they rejoice —

49 Though they were before this, before it was sent down upon them, in sure despair.

50 Look then at the signs of Allāh's mercy, how He gives life to the earth after its death. Surely He is the Quickener of the dead; and He is Possessor of power over all things.

51 And if We send a wind and they see it yellow, they would after that certainly continue to disbelieve.

52 So surely thou canst not make the dead to hear, nor canst thou make the deaf to hear the call, when they turn back retreating.

53 Nor canst thou guide the blind out of their error. Thou canst make none to hear but those who believe in Our messages, so they submit.

SECTION 6:
Overthrow of Opposition

54 Allāh is He Who created you from a state of weakness, then He gave strength after weakness, then ordained weakness and hoary hair after strength. He creates what He pleases, and He is the Knowing, the Powerful.

55 And the day when the Hour comes, the guilty will

swear: They did not tarry but an hour. Thus are they ever turned away.

56 And those who are given knowledge and faith will say: Certainly you tarried according to the ordinance of Allāh till the day of Resurrection — so this is the day of Resurrection — but you did not know.

57 So that day their excuse will not profit those who were unjust, nor will they be granted goodwill.

58 And certainly We have set forth for men in this Qur'ān every kind of parable. And if thou bring them a sign, those who disbelieve would certainly say: You are naught but deceivers.

59 Thus does Allāh seal the hearts of those who know not.

60 So be patient; surely the promise of Allāh is true; and let not those disquiet thee who have no certainty.

Chapter 31

Luqmān

(Revealed at Makkah: 4 *sections*; 34 *verses*)

SECTION 1:
Believers will be successful

In the name of Allāh, the Beneficent, the Merciful.

1 I, Allāh, am the Best Knower.

2 These are the verses of the Book of Wisdom —

3 A guidance and a mercy for the doers of good,

4 Who keep up prayer and pay the poor-rate and who are certain of the Hereafter.

5 These are on a guidance from their Lord, and these are they who are successful.

6 And of men is he who takes instead frivolous discourse to lead astray from Allāh's path without knowledge, and to make it a mockery. For such is an abasing chastisement.

7 And when Our messages are recited to him, he turns back proudly, as if he had not heard them, as if there were deafness in his ears; so announce to him a painful chastisement.

8 Those who believe and do good, for them are Gardens of bliss,

9 To abide therein. A promise of Allāh in truth! And He is the Mighty, the Wise.

10 He created the heavens without pillars that you see, and cast mountains on the earth lest it should be convulsed with you, and He spread on it animals of every kind. And We send down water from the clouds, then cause to grow therein of every noble kind.

11 This is Allāh's creation; now show Me that which those besides Him have created. Nay, the unjust are in manifest error.

SECTION 2:
Luqmān's Advice to his Son

12 And certainly We gave Luqmān wisdom, saying: Give thanks to Allāh. And whoever is thankful, is thankful for his own soul; and whoever denies, then surely Allāh is Self-Sufficient, Praised.

13 And when Luqmān said to his son, while he admonished him: O my son, ascribe no partner to Allāh. Surely ascribing partners (to Him) is a grievous iniquity.

14 And We have enjoined on man concerning his parents — his mother bears him with faintings upon faintings and his weaning takes two years — saying: Give thanks to Me and to thy parents. To Me is the eventual coming.

15 *And if they strive with thee to make thee associate with Me that of which thou hast no knowledge, obey them not, and keep kindly company with them in this world, and follow the way of him who turns to Me;* then to Me is your return, then I shall inform you of what you did.

16 O my son, even if it be the weight of a grain of mustard-seed, even though it be in a rock, or in the heaven or in the earth, Allāh will bring it forth. Surely Allāh is Knower of subtilities, Aware.

17 O my son, keep up prayer and enjoin good and forbid evil, and bear patiently that which befalls thee. Surely this is an affair of great resolution.

18 And turn not thy face away from people in contempt, nor go about in the land exultingly. Surely Allāh loves not any self-conceited boaster.

19 And pursue the right course in thy going about and lower thy voice. Surely the most hateful of voices is braying of asses.

SECTION 3:
Greatness of Divine Power

20 See you not that Allāh has made subservient to you whatever is in the heavens and whatever is in the earth, and granted to you His favours complete outwardly and inwardly? And among men is he who disputes concerning Allāh without knowledge or guidance or a Book giving light.

21 And when it is said to them, Follow that which Allāh has revealed, they say: Nay, we follow that wherein we found our fathers. What! Though the devil calls them to the chastisement of the burning Fire!

22 And whoever submits himself to Allāh and does good (to others), he indeed takes hold of the firmest handle. And Allāh's is the end of affairs.

23 And whoever disbelieves, let not his disbelief grieve thee. To Us is their return, then We shall inform them of what they did. Surely Allāh is Knower of what they did. Surely Allāh is Knower of what is in the breasts.

24 We give them to enjoy a little, then We shall drive them to a severe chastisement.

25 And if thou ask them who created the heavens and the earth? they will say: Allāh. Say: Praise be to Allāh! Nay, most of them know not.

26 To Allāh belongs whatever is in the heavens and the earth. Surely Allāh is the Self-Sufficient, the Praised.

27 And if all the trees in the earth were pens, and the sea with seven more seas added to it (were ink), the words of Allāh would not be exhausted. Surely Allāh is Mighty, Wise.

28 Your creation or your raising is only like a single soul. Surely Allāh is Hearing, Seeing.

29 Seest thou not that Allāh makes the night to enter into the day, and He makes the day to enter into the night, and He has made the sun and the moon subservient (to you) — each pursues its course till an appointed time — and that Allāh is Aware of what you do?

30 This is because Allāh is the Truth, and that which they call upon besides Him is falsehood, and that Allāh is the High, the Great.

SECTION 4:
The Doom comes

31 Seest thou not that the ships glide on the sea by Allāh's grace, that He may show you of His signs? Surely there are signs in this for every patient endurer, grateful one.

32 And when a wave like awnings covers them, they call upon Allāh, being sincere to Him in obedience. But when He brings them safe to land, some of them follow the middle course. And none denies Our signs but every perfidious, ungrateful one.

33 O people, keep your duty to your Lord and dread the day when no father can avail his son in aught, nor the child will avail his father. Surely the promise of Allāh is true, so let not this world's life deceive you, nor let the arch-deceiver deceive you about Allāh.

34 Surely Allāh is He with Whom is the knowledge of the Hour, and He sends down the rain, and He knows what is in the wombs. And no one knows what he will earn on the morrow. And no one knows in what land he will die. Surely Allāh is Knowing, Aware.

Chapter 32
Al-Sajdah: **The Adoration**

(Revealed at Makkah: 3 *sections*; 30 *verses*)

SECTION 1:
Islām will be established

In the name of Allāh, the Beneficent, the Merciful.

1 I, Allāh, am the Best Knower.

2 The revelation of the Book, there is no doubt in it, is from the Lord of the worlds.

3 Or do they say: He has forged it? Nay, it is the Truth from thy Lord that thou mayest warn a people to whom no warner has come before thee that they may walk aright.

4 Allāh is He Who created the heavens and the earth and what is between them in six periods, and He is established on the Throne of Power. You have not besides Him a guardian or an intercessor. Will you not then mind?

5 He orders the Affair from the heaven to the earth; then it will ascend to Him in a day the measure of which is a thousand years as you count.

6 Such is the Knower of the unseen and the seen, the Mighty, the Merciful,

7 Who made beautiful everything that He created, and He began the creation of man from dust.

8 Then He made his progeny of an extract, of worthless water.

9 Then He made him complete and breathed into him of His spirit, and gave you ears and eyes and hearts; little it is that you give thanks!

10 And they say: When we are lost in the earth, shall we then be in a new creation? Nay, they are disbelievers in the meeting with their Lord.

11 Say: The angel of death, who is given charge

of you, will cause you to die, then to your Lord you will be returned.

SECTION 2:
Believers and Disbelievers — a Comparison

12 And couldst thou but see when the guilty hang their heads before their Lord: Our Lord, we have seen and heard, so send us back, we will do good; we are (now) certain.

13 And if We had pleased, We could have given every soul its guidance, but the word from Me was just: I will certainly fill hell with the jinn and men together.

14 So taste, because you forgot the meeting of this Day of yours; surely We forsake you; and taste the abiding chastisement for what you did.

15 Only they believe in Our messages who, when they are reminded of them, fall down prostrate and celebrate the praise of their Lord, and they are not proud.

16 They forsake (their) beds, calling upon their Lord in fear and in hope, and spend out of what We have given them.

17 So no soul knows what refreshment of the eyes is hidden for them: a reward for what they did.

18 Is he then, who is a believer, like him who is a transgressor? They are not equal.

19 As for those who believe and do good deeds, for them are Gardens, a refuge — an entertainment for what they did.

20 And as for those who transgress, their refuge is the Fire. Whenever they desire to go forth from it, they are brought back into it, and it is said to them: Taste the chastisement of the Fire, which you called a lie.

21 And certainly We will make them taste the nearer punishment before the greater chastisement, that haply they may turn.

22 And who is more iniquitous than he who is reminded of the messages of his Lord, then he turns away from them? Surely

THE ADORATION

We exact retribution from the guilty.

SECTION 3:
Dead Earth will receive Life

23 And We indeed gave Moses the Book — so doubt not the meeting with Him — and We made it a guide for the Children of Israel.

24 And We made from among them leaders to guide by Our command when they were patient. And they were certain of Our messages.

25 Surely thy Lord will judge between them on the day of Resurrection concerning that wherein they differed.

26 Is it not clear to them, how many of the generations, in whose abodes they go about, We destroyed before them? Surely there are signs in this. Will they not then hear?

27 See they not that We drive the water to a land having no herbage, then We bring forth thereby seed-produce, of which their cattle and they themselves eat. Will they not then see?

28 And they say: When will this victory come, if you are truthful?

29 Say: On the day of victory the faith of those who (now) disbelieve will not profit them, nor will they be respited.

30 So turn away from them and wait, surely they too are waiting.

CHAPTER 33
Al-Aḥzāb: **The Allies**

(REVEALED AT MADĪNAH: 9 *sections*; 73 *verses*)

SECTION 1:
Spiritual and Physical Relationship

In the name of Allāh, the Beneficent, the Merciful.

1 O Prophet, keep thy duty to Allāh and obey not the disbelievers and the hypocrites. Surely Allāh is ever Knowing, Wise;

2 And follow that which is revealed to thee from thy Lord. Surely Allāh is ever Aware of what you do;

3 And trust in Allāh. And Allāh is enough as having charge (of affairs).

4 Allāh has not made for any man two hearts within him; nor has He made your *wives whom you desert by* Ẓihār, your mothers, nor has He made those whom you assert (to be your sons) your sons. These are the words of your mouths. And Allāh speaks the truth and He shows the way.

5 Call them by (the names of) their fathers; this is more equitable with Allāh; but if you know not their fathers, then they are your brethren in faith and your friends. And there is no blame on you in that wherein you make a mistake, but (you are answerable for) that which your hearts purpose. And Allāh is ever Forgiving, Merciful.

6 The Prophet is closer to the faithful than their own selves, and his wives are (as) their mothers. And the possessors of relationship are closer one to another in the ordinance of Allāh than (other) believers, and those who fled (their homes), except that you do some good to your friends. This is written in the Book.

7 And when We took a covenant from the prophets and from thee, and from Noah and Abraham and

Moses and Jesus, son of Mary, and We took from them a solemn covenant,

8 That He may question the truthful of their truth, and He has prepared for the disbelievers a painful chastisement.

SECTION 2:
The Allies' Attack on Madīnah

9 O you who believe, call to mind the favour of Allāh to you when there came against you hosts, so We sent against them a strong wind and hosts that you saw not. And Allāh is ever Seer of what you do.

10 When they came upon you from above you and from below you, and when the eyes turned dull and the hearts rose up to the throats, and you began to think diverse thoughts about Allāh.

11 There were the believers tried and they were shaken with a severe shaking.

12 And when the hypocrites and those in whose hearts was a disease began to say: Allāh and His Messenger did not promise us (victory) but only to deceive.

13 And when a party of them said: O people of Yathrib, you cannot make a stand, so go back. And a party of them asked permission of the Prophet, saying, Our houses are exposed. And they were not exposed. They only desired to run away.

14 And if an entry were made upon them from the outlying parts of it, then they were asked to wage war (against the Muslims), they would certainly have done it, and they would not have stayed in it but a little while.

15 And they had indeed made a covenant with Allāh before (that) they would not turn (their) backs. And a covenant with Allāh must be answered for.

16 Say: Flight will not profit you, if you flee from death or slaughter, and then you will not be allowed to enjoy yourselves but a little.

17 Say: Who is it that can protect you from Allāh, if

He intends harm for you or He intends to show you mercy? And they will not find for themselves a guardian or a helper besides Allāh.

18 Allāh indeed knows those among you who hinder others and those who say to their brethren, Come to us. And they come not to the fight but a little,

19 Being niggardly with respect to you. But when fear comes, thou wilt see them looking to thee, their eyes rolling like one swooning because of death. But when fear is gone they smite you with sharp tongues, being covetous of wealth. These have not believed, so Allāh makes their deeds naught. And that is easy for Allāh.

20 They think the allies are not gone, and if the allies should come (again), they would fain be in the deserts with the desert Arabs, asking for news about you. And if they were among you, they would not fight save a little.

SECTION 3:
Allies' Flight: Quraiẓah punished

21 Certainly you have in the Messenger of Allāh an excellent exemplar for him who hopes in Allāh and the Latter day, and remembers Allāh much.

22 And when the believers saw the allies, they said: This is what Allāh and His Messenger promised us, and Allāh and His Messenger spoke the truth. And it only added to their faith and submission.

23 Of the believers are men who are true to the covenant they made with Allāh; so of them is he who has accomplished his vow, and of them is he who yet waits, and they have not changed in the least —

24 That Allāh may reward the truthful for their truth, and chastise the hypocrites, if He please, or turn to them (mercifully). Surely Allāh is ever Forgiving, Merciful.

25 And Allāh turned back the disbelievers in their rage — they gained no advantage. And Allāh sufficed the believers in fighting. And Allāh is ever Strong, Mighty.

26 And He drove down those of the People of the Book who backed them from their fortresses and He cast awe into their hearts; some you killed and you took captive some.

27 And He made you heirs to their land and their dwellings and their property, and (to) a land which you have not yet trodden. And Allāh is ever Possessor of power over all things.

SECTION 4:
Prophet's Domestic Simplicity

28 O Prophet, say to thy wives: If you desire this world's life and its adornment, come, I will give you a provision and allow you to depart a goodly departing.

29 And if you desire Allāh and His Messenger and the abode of the Hereafter, then surely Allāh has prepared for the doers of good among you a mighty reward.

30 O wives of the Prophet, whoever of you is guilty of manifestly improper conduct, the chastisement will be doubled for her. And this is easy for Allāh.

Part 22

31 And whoever of you is obedient to Allāh and His Messenger and does good, We shall give her a double reward, and We have prepared for her an honourable sustenance.

32 O wives of the Prophet, you are not like any other women. If you would keep your duty, be not soft in speech, lest he in whose heart is a disease yearn; and speak a word of goodness.

33 And stay in your houses and display not (your beauty) like the displaying of the ignorance of yore; and keep up prayer, and pay the poor-rate, and obey Allāh and His Messenger. Allāh only desires to take away uncleanness from you, O people of the household, and to purify you a (thorough) purifying.

34 And remember that which is recited in your

houses of the messages of Allāh and the Wisdom. Surely Allāh is ever Knower of subtilities, Aware.

SECTION 5:
Prophet's Marriage with Zainab

35 Surely the men who submit and the women who submit, and the believing men and the believing women, and the obeying men and the obeying women, and the truthful men and the truthful women, and the patient men and the patient women, and the humble men and the humble women, and the charitable men and the charitable women, and the fasting men and the fasting women, and the men who guard their chastity and the women who guard, and the men who remember Allāh much and women who remember — Allāh has prepared for them forgiveness and a mighty reward.

36 And it behoves not a believing man or a believing woman, when Allāh and His Messenger have decided an affair, to exercise a choice in their matter. And whoever disobeys Allāh and His Messenger, he surely strays off to manifest error.

37 And when thou saidst to him to whom Allāh had shown favour and to whom thou hadst shown a favour: Keep thy wife to thyself and keep thy duty to Allāh; and thou concealedst in thy heart what Allāh would bring to light, and thou fearedst men, and Allāh has a greater right that thou shouldst fear Him. So when Zaid dissolved her marriage-tie, We gave her to thee as a wife, so that there should be no difficulty for the believers about the wives of their adopted sons, when they have dissolved their marraige-tie. And Allāh's command is ever performed.

38 There is no harm for the Prophet in that which Allāh has ordained for him. Such has been the way of Allāh with those who have gone before. And the command of Allāh is a decree that is made absolute —

39 Those who deliver the messages of Allāh and fear Him, and fear none but Allāh. And Allāh is

Sufficient to take account.

40 Muḥammad is not the father of any of your men, but he is the Messenger of Allāh and the Seal of the prophets. And Allāh is ever Knower of all things.

SECTION 6:
The Prophet's Marriages

41 O you who believe, remember Allāh with much remembrance,

42 And glorify Him morning and evening.

43 He it is Who sends blessings on you, and (so do) His angels, that He may bring you forth out of darkness into light. And He is ever Merciful to the believers.

44 Their salutation on the day they meet Him will be, Peace! and He has prepared for them an honourable reward.

45 O Prophet, surely We have sent thee as a witness, and a bearer of good news and a warner,

46 And as an inviter to Allāh by His permission, and as a light-giving sun,

47 And give the believers the good news that they will *have great grace from Allāh.*

48 And obey not the disbelievers and the hypocrites, and disregard their annoying talk, and rely on Allāh. and Allāh is enough as having charge (of affairs).

49 O you who believe, when you marry believing women, then divorce them before you touch them, you have in their case no term which you should reckon. But make provision for them and set them free in a goodly manner.

50 O Prophet, We have made lawful to thee thy wives whom thou hast given their dowries, and those whom thy right hand possesses, out of those whom Allāh has given thee as prisoners of war, and the daughters of thy paternal uncle and the daughters of thy paternal aunts, and the daughters of thy maternal uncle and the daughters of thy maternal aunts who fled with thee; and a believing woman, if she gives herself to the Prophet, if the Prophet desires to marry her. (It is) especially for thee, not for the believers — We know what We have ordained for them concerning their wives and those whom their right hands possess in order that no blame may attach to thee. And Allāh is ever Forgiving, Merciful.

51 Thou mayest put off whom thou pleasest of them, and take to thee whom thou pleasest. And whom thou desirest of those whom thou hadst separated provisionally, no blame attaches to thee. This is most proper so that their eyes may be cool and they may not grieve, and that they should be pleased, all of them, with what thou givest them. And Allāh knows what is in your hearts. And Allāh is ever Knowing, Forbearing.

52 It is not allowed to thee to take wives after this, nor to change them for other wives, though their beauty be pleasing to thee, except those whom thy right hand possesses. And Allāh is ever Watchful over all things.

SECTION 7:
Rules of Conduct in Domestic Relations

53 O you who believe, enter not the houses of the Prophet unless permission is given to you for a meal, not waiting for its cooking being finished — but when you are invited, enter, and when you have taken food, disperse — not seeking to listen to talk. Surely this gives the Prophet trouble, but he forbears from you, and Allāh forbears not from the truth. And when you ask of them any goods, ask of them from behind a curtain. This is purer for your hearts and their hearts. And it behoves you not to give trouble to the Messenger of Allāh, nor to marry his wives after him ever. Surely this is grievous in the sight of Allāh.

54 If you do a thing openly or do it in secret, then surely Allāh is ever Knower of all things.

55 There is no blame on them in respect of their fathers, nor their sons, nor their brothers, nor their brothers' sons, nor their sisters' sons, nor their own women, nor of what their right hands possess — and (ye women) keep your duty to Allāh. Surely Allāh is ever Witness over all things.

56 Surely Allāh and His angels bless the Prophet. O you who believe, call for blessings on him and salute him with a (becoming) salutation.

57 Surely those who annoy Allāh and His Messenger, Allāh has cursed them in this world and the Hereafter, and He has prepared for them an abasing chastisement.

58 And those who annoy believing men and believing women undeservedly, they bear the guilt of slander and manifest sin.

SECTION 8:
Those who spread Evil Reports

59 O Prophet, tell thy wives and thy daughters and the women of believers to let down upon them their over-garments. This is more proper, so that they may be known, and not be given trouble. And Allāh is ever Forgiving, Merciful.

60 If the hypocrites and those in whose hearts is a disease and the agitators in Madīnah desist not, We shall certainly urge thee on against them, then they shall not be thy neighbours in it but for a little while —

61 Accursed, wherever they are found they will be seized and slain.

62 That was the way of Allāh concerning those who have gone before; and thou wilt find no change in the way of Allāh.

63 Men ask thee about the Hour. Say: The knowledge of it is only with Allāh. And what will make thee comprehend that the Hour may be nigh?

64 Surely Allāh has cursed the disbelievers and prepared for them a burning Fire,

65 To abide therein for a long time; they will find no protector nor helper.

66 On the day when their leaders are turned back into the Fire, they say: O would that we had obeyed Allāh and obeyed the Messenger!

67 And they say: Our

Lord, we only obeyed our leaders and our great men, so they led us astray from the path.

68 Our Lord, give them a double chastisement and curse them with a great curse.

SECTION 9:
An Exhortation to the Faithful

69 O you who believe, be not like those who maligned Moses, but Allāh cleared him of what they said. And he was worthy of regard with Allāh.

70 O you who believe, keep your duty to Allāh and speak straight words:

71 He will put your deeds into a right state for you, and forgive you your sins. And whoever obeys Allāh and His Messenger, he indeed achieves a mighty success.

72 Surely We offered the trust to the heavens and the earth and the mountains, but they refused to be unfaithful to it and feared from it, and man has turned unfaithful to it. Surely he is ever unjust, ignorant —

73 That Allāh may chastise the hypocritical men and the hypocritical women and the polytheistic men and the polytheistic women, and Allāh will turn (mercifully) to the believing men and the believing women. And Allāh is ever Forgiving, Merciful.

CHAPTER 34
Al-Saba': The Saba'
(REVEALED AT MAKKAH: 6 *sections*; 54 *verses*)

SECTION 1:
Judgment is certain

In the name of Allāh, the Beneficent, the Merciful.

1 Praise be to Allāh! Whose is whatsoever is in the heavens and whatsoever is in the earth, and to Him be praise in the Hereafter! And He is the Wise, the Aware.

2 He knows that which goes down into the earth and that which comes out of it, and that which comes down from heaven and that which goes up to it. And He is the Merciful, the Forgiving.

3 And those who disbelieve say: The Hour will never come to us. Say: Yea, by my Lord, the Knower of the unseen! it will certainly come to you. Not an atom's weight escapes Him in the heavens or in the earth, nor is there less than that nor greater, but (all) is in a clear book,

4 That He may reward those who believe and do good. For them is forgiveness and an honourable sustenance.

5 And those who strive hard in opposing Our Messages, for them is a painful chastisement of an evil kind.

6 And those who have been given knowledge see that what is revealed to thee from thy Lord, is the Truth and it guides into the path of the Mighty, the Praised.

7 And those who disbelieve say: Shall we show to you a man who informs you that, when you are scattered the utmost scattering, you will then be in a new creation?

8 Has he forged a lie against Allāh or is there madness in him? Nay, those who believe not in the Hereafter are in torment and in far error.

373

9 See they not what is before them and what is behind them of the heaven and the earth? If We please, We can make them low in the land or bring down upon them a portion of heaven. Surely there is a sign in this for every servant turning (to Allāh).

SECTION 2:
Favours followed by Retribution

10 And certainly We gave David abundance from Us: O mountains, repeat praises with him, and the birds, and We made the iron pliant to him,

11 Saying: Make ample (coats of mail), and assign a time to the making of coats of mail and do ye good. Surely I am Seer of what you do.

12 And (We made) the wind (subservient) to Solomon; it made a month's journey in the morning and a month's journey in the evening; and We made a fountain of molten brass to flow for him. And of the jinn there were those who worked before him by the command of his Lord. And whoever turned aside from Our command from among them, We made him taste of the chastisement of burning.

13 They made for him what he pleased, of synagogues and images, and bowls (large) as watering-troughs and fixed cooking-pots. Give thanks, O people of David! And very few of My servants are grateful.

14 But when We decreed death for him, naught showed them his death but a creature of the earth that ate away his staff. So when it fell down, the jinn saw clearly that, if they had known the unseen, they would not have tarried in humiliating torment.

15 Certainly there was a sign for Saba' in their abode — two gardens on the right and the left. Eat of the sustenance of your Lord and give thanks to Him. A good land and a Forgiving Lord!

16 But they turned aside, so We sent upon them a violent torrent, and in place of their two gardens We gave them two gardens yielding bitter fruit and (growing) tamarisk and a few lote-trees.

17 *With this We requited them because they were ungrateful; and We punish none but the ingrate.*

18 And We made between them and the towns which We had blessed, (other) towns easy to be seen, and We apportioned the journey therein: Travel through them nights and days, secure.

19 But they said: Our Lord, make longer stages between our journeys. And they wronged themselves; so We made them stories and scattered them a total scattering. Surely there are signs in this for every patient, grateful one.

20 And the devil indeed found true his conjecture concerning them, so they follow him, except a party of the believers.

21 And he has no authority over them, but that We may know him who believes in the Hereafter from him who is in doubt concerning it. And thy Lord is the Preserver of all things.

SECTION 3:
A Victory for the Muslims

22 *Say: Call upon those whom you assert besides Allāh; they control not the weight of an atom in the heavens or in the earth, nor have they any partnership in either, nor has He a helper among them.*

23 And intercession avails naught with Him, save of him whom He permits. Until when fear is removed from their hearts, they say: What is it that your Lord said? They say: The Truth. And He is the Most High, the Great.

24 Say: Who gives you sustenance from the heavens and the earth? Say: Allāh. And surely we or you are on a right way or in manifest error.

25 Say: You will not be asked of what we are guilty, nor shall we be asked of what you do.

26 Say: Our Lord will gather us together, then He will judge between us with truth. And He is the Best Judge, the Knower.

27 Say: Show me those

whom you join with Him as associates. By no means (can you)! Nay, He is Allāh, the Mighty, the Wise.

28 And We have not sent thee but as a bearer of good news and as a warner to all mankind, but most men know not.

29 And they say: When will this promise be (fulfilled), if you are truthful?

30 Say: You have the appointment of a day which you cannot postpone by an hour, nor hasten on.

SECTION 4:
The Leaders of Evil

31 And those who disbelieve say: We believe not in this Qur'ān, nor in that which is before it. And if thou couldst see when the wrongdoers *are made to* stand before their Lord, throwing back the blame one to another! Those who were reckoned weak say to those who were proud: Had it not been for you, we would have been believers.

32 Those who were proud say to those who were deemed weak: Did we turn you away from the guidance after it had come to you? Nay, you (yourselves) were guilty.

33 And those who were deemed weak say to those who were proud: Nay, (it was your) planning by night and day when you told us to disbelieve in Allāh and to set up likes with Him. And they will manifest regret when they see the chastisement. And We put shackles on the necks of those who disbelieve. They will not be requited but for what they did.

34 And We never sent a warner to a town but those who led easy lives in it said: We are disbelievers in that with which you are sent.

35 And they say: We have more wealth and children, and we cannot be punished.

36 Say: Surely my Lord amplifies and straitens provision for whom He pleases, but most men know not.

SECTION 5:
Wealth does not stand for Greatness

37 And it is not your wealth, nor your children, that bring you near to Us in rank; but whoever believes and does good, for such is a double reward for what they do, and they are secure in the highest places.

38 And those who strive in opposing Our messages, they will be brought to the chastisement.

39 Say: Surely my Lord amplifies provision for whom He pleases of His servants and straitens (it) for him. And whatsoever you spend, He increases it in reward, and He is the Best of Providers.

40 And on the day when He will gather them all together, then will He say to the angels: Did these worship you?

41 They will say: Glory be to Thee! Thou art our Protecting Friend, not they; nay, they worshipped the jinn; most of them were believers in them.

42 So on that day you will not control profit nor harm for one another. And We will say to those who were iniquitous: Taste the chastisement of the Fire, which you called a lie.

43 And when Our clear messages are recited to them, they say: This is naught but a man who desires to turn you away from that which your fathers worshipped. And they say: This is naught but a forged lie! And those who disbelieve say of the Truth when it comes to them: This is only clear enchantment!

44 And We have not given them any Books which they read, nor did We send to them before thee a warner.

45 And those before them rejected (the truth), and these have not yet attained a tenth of that which We gave them, but they gave the lie to My messengers. How (terrible) was then My disapproval!

SECTION 6:
Truth will prosper

46 Say: I exhort you only to one thing, that you rise

up for Allāh's sake by twos and singly; then ponder! There is no madness in your companion. He is only a warner to you before a severe chastisement.

47 Say: Whatever reward I ask of you, that is only for yourselves. My reward is only with Allāh, and He is a Witness over all things.

48 Say: Surely my Lord casts the Truth, the great Knower of the unseen.

49 Say: The Truth has come, and falsehood neither originates, nor reproduces.

50 Say: If I err, I err only to my own loss; and if I go aright, it is because of what my Lord reveals to me. Surely He is Hearing, Nigh.

51 And couldst thou see when they become terrified, but (then) there will be no escape and they will be seized from a near place;

52 And they will say: We believe in it. And how can they attain (to faith) from a distant place?

53 And they indeed disbelieved in it before, and they utter conjectures with regard to the unseen from a distant place.

54 And a barrier is placed between them and that which they desire, as was done with their partisans before. Surely they are in a disquieting doubt.

CHAPTER 35
Al-Fāṭir: **The Originator**

(REVEALED AT MAKKAH: 5 *sections*; 45 *verses*)

SECTION 1:
Divine Favours

In the name of Allāh, the Beneficent, the Merciful.

1 Praise be to Allāh, the Originator of the heavens and the earth, the Maker of the angels, messengers flying on wings, two, and three, and four. He increases in creation what He pleases. Surely Allāh is Possessor of power over all things.

2 Whatever Allāh grants to men of (His) mercy, there is none to withhold it, and what He withholds, none can grant thereafter. And He is the Mighty, the Wise.

3 O men, call to mind the favour of Allāh to you. Is there any Creator besides Allāh who provides for you from the heaven and the earth? There is no God but He. How are you then turned away?

4 And if they reject thee — truly messengers before thee were rejected. And to Allāh are all affairs returned.

5 O men, surely the promise of Allāh is true, so let not the life of this world deceive you. And let not the arch-deceiver deceive you about Allāh.

6 Surely the devil is your enemy, so take him for an enemy. He only invites his party to be companions of the burning Fire.

7 Those who disbelieve, for them is a severe chastisement. And those who believe and do good, for them is forgiveness and a great reward.

SECTION 2:
Truth will prevail

8 Is he whose evil deed is made fair-seeming to him so that he considers it good? — Now surely Allāh leaves in error whom He pleases and guides aright whom He pleases, so let not thy soul waste in grief for them. Surely Allāh is Knower of what they do.

9 And Allāh is He Who sends the winds, so they raise a cloud, then We drive it on to a dead land, and therewith give life to the earth after its death. Even so is the quickening.

10 Whoever desires might, then to Allāh belongs the might wholly. To Him do ascend the goodly words, and the goodly deed — He exalts it. And those who plan evil — for them is a severe chastisement. And their plan will perish.

11 And Allāh created you from dust, then from the life-germ, then He made you pairs. And no female bears, nor brings forth, except with His knowledge. And no one living long is granted a long life, nor is aught diminished of one's life, but it is all in a book. Surely this is easy to Allāh.

12 And the two seas are not alike: the one sweet, very sweet, pleasant to drink; and the other salt, bitter. Yet from both you eat fresh flesh and bring forth ornaments which you wear. And thou seest the ships cleave through it, that you may seek of His bounty and that you may give thanks.

13 He causes the night to enter in upon the day, and causes the day to enter in upon the night, and He has made subservient the sun and the moon, each one moves to an appointed time. This is Allāh, your Lord; His is the kingdom. And those whom you call upon besides Him own not a straw.

14 If you call on them, they hear not your call; and if they heard, they could not answer you. And on the day of Resurrection they will *deny* your associating them (with Allāh). And none can inform thee like the All-Aware One.

SECTION 3:
A New Generation will be raised

15 O men, it is you that

THE ORIGINATOR

have need of Allāh, and Allāh is the Self-Sufficient, *the Praised One.*

16 If He please, He will remove you and bring a new creation.

17 And this is not hard to Allāh.

18 And no burdened soul can bear another's burden. And if one weighed down by a burden calls another to carry his load, naught of it will be carried, even though he be near of kin. Thou warnest only those who fear their Lord in secret and keep up prayer. And whoever purifies himself, purifies himself only for his own good. And to Allāh is the eventual coming.

19 And the blind and the seeing are not alike,

20 Nor the darkness and the light,

21 Nor the shade and the heat.

22 Neither are the living and the dead alike. Surely Allāh makes whom He pleases hear, and thou canst not make those hear who are in the graves.

23 Thou art naught but a warner.

24 Surely We have sent thee with the Truth as a bearer of good news and a warner. And there is not a people but a warner has gone among them.

25 And if they reject thee, those before them also rejected — their messengers came to them with clear arguments, and with scriptures, and with the illuminating Book.

26 Then I seized those who disbelieved, so how (terrible) was My disapproval!

SECTION 4: The Elect

27 Seest thou not that Allāh sends down water from the clouds, then We bring forth therewith fruits of various hues? And in the mountains are streaks, white and red, of various hues and (others) intensely black.

28 And of men and beasts and cattle there are various colours likewise. Those of His servants only who are possessed of knowledge fear Allāh. Surely Allāh is Mighty, Forgiving.

29 Surely those who

recite the Book of Allāh and keep up prayer and spend out of what We have given them, secretly and openly, hope for a gain which perishes not —

30 That He may pay them back fully their rewards and give them more out of His grace. Surely He is Forgiving, Multiplier of reward.

31 And that which We have revealed to thee of the Book, that is the truth, verifying that which is before it. Surely Allāh is Aware, Seer of His servants.

32 Then We have given the Book as inheritance to those whom We have chosen from among Our servants: so of them is he who wrongs himself, and of them is he who takes a middle course, and of them is he who is foremost in deeds of goodness by Allāh's permission. *That* is the great grace,

33 Gardens of perpetuity, which they enter — they are made to wear therein bracelets of gold and pearls, and their dress therein is silk.

34 And they say: Praise be to Allāh, Who has removed grief from us! Surely our Lord is Forgiving, Multiplier of reward,

35 Who out of His grace has made us alight in a house abiding for ever; therein toil touches us not nor does fatigue afflict us therein.

36 And those who disbelieve, for them is Fire of hell; it is not finished with them so that they should die, nor is chastisement thereof lightened to them. Thus We deal retribution on every ungrateful one.

37 And therein they cry for succour: Our Lord, take us out! we will do good deeds other than those which we used to do! Did We not give you a life long enough, for him to be mindful who would mind? And there came to you the warner. So taste; because for the iniquitous there is no helper.

SECTION 5:
Punishment due to Evil Deeds

38 Surely Allāh is the Knower of the unseen in the

heavens and the earth. *Surely He is Knower of what is in the hearts.

39 He it is Who made you successors in the earth. So whoever disbelieves, his disbelief is against himself. And their disbelief increases the disbelievers with their Lord in naught but hatred; and their disbelief increases the disbelievers in naught but loss.

40 Say: Have you seen your associates which you call upon besides Allāh? Show me what they have created of the earth! Or have they any share in the heavens? Or, have We given them a Book so that they follow a clear argument thereof? Nay, the wrongdoers hold out promises one to another only to deceive.

41 Surely Allāh upholds the heavens and the earth lest they come to naught. And if they come to naught, none can uphold them after Him. Surely He is ever Forebearing, Forgiving.

42 And they swore by Allāh, their strongest oaths, that, if a warner came to them, they would be better guided than any of the nations. But when a warner came to them, it increased them in naught but aversion,

43 Behaving proudly in the land and planning evil. And the evil plan besets none save the authors of it. So they wait for naught but the way of the ancients. But thou wilt find no alteration in the course of Allāh; and thou wilt find no change in the course of Allāh.

44 Have they not travelled in the land and seen what was the end of those before them — and they were stronger than those in power? And Allāh is not such that anything in the heavens or the earth can escape Him. Surely He is ever Knowing, Powerful.

45 And were Allāh to punish men for what they earn, He would not leave on the back of it any creature, but He respites them till an appointed term; so when their doom comes, then surely Allāh is ever Seer of His servants.

Chapter 36
Yā Sīn

(Revealed at Makkah: 5 *sections*; 83 *verses*)

SECTION 1:
Truth of the Qur'ān

In the name of Allāh, the Beneficent, the Merciful.

1 O man,

2 By the Qur'ān, full of wisdom!

3 Surely thou art one of the messengers,

4 On a right way.

5 A revelation of the Mighty, the Merciful,

6 That thou mayest warn a people whose fathers were not warned, so they are heedless.

7 The word has indeed proved true of most of them, so they believe not.

8 Surely We have placed on their necks chains reaching up to the chins, so they have their heads raised aloft.

9 And We have set a barrier before them and a barrier behind them, thus We have covered them, so that they see not.

10 And it is alike to them whether thou warn them or warn them not — they believe not.

11 Thou canst warn him only who follows the Reminder and fears the Beneficent in secret; so give him good news of forgiveness and a generous reward.

12 Surely We give life to the dead, and We write down that which they send before and their footprints, and We record everything in a clear writing.

SECTION 2:
Confirmation of the Truth

13 And set out to them a parable of the people of the town, when apostles came to it.

14 When We sent to them two, they rejected them

YĀ SĪN

both; then We strengthened (them) with a third, so they said: Surely we are sent to you.

15 They said: You are only mortals like ourselves, nor has the Beneficent revealed anything — you only lie.

16 They said: Our Lord knows that we are surely sent to you.

17 And our duty is only a clear deliverance (of the message).

18 They said: Surely we augur evil from you. If you desist not, we will surely stone you, and a painful chastisement from us will certainly afflict you.

19 They said: Your evil fortune is with you. What! If you are reminded! Nay, you are an extravagant people.

20 And from the remote part of the city there came a man running. He said: O my people, follow the apostles.

21 Follow him who asks of you no reward, and they are on the right course.

Part 23

22 And what reason have I that I should not serve Him Who created me and to Whom you will be brought back.

23 Shall I take besides Him gods whose intercession, if the Beneficent should desire to afflict me with harm, will avail me naught, nor can they deliver me?

24 Then I shall surely be in clear error.

25 Surely I believe in your Lord, so hear me.

26 It was said: Enter the Garden. He said: Would that my people knew,

27 How my Lord has forgiven me and made me of the honoured ones!

28 And We sent not down upon his people after him any host from heaven, nor do We ever send.

29 It was naught but a single cry, and lo! they were still.

30 Alas for the servants! Never does a messenger come to them but they mock him.

31 See they not how

many generations We destroyed before them, that they return not to them?

32 And all — surely all — will be brought before Us.

SECTION 3:
Signs of the Truth

33 And a sign to them is the dead earth: We give life to it and bring forth from it grain so they eat of it.

34 And We make therein gardens of date-palms and grapes and We make springs to flow forth therein,

35 That they may eat of the fruit thereof, and their hands made it not. Will they not then give thanks?

36 Glory be to Him Who created pairs of all things, of what the earth grows, and of their kind and of what they know not!

37 And a sign to them is the night: We draw forth from it the day, then lo! they are in darkness;

38 And the sun moves on to its destination. That is the ordinance of the Mighty, the Knower.

39 And the moon, We have ordained for it stages till it becomes again as an old dry palm-branch.

40 Neither is it for the sun to overtake the moon, nor can the night outstrip the day. And all float on in an *orbit*.

41 And a sign to them is that We bear their offspring in the laden ship,

42 And We have created for them the like thereof, whereon they ride.

43 And if We please, We may drown them, then there is no succour for them, nor can they be rescued —

44 But by mercy from Us and for enjoyment till a time.

45 And when it is said to them: Guard against that which is before you and that which is behind you, that mercy may be shown to you.

46 And there comes to them no message of the messages of their Lord but they turn away from it.

47 And when it is said to them: Spend out of that which Allāh has given you, those who disbelieve say to those who believe: Shall we feed him whom, if Allāh please, He could feed? You are in naught but clear error.

48 And they say: When will this promise come to pass, if you are truthful?

49 They await but a single cry, which will overtake them while they contend.

50 So they will not be able to make a bequest, nor will they return to their families.

SECTION 4:
Reward and Punishment

51 And the trumpet is blown, when lo! from their graves they will hasten on to their Lord.

52 They will say: O woe to us! Who has raised us up from our sleeping-place? This is what the Beneficent promised and the messengers told the truth.

53 It is but a single cry, when lo! they are all brought before Us.

54 So this day no soul is wronged in aught; and you are not rewarded aught but for what you did.

55 Surely the owners of the Garden are on that day in a happy occupation.

56 They and their wives are in shades, reclining on raised couches.

57 They have fruits therein, and they have whatever they desire.

58 Peace! A word from a Merciful Lord.

59 And withdraw to-day, O guilty ones!

60 Did I not charge you, O children of Adam, that you serve not the devil? Surely he is your open enemy.

61 And that you serve Me. This is the right way.

62 And certainly he led astray numerous people from among you. Could you not then understand?

63 This is the hell which you were promised.

64 Enter it this day because you disbelieved.

65 That day We shall seal their mouths, and their hands will speak to Us, and their feet will bear witness as to what they earned.

66 And if We pleased, We would put out their eyes, then they would strive to get first to the way, but how should they see?

67 And if We pleased, We would transform them in their place, then they would not be able to go on, or turn back.

SECTION 5:
The Resurrection

68 And whomsoever We cause to live long, We reduce to an abject state in creation. Do they not understand?

69 And We have not taught him poetry, nor is it meet for him. This is naught but a Reminder and a plain Qur'ān,

70 To warn him who would have life, and (that) the word may prove true against the disbelievers.

71 See they not that We have created cattle for them, out of what Our hands have wrought, so they are their masters?

72 And We have subjected them to them, so some of them they ride, and some they eat.

73 And therein they have advantages and drinks. Will they not then give thanks?

74 And they take gods besides Allāh that they may be helped.

75 They are not able to help them, and they are a host brought up before them.

76 So let not their speech grieve thee. Surely We know what they do in secret and what they do openly.

77 Does not man see that We have created him from the small life-germ? Then lo! he is an open disputant.

78 And he strikes out a likeness for Us and forgets his own creation. Says he: Who will give life to the bones, when they are rotten?

79 Say: He will give life to them, Who brought them into existence at first, and He is Knower of all creation,

80 Who produced fire for you out of the green tree, so that with it you kindle.

81 Is not He Who created the heavens and the earth able to create the like of them? Yea! And He is the Creator (of all), the Knower.

82 His command, when He intends anything, is only to say to it, Be, and it is.

83 So glory be to Him in Whose hand is the kingdom of all things! and to Him you will be returned.

CHAPTER 37

Al-Ṣāffāt: Those Ranging in Ranks

(REVEALED AT MAKKAH: 5 *sections*; 182 *verses*)

SECTION 1: Unity will prevail

In the name of Allāh, the Beneficent, the Merciful.

1 By those ranging in ranks,

2 And those who restrain holding in restraint,

3 And those who recite the Reminder,

4 Surely your God is One.

5 The Lord of the heavens and the earth and what is between them, and the Lord of the eastern lands.

6 Surely We have adorned the lower heaven with an adornment, the stars,

7 And (there is) a safeguard against every rebellious devil.

8 They cannot listen to the exalted assembly and they are reproached from every side,

9 Driven off; and for them is a perpetual chastisement,

10 Except him who snatches away but once, then there follows him a brightly shining flame.

11 So ask them whether they are stronger in creation or those (others) whom We have created. Surely We created them of firm clay.

12 Nay, thou wonderest, while they mock,

13 And when they are reminded, they mind not,

14 And when they see a sign, they seek to scoff.

15 And say: This is nothing but clear enchantment.

16 When we are dead and *have* become dust and bones, shall we then be raised,

17 Or our fathers of yore?

18 Say: Yea, and you will be humiliated.

19 So it will be but one

THOSE RANGING IN RANKS

cry, when lo! they will see.

20 And they will say: O woe to us! This is the day of Requital.

21 This is the day of Judgment, which you called a lie.

SECTION 2:
The Judgment

22 Gather together those who did wrong and their associates, and what they worshipped

23 Besides Allāh, then lead them to the way to hell.

24 And stop them, for they shall be questioned:

25 What is the matter with you that you help not one another?

26 Nay, on that day they will be submissive.

27 And some of them will turn to others mutually questioning —

28 Saying: Surely you used to come to us from the right side.

29 They will say: Nay, you (yourselves) were not believers.

30 And we had no authority over you, but you were an inordinate people.

31 So the word of our Lord has proved true against us: we shall surely taste.

32 We led you astray, for we ourselves were erring.

33 So, that day they will be sharers in the chastisement.

34 Thus do We deal with the guilty.

35 They indeed were arrogant, when it was said to them: There is no god but Allāh;

36 And said: Shall we give up our gods for a mad poet?

37 Nay, he has brought the Truth and verifies the messengers.

38 Surely you will taste the painful chastisement.

39 And you are requited naught but for what you did —

40 Save the servants of Allāh, the purified ones.

41 For them is a known sustenance:

42 Fruits. And they are honoured,

43 In Gardens of delight,

44 On thrones, facing each other.

45 A bowl of running water will be made to go round them,

46 White, delicious to those who drink.

47 It deprives not of reason, nor are they exhausted therewith.

48 And with them are those modest in gaze, having beautiful eyes,

49 As if they were eggs, carefully protected.

50 Then some of them will turn to others, questioning mutually.

51 A speaker of them will say: Surely I had a comrade,

52 Who said: Art thou indeed of those who accept?

53 When we are dead and *have become dust and* bones, shall we then be requited?

54 He will say: Will you look?

55 Then he looked down and saw him in the midst of hell.

56 He will say: By Allāh! thou hadst almost caused me to perish;

57 And had it not been for the favour of my Lord, I should have been among those brought up.

58 Are we not to die,

59 Except our previous death? And are we not to be chastised?

60 Surely this is the mighty achievement.

61 For the like of this, then, let the workers work.

62 Is this the better entertainment or the tree of Zaqqūm?

63 Surely We have made it a trial for the wrongdoers.

64 It is a tree that grows in the bottom of hell —

65 Its produce is as it were the heads of serpents.

66 Then truly they will eat of it and fill (their) bellies with it.

67 Then surely they shall have after it a drink of boiling water.

68 Then their return is surely to the flaming Fire.

69 They indeed found their fathers astray,

70 So in their footsteps

THOSE RANGING IN RANKS

they are hastening on.

71 And most of the ancients surely went astray before them,

72 And indeed We sent among them warners.

73 Then see what was the end of those warned —

74 Except the servants of Allāh, the purified ones.

SECTION 3:
Noah and Abraham

75 And Noah certainly called upon Us, and excellent Answerer of prayers are We!

76 And We delivered him and his people from the great distress;

77 And made his offspring the survivors,

78 And left for him (praise) among the later generations,

79 Peace be to Noah among the nations!

80 Thus indeed do We reward the doers of good.

81 Surely he was of Our believing servants.

82 Then We drowned the others.

83 And surely of his party was Abraham.

84 When he came to his Lord with a secure heart,

85 When he said to his sire and his people: What is it that you worship?

86 A lie — gods besides Allāh do you desire?

87 What is then your idea about the Lord of the worlds?

88 Then he glanced a glance at the stars,

89 And said: Surely I am sick (of your deities).

90 So they turned their backs on him, going away.

91 Then he turned to their gods and said: Do you not eat?

92 What is the matter with you that you speak not?

93 So he turned upon them, smiting with the right hand.

94 Then they came to him, hastening.

95 He said: Do you worship that which you hew out?

96 And Allāh has created you and what you make.

97 They said: Build for

him a building, then cast him into the flaming fire.

98 And they designed a plan against him, but We brought them low.

99 And he said: Surely I flee to my Lord — He will guide me.

100 My Lord, grant me a doer of good deeds.

101 So We gave him the good news of a forbearing son.

102 But when he became of age to work with him, he said: O my son, I have seen in a dream that I should sacrifice thee: so consider what thou seest. He said: O my father, do as thou art commanded: if Allāh please, thou wilt find me patient.

103 So when they both submitted and he had thrown him down upon his *forehead*,

104 And We called out to him saying, O Abraham,

105 Thou hast indeed fulfilled the vision. Thus do We reward the doers of good.

106 Surely this is a manifest trial.

107 And We ransomed him with a great sacrifice.

108 And We granted him among the later generations (the salutation),

109 Peace be to Abraham!

110 Thus do We reward the doers of good.

111 Surely he was one of Our believing servants.

112 And We gave him the good news of Isaac, a prophet, a righteous one.

113 And We blessed him and Isaac. And of their offspring some are doers of good, but some are clearly unjust to themselves.

SECTION 4:
Moses, Aaron, Elias and Lot

114 And certainly We conferred a favour on Moses and Aaron.

115 And We delivered them, and their people from the mighty distress.

116 And We helped them, so they were the vanquishers.

117 And We gave them both the clear Book.

118 And We guided them on the right way.

119 And We granted them among the later generations (the salutation),

120 Peace be to Moses and Aaron!

121 Thus do We reward the doers of good.

122 Surely they were both of Our believing servants.

123 And Elias was surely of those sent.

124 When he said to his people: Will you not guard against evil?

125 Do you call upon Ba'l and forsake the Best of the creators,

126 Allāh, your Lord and the Lord of your fathers of yore?

127 But they rejected him, so they shall be brought up,

128 But not the servants of Allāh, the purified ones.

129 And We granted him among the later generations (the salutation),

130 Peace be to Elias!

131 Even thus We reward the doers of good.

132 Surely he was one of Our believing servants.

133 And Lot was surely of those sent.

134 When We delivered him and his people, all —

135 Except an old woman among those who remained behind.

136 Then We destroyed the others.

137 And surely you pass by them in the morning,

138 And at night. Do you not then understand?

SECTION 5:
Jonah and the Prophet's Triumph

139 And Jonah was surely of those sent.

140 When he fled to the laden ship,

141 So he shared with others but was of those cast away.

142 So the fish took him into its mouth while he was blameable.

143 But had he not been of those who glorify (Us),

144 He would have tarried in its belly till the day when they are raised.

145 Then We cast him on the naked shore, while he was sick.

146 And We caused a gourd to grow up for him.

147 And We sent him to a hundred thousand or more.

148 And they believed, so We gave them provision till a time.

149 Now ask them whether thy Lord has daughters and they have sons?

150 Or did We create the angels females, while they witnessed?

151 Now surely it is of their own lie that they say:

152 Allāh has begotten. And truly they are liars.

153 Has He preferred daughters to sons?

154 What is the matter with you? How you judge!

155 Will you not then mind?

156 Or have you a clear authority?

157 Then bring your Book, if you are truthful.

158 And they assert a relationship between Him and the jinn. And certainly the jinn know that they will be brought up (for judgment)—

159 Glory be to Allāh from what they describe!—

160 But not so the servants of Allāh, the purified ones.

161 So surely you and that which you serve,

162 Not against Him can you cause (any) to fall into trial,

163 Save him who will burn in the flaming Fire.

164 And there is none of us but has an assigned place,

165 And verily we are ranged in ranks,

166 And we truly glorify (Him).

167 And surely they used to say:

168 Had we a reminder from those of yore,

169 We would have been sincere servants of Allāh.

170 But (now) they disbelieve in it, so they will come

to know.

171 And certainly Our word has already gone forth to Our servants, to those sent,

172 That they, surely they, will be helped,

173 And Our hosts, surely they, will be triumphant.

174 So turn away from them till a time,

175 And watch them, they too will see.

176 Would they hasten on Our chastisement?

177 So when it descends in their court, evil will be the morning of the warned ones.

178 And turn away from *them till a time,*

179 And watch, for they too will see.

180 Glory be to thy Lord, the Lord of Might, above what they describe!

181 And peace be to those sent!

182 And praise be to Allāh, the Lord of the worlds!

Chapter 38
Ṣād

(Revealed at Makkah: 5 *sections*; 88 *verses*)

SECTION 1: The Enemy's Discomfiture

In the name of Allāh, the Beneficent, the Merciful.

1 Truthful God! By the Qur'ān, possessing eminence!

2 Nay, those who disbelieve are in self-exaltation and opposition.

3 How many a generation We destroyed before them, then they cried when there was no longer time for escape!

4 And they wonder that a warner from among themselves has come to them, and the disbelievers say: This is an enchanter, a liar.

5 Makes he the gods a single God? Surely this is a strange thing.

6 And the chiefs among them say: Go and steadily adhere to your gods: surely this is a thing intended.

7 We never heard of this in the former faith: this is nothing but a forgery.

8 Has the Reminder been revealed to him from among us? Nay, they are in doubt as to My Reminder. Nay, they have not yet tasted My chastisement.

9 Or, have they the treasures of the mercy of thy Lord, the Mighty, the Great Giver?

10 Or is the kingdom of the heavens and the earth and what is between them theirs? Then let them rise higher in means.

11 What an army of the allies is here put to flight!

12 The people of Noah, and 'Ād, and Pharaoh, the lord of hosts, rejected (prophets) before them,

13 And Thamūd and the people of Lot and the dwellers of the grove. These were the parties (opposing Truth).

ṢĀD

14 Not one of them but rejected the messengers, so just was My retribution.

SECTION 2:
David's Enemies

15 And these wait but for one cry, wherein there is no delay.

16 And they say: Our Lord, hasten on for us our portion before the day of Reckoning.

17 Bear patiently what they say, and remember Our servant David, the possessor of power. He ever turned (to Allāh).

18 Truly We made the mountains subject to him, glorifying (Allāh) at nightfall and sunrise,

19 And the birds gathered together. All were obedient to him.

20 And We strengthened his kingdom and We gave him wisdom and a clear judgment.

21 And has the story of the adversaries come to thee? When they made an entry into the private chamber by climbing the wall —

22 When they came upon David so he was afraid of them. They said: Fear not; two litigants, of whom one has wronged the other, so decide between us with justice, and act not unjustly, and guide us to the right way.

23 This is my brother. He has ninety-nine ewes and I have a single ewe. Then he said, Make it over to me, and he has prevailed against me in dispute.

24 He said: Surely he has wronged thee in demanding thy ewe (to add) to his own ewes. And surely many partners wrong one another save those who believe and do good, and very few are they! And David knew that We had tried him, so he asked his Lord for protection, and he fell down bowing and turned (to God).

25 So We gave him this protection, and he had a nearness to Us and an excellent resort.

26 O David, surely We have made thee a ruler in the land; so judge between men justly and follow not desire, lest it lead thee astray from the path of Allāh. Those who go astray from the path of Allāh, for them is surely a severe chastisement because they forgot the day of Reckoning.

SECTION 3:
Solomon and his Enemies

27 And We created not the heaven and the earth and what is between them *in vain*. That is the opinion of those who disbelieve. So woe to those who disbelieve on account of the Fire!

28 Shall We treat those who believe and do good like the mischief-makers in the earth? Or shall We make the dutiful like the wicked?

29 (This is) a Book that We have revealed to thee abounding in good, that they may ponder over its verses, and that the men of understanding may mind.

30 And We gave to David Solomon. Most excellent the servant! Surely he ever turned (to Allāh).

31 When well-bred, swift (horses) were brought to him at evening —

32 So he said, I love the good things on account of the remembrance of my Lord — until they were hidden behind the veil.

33 (He said): Bring them back to me. So he began to stroke (their) legs and necks.

34 And certainly We tried Solomon, and We put on *his* throne a (mere) body, so he turned (to Allāh).

35 He said: My Lord, forgive me and grant me a kingdom which is not fit for anyone after me; surely Thou art the Great Giver.

36 So We made the wind subservient to him, running gently by His command wherever he desired,

37 And the devils, every builder and diver,

38 And others fettered in chains.

39 This is Our free gift, so give freely or withhold, *without reckoning*.

40 And surely he had a nearness to Us and an excellent resort.

SECTION 4: Job —
Triumph of the Righteous

41 And remember Our servant Job. When he cried

to his Lord: The devil has afflicted me with toil and torment.

42 Urge with thy foot; here is a cool washing-place and a drink.

43 And We gave him his people and the like of them with them, a mercy from Us, and a reminder for men of understanding.

44 And take in thy hand few worldly goods and earn goodness therewith and incline not to falsehood. Surely We found him patient; most excellent the servant! Surely he (ever) turned (to Us).

45 And remember Our servants Abraham and Isaac and Jacob, men of power and insight.

46 We indeed purified them by a pure quality, the keeping in mind of the (final) abode.

47 And surely they were with Us, of the elect, the best.

48 And remember Ishmael and Elisha and Dhu-l-Kifl; and they were all of the best.

49 This is a reminder. And surely there is an excellent resort for the dutiful:

50 Gardens of perpetuity — the doors are opened for them.

51 Reclining therein, calling therein for many fruits and drink.

52 And with them are those modest in gaze, equals in age.

53 This is what you are promised for the day of Reckoning.

54 Surely this is Our sustenance; it will never come to an end —

55 This (is for the good)! And surely there is an evil resort for the inordinate —

56 Hell. They will enter it. So evil is the resting-place.

57 This — so let them taste it, boiling and intensely cold (drink),

58 And other similar (punishment), of various sorts.

59 This is an army rushing headlong with you — no welcome for them! Surely they will burn in fire.

60 They say: Nay! you — no welcome to you! You

prepared it for us, so evil is the resting-place.

61 They say: Our Lord, whoever prepared it for us, give him more, a double, punishment in the Fire.

62 And they say: What is the matter with us? — we see not men whom we used to count among the vicious.

63 Did we (only) take them in scorn, or do our eyes miss them?

64 That surely is the truth — the contending one with another of the inmates of the Fire.

SECTION 5:
Opposition to Prophets

65 Say: I am only a warner; and there is no God but Allāh, the One, the Subduer (of all) —

66 The Lord of the heavens and the earth and what *is between* them, the Mighty, the Forgiving.

67 Say: It is a message of importance,

68 From which you turn away.

69 I have no knowledge of the exalted chiefs when they contend.

70 Only this is revealed to me that I am a plain warner.

71 When thy Lord said to the angels: Surely I am going to create a mortal from dust.

72 So when I have made him complete and breathed into him of My spirit, fall down submitting to him.

73 And the angels submitted, all of them,

74 But not Iblīs. He was proud and he was one of the disbelievers.

75 He said: O Iblīs, what prevented thee from submitting to him whom I created with both My hands? Art thou proud or art thou of the exalted ones?

76 He said: I am better than he; Thou hast created me of fire, and him Thou didst create of dust.

77 He said: Go forth from hence! surely thou art driven away;

78 And surely My curse is on thee to the day of Judgment.

79 He said: My Lord, respite me to the day that they are raised.

80 He said: Surely thou

art of the respited ones.

81 Till the day of the time made known.

82 He said: Then, by Thy Might! I will surely lead them all astray,

83 Except Thy servants from among them, the purified ones.

84 He said: The Truth is, and the truth I speak —

85 That I shall fill hell with thee and with all those among them who follow thee.

86 Say: I ask you no reward for it; nor am I of the impostors.

87 It is naught but a Reminder to the nations.

88 And certainly you will come to know about it after a time.

CHAPTER 39
Al-Zumar: **The Companies**

(REVEALED AT MAKKAH: 8 *sections*; 75 *verses*)

SECTION 1:
Obedience to Allāh

In the name of Allāh, the Beneficent, the Merciful.

1 The revelation of the Book is from Allāh, the Mighty, the Wise.

2 Surely We have revealed to thee the Book with truth, so serve Allāh, being sincere to Him in obedience.

3 Now surely sincere obedience is due to Allāh (alone). And those who choose protectors besides Him (say): We serve them only that they may bring us nearer to Allāh. Surely Allāh will judge between them in that in which they differ. Surely Allāh guides not him who is a liar, ungrateful.

4 If Allāh desired to take a son to Himself, He could have chosen those He pleased out of those whom He has created — Glory be to Him! He is Allāh, the One, the Subduer (of all).

5 He has created the heavens and the earth with truth; He makes the night cover the day and makes the day overtake the night, and He has made the sun and the moon subservient; each one moves on to an assigned term. Now surely He is the Mighty, the Forgiver.

6 He created you from a single being, then made its mate of the same (kind). And He sent down for you eight of the cattle in pairs. He creates you in the wombs of your mothers — creation after creation — in triple darkness. That is Allāh, your Lord; His is the kingdom. There is no God but He. How are you then turned away?

7 If you are ungrateful, then surely Allāh is above need of you. And He likes not ungratefulness in His servants. And if you are grateful, He likes it for you. And no bearer of a burden will bear another's burden. Then to your Lord is your return, then will He inform you of what you did. Surely He is Knower of what is in the breasts.

8 And when distress afflicts a man he calls upon his Lord, turning to Him; then when He grants him a favour from Him, he forgets that for which he called upon Him before, and sets up rivals to Allāh that he may cause (men) to stray from His path. Say: Enjoy thine ungratefulness for a little, surely thou art of the companions of the Fire.

9 Is he who is obedient during hours of the night, prostrating himself and standing, taking care of the Hereafter and hoping for the mercy of his Lord—? Say: Are those who know and those who know not alike? Only men of understanding mind.

SECTION 2: Believers and Disbelievers

10 Say: O My servants who believe, keep your duty to your Lord. For those who do good in this world is good, and Allāh's earth is spacious. Truly the steadfast will be paid their reward without measure.

11 Say: I am commanded to serve Allāh, being sincere to Him in obedience,

12 And I am commanded to be the first of those who submit.

13 Say: I fear, if I disobey my Lord, the chastisement of a grevious day.

14 Say: Allāh I serve, being sincere to Him in my obedience.

15 Serve then what you will besides Him. Say: The losers surely are those who lose themselves and their people on the day of Resurrection. Now surely that is the manifest loss!

16 They shall have coverings of fire above them and coverings beneath them. With that Allāh makes His servants to fear; so keep your duty to Me, O My servants.

17 And those who eschew the worship of the idols and turn to Allāh, for them is good news. So give good news to My servants,

18 Who listen to the Word, then follow the best of it. Such are they whom Allāh has guided, and such are the men of understanding.

19 He against whom the sentence of chastisement is due — canst thou save *him* who is in the Fire?

20 But those who keep their duty to their Lord, for them are high places, above them higher places, built (for them), wherein rivers flow. (It is) the promise of Allāh. Allāh fails not in (His) promise.

21 Seest thou not that Allāh sends down water from the clouds, then makes it go down into the earth in springs, then brings forth therewith herbage of various hues; then it withers *so that thou seest it turn yellow*, then He makes it chaff? Surely there is a reminder in this for men of understanding.

SECTION 3:
A Perfect Guidance

22 Is he whose breast Allāh has opened to Islām so that he follows a light from his Lord—? So woe to those whose hearts are hardened against the remembrance of Allāh! Such are in clear error.

23 Allāh has revealed the best announcement, a Book consistent, repeating (its injunctions), whereat do shudder the skins of those who fear their Lord, then their skins and their hearts soften to Allāh's remembrance. This is Allāh's guidance — He guides with it whom Hepleases. And he whom Allāh leaves in error, there is no guide for him.

24 Is then he who has to guard himself with his own person against the evil chastisement of the Resurrection day—? And it will be said to the iniquitous: Taste what you earned.

25 Those before them denied, so the chastisement came to them from whence they perceived not.

26 So Allāh made them taste disgrace in this world's life, and certainly the chastisement of the Hereafter is greater. Did they but know!

27 And certainly We have set forth for men in this Qur'ān similitudes of every sort that they may mind.

28 An Arabic Qur'ān without any crookedness, that they may guard against evil.

29 Allāh sets forth a parable: A man belonging to partners differing with one another, and a man (devoted) wholly to one man. Are the two alike in condition? Praise be to Allāh! Nay, most of them know not.

30 Surely thou wilt die and they (too) will die;

31 Then surely on the day of Resurrection you will contend one with another before your Lord.

Part 24

SECTION 4: Rejectors will be Abased

32 Who is then more unjust than he who utters a lie against Allāh and denies the truth, when it comes to him? Is there not in hell an abode for the disbelievers?

33 And he who brings the truth and accepts the truth — such are the dutiful.

34 They shall have with their Lord what they please. *Such is the reward of the doers of good* —

35 That Allāh may ward off from them the worst of what they did, and give them their reward for the best of what they did.

36 Is not Allāh sufficient for His servant? And they seek to frighten thee with those besides Him. And whomsoever Allāh leaves in error, there is no guide for him.

37 And whom Allāh guides, there is none that can lead him astray. Is not Allāh Mighty, the Lord of retribution?

38 And if thou ask them, Who created the heavens and the earth? They will say: Allāh. Say: See you then that those you call upon besides Allāh, would they, if Allāh desire to afflict me with harm, remove His harm? Or if He desire to show me mercy, could they withhold His mercy? Say: Allāh is sufficient for me. On Him do the reliant rely.

39 Say: O people, work in

your place. Surely I am a worker, so you will come to know,

40 Who it is to whom there comes a chastisement abasing him, and on whom falls a lasting chastisement.

41 Surely We have revealed to thee the Book with truth for (the good of) men. So whoever follows the right way, it is for his own soul, and whoever errs, he errs only to its detriment. And thou art not a custodian over them.

SECTION 5:
Punishment cannot be Averted

42 Allāh takes (men's) souls at the time of their death, and those that die not, during their sleep. Then He withholds those on whom He has passed the decree of death and sends *the others back* till an appointed term. Surely there are signs in this for a people who reflect.

43 Or, take they intercessors besides Allāh? Say: What! Even though they control naught, nor do they understand.

44 Say: Allāh's is the intercession altogether. His is the kingdom of the heavens and the earth. Then to Him you will be returned.

45 And when Allāh alone is mentioned, the hearts of those who believe not in the Hereafter shrink, and when those besides Him are mentioned, lo! they are joyful.

46 Say: O Allāh, Originator of the heavens and the earth, Knower of the unseen and the seen, Thou judgest between Thy servants as to that wherein they differ.

47 And had those who do wrong all that is in the earth and the like of it with it, they would certainly offer it as ransom from the evil of the chastisement on the day of Resurrection. And what they never thought of shall become plain to them from Allāh.

48 And the evil of what they wrought will become plain to them, and that which they mocked at will beset them.

49 So when harm afflicts a man he calls upon Us; then, when We give him a boon from Us, he says: I have been given it only by means of knowledge. Nay, it is a trial, but most of them know not.

50 Those before them did say it indeed, but what they earned availed them not.

51 So there befell them the evil which they had earned. And those who are unjust from among these, there shall befall them the evil which they earn, and they shall not escape.

52 Know they not that Allāh gives ample subsistence to whom He pleases, and He straitens; surely there are signs in this for a people who believe.

SECTION 6:
Divine Mercy

53 Say: O My servants who have been prodigal regarding their souls, despair not of the mercy of Allāh; surely Allāh forgives sins altogether. He is indeed the Forgiving, the Merciful.

54 And turn to your Lord and submit to Him before chastisement comes to you, then you will not be helped.

55 And follow the best that has been revealed to *you from your Lord before* chastisement comes to you all of a sudden, while you perceive not —

56 Lest a soul should say: O woe is me, that I fell short of my duty to Allāh! and surely I was of those who laughed to scorn;

57 Or it should say: Had Allāh guided me, I should have been dutiful.

58 Or it should say, when it sees the chastisement: Had I another chance I should be a doer of good.

59 Aye! My messages came to thee, but thou didst reject them, and wast proud and wast of the disbelievers.

60 And on the day of Resurrection thou wilt see those who lied against Allāh, their faces will be blackened. Is there not in hell an abode for the proud?

61 And Allāh delivers those who keep their duty with their achievement — evil touches them not, nor do they grieve.

62 Allāh is the Creator of all things and He has charge over everything.

63 His are the treasures of the heavens and the earth. And those who disbelieve in the messages of Allāh, such are the losers.

SECTION 7:
The Final Judgment

64 Say: Do you bid me serve others than Allāh, O ye ignorant ones?

65 And certainly, it has been revealed to thee and to those before thee: If thou associate (with Allāh), thy work would certainly come to naught and thou wouldst be a loser.

66 Nay, but serve Allāh alone and be of the thankful.

67 And they honour not Allāh with the honour due to Him; and the whole earth will be in His grip on the day of Resurrection and the heavens rolled up in His right hand. Glory be to Him! and highly exalted is He above what they associate (with Him).

68 And the trumpet is blown, so all those in the heavens and all those in the earth will swoon, except such as Allāh please. Then it will be blown again, when lo! they stand up, awaiting.

69 And the earth beams with the light of its Lord, and the Book is laid down, and the prophets and the witnesses are brought up, and judgment is given between them with justice, and they are not wronged.

70 And every soul is paid back fully for what it did, and He knows best what they do.

SECTION 8:
Each Party meets with its Desert

71 And those who disbelieve are driven to hell in companies; until, when they come to it, its doors are opened, and the keepers of it say to them: Did not there come to you messengers from among you reciting to you the messages of your Lord and warning you of the meeting of this day of yours? They say: Yea. But the word of punishment proved true against the disbelievers.

72 It is said: Enter the gates of hell to abide therein; so evil is the abode of the proud.

73 And those who keep their duty to their Lord are conveyed to the Garden in companies until when they come to it, and its doors are opened and the keepers of it say to them: Peace be to you! you led pure lives; so enter it to abide.

74 And they say: Praise be to Allāh! Who has made good to us His promise, and He has made us inherit the land; we abide in the Garden where we please. So goodly is the reward of the workers.

75 And thou seest the angels going round about the Throne of Power, glorifying their Lord with praise. And they are judged with justice, and it is said: Praise be to Allāh, the Lord of the worlds!

CHAPTER 40
Al-Mu'min: **The Believer**

(REVEALED AT MAKKAH: 9 *sections*; 85 *verses*)

SECTION 1:
Protection of the Faithful

In the name of Allāh, the Beneficent, the Merciful.

1 Beneficent God!

2 The revelation of the Book is from Allāh, the Mighty, the Knowing,

3 Forgiver of sin and Acceptor of repentence, Severe to punish, Lord of bounty. There is no God but He; to Him is the eventual coming.

4 None dispute concerning the messages of Allāh but those who disbelieve, so let not their control in the land deceive thee.

5 Before them the people of Noah and the parties after them rejected (prophets), and every nation purposed against its messenger to destroy him, and disputed by means of falsehood to render null thereby the truth, so I seized them; how (terrible) was then My retribution!

6 And thus did the word of thy Lord prove true against those who disbelieve that they are the companions of the Fire.

7 Those who bear the Throne of Power and those around it celebrate the praise of their Lord and believe in Him and ask protection for those who believe: Our Lord, Thou embracest all things in mercy and knowledge, so protect those who turn (to Thee) and follow Thy way, and save them from the chastisement of hell.

8 Our Lord, make them enter the Gardens of perpetuity, which Thou hast promised them and such of their fathers and their wives and their offspring as are good. Surely Thou art the Mighty, the Wise.

9 And guard them from

evil, and whom Thou guardest from evil this day, Thou hast indeed mercy on him. And that is the mighty achievement.

SECTION 2:
Failure of Opponents

10 Those who disbelieve are told: Certainly Allāh's hatred (of you), when you were called upon to the faith and you rejected, was much greater than your hatred (now) of yourselves.

11 They say: Our Lord, twice hast Thou made us die, and twice hast Thou given us life; so we confess our sins. Is there then a way of escape?

12 That is because when Allāh alone was called upon, you disbelieved, and when associates were given to Him, you believed. So judgment belongs to Allāh, the High, the Great.

13 He it is Who shows you His signs and sends down for you sustenance from heaven, and none minds but he who turns (to Him).

14 So call upon Allāh, being sincere to Him in obedience, though the disbelievers are averse —

15 Exalter of degrees, Lord of the Throne of Power, He makes the spirit to light by His command upon whom He pleases of His servants, that he may warn (men) of the day of Meeting —

16 The day when they come forth. Nothing concerning them remains hidden from Allāh. To whom belongs the kingdom this day? To Allāh, the One, the Subduer (of all).

17 This day every soul is rewarded what it has earned. No injustice this day! Surely Allāh is Swift *in Reckoning*.

18 And warn them of the day that draws near, when hearts, grieving inwardly, rise up to the throats. The iniquitous will have no friend, nor any intercessor who should be obeyed.

19 He knows the dishonesty of eyes and that which the breasts conceal.

20 And Allāh judges with truth. And those whom they call upon besides Him judge naught! Surely Allāh is the Hearing, the Seeing.

SECTION 3:
A Warning in Moses' History

21 Have they not travelled in the land and seen what was the end of those *who were before them?* Mightier than these were they in strength and in fortifications in the land, but Allāh destroyed them for their sins. And they had none to protect them from Allāh.

22 That was because there came to them their messengers with clear arguments, but they disbelieved, so Allāh destroyed them. Surely He is Strong, Severe in Retribution.

23 And certainly We sent Moses with Our messages and clear authority,

24 To Pharaoh and Hāmān and Korah, but they said: A lying enchanter!

25 So when he brought to them the Truth from Us, they said: Slay the sons of those who believe with him and keep their women alive. And the plot of the disbelievers is bound to fail.

26 And Pharaoh said: Leave me to slay Moses and let him call upon his Lord. Surely I fear that he will change your religion or that he will make mischief to appear in the land.

27 And Moses said: Truly I seek refuge in my Lord and your Lord from every proud one who believes not in the day of Reckoning.

SECTION 4:
A Believer of Pharaoh's People

28 And a believing man of Pharaoh's people, who hid his faith, said: Will you slay a man because he says, My Lord is Allāh, and indeed he has brought you clear arguments from your Lord? And if he be a liar, on him will be his lie, and if he be truthful, there will befall you some of that which he threatens you with. Surely Allāh guides not one who is a prodigal, a liar.

29 O my people, yours is the kingdom this day, being masters in the land, but who will help us against the punishment of Allāh, if it comes to us? Pharaoh said:

THE BELIEVER

I only show you that which I see and I guide you only to the right way.

30 And he who believed said: O my people, surely I fear for you the like of what befell the parties,

31 The like of what befell the people of Noah and 'Ād and Thamūd and those after them. And Allāh wishes no injustice to (His) servants.

32 And, O my people, I fear for you the day of Calling out —

33 The day on which you will turn back retreating, having none to save you from Allāh; and whomsoever Allāh leaves in error there is no guide for him.

34 And Joseph indeed came to you before with clear arguments, but you ever remained in doubt as to what he brought you; until, when he died, you said: Allāh will never raise a messenger after him. Thus does Allāh leave him in error who is a prodigal, a doubter —

35 Those who dispute concerning the messages of Allāh without any authority that has come to them. Greatly hated is it by Allāh and by those who believe. Thus does Allāh seal every *heart, of a proud, haughty* one.

36 And Pharaoh said: O Hāmān, build for me a tower that I may attain the means of access —

37 The means of access to the heavens, then reach the God of Moses, and I surely think him to be liar. And thus the evil of his deed was made fair-seeming to Pharaoh, and he was turned aside from the way. And the plot of Pharaoh ended in naught but ruin.

SECTION 5:
The End of Pharaoh's People

38 And he who believed said: O my people, follow me I will guide you to the right way.

39 O my people, this life of the world is but a (passing) enjoyment, and the Hereafter, that is the abode to settle.

40 Whoever does evil, he is requited only with the like of it; and whoever does good, whether male or female, and he is a believer, these shall enter the Garden, to be given therein sustenance without measure.

41 And O my people, how is it that I call you to salvation and you call me to the Fire?

42 You call me to disbelieve in Allāh and to associate with Him that of which I have no knowledge, and I call you to the Mighty, the Forgiving.

43 Without doubt that which you call me to has no title to be called to in this world, or in the Hereafter, and our return is to Allāh, and the prodigals are companions of the Fire.

44 So you will remember what I say to you, and I entrust my affair to Allāh. Surely Allāh is Seer of the servants.

45 So Allāh protected him from the evil that they planned; and evil chastisement overtook Pharaoh's people —

46 The Fire. They are brought before it (every) morning and evening, and on the day when the Hour comes to pass: Make Pharaoh's people enter the severest chastisement.

47 And when they contend one with another in the Fire, the weak saying to those who were proud: Surely we were your followers; will you then avert from us a portion of the Fire?

48 Those who were proud say: Now we are all in it: Allāh has indeed judged between the servants.

49 And those in the Fire will say to the guards of hell: Pray to your Lord to lighten our chastisement for a day.

50 They will say: Did not your messengers come to you with clear arguments? They will say: Yea. They will say: Then pray. And the prayer of the disbelievers goes only astray.

SECTION 6:
Messengers Receive Divine Help

51 We certainly help Our messengers, and those who believe, in this world's life and on the day when the witnesses arise —

52 The day on which their

THE BELIEVER

excuse will not benefit the unjust, and for them is a curse and for them is the evil abode.

53 And We indeed gave Moses the guidance, and We made the Children of Israel inherit the Book —

54 A guidance and a reminder for men of understanding.

55 So be patient; surely the promise of Allāh is true; and ask protection for thy sin and celebrate the praise of thy Lord in the evening and the morning.

56 Those who dispute about the messages of Allāh without any authority having come to them, there is naught in their breasts but (a desire) to become great, which they will never attain. So seek refuge in Allāh. Surely He is the Hearing, the Seeing.

57 Assuredly the creation of the heavens and the earth is greater than the creation of men; but most people know not.

58 And the blind and the seeing are not alike, nor those who believe and do good and the evildoers. Little do you mind!

59 The Hour is surely coming — there is no doubt therein — but most people believe not.

60 And your Lord says: Pray to Me, I will answer you. Those who disdain My service will surely enter hell, abased.

SECTION 7:
The Power of Allāh

61 Allāh is He Who made for you the night for resting in and the day for seeing. Surely Allāh is Full of grace to men, but most men give not thanks.

62 That is Allāh, your Lord, the Creator of all things. There is no God but He. Whence are you then turned away?

63 Thus are turned away those who deny the messages of Allāh.

64 Allāh is He Who made the earth a resting-place for you and the heaven a structure, and He formed you, then made goodly your forms, and He provided you with goodly things. That is Allāh, your Lord — so blessed is Allāh, the Lord of the worlds.

65 He is the Living, there is no God but He; so call on Him, being sincere to Him in obedience. Praise be to Allāh, the Lord of the worlds!

66 Say: I am forbidden to serve those whom you call upon besides Allāh, when clear arguments have come to me from my Lord; and I am commanded to submit to the Lord of the worlds.

67 He it is Who created you from dust, then from a small life-germ, then from a clot, then He brings you forth as a child, then that you may attain your maturity, then that you may be old; and of you are some who die before and that you may reach an appointed term, and that you may understand.

68 He it is Who gives life *and causes death,* so when He decrees an affair, He only says to it, Be, and it is.

SECTION 8:
The End of Opposition

69 Seest thou not those who dispute concerning the messages of Allāh? How are they turned away?—

70 Those who reject the Book and that with which We have sent Our messengers. But they shall soon know.

71 When the fetters are on their necks and the chains. They are dragged.

72 Into hot water; then in the Fire they are burned.

73 Then it is said to them: Where is that which you used to set up

74 Besides Allāh? They will say: They have failed us; nay, we used not to call upon anything before. Thus does Allāh confound the disbelievers.

75 That is because you exulted in the land unjustly and because you behaved insolently.

76 Enter the gates of hell to abide therein; so evil is the abode of the proud.

77 Therefore be patient, surely the promise of Allāh is true. But whether We make thee see part of what We threaten them with, or cause thee to die, to Us shall they be returned.

78 And certainly We sent

THE BELIEVER

messengers before thee — of them are those We have mentioned to thee and of them are those We have not mentioned to thee. Nor was it possible for a messenger to bring a sign except with Allāh's permission; so when Allāh's command comes, judgment is given with truth, and those who treat (it) as a lie are lost.

SECTION 9:
The End of Opposition

79 Allāh is He Who made the cattle for you that you may ride on some of them, and some of them you eat.

80 And there are advantages in them for you, and that you may attain through them a need which is in your breasts, and on them and on ships you are borne.

81 And He shows you His signs; which then of Allāh's signs will you deny?

82 Do they not travel in the land and see what was the end of those before them? They were more numerous than these and greater in strength and in fortifications in the land, but what they earned availed them not.

83 Then when their messengers came to them with clear arguments, they exulted in what they had with them of knowledge and that at which they used to mock befell them.

84 So when they saw Our punishment, they said: We believe in Allāh alone, and we deny what we used to associate with Him.

85 But their faith could not profit them when they saw Our punishment. Such is Allāh's law, which ever takes its course in the matter of His servants; and there the disbelievers are lost.

CHAPTER 41
Ḥā Mīm

(REVEALED AT MAKKAH: 6 *sections*; 54 *verses*)

SECTION 1:
Invitation to the Truth

In the name of Allāh, the Beneficent, the Merciful.

1 Beneficent God!

2 A revelation from the Beneficent, the Merciful.

3 A Book of which the verses are made plain, an Arabic Qur'ān for a people who know —

4 Good news and a warning. But most of them turn away, so they hear not.

5 And they say: Our hearts are under coverings from that to which thou callest us, and there is a deafness in our ears, and there is a veil between us and thee, so act, we too are acting.

6 Say: I am only a mortal like you. It is revealed to me that your God is one God, so keep in the straight path to Him, and ask His protection. And woe to the polytheists!

7 Who give not the poor-rate, and who are disbelievers in the Hereafter.

8 Those who believe and do good, for them is surely a reward never to be cut off.

SECTION 2:
The Warning

9 Say: Do you indeed disbelieve in Him Who created the earth in two days, and do you set up equals with Him? That is the Lord of the worlds.

10 And He made in it mountains above its surface, and He blessed therein and ordained therein its foods, in four days; alike for (all) seekers.

11 Then He directed Himself to the heaven and it was a vapour, so He said to it and to the earth: Come both, willingly or unwillingly. They both said: We come willingly.

HĀ MĪM

12 So He ordained them seven heavens in two days, and revealed in every heaven its affair. And We adorned the lower heaven with lights, and (made it) to guard. That is the decree of the Mighty, the Knowing.

13 But if they turn away, then say: I warn you of a scourge like the scourge of 'Ād and Thamūd.

14 When messengers came to them from before them and behind them, saying, Serve nothing but Allāh, they said: If our Lord had pleased, He would have sent down angels. So we are disbelievers in that with which you are sent.

15 Then as to 'Ād, they were unjustly proud in the land, and said: Who is mightier than we in power? See they not that Allāh Who created them is mightier than they in power? And they denied Our messages.

16 So We sent on them a furious wind in unlucky days that We might make them taste the chastisement of abasement in this world's life. And the chastisement of the Hereafter is truly more abasing, and they will not be helped.

17 And as for Thamūd, We showed them the right way, but they preferred blindness to guidance, so the scourge of an abasing chastisement overtook them for what they had earned.

18 And We delivered those who believed and kept their duty.

SECTION 3:
Man's Evidence against Himself

19 And the day when the enemies of Allāh are gathered to the Fire, they will be formed into groups.

20 Until, when they come to it, their ears and their eyes and their skins will bear witness against them as to what they did.

21 And they will say to their skins: Why bear ye witness against us? They will say: Allāh Who makes everything speak has made us speak, and He created you at first, and to Him you are returned.

22 And you did not cover yourselves lest your ears and your eyes and your skins should bear witness against you, but you thought that Allāh knew not much of what you did.

23 And that, your (evil) thought which you entertained about your Lord, ruined you, so have you become of the lost ones.

24 Then if they are patient, the Fire is their abode. And if they ask for goodwill, they are not of those who are granted goodwill.

25 And We have appointed for them comrades, so they make fair-seeming to them what is before them and what is behind them, and the word proved true against them among the nations of jinn and men that have passed away before them: they are surely losers.

SECTION 4:
Believers Strengthened

26 And those who disbelieve say: Listen not to this Qur'ān but make noise therein, perhaps you may overcome.

27 So We shall certainly make those who disbelieve taste a severe chastisement, and We shall certainly requite them for the worst of what they did.

28 That is the reward of Allāh's enemies — the Fire. For them therein is the home to abide. A requital for their denying Our messages.

29 And those who disbelieve will say: Our Lord, show us those who led us astray from among the jinn and the men that we may trample them under our feet, so that they may be of the lowest.

30 Those who say, Our Lord is Allāh, then continue in the right way, the angels descend upon them saying: Fear not, nor be grieved, and receive good news of the Garden which you were promised.

31 We are your friends in this world's life and in the Hereafter, and you have therein what your souls desire, and you have therein what you ask for.

32 A welcome gift from the Forgiving, the Merciful.

SECTION 5:
Effect of the Revelation

33 And who is better in *speech than one who calls* to Allāh and does good, and says: I am surely of those who submit?

34 And not alike are the good and the evil. Repel (evil) with that which is best, when lo! he between whom and thee is enmity will be as if he were a warm friend.

35 And none is granted it but those who are patient, and none is granted it but the owner of a mighty good fortune.

36 And if a false imputation from the devil afflict thee, seek refuge in Allāh. Surely He is the Hearing, the Knowing.

37 And of His signs are the night and the day and the sun and the moon. Adore not the sun nor the moon, but adore Allāh Who created them, if He it is that you serve.

38 But if they are proud, yet those with thy Lord glorify Him night and day, and they tire not.

39 And of His signs is this, that thou seest the earth still, but when We send down water thereon, it stirs and swells. He Who gives it life is surely the Giver of life to the dead. Surely He is Possessor of power over all things.

40 Those who distort Our messages are not hidden from Us. Is he then who is cast into the Fire better or he who comes safe on the day of Resurrection? Do what you like, surely He is Seer of what you do.

41 Those who disbelieve in the Reminder when it comes to them, and surely it is an Invincible Book:

42 Falsehood cannot come at it from before or behind it: a revelation from the Wise, the Praised One.

43 Naught is said to thee but what was said to messengers before thee. Surely thy Lord is the Lord of Forgiveness and the Lord of painful Retribution.

44 And if We had made it a Qur'ān in a foreign tongue, they would have said: Why have not its messages been made clear? What! a foreign (tongue) and an Arab! Say: It is to those who believe a guidance and a healing, and those who believe not, there is a deafness in their ears and it is obscure to them. These are called to from a place afar.

SECTION 6:
Gradual Spread of Truth

45 And indeed We gave Moses the Book, but differences arose therein. And had not a word already gone forth from thy Lord, judgment would have been given between them. And surely they are in a disquieting doubt about it.

46 Whoever does good, it is for his own soul; and whoever does evil, it is against it. And thy Lord is not in the least unjust to the servants.

Part 25

47 To Him is referred the knowledge of the Hour. And no fruit comes forth from its coverings, nor does a female bear or bring forth but with His knowledge. And on the day when He calls out to them: Where are My associates? they will say: We declare to Thee, not one of us can bear witness.

48 And those whom they called upon before will fail them, and they will know that they cannot escape.

49 Man tires not of praying for good, but, if evil touch him, he is despairing, hopeless.

50 And if We make him taste mercy from Us after distress has touched him, he says: This is due to me, and I think not that the Hour will come to pass; and if I am sent back to my Lord, I shall have sure good with Him. So We shall certainly inform those who disbelieve of what they do, and We shall make them taste of hard chastisement.

51 And when We show favour to man, he turns away and withdraws himself; but when evil touches him, he is full of lengthy supplications.

52 Say: See you, if it is from Allāh, then you disbelieve in it, who is in greater error than he who is in opposition far away?

53 We will soon show them Our signs in farthest

regions and among their own people, until it is quite clear to them that it is the Truth. Is it not enough that *thy Lord is a Witness over all things?*

54 Now surely they are in doubt as to the meeting with their Lord. Lo! He surely encompasses all things.

CHAPTER 42
Al-Shūrā: The Counsel

(REVEALED AT MAKKAH: 5 *sections*; 53 *verses*)

SECTION 1:
Divine Mercy in giving Warning

In the name of Allāh, the *Beneficent, the Merciful.*

1 Beneficent God!

2 Knowing, Hearing, Powerful God!

3 Thus does Allāh, the Mighty, the Wise, reveal to thee, and (He revealed) to those before thee.

4 To Him belongs whatever is in the heavens and whatever is in the earth; and He is the High, the Great.

5 The heavens may almost be rent asunder above them, while the angels celebrate the praise *of their Lord and ask for-*giveness for those on earth. Now surely Allāh is the Forgiving, the Merciful.

6 And those who take protectors besides Him — Allāh watches over them; and thou hast not charge over them.

7 And thus have We revealed to thee an Arabic Qur'ān, that thou mayest *warn the mother-town and* those around it, and give warning of the day of Gathering, wherein is no doubt. A party will be in the Garden and (another) party in the burning Fire.

8 And if Allāh had pleased, He would surely have made them a single nation, but He admits whom He pleases to His mercy. And the wrongdoers have no protector nor helper.

9 Or have they taken protectors besides Him? But Allāh is the Protector, and He gives life to the dead, and He is Possessor of power over all things.

SECTION 2:
Judgment is Given

10 And in whatever you

differ, the judgment thereof is with Allāh. That is Allāh, my Lord; on Him I rely, and to Him I turn.

11 The Originator of the heavens and the earth. He has made for you pairs from among yourselves, and pairs of the cattle, too, multiplying you thereby. Nothing is like Him; and He is the Hearing, the Seeing.

12 His are the treasures of the heavens and the earth — He amplifies and straitens subsistence for whom He pleases. Surely He is Knower of all things.

13 He has made plain to you the religion which He enjoined upon Noah and which We have revealed to thee, and which We enjoined on Abraham and Moses and Jesus — to establish religion and not to be divided therein. Hard for the polytheists is that to which thou callest them. Allāh chooses for Himself whom He pleases, and guides to Himself him who turns (to Him).

14 And they were not divided until after knowledge had come to them, out of envy among themselves. And had not a word gone forth from thy Lord for an appointed term, the matter would surely have been judged between them. And those who were made to inherit the Book after them are surely in disquieting doubt about it.

15 To this then go on inviting, and be steadfast as thou art commanded, and follow not their low desires, and say: I believe in what Allāh has revealed of the Book, and I am commanded to do justice between you. Allāh is our Lord and your Lord. For us are our deeds; and for you your deeds. There is no con-*tention* between us and you. Allāh will gather us together, and to Him is the eventual coming.

16 And those who dispute about Allāh after obedience has been rendered to Him, their plea is null with their Lord, and upon them is wrath, and for them is severe chastisement.

17 Allāh is He Who revealed the Book with truth, and the Balance; and what will make thee know that perhaps the Hour is

18 Those who believe not in it would hasten it on, and those who believe are in fear from it, and they know that it is the Truth. Now surely those who dispute concerning the Hour are far astray.

19 Allāh is Benignant to His servants; He gives sustenance to whom He pleases; and He is the Strong, the Mighty.

SECTION 3:
Allāh's Dealing is Just

20 Whoso desires the tilth of the Hereafter, We give him increase in his tilth; and whoso desires the tilth of this world, We give him thereof; and he has no portion in the Hereafter.

21 Or have they associates who have prescribed for them any religion that Allāh does not sanction? And were it not for the word of judgment, it would have been decided between them. And surely for the wrongdoers is a painful chastisement.

22 Thou seest the unjust fearing on account of what they have earned, and it must befall them. And those who believe and do good are in the meadows of the Gardens — they have what they please with their Lord. That is the great grace.

23 This it is of which Allāh gives the good news to His servants, who believe and do good. Say: I ask of you naught in return for it but love for relatives. And whoever earns good, We give him more of good therein. Surely Allāh is Forgiving, Grateful.

24 Or say they: He has forged a lie against Allāh? So, if Allāh please, He would seal thy heart (against them). And Allāh blots out the falsehood and confirms the Truth with His words. Surely He is Knower of what is in the breasts.

25 And He it is Who accepts repentence from His servants and pardons evil deeds, and He knows what you do;

26 And He answers those who believe and do good deeds, and gives them more out of His grace. And for the disbelievers is a severe chastisement.

27 And if Allāh were to amplify the provision for His servants, they would rebel in the earth; but He sends (it) down by measure, as He pleases. Surely He is Aware, Seer of His servants.

28 And He it is Who sends down the rain after they have despaired, and He unfolds His mercy. And He is the Friend, the Praised One.

29 And of His signs is the creation of the heavens and the earth and what He has spread forth in both of them of living beings. And He is All-powerful to gather them together, when He will.

SECTION 4:
Believers should be Patient

30 And whatever misfortune befalls you, it is on account of what your hands have wrought and He pardons much.

31 And you cannot escape in the earth, and besides Allāh you have no protector nor helper.

32 And of His signs are the ships, like mountains on the sea.

33 If He will, He stills the wind so that they lie motionless on its back. Surely there are signs in this for every patient, grateful one,

34 Or He causes them to perish for what they have earned, and He pardons much;

35 And (that) those who dispute about Our messages may know. There is no refuge for them.

36 So whatever you are given is but a provision of this world's life, and that which Allāh has is better and more lasting for those who believe and rely on their Lord;

37 And those who shun the great sins and indecencies, and whenever they are angry they forgive;

38 And those who respond to their Lord and keep up prayer, and whose affairs are (decided) by counsel among themselves, and who spend out of what We have given them;

39 And those who, when great wrong afflicts them,

defend themselves.

40 And the recompense of evil is punishment like it; but whoever forgives and amends, his reward is with Allāh. Surely He loves not the wrongdoers.

41 And whoever defends himself after his being oppressed, these it is against whom there is no way (of blame).

42 The way (of blame) is only against those who oppress men and revolt in the earth unjustly. For such there is a painful chastisement.

43 And whoever is patient and forgives — that surely is an affair of great resolution.

SECTION 5:
Revelation guides aright

44 And he whom Allāh leaves in error, has no friend after Him. And thou wilt see the iniquitous, when they see the chastisement, saying: Is there any way of return?

45 And thou wilt see them brought before it, humbling themselves because of abasement, looking with a faint glance. And those who believe will say: Surely the losers are they who lose themselves and their followers on the Resurrection day. Now surely the iniquitous are in lasting chastisement.

46 And they will have no friends to help them besides Allāh. And he whom Allāh leaves in error cannot find a way.

47 Hearken to your Lord before there comes from Allāh the day which there is no averting. You will have no refuge on that day, nor will it be yours to make a denial.

48 But if they turn away, We have not sent thee as a watcher over them. Thy duty is only to deliver (the message). And surely when We make man taste mercy from Us, he rejoices thereat; and if an evil afflicts them on account of what their hands have sent before, then surely man is ungrateful.

49 Allāh's is the kingdom of the heavens and the earth. He creates what He pleases. He grants females to whom He pleases and grants males to whom He pleases,

50 Or He grants them both males and females, and He makes whom He pleases, barren. Surely He is Knower, Powerful.

51 And it is not vouchsafed to a mortal that Allāh should speak to him, except by revelation or from behind a veil, or by sending a messenger and revealing by His permission what He pleases. Surely He is High, Wise.

52 And thus did We reveal to thee an inspired Book by Our command. *Thou knewest not what the Book was, nor (what) Faith (was)*, but We made it a light, guiding thereby whom We please of Our servants. And surely thou guidest to the right path —

53 The path of Allāh, to Whom belongs whatsoever is in the heavens and whatsoever is in the earth. Now surely to Allāh do all affairs eventually come.

Chapter 43
Zukhruf: Gold

(Revealed at Makkah: 7 *sections*; 89 *verses*)

SECTION 1:
Revelation is a Divine Favour

In the name of Allāh, the Beneficent, the Merciful.

1 Beneficent God!

2 By the Book that makes manifest!

3 Surely We have made it an Arabic Qur'ān that you may understand.

4 And it is in the Original of the Book with Us, truly elevated, full of wisdom.

5 Shall We then turn away the Reminder from you altogether because you are a prodigal people?

6 And how many a prophet did We send among the ancients!

7 And no prophet came to them but they mocked him.

8 Then We destroyed those stronger than these in prowess, and the example of the ancients has gone before.

9 And if thou ask them, Who created the heavens and the earth? they would say: The Mighty, the Knowing One, has created them,

10 Who made the earth a resting-place for you, and made in it ways for you that you might go aright.

11 And Who sends down water from the cloud according to a measure, then We raise to life thereby a dead land; even so will you be brought forth.

12 And Who created pairs of all things, and made for you ships and cattle on which you ride,

13 That you may sit firm on their backs, then remember the favour of your Lord, when you are firmly seated thereon, and say: Glory be to Him Who made this subservient to us and we were not able to do it,

14 And surely to our Lord we must return.

15 And they assign to Him a part of His servants. Man, to be sure, is clearly ungrateful.

SECTION 2:
Polytheism condemned

16 Or has He taken daughters to Himself of what He creates and chosen you to have sons?

17 And when one of them is given news of that of which he sets up a likeness for the Beneficent, his face becomes black and he is full of rage.

18 Is one decked with ornaments and unable to make plain speech in disputes (a partner with God)?

19 And they make the angels, who are the servants of the Beneficent, females. Did they witness their creation? Their evidence will be recorded and they will be questioned.

20 And they say: If the Beneficent had pleased, we should not have worshipped them. They have no knowledge of this; they only lie.

21 Or have We given them a Book before it so that they hold fast to it?

22 Nay, they say: We found our fathers on a course, and surely we are guided by their footsteps.

23 And thus, We sent not before thee a warner in a town, but its wealthy ones said: Surely we found our fathers following a religion, and we follow their footsteps.

24 (The warner) said: And even if I bring to you a better guide than that which you found your fathers following? They said: We surely disbelieve in that with which you are sent.

25 So We exacted retribution from them, then see what was the end of the rejectors!

SECTION 3:
Allāh's Choice of a Prophet

26 And when Abraham said to his sire and his people: I am clear of what you worship,

27 Save Him Who created me, for surely He will

28 And he made it a word to continue in his posterity that they might return.

29 Nay! I let these and their fathers enjoy till there came to them the Truth and a Messenger making manifest.

30 And when the Truth came to them they said: This is enchantment, and surely we are disbelievers in it.

31 And they say: Why was not this Qur'ān revealed to a man of importance in the two towns?

32 Do they apportion the mercy of thy Lord? We portion out among them their livelihood in the life of this world, and We exalt some of them above others in rank, that some of them may take others in service. And the mercy of thy Lord is better than that which they amass.

33 And were it not that all people would become one (disbelieving) community, We would provide for those who disbelieve in the Beneficent, roofs of silver for their houses and stairs (of silver) by which they ascend,

34 And (of silver) the doors of their houses and the couches on which they recline,

35 And of gold. And all this is naught but a provision of this world's life; and the Hereafter is with thy Lord only for the dutiful.

SECTION 4:
Opposition to Truth is punished

36 And whoever turns himself away from the remembrance of the Beneficent, We appoint for him a devil, so he is his associate.

37 And surely they hinder them from the (right) path, and they think that they are guided aright.

38 Until when he comes to Us, he says: O would that between me and thee were the distance of the East and the West! so evil is the associate!

39 And as you did wrong, it will profit you naught this day that you are sharers in the chastisement.

40 Canst thou then make the deaf to hear or guide the blind and him who is in clear error?

41 So if We take thee away, still We shall exact retribution from them,

42 Or We shall show thee that which We promise them— surely We are Possessors of power over them.

43 So hold fast to that which has been revealed to thee; surely thou art on the right path.

44 And surely it is a reminder for thee and thy people, and you will be questioned.

45 And ask those of Our messengers whom We sent before thee: Did We ever appoint gods to be worshipped besides the Beneficent?

SECTION 5:
Pharaoh's Opposition to Moses

46 And truly We sent Moses with Our messages to Pharaoh and his chiefs, so he said: I am the messenger of the Lord of the worlds.

47 But when he brought them Our signs, lo! they laughed at them.

48 And We showed them not a sign but it was greater than its fellow, and We seized them with chastisement that they might turn.

49 And they said: O enchanter, call on thy Lord for us, as He has made the covenant with thee; we shall surely follow guidance.

50 But when We removed from them the chastisement, lo! they broke the pledge.

51 And Pharaoh proclaimed amongst his people, saying: O my people, is not the kingdom of Egypt mine and these rivers flowing beneath me? Do you not see?

52 Rather I am better than this (fellow) who is contemptible, and can hardly express himself clearly.

53 Why, then, have bracelets of gold not been bestowed on him, or angels come along with him in procession?

54 So he incited his people to levity and they

obeyed him. Surely they were a transgressing people.

55 Then when they displeased Us, We exacted retribution from them, so We drowned them all together.

56 And We made them a thing past and an example for later generations.

SECTION 6:
Jesus as Prophet

57 And when the son of Mary is mentioned as an example, lo! thy people raise a clamour thereat.

58 And they say: Are our gods better, or is he? They set it forth to thee only by way of disputation. Nay, they are a contentious people.

59 He was naught but a servant on whom We bestowed favour and We made him an example for *the Children of Israel;*

60 And if We pleased, We could make among you angels to be (Our) vicegerents in the land.

61 And this (revelation) is surely knowledge of the Hour, so have no doubt about it and follow me. This is the right path.

62 And let not the devil hinder you; surely he is your open enemy.

63 And when Jesus came with clear arguments, he said: I have come to you indeed with wisdom, and to make clear to you some of that about which you differ. So keep your duty to Allāh and obey me.

64 Surely Allāh is my Lord and your Lord, so serve Him. This is the right path.

65 But parties among them differed, so woe to those who did wrong for the chastisement of a painful day!

66 Wait they for aught but the Hour, that it should come on them all of a sudden, while they perceive not?

67 Friends on that day will be foes one to another, except those who keep their duty.

SECTION 7:
The two Parties

68 O My servants, there is no fear for you this day,

nor will you grieve —

69 Those who believed in Our messages and submitted (to Us),

70 Enter the Garden, you and your wives, being made happy.

71 Sent round to them are golden bowls and drinking-cups, and therein is that which (their) souls yearn for and the eyes delight in, and therein you will abide.

72 And this is the Garden, which you are made to inherit on account of what you did.

73 For you therein is abundant fruit to eat thereof.

74 Surely the guilty will abide in the chastisement of hell.

75 It is not abated for them and they will therein despair.

76 And We wronged them not but they were themselves the wrongdoers.

77 And they cry: O Mālik, let thy Lord make an end of us. He will say: You shall stay (here).

78 Certainly We bring the Truth to you, but most of you are averse to the Truth.

79 Or have they settled an affair? But it is We Who settle (affairs).

80 Or do they think that We hear not their secrets and their private counsels? Aye, and Our messengers with them write down.

81 Say: The Beneficent has no son; so I am the foremost of those who serve (God).

82 Glory to the Lord of the heavens and the earth, the Lord of the Throne of Power, from what they describe!

83 So let them talk and sport until they meet their day which they are promised.

84 And He it is Who is God in the heavens and God in the earth. And He is the Wise, the Knowing.

85 And blessed is He Whose is the kingdom of the heavens and the earth and all between them; and with Him is the knowledge of the Hour, and to Him you will be returned.

86 And those whom they call upon besides Him control not intercession, but he who bears witness to the Truth and they know (him).

87 And if thou wert to ask them who created them, they would say: Allāh. How are they then turned back?

88 And his cry — O my Lord, these are a people who believe not!

89 So turn away from them and say, Peace! They will soon come to know.

Chapter 44
Al-Dukhān: The Drought

(REVEALED AT MAKKAH: 3 *sections*; 59 *verses*)

SECTION 1:
Lighter Punishment followed by Severer

In the name of Allāh, the Beneficent, the Merciful.

1 Beneficent God!

2 By the Book that makes manifest!

3 We revealed it on a blessed night — truly We are ever warning.

4 Therein is made clear every affair full of wisdom —

5 A command from Us — truly We are ever sending messengers —

6 A mercy from thy Lord — truly He is the Hearing, the Knowing,

7 The Lord of the heavens and the earth and what is between them, if you would be sure.

8 There is no God but He; He gives life and causes death — your Lord and the Lord of your fathers of yore.

9 Nay, in doubt they sport.

10 So wait for the day when the heaven brings a clear drought,

11 Enveloping men. This is a painful chastisement.

12 Our Lord, remove from us the chastisement — surely we are believers.

13 When will they be reminded? And a Messenger has indeed come, making clear;

14 Yet they turned away from him and said: One taught (by others), a madman!

15 We shall remove the chastisement a little, (but) you will surely return (to evil).

16 On the day when We seize (them) with the most violent seizing; surely We shall exact retribution.

17 And certainly We tried before them Pharaoh's people, and a noble messenger came to them,

18 Saying: Deliver to me the servants of Allāh. Surely I am a faithful messenger to you.

19 And exalt not yourselves against Allāh. Surely I bring to you a clear authority.

20 And I take refuge with my Lord and your Lord, lest you stone me to death.

21 And if you believe not in me, leave me alone.

22 Then he called upon his Lord: These are a guilty people.

23 So go forth with My servants by night; surely you will be pursued.

24 And leave the sea behind calm. Surely they are a host to be drowned.

25 *How many of the gardens and springs they left behind!*

26 And cornfields and noble places!

27 And goodly things wherein they rejoiced!

28 Thus (it was). And We made other people inherit them.

29 So the heaven and the earth wept not for them, nor were they respited.

SECTION 2:
Good and Evil Rewarded

30 And We indeed delivered the Children of Israel from the abasing chastisement,

31 From Pharaoh. Surely he was haughty, prodigal.

32 And certainly We chose them above the nations, having knowledge.

33 And We gave them signs wherein was clear blessing.

34 These do indeed say:

35 There is naught but our first death and we shall not be raised again.

36 So bring our fathers (back), if you are truthful.

37 Are they better or the people of Tubba‛, and those before them? We destroyed them, for surely they were guilty.

38 And We did not create the heavens and the earth and that which is between them in sport.

THE DROUGHT

39 We created them not but with truth, but most of them know not.

40 Surely the day of Decision is the term for them all,

41 The day when friend will avail friend in naught, nor will they be helped —

42 Save those on whom Allāh has mercy. Surely He is the Mighty, the Merciful.

SECTION 3:
Good and Evil Rewarded

43 Surely the tree of Zaqqūm

44 Is the food of the sinful,

45 Like molten brass; it seethes in (their) bellies

46 Like boiling water.

47 Seize him, then drag him into the midst of hell;

48 Then pour on his head of the torment of boiling water —

49 Taste — thou art forsooth the mighty, the honourable!

50 Surely this is what you doubted.

51 Those who keep their duty are indeed in a secure place —

52 In gardens and springs,

53 Wearing fine and thick silk, facing one another —

54 Thus (shall it be). And We shall join them to pure, beautiful ones.

55 They call therein for every fruit in security —

56 They taste not therein death, except the first death; and He will save them from the chastisement of hell —

57 A grace from thy Lord. This is the great achievement.

58 So We have made it easy in thy tongue that they may mind.

59 Wait then; surely they (too) are waiting.

CHAPTER 45
Al-Jāthiyah: **The Kneeling**

(REVEALED AT MAKKAH: 4 *sections*; 37 *verses*)

SECTION 1:
Denial of Revelation

In the name of Allāh, the Beneficent, the Merciful.

1 Beneficent God!

2 The revelation of the Book is from Allāh, the Mighty, the Wise.

3 Surely in the heavens and the earth are signs for believers.

4 And in your creation and in the animals He spreads abroad are signs for a people who are sure;

5 And (in) the variation of the night and the day and (in) the sustenance which Allāh sends down from the heaven, then gives life *thereby to the earth after its* death, and (in) the changing of the winds, are signs for a people who understand.

6 These are the messages of Allāh, which We recite to thee with truth. In what announcement will they then believe after Allāh and His signs?

7 Woe to every sinful liar!

8 Who hears the messages of Allāh recited to him then persists in haughtiness, as though he had not heard them. So announce to him a painful chastisement.

9 And when he comes to know of any of Our messages, he takes them for a jest. For such is an abasing chastisement.

10 In front of them is hell, and that which they have earned will avail them naught, nor those whom they take for protectors besides Allāh, and for them is a grievous chastisement.

11 This is guidance; and those who disbelieve in the messages of their Lord, for them is a painful chastisement of an evil (kind).

SECTION 2:
Truth of the Revelation

12 Allāh is He Who made subservient to you the sea that the ships may glide therein by His command, and that you may seek of His grace, and that you may give thanks.

13 And He has made subservient to you whatsoever is in the heavens and whatsoever is in the earth, all, from Himself. Surely there are signs in this for a people who reflect.

14 Tell those who believe to forgive those who fear not the days of Allāh that He may reward a people for what they earn.

15 Whoever does good it is for himself, and whoever does evil, it is against himself; then to your Lord you will be brought back.

16 And certainly We gave the Children of Israel the Book and judgment and prophethood and provided them with good things, and made them excel the nations.

17 And We gave them clear arguments in the Affair. So they differed not until after knowledge had come to them, out of envy among themselves. Surely thy Lord will judge between them on the day of Resurrection concerning that wherein they differed.

18 Then We made thee follow a course in the Affair, so follow it, and follow not the low desires of those who know not.

19 Surely they can avail thee naught against Allāh. And surely the wrongdoers are friends of each other, and Allāh is the Friend of the dutiful.

20 These are clear proofs for men, and a guidance and a mercy for a people who are sure.

21 Or do those who do evil deeds think that We shall make them as those who believe and do good — their life and their death being equal? Evil is what they judge!

SECTION 3:
Denial of Judgment

22 And Allāh created the heavens and the earth with truth, and that every soul may be rewarded for what it has earned, and they will not be wronged.

23 Seest thou him who takes his desire for his god, and Allāh leaves him in error knowingly, and seals his hearing and his heart and puts a covering on his sight? Who can then guide him after Allāh? Will you not mind?

24 And they say: There is naught but our life of the world; we die and we live and nothing destroys us but time, and they have no knowledge of that; they only conjecture.

25 And when Our clear messages are recited to them, their only argument is that they say: Bring (back) our fathers, if you are truthful.

26 Say: Allāh gives you life, then makes you die, then will He gather you to the day of Resurrection, wherein is no doubt, but most people know not.

SECTION 4:
The Doom

27 And Allāh's is the kingdom of the heavens and the earth. And on the day when the Hour comes to pass, on that day will the followers of falsehood perish.

28 And thou wilt see every nation kneeling down. Every nation will be called to its record. This day you are requited for what you did.

29 This is Our record that speaks against you with truth. Surely We wrote what you did.

30 Then as to those who believed and did good, their Lord will admit them to His mercy. That is the manifest achievement.

31 And as to those who disbelieved — were not My messages recited to you? But you were proud and you were a guilty people.

32 And when it was said, Surely the promise of Allāh is *true* and the Hour — there is no doubt about it, you said: We know not what the Hour is. We think (it) only a conjecture and we are not at all sure.

33 And the evil of what they did will become manifest to them, and that at which they mocked will encompass them.

34 And it will be said: This day We forsake you as you neglected the meeting of this day of yours, and your abode is the Fire, and you have no helpers.

35 That is because you made the messages of Allāh a jest and the life of this world deceived you. So on that day they shall not be taken out of it, nor shall *they be granted goodwill*.

36 So praise be to Allāh, the Lord of the heavens and the Lord of the earth, the Lord of the worlds!

37 And to Him belongs greatness in the heavens and the earth; and He is the Mighty, the Wise.

Part 26

CHAPTER 46
Al-Aḥqāf: **The Sandhills**

(REVEALED AT MAKKAH: 4 *sections*; 35 *verses*)

SECTION 1:
Truth of Revelation

In the name of Allāh, the Beneficent, the Merciful.

1 Beneficent God!

2 The revelation of the Book is from Allāh, the Mighty, the Wise.

3 We created not the heavens and the earth and all between them save with truth and for an appointed term. And those who disbelieve turn away from that whereof they are warned.

4 Say: Have you considered that which you invoke besides Allāh? Show me what they have created of the earth, or have they a share in the heavens? Bring me a Book before this or any relics of knowledge, if you are truthful.

5 And who is in greater error than he who invokes besides Allāh such as answer him not till the day of Resurrection, and they are heedless of their call?

6 And when men are gathered together, they will be their enemies, and will deny their worshipping (them).

7 And when Our clear messages are recited to them, those who disbelieve say of the Truth when it comes to them: This is clear enchantment.

8 Nay, they say: He has forged it. Say: If I have forged it, you control naught for me from Allāh. He knows best what you utter concerning it. He is *enough as a* witness between me and you. And He is the Forgiving, the Merciful.

9 Say: I am not the first of the messengers, and I know not what will be done with me or with you. I follow naught but that which is *revealed to me*, and I am but a *plain warner*.

10 Say: See you if it is from Allāh, and you disbelieve in it, and a witness from among the Children of Israel has borne witness of one like him, so he believed, while you are big with pride. Surely Allāh guides not the iniquitous people.

SECTION 2:
Witness of Truth

11 And those who disbelieve say of those who believe: If it had been a good, they would not have attained it before us. And as they are not guided thereby, they say: It is an old lie.

12 And before it was the Book of Moses, a guide and a mercy. And this is a Book verifying (it) in the Arabic language, that it may warn those who do wrong, and as good news for the doers of good.

13 Surely those who say, Our Lord is Allāh, then continue on the right way, on them is no fear, nor shall they grieve.

14 These are the owners of the Garden, abiding *therein* — *a reward for what they did*.

15 And We have enjoined on man the doing of good to his parents. His mother bears him with trouble and she brings him forth in pain. And the bearing of him and the weaning of him is thirty months. Till, when he attains his maturity and reaches forty years, he says: My Lord, grant me that I may give thanks for Thy favour, which Thou hast bestowed on me and on my parents, and that I may do good which pleases Thee; and be good to me in respect of my offspring. Truly I turn to Thee, and truly I am of those who submit.

16 These are they from whom We accept the best of what they do and pass by their evil deeds — among the owners of the Garden. A promise of truth, which they were promised.

17 And he who says to his parents: Fie on you! Do you threaten me that I shall be brought forth, when generations have passed away before me? And they both call for Allāh's aid: Woe to thee! Believe; surely the promise of Allāh is true. But he says: This is nothing but stories of the ancients.

18 These are they against whom the word proves true, among nations of the jinn and the men that have passed away before them. Surely they are losers.

19 And for all are degrees according to what they do, and that He may pay them for their deeds and they will not be wronged.

20 And on the day when those who disbelieve are brought before the Fire: You did away with your good things in your life of the world and you enjoyed them; so this day you are rewarded with the chastisement of abasement because you were unjustly proud in *the land* and because you transgressed.

SECTION 3:
The Fate of 'Ād

21 And mention the brother of 'Ād; when he warned his people in the sandy plains — and warners indeed came before him and after him — saying: Serve none but Allāh. Surely I fear for you the chastisement of a grievous day.

22 They said: Hast thou come to us to turn us away from our gods? Then bring us that with which thou threatenest us, if thou art truthful.

23 He said: The knowledge is only with Allāh, and I deliver to you that wherewith I am sent, but I see you are an ignorant people.

24 So when they saw it — a cloud advancing towards their valleys, they said: This is a cloud bringing us rain. Nay, it is that which you sought to hasten, a wind wherein is painful chastisement.

25 Destroying everything by the command of its Lord. So at dawn naught could be seen except their dwellings. Thus do We reward the guilty people.

26 And certainly We had given them power in matters in which We have not empowered you, and We had given them ears and eyes and hearts, but neither their ears, nor their eyes, nor their hearts availed them aught, since they denied the messages of Allāh, and that which they mocked at encompassed them.

SECTION 4:
A Warning

27 And certainly We destroyed the towns round about you, and We repeat the messages that they may turn.

28 Then why did those whom they took for gods besides Allāh to draw (them) nigh (to Him) not help them? Nay, they failed them. And this was their lie and what they forged.

29 And when We turned towards thee a party of the jinn, who listened to the Qur'ān; so when they were in its presence, they said: Be silent. Then when it was finished, they turned back to their people warning (them).

30 They said: O our people, we have heard a Book revealed after Moses, verifying that which is before it, guiding to the truth and to a right path.

31 O our people, accept the Inviter to Allāh and believe in Him. He will forgive you some of your sins and protect you from a painful chastisement.

32 And whoever accepts not the Inviter to Allāh, he cannot escape in the earth, nor has he protectors besides Him. These are in manifest error.

33 See they not that Allāh, Who created the heavens and the earth and was not tired by their creation, is able to give life to the dead? Aye, He is surely Possessor of power over all things.

34 And on the day when those who disbelieve are brought before the Fire: Is it not true? They will say: Yea, by our Lord! He will say: Then taste the chastisement, because you disbelieved.

35 So have patience, as men of resolution, the messengers, had patience, and seek not to hasten on for them (their doom). On the day when they see that which they are promised, (it will be) as if they had not tarried save an hour of the day. (Thine is) to deliver. Shall then any be destroyed save the transgressing people?

CHAPTER 47
Muḥammad

(REVEALED AT MADĪNAH: 4 *sections*; 38 *verses*)

SECTION 1:
Opponents will perish in War

In the name of Allāh, the Beneficent, the Merciful.

1 Those who disbelieve and turn (men) from Allāh's way, He will destroy their works.

2 And those who believe and do good, and believe in that which has been revealed to Muḥammad — and it is the Truth from their Lord — He will remove their evil from them and improve their condition.

3 That is because those who disbelieve follow falsehood, and those who believe follow the Truth from their Lord. Thus does Allāh set forth their descriptions for men.

4 So when you meet in battle those who disbelieve, smite the necks; then, when you have overcome them, make (them) prisoners, and afterwards (set them free) as a favour or for ransom till the war lay down its burdens. That (shall be so). And if Allāh please, He would certainly exact retribution from them, but that He may try some of you by means of others. And those who are slain in the way of Allāh, He will never allow their deeds to perish.

5 He will guide them and improve their condition.

6 And make them enter the Garden, which He has made known to them.

7 O you who believe, if you help Allāh, He will help you and make firm your feet.

8 And those who disbelieve, for them is destruction, and He will destroy their works.

9 That is because they hate that which Allāh reveals, so He has rendered

10 Have they not travelled in the land and seen what was the end of those before them? Allāh destroyed them. And for the disbelievers is the like thereof.

11 That is because Allāh is the Patron of those who believe, and because the disbelievers have no patron.

SECTION 2:
Oppressors shall be brought low

12 Surely Allāh will make those who believe and do good enter Gardens wherein flow rivers. And those who disbelieve enjoy themselves and eat as the cattle eat, and the Fire is their abode.

13 And how many a town, more powerful than thy town which has driven *thee out* — We destroyed them, so there was no helper for them.

14 Is then he who has a clear argument from his Lord like him to whom his evil conduct is made fair-seeming; and they follow their low desires.

15 A parable of the Garden which the dutiful are promised: Therein are rivers of water not altering for the worse, and rivers of milk whereof the taste changes not, and rivers of wine delicious to the drinkers, and rivers of honey clarified; and for them therein are all fruits and protection from their Lord. (Are these) like those who abide in the Fire and who are made to drink boiling water, so it rends their bowels asunder?

16 And there are those of them who seek to listen to thee, till, when they go forth from thee, they say to those who have been given knowledge: What was it that he said just now? These are they whose hearts Allāh has sealed and they follow their low desires.

17 And those who follow guidance, He increases them in guidance and grants them their observance of duty.

18 Wait they for aught but the Hour that it should come upon them of a sudden? Now tokens thereof have already come. But how will they have their reminder, when it comes on them?

19 So know that there is no god but Allāh and ask protection for thy sin and for the believing men and the believing women. And Allāh knows your moving about and your staying (in a place).

SECTION 3:
The Weak-hearted Ones

20 And those who believe say: Why is not a chapter revealed? But when a decisive chapter is revealed, and fighting is mentioned therein, thou seest those in whose hearts is a disease look to thee with the look of one fainting at death. So woe to them!

21 Obedience and a gentle word (was proper). Then when the affair is settled, it is better for them if they remain true to Allāh.

22 But if you turn away, you are sure to make mischief in the land and cut off the ties of kinship!

23 Those it is whom Allāh has cursed, so He has made them deaf and blinded their eyes.

24 Do they not reflect on the Qur'ān? Or, are there locks on the hearts?

25 Surely those who turn back after guidance is manifest to them, the devil embellishes it for them; and lengthens false hopes for them.

26 That is because they say to those who hate what Allāh has revealed: We will obey you in some matters. And Allāh knows their secrets.

27 But how will it be when the angels cause them to die, smiting their faces and their backs?

28 That is because they follow that which displeases Allāh and are averse to His pleasure, so He makes their deeds fruitless.

SECTION 4:
An Exhortation

29 Or do those in whose hearts is a disease think that Allāh will not bring forth their spite?

30 And if We please, We could show them to thee so that thou shouldst know them by their marks. And certainly thou canst recognize them by the tone of (their) speech. And Allāh knows your deeds.

31 And certainly We shall try you, till We know those among you who strive hard, and the steadfast, and manifest your news.

32 Surely those who disbelieve and hinder (men) from Allāh's way and oppose the Messenger after guidance is quite clear to them, cannot harm Allāh in any way, and He will make their deeds fruitless.

33 O you who believe, obey Allāh and obey the Messenger and make not your deeds vain.

34 Surely those who disbelieve and hinder (men) from Allāh's way, then die disbelievers, Allāh will not forgive them.

35 And be not slack so as to cry for peace — and you are the uppermost — and Allāh is with you, and He will not bring your deeds to naught.

36 The life of this world is but idle sport and play, and, if you believe and keep your duty, He will give you your reward, and He does not ask of you your wealth.

37 If He should ask you for it and press you, you will be niggardly, and He will bring forth your malice.

38 Behold! you are those who are called to spend in Allāh's way, but among you are those who are niggardly; and whoever is niggardly, is niggardly against his own soul. And Allāh is Self-Sufficient and you are needy. And if you turn back He will bring in your place *another people*, then they will not be like you.

CHAPTER 48
Al-Fatḥ: **The Victory**

(Revealed at Madīnah: 4 *sections*; 29 *verses*)

SECTION 1: Ḥudaibiyah Truce was a Victory

In the name of Allāh, the Beneficent, the Merciful.

1 Surely We have granted thee a clear victory,

2 That Allāh may cover for thee thy (alleged) shortcomings in the past and those to come, and complete His favour to thee and guide thee on a right path,

3 And that Allāh might *help thee* with a mighty help.

4 He it is Who sent down tranquillity into the hearts of the believers that they might add faith to their faith. And Allāh's are the hosts of the heavens and the earth, and Allāh is ever Knowing, Wise —

5 That He may cause the believing men and the believing women to enter Gardens wherein flow rivers to abide therein and remove from them their evil. And that is a grand achievement with Allāh,

6 And (that) He may chastise the hypocritical men and the hypocritical women, and the polytheistic men and the polytheistic women, the entertainers of evil thoughts about Allāh. On them is the evil turn, and Allāh is wroth with them and has cursed them and prepared hell for them; and evil is the resort.

7 And Allāh's are the hosts of the heavens and the earth; and Allāh is ever Mighty, Wise.

8 Surely We have sent thee as a witness and as a bearer of good news and as a warner,

9 That you may believe in Allāh and His Messenger and may aid him and revere him. And (that) you may declare His glory, morning

and evening.

10 Those who swear allegiance to thee do but swear allegiance to Allāh. The hand of Allāh is above their hands. So whoever breaks (his faith), he breaks it only to his soul's injury. And whoever fulfils his covenant with Allāh, He will grant him a mighty reward.

SECTION 2:
The Defaulters

11 Those of the dwellers of the desert who lagged behind will say to thee: Our property and our families kept us busy, so ask forgiveness for us. They say with their tongues what is not in their hearts. Say: Then who can control aught for you from Allāh, if He intends to do you harm or if He intends to do you good. Nay, Allāh is ever Aware of what you do.

12 Nay, you thought that the Messenger and the believers would never return to their families, and that was made fair-seeming in your hearts, and you thought an evil thought, and you are a people doomed to perish.

13 And whoever believes not in Allāh and His Messenger — then surely We have prepared burning Fire for the disbelievers.

14 And Allāh's is the kingdom of the heavens and the earth. He forgives whom He pleases and chastises whom He pleases. And Allāh is ever Forgiving, Merciful.

15 Those who lagged behind will say, when you set forth to acquire gains: Allow us to follow you. They desire to change the word of Allāh. Say: You shall not follow us. Thus did Allāh say before. But they will say: Nay, you are jealous of us. Nay, they understand not but a little.

16 Say to those of the dwellers of the desert who lagged behind: You will soon be called against a people of mighty prowess to fight against them until they submit. Then if you obey, Allāh will grant you a good reward; but, if you turn back as you turned back before, He will chastise you with a painful chastisement.

17 There is no blame on

THE VICTORY

the blind, nor is there blame on the lame, nor is there blame on the sick. And whoever obeys Allāh and His Messenger, He will cause him to enter Gardens wherein flow rivers. And whoever turns back, He will chastise him with a painful chastisement.

SECTION 3:
More Victories for Islām

18 Allāh indeed was well pleased with the believers, when they swore allegiance to thee under the tree, and He knew what was in their hearts, so He sent down tranquillity on them and rewarded them with a near victory,

19 And many gains which they will acquire. And Allāh is ever Mighty, Wise.

20 Allāh promised you many gains which you will acquire, then He hastened this on for you, and held back the hands of men from you; and that it may be a sign for the believers and that He may guide you on a right path,

21 And others which you have not yet been able to achieve — Allāh has surely encompassed them. And Allāh is ever Powerful over all things.

22 And if those who disbelieve fight with you, they will certainly turn (their) backs, then they will find no protector nor helper.

23 (Such has been) the course of Allāh that has run before, and thou wilt not find a change in Allāh's course.

24 And He it is Who held back their hands from you and your hands from them in the valley of Makkah after He had given you victory over them. And Allāh is ever Seer of what you do.

25 It is they who disbelieved and debarred you from the Sacred Mosque — and the offering withheld from reaching its goal. And were it not for the believing men and the believing women, whom, not having known, you might have trodden down and thus something hateful might have afflicted you on their account without knowledge — so that Allāh may admit to His mercy whom He pleases. Had they been apart, We would surely have chastised those who disbelieved from among them with a painful chastisement.

26 When those who disbelieved harboured disdain in their hearts, the disdain of Ignorance, but Allāh sent down His tranquillity on His Messenger and on the believers and made them keep the word of observance of duty, and they were entitled to it and worthy of it. And Allāh is ever Knower of all things.

SECTION 4:
Ultimate Triumph of Islām

27 Allāh indeed fulfilled the vision for His Messenger with truth. You shall certainly enter the Sacred Mosque, if Allāh please, in security, your heads shaved and hair cut short, not fearing. But He knows what you know not, so He has ordained a near victory before that.

28 He it is Who has sent His Messenger with the guidance and the Religion of Truth that He may make it prevail over all religions. And Allāh is enough for a witness.

29 Muḥammad is the Messenger of Allāh, and those with him are firm of heart against the disbelievers, compassionate among themselves. Thou seest them bowing down, prostrating themselves, seeking Allāh's grace and pleasure. Their marks are on their faces in consequence of prostration. That is their description in the Torah — and their description in the Gospel — like seed-produce that puts forth its sprout, then strengthens it, so it becomes stout and stands firmly on its stem, delighting the sowers that He may enrage the disbelievers on account of them. Allāh has promised such of them as believe and do good, forgiveness and a great reward.

CHAPTER 49
Al-Ḥujurāt: **The Apartments**

(REVEALED AT MADĪNAH: 2 *sections*; 18 verses)

SECTION 1:
Respect for the Prophet

In the name of Allāh, the Beneficent, the Merciful.

1 O you who believe, be not forward in the presence of Allāh and His Messenger, and keep your duty to Allāh. Surely Allāh is Hearing, Knowing.

2 O you who believe, raise not your voices above the Prophet's voice, nor speak loudly to him as you speak loudly one to another, lest your deeds become null, while you perceive not.

3 Surely those who lower their voices before Allāh's Messenger are they whose hearts Allāh has proved for dutifulness. For them is forgiveness and a great reward.

4 Those who call out to thee from behind the private apartments, most of them have no sense.

5 And if they had patience till thou come out to them, it would be better for them. And Allāh is Forgiving, Merciful.

6 O you who believe, if an unrighteous man brings you news, look carefully into it, lest you harm a people in ignorance, then be sorry for what you did.

7 And know that among you is Allāh's Messenger. Were he to obey you in many a matter, you would surely fall into distress; but Allāh has endeared the faith to you and has made it seemly in your hearts, and He has made hateful to you disbelief and transgression and disobedience. Such are those who are rightly guided.

8 A grace from Allāh and a favour. And Allāh is Knowing, Wise.

9 And if two parties of the believers quarrel, make

peace between them. Then if one of them does wrong to the other, fight that which does wrong, till it return to Allāh's command. Then, if it returns, make peace between them with justice and act equitably. Surely Allāh loves the equitable.

10 The believers are brethren so make peace between your brethren, and keep your duty to Allāh that mercy may be had on you.

SECTION 2:
Respect for Muslim Brotherhood

11 O you who believe, let not people laugh at people, perchance they may be better than they; nor let women (laugh) at women, perchance they may be better than they. Neither find fault with your own people, nor call one another by nicknames. Evil is a bad name after faith; and whoso turns not, these it is that are the iniquitous.

12 O you who believe, avoid most of suspicion, for surely suspicion in some cases is sin; and spy not nor let some of you backbite others. Does one of you like to eat the flesh of his dead brother? You abhor it! And keep your duty to Allāh, surely Allāh is Oft-returning (to mercy), Merciful.

13 O mankind, surely We have created you from a male and a female, and made you tribes and families that you may know each other. Surely the noblest of you with Allāh is the most dutiful of you. Surely Allāh is Knowing, Aware.

14 The dwellers of the desert say: We believe. Say: You believe not, but say, We submit; and faith has not yet entered into your hearts. And if you obey Allāh and His Messenger, He will not diminish aught of your deeds. Surely Allāh is Forgiving, Merciful.

15 The believers are those only who believe in Allāh and His Messenger, then they doubt not, and struggle hard with their wealth and their lives in the way of Allāh. Such are the truthful ones.

16 Say: Would you apprise Allāh of your religion? and Allāh knows what is in the heavens and what is in the earth. And Allāh is Knower of all things.

17 They presume to lay thee under an obligation by becoming Muslims. Say: Lay me not under an obligation by your Islām; rather Allāh lays you under an obligation by guiding you to the faith, if you are truthful.

18 Surely Allāh knows the unseen of the heavens and the earth. And Allāh is Seer of what you do.

CHAPTER 50
Qāf

(REVEALED AT MAKKAH: 3 *sections*; 45 *verses*)

SECTION 1:
The Resurrection

In the name of Allāh, the Beneficent, the Merciful.

1 Almighty (God)! By the glorious Qur'ān!

2 Nay, they wonder that a warner has come to them from among themselves; so the disbelievers say: This is a wonderful thing!

3 When we die and become dust — that is a far return.

4 We know indeed what the earth diminishes of them and with Us is a book that preserves.

5 Nay, they reject the Truth when it comes to them, so they are in a state of confusion.

6 Do they not look at the sky above them? — how We have made it and adorned it and it has no gaps.

7 And the earth, We have spread it out, and cast therein mountains, and We have made to grow therein of every beautiful kind —

8 To give sight and as a reminder to every servant who turns (to Allāh).

9 And We send down from the clouds water abounding in good, then We cause to grow thereby gardens and the grain that is reaped,

10 And the tall palm-trees having flower spikes piled one above another —

11 A sustenance for the servants, and We give life thereby to a dead land. Thus is the rising.

12 Before them the people of Noah rejected (the Truth) and (so did) the dwellers of al-Rass and Thamūd

13 And 'Ād and Pharaoh and Lot's brethren,

14 And the dwellers of

the grove and the people of Tubba'. They all rejected the messengers, so My threat came to pass.

15 Were We then fatigued with the first creation? Yet they are in doubt about a new creation.

SECTION 2:
The Resurrection

16 And certainly We created man, and We know what his mind suggests to him — and We are nearer to him than his life-vein.

17 When the two receivers receive, sitting on the right and on the left,

18 He utters not a word but there is by him a watcher at hand.

19 And the stupor of death comes in truth; that is what thou wouldst shun.

20 And the trumpet is blown. That is the day of threatening.

21 And every soul comes, with it a driver and a witness.

22 Thou wast indeed heedless of this, but now We have removed from thee thy veil, so thy sight is sharp this day.

23 And his companion will say: This is what is ready with me.

24 Cast into hell every ungrateful, rebellious one,

25 Forbidder of good, exceeder of limits, doubter,

26 Who sets up another god with Allāh, so cast him into severe chastisement.

27 His companion will say: Our Lord, I did not cause him to rebel but he himself went far in error.

28 He will say: Dispute not in My presence, and indeed I gave you warning beforehand.

29 My sentence cannot be changed, nor am I in the least unjust to the servants.

SECTION 3:
The Resurrection

30 On the day when We say to hell: Art thou filled up? And it will say: Are there any more?

31 And the Garden is brought near for those who guard against evil — (it is) not distant.

32 This is what you are

promised — for everyone turning (to Allāh), keeping (the limits) —

33 Who fears the Beneficent in secret, and comes with a penitent heart:

34 Enter it in peace. That is the day of abiding.

35 For them therein is all they wish, and with Us is yet more.

36 And how many a generation We destroyed before them who were mightier in prowess than they! so they went about in the lands. Is there a place of refuge?

37 Surely there is a reminder in this for him who has a heart or he gives ear and is a witness.

38 And certainly We created the heavens and the earth and what is between them in six periods, and no fatigue touched Us.

39 So bear with what they say, and celebrate the praise of thy Lord before the rising of the sun and before the setting.

40 And glorify Him in the night and after prostration.

41 And listen on the day when the crier cries from a near place —

42 The day when they hear the cry in truth. That is the day of coming forth.

43 Surely We give life and cause to die, and to Us is the eventual coming —

44 The day when the earth cleaves asunder from them, hastening forth. That is a gathering easy to Us.

45 We know best what they say, and thou art not one to compel them. So remind by means of the Qur'ān him who fears My threat.

CHAPTER 51
Al-Dhāriyāt: **The Scatterers**

(REVEALED AT MAKKAH: 3 *sections*; 60 *verses*)

SECTION 1:
Falsehood is doomed

In the name of Allāh, the Beneficent, the Merciful.

1 By those scattering broadcast!

2 And those bearing the load!

3 And those running easily!

4 And those distributing the Affair!—

5 What you are promised is surely true,

6 And the Judgment will surely come to pass.

7 By the heaven full of paths!

8 Surely you are of varying opinion —

9 He is turned away from it who would be turned away.

10 Cursed be the liars!

11 Who are in an abyss, neglectful;

12 They ask: When is the day of Judgment?

13 (It is) the day when they are tried at the Fire.

14 Taste your persecution! This is what you would hasten on.

15 Surely the dutiful are amidst Gardens and fountains,

16 Taking that which their Lord gives them. Surely they were before that the doers of good.

17 They used to sleep but little at night.

18 And in the morning they asked (Divine) protection.

19 And in their wealth there was a due share for the beggar and for one who is denied (good).

20 And in the earth are signs for those who are sure,

21 And in yourselves — do you not see?

22 And in the heavens is your sustenance and that which you are promised.

23 So by the Lord of the heavens and the earth! it is surely the truth, just as you speak.

SECTION 2:
The Fate of previous Nations

24 Has the story of Abraham's honoured guests reached thee?

25 When they came to him, they said: Peace! Peace! said he. Strangers!

26 Then he turned aside to his family and brought a fat calf.

27 So he placed it before them. He said: Will you not eat?

28 So he conceived a fear of them. They said: Fear not. And they gave him the good news of a boy possessing knowledge.

29 Then his wife came up in grief, and she smote her face and said: A barren old woman!

30 They said: Thus says thy Lord. Surely He is the Wise, the Knowing.

Part 27

31 He said: what is your errand, O messengers!

32 They said: We have been sent to a guilty people

33 That we may send upon them stones of clay,

34 Marked from thy Lord for the prodigal.

35 Then We brought forth such believers as were there.

36 And We found there but a (single) house of Muslims.

37 And We left therein a sign for those who fear the painful chastisement.

38 And in Moses, when We sent him to Pharaoh with clear authority.

39 But he turned away on account of his might and said: An enchanter or a madman!

40 So We seized him and his hosts and hurled them into the sea, and he was blameable.

41 And in 'Ād, when We sent upon them the destructive wind.

42 It spared naught that it came against, but it made it like ashes.

THE SCATTERERS

43 And in Thamūd, when it was said to them: Enjoy yourselves for a while.

44 But they revolted against the commandment of their Lord, so the punishment overtook them, while they saw.

45 So they were unable to rise up, nor could they defend themselves;

46 And the people of Noah before. Surely they were a transgressing people.

SECTION 3:
Judgment is sure

47 And the heaven, We raised it high with power, and We are Makers of the vast extent.

48 And the earth, We have spread it out. How well We prepared it!

49 And of everything We have created pairs that you may be mindful.

50 So flee to Allāh. Surely I am a plain warner to you from Him.

51 And do not set up with Allāh another god. Surely I am a plain warner to you from Him.

52 Thus there came not a messenger to those before them but they said: An enchanter or a madman!

53 Have they charged each other with this? Nay, they are an inordinate people.

54 So turn away from them, for thou art not to blame;

55 And remind, for reminding profits the believers.

56 And I have not created the jinn and the men except that they should serve Me.

57 I desire no sustenance from them, nor do I desire *that they should* feed Me.

58 Surely Allāh is the Bestower of sustenance, the Lord of Power, the Strong.

59 Surely the lot of the wrongdoers is as was the lot of their companions, so let them not ask Me to hasten on.

60 Woe, then, to those who disbelieve because of that day of theirs which they are promised!

CHAPTER 52
Al-Ṭūr: The Mountain

(REVEALED AT MAKKAH: 2 *sections*; 49 *verses*)

SECTION 1:
Success of the Faithful

In the name of Allāh, the Beneficent, the Merciful.

1 By the Mountain!

2 And a Book written

3 On unfolded vellum!

4 And the frequented House,

5 And the elevated canopy,

6 And the swollen sea!

7 The chastisement of thy Lord will surely come to pass —

8 There is none to avert it;

9 On the day when the heaven will be in a state of commotion,

10 *And the mountains will pass away, fleeing.*

11 Woe on that day to the deniers,

12 Who amuse themselves by vain talk.

13 The day when they are driven to hell-fire with violence.

14 This is the Fire, which you gave the lie to.

15 Is it magic or do you not see?

16 Burn in it, then bear (it) patiently, or bear (it) not, it is the same to you. You are requited only for what you did.

17 The dutiful will be surely in Gardens and bliss,

18 Rejoicing because of what their Lord has given them; and their Lord saved them from the chastisement of the burning Fire.

19 Eat and drink with pleasure for what you did,

20 Reclining on thrones set in lines, and We shall join them to pure, beautiful ones.

21 And those who believe and whose offspring follow them in faith — We unite with them their offspring

and We shall deprive them of naught of their work. Every man is pledged for *what* he does.

22 And We shall aid them with fruit and flesh, as they desire.

23 They pass therein from one to another a cup, wherein is neither vanity, nor sin.

24 And round them go boys of theirs as if they were hidden pearls.

25 And they will advance to each other, questioning —

26 Saying: Surely we feared before on account of our families.

27 But Allāh has been gracious to us and He has saved us from the chastisement of the hot wind.

28 Surely we called upon Him before. Surely, He is the Benign, the Merciful.

SECTION 2:
Opponents are doomed

29 So remind for, by the grace of thy Lord, thou art no soothsayer, nor madman.

30 Or say they: A poet — we wait for him the evil accidents of time.

31 Say: Wait, I too wait along with you.

32 Or do their understandings bid them this? Or are they an inordinate people?

33 Or say they: He has forged it. Nay, they have no faith.

34 Then let them bring a saying like it, if they are truthful.

35 Or were they created without a (creative) agency? Or are they the creators?

36 Or did they create the heavens and the earth? Nay, they are sure of nothing.

37 Or have they the treasures of thy Lord with them? Or have they absolute authority?

38 Or have they the means by which they listen? Then let their listener bring a clear authority.

39 Or has He daughters and you have sons?

40 Or askest thou a reward from them so that they are over-burdened by a debt?

41 Or possess they the unseen, so they write (it) down?

42 Or do they intend a plot? But those who disbelieve will be the ensnared ones in the plot.

43 Or have they a god other than Allāh? Glory be to Allāh from what they set up (with Him)!

44 And if they were to see a portion of the heaven coming down, they would say: Piled-up clouds!

45 Leave them then till they meet that day of theirs wherein they are smitten with punishment:

46 The day when their struggle will avail them naught, nor will they be helped.

47 And surely for those who do wrong there is a chastisement besides that; but most of them know not.

48 And wait patiently for the judgment of thy Lord, for surely thou art before Our eyes, and celebrate the praise of thy Lord, when thou risest,

49 And in the night, give Him glory, too, and at the setting of the stars.

CHAPTER 53
Al-Najm: **The Star**

(REVEALED AT MAKKAH: 3 *sections*; 62 *verses*)

SECTION 1:
Eminence to be attained by the Prophet

In the name of Allāh, the Beneficent, the Merciful.

1 By the star when it sets!

2 Your companion errs not, nor does he deviate.

3 Nor does he speak out of desire.

4 It is naught but revelation that is revealed —

5 One Mighty in Power has taught him,

6 The Lord of Strength. So he attained to perfection,

7 And he is in the highest part of the horizon.

8 Then he drew near, drew nearer yet,

9 So he was the measure of two bows or closer still.

10 So He revealed to His servant what He revealed.

11 The heart was not untrue in seeing what he saw.

12 Do you then dispute with him as to what he saw?

13 And certainly he saw Him in another descent,

14 At the farthest lote-tree.

15 Near it is the Garden of Abode.

16 When that which covers covered the lote-tree;

17 The eye turned not aside, nor did it exceed the limit.

18 Certainly he saw of the greatest signs of his Lord.

19 Have you then considered Lāt and 'Uzzā,

20 And another, the third, Manāt?

21 Are the males for you and for Him the females?

22 This indeed is an unjust division!

23 They are naught but names which you have named, you and your fathers — Allāh has sent no authority for them. They

follow but conjecture and what (their) souls desire. And certainly the guidance has come to them from their Lord.

24 Or shall man have what he wishes?

25 But for Allāh is the Hereafter and the former (life).

SECTION 2:
Nothing avails against Truth

26 And how many angels are in the heavens, whose intercession avails naught except after Allāh gives permission to whom He pleases and chooses.

27 Surely those who believe not in the Hereafter name the angels with female names.

28 And they have no knowledge of it. They follow but conjecture, and surely conjecture avails naught against Truth.

29 So shun him who turns his back upon Our Reminder, and desires nothing but this world's life.

30 That is their goal of knowledge. Surely thy Lord knows best him who strays from His path and He knows best him who goes aright.

31 And Allāh's is whatever is in the heavens and whatever is in the earth, that He may reward those who do evil for that which they do, and reward those who do good with goodness.

32 Those who avoid the great sins and the indecencies, but the passing idea— surely thy Lord is Liberal in Forgiving. He knows you best when He brings you forth from the earth and when you are embryos in the wombs of your mothers; so ascribe not purity to yourselves. He knows him best who guards against evil.

SECTION 3:
Allāh's Power manifested in destruction of Falsehood

33 Seest thou him who turns back,

34 And gives a little, then withholds?

35 Has he the knowledge of the unseen so that he can see?

36 Or has he not been informed of what is in the scriptures of Moses,

37 And (of) Abraham who fulfilled (commandments)?

38 That no bearer of burden bears another's burden:

39 And that man can have nothing but what he strives for:

40 And that his striving will soon be seen.

41 Then he will be rewarded for it with the fullest reward:

42 And that to thy Lord is the goal:

43 And that He it is Who makes (men) laugh and makes (them) weep:

44 And that He it is Who causes death and gives life:

45 And that He creates pairs, the male and the female:

46 From the small life-germ when it is adapted:

47 And that He has ordained the second bringing forth:

48 And that He it is Who gives wealth and contentment:

49 And that He is the Lord of Sirius:

50 And that He destroyed the first 'Ād:

51 And Thamūd, so He spared not:

52 And the people of Noah before. Surely they were most iniquitous and inordinate.

53 And the overthrown cities, He hurled down:

54 So there covered them that which covered.

55 Which, then, of thy Lord's benefits wilt thou dispute?

56 This is a warner of the warners of old.

57 The near Event draws nigh.

58 There is none besides Allāh to remove it.

59 Wonder you then at this announcement?

60 And do you laugh and not weep,

61 While you sport?

62 So bow down in prostration before Allāh and serve (Him).

Chapter 54
Al-Qamar: The Moon

(Revealed at Makkah: 3 *sections*; 55 *verses*)

SECTION 1:
Judgment to overtake opponents

In the name of Allāh, the Beneficent, the Merciful.

1 The hour drew nigh and the moon was rent asunder.

2 And if they see a sign, they turn away and say: Strong enchantment!

3 And they deny and follow their low desires; and every affair is settled.

4 And certainly narratives have come to them, which should deter —

5 Consummate wisdom — but warnings avail not;

6 So turn away from them. On the day when the *Inviter invites them to a* hard task —

7 Their eyes cast down, they will go forth from their graves as if they were scattered locusts,

8 Hastening to the Inviter. The disbelievers will say: This is a hard day!

9 Before them the people of Noah rejected — they rejected Our servant and called (him) mad, and he was driven away.

10 So he called upon his Lord: I am overcome, so do Thou help.

11 Then We opened the gates of heaven with water pouring down,

12 And made water to flow forth in the land in springs, so the water gathered together according to a measure already ordained.

13 And We bore him on that which was made of planks and nails,

14 Floating on, before Our eyes — a reward for him who was denied.

15 And certainly We left it as a sign, but is there any that will mind?

16 How (terrible) was

THE MOON

17 And certainly We have made the Qur'ān easy to remember, but is there any one who will mind?

18 'Ād denied, so how terrible was My chastisement and My warning!

19 Surely We sent on them a furious wind in a day of bitter ill-luck,

20 Tearing men away as if they were the trunks of palm-trees torn up.

21 How (terrible) was then My chastisement and My warning!

22 And certainly We have made the Qur'ān easy to remember, but is there any one who will mind?

SECTION 2:
Thamūd and Lot's People

23 Thamūd rejected the warning.

24 So they said: What! A single mortal from among us! Shall we follow him? We shall then be in sure error and distress.

25 Has the reminder been sent to him from among us? Nay, he is an insolent liar!

26 Tomorrow they will know who is the liar, the insolent one.

27 Surely We are going to send the she-camel as a trial for them; so watch them and have patience.

28 And inform them that the water is shared between them; every share of the water shall be attended.

29 But they called their companion, so he took (a sword) and hamstrung (her).

30 How (terrible) was then My chastisement and My warning!

31 Surely We sent upon them a single cry, so they were like the dry fragments of trees, which the maker of an enclosure collects.

32 And certainly We have made the Qur'ān easy to remember, but is there any one who will mind?

33 The people of Lot treated the warning as a lie.

34 Surely We sent upon them a stone-storm, except Lot's followers; We saved them a little before daybreak —

35 A favour from Us.

Thus do We reward him who gives thanks.

36 And certainly he warned them of Our violent seizure, but they disputed the warning.

37 And certainly they endeavoured to turn him from his guests, but We blinded their eyes; so taste My chastisement and My warning.

38 And certainly a lasting chastisement overtook them in the morning.

39 So taste My chastisement and My warning.

40 And certainly We have made the Qur'ān easy to remember, but is there any one who will mind?

SECTION 3:
Pharaoh and the Prophet's Opponents

41 And certainly the *warning came to Pharaoh*'s people.

42 They rejected all Our signs, so We overtook them with the seizing of the Mighty, the Powerful.

43 Are your disbelievers better than these, or have you an immunity in the scriptures?

44 Or say they: We are a host allied together to help each other?

45 Soon shall the hosts be routed, and they will show (their) backs.

46 Nay, the Hour is their promised time, and the Hour is most grievous and bitter.

47 Surely the guilty are in error and distress.

48 On the day when they are dragged into the Fire upon their faces: Taste the touch of hell.

49 Surely We have created everything according to a measure.

50 And Our command is but once, as the twinkling of an eye.

51 And certainly We destroyed your fellows, but is there anyone who will mind?

52 And everything they do is in the writings.

53 And everything small and great is written down.

54 Surely the dutiful will be among Gardens and rivers,

55 In the seat of truth, with a most Powerful King.

CHAPTER 55
Al-Raḥmān: **The Beneficent**

(REVEALED AT MAKKAH: 3 *sections*; 78 verses)

SECTION 1:
Divine Beneficence

In the name of Allāh, the Beneficent, the Merciful.

1 The Beneficent

2 Taught the Qur'ān.

3 He created man,

4 Taught him expression.

5 The sun and the moon follow a reckoning,

6 And the herbs and the trees adore (Him).

7 And the heaven, He raised it high, and He set up the measure,

8 That you may not exceed the measure,

9 And keep up the balance with equity, nor fall short in the measure.

10 And the earth, He has set it for (His) creatures;

11 Therein is fruit and palms having sheathéd clusters,

12 And the grain with (its) husk and fragrance.

13 Which then of the bounties of your Lord will you deny?

14 He created man from dry clay like earthen vessels,

15 And He created the jinn of a flame of fire.

16 Which then of the bounties of your Lord will you deny?

17 Lord of the two Easts, and Lord of the two Wests.

18 Which then of the bounties of your Lord will you deny?

19 He has made the two seas to flow freely — they meet:

20 Between them is a barrier which they cannot pass.

21 Which then of the bounties of your Lord will you deny?

22 There come forth from them both, pearls large and small.

23 Which then of the bounties of your Lord will you deny?

24 And His are the ships reared aloft in the sea like mountains.

25 Which then of the bounties of your Lord will you deny?

SECTION 2:
Judgment of the Guilty

26 Everyone on it passes away —

27 And there endures forever the person of thy Lord, the Lord of glory and honour.

28 Which then of the bounties of your Lord will you deny?

29 All those in the heavens and the earth ask of Him. Every moment He is in a state (of glory).

30 *Which then of the bounties of your Lord will you deny?*

31 Soon shall We apply Ourselves to you, O you two armies.

32 Which then of the bounties of your Lord will you deny?

33 O assembly of jinn and men, if you are able to pass through the regions of the heavens and the earth, then pass through. You cannot pass through but with authority.

34 Which then of the bounties of your Lord will you deny?

35 The flames of fire and sparks of brass will be sent upon you, then you will not be able to defend yourselves.

36 Which then of the bounties of your Lord will you deny?

37 So when the heaven is rent asunder, so it becomes red like red hide.

38 Which then of the bounties of your Lord will you deny?

39 So on that day neither man nor jinni will be asked about his sin.

40 Which then of the bounties of your Lord will you deny?

41 The guilty will be known by their marks, so they shall be seized by the forelocks and the feet.

42 Which then of the

THE BENEFICENT

bounties of your Lord will you deny?

43 This is the hell which the guilty deny.

44 Round about shall they go between it and hot, boiling water.

45 Which then of the bounties of your Lord will you deny?

SECTION 3:
Reward of the Righteous

46 And for him who fears to stand before his Lord are two Gardens.

47 Which then of the bounties of your Lord will you deny?

48 Full of varieties.

49 Which then of the bounties of your Lord will you deny?

50 Therein are two fountains flowing.

51 Which then of the bounties of your Lord will you deny?

52 Therein are pairs of every fruit.

53 Which then of the bounties of your Lord will you deny?

54 Reclining on beds, whose inner coverings are of silk brocade. And the fruits of the two Gardens are within reach.

55 Which then of the bounties of your Lord will you deny?

56 Therein are those restraining their glances, whom no man nor jinni has touched before them.

57 Which then of the bounties of your Lord will you deny?

58 As though they were rubies and pearls.

59 Which then of the bounties of your Lord will you deny?

60 Is the reward of goodness aught but goodness?

61 Which then of the bounties of your Lord will you deny?

62 And besides those are two (other) Gardens.

63 Which then of the bounties of your Lord will you deny?

64 Inclining to blackness.

65 Which then of the bounties of your Lord will you deny?

66 Therein are two

springs gushing forth.

67 Which then of the bounties of your Lord will you deny?

68 Therein are fruits and palms and pomegranates.

69 Which then of the bounties of your Lord will you deny?

70 Therein are goodly beautiful ones.

71 Which then of the bounties of your Lord will you deny?

72 Pure ones confined to pavilions.

73 Which then of the bounties of your Lord will you deny?

74 Before them man has not touched them, nor jinni.

75 Which then of the bounties of your Lord will you deny?

76 Reclining on green cushions and beautiful carpets.

77 Which then of the bounties of your Lord will you deny?

78 Blessed be the name of thy Lord, the Lord of Glory and Honour!

Chapter 56
Al-Wāqi'ah: **The Event**

(Revealed at Makkah: 3 *sections*; 96 *verses*)

SECTION 1:
Three Classes of Men

In the name of Allāh, the Beneficent, the Merciful.

1 When the Event comes to pass —

2 There is no belying its coming to pass —

3 Abasing (some), exalting (others) —

4 When the earth is shaken with a (severe) shaking,

5 And the mountains are crumbled to pieces,

6 So they are as scattered dust,

7 And you are three sorts.

8 So those on the right-hand; how (happy) are those on the right-hand!

9 And those on the left; how (wretched) are those on the left!

10 And the foremost are the foremost —

11 These are drawn nigh (to Allāh).

12 In Gardens of bliss.

13 A multitude from among the first,

14 And a few from among those of later times,

15 On thrones inwrought,

16 Reclining on them, facing each other.

17 Round about them will go youths never altering in age,

18 With goblets and ewers, and a cup of pure drink —

19 They are not affected with headache thereby, nor are they intoxicated,

20 And fruits that they choose,

21 And flesh of fowl that they desire,

22 And pure, beautiful ones,

23 Like hidden pearls.

24 A reward for what they did.

25 They hear therein no vain or sinful talk —

26 But only the saying, Peace! Peace!

27 And those on the right hand; how (happy) are those on the right hand!

28 Amid thornless lote-trees,

29 And clustered banana-trees,

30 And extensive shade,

31 And water gushing,

32 And abundant fruit,

33 Neither intercepted, nor forbidden,

34 And exalted couches.

35 Surely We have created them a (new) creation,

36 So We have made them virgins,

37 Loving, equals in age,

38 For those on the right hand.

39 A multitude from among the first,

40 And a multitude from among those of later times.

SECTION 2:
The Guilty

41 And those on the left hand; how (wretched) are those on the left hand!

42 In hot wind and boiling water,

43 And shadow of black smoke,

44 Neither cool nor refreshing.

45 Surely they lived before that in ease.

46 And they persisted in the great violation.

47 And they used to say: When we die and become dust and bones, shall we then indeed be raised?

48 Or our fathers of yore?

49 Say: The ancients and those of later times

50 Will surely be gathered together for the appointed hour of a known day.

51 Then shall you, O you who err and deny,

52 Eat of the tree of Zaqqūm,

53 And fill (your) bellies with it;

54 Then drink after it of boiling water;

55 And drink as drinks the thirsty camel.

56 This is their entertainment on the day of Requital.

57 We have created you, why do you not then accept?

58 See you that which you emit?

59 Is it you that create it or are We the Creator?

60 We have ordained death among you and We are not to be overcome,

61 That We may change your state and make you grow into what you know not.

62 And certainly you know the first growth, why do you not then mind?

63 See you what you sow?

64 Is it you that cause it to grow, or are We the Causer of growth?

65 If We pleased, We would make it chaff, then would you lament:

66 Surely we are burdened with debt:

67 Nay, we are deprived.

68 See you the water which you drink?

69 Do you bring it down from the clouds, or are We the Bringer?

70 If We pleased, We could make it saltish; why give you not thanks?

71 See you the fire which you kindle?

72 Is it you that produce the trees for it, or are We the Producer?

73 We have made it a reminder and an advantage for the wayfarers of the desert.

74 So glorify the name of thy Lord, the Incomparably Great.

SECTION 3:
Judgment is Inevitable

75 But nay, I swear by revelation of portions (of the Qur'ān)!—

76 And it is a great oath indeed, if you knew —

77 Surely it is a bounteous Qur'ān,

78 In a book that is protected,

79 Which none touches save the purified ones.

80 A revelation from the Lord of the worlds.

81 Is it this announcement that you disdain?

82 And make your denial your means of subsistence.

83 Why is it not then that when it comes up to the throat,

84 And you at that time look on —

85 And We are nearer to it than you, but you see not —

86 Why then, if you are not held under authority,

87 Do you not send it back, if you are truthful?

88 Then if he is one of those drawn nigh (to Allāh),

89 Then happiness and bounty and a Garden of bliss.

90 And if he is one of those on the right hand,

91 Then peace to thee from those on the right hand.

92 And if he is one of the rejectors, the erring ones,

93 He has an entertainment of boiling water,

94 And burning in hell.

95 Surely this is a certain truth.

96 So glorify the name of thy Lord, the Incomparably Great.

CHAPTER 57
Al-Ḥadīd: **Iron**

(Revealed at Madīnah: 4 *sections*; 29 *verses*)

SECTION 1:
Establishment of the Kingdom of God

In the name of Allāh, the Beneficent, the Merciful.

1 Whatever is in the heavens and the earth declares the glory of Allāh, and He is the Mighty, the Wise.

2 His is the kingdom of the heavens and the earth. He gives life and causes death; and He is Possessor of power over all things.

3 He is the First and the Last and the Manifest and the Hidden, and He is Knower of all things.

4 He it is Who created the heavens and the earth in six periods, and He is established on the Throne of Power. He knows that which goes down into the earth and that which comes forth out of it, and that which comes down from heaven and that which goes up to it. And He is with you wherever you are. And Allāh is Seer of what you do.

5 His is the kingdom of the heavens and the earth; and to Allāh are (all) affairs returned.

6 He causes the night to pass into the day, and causes the day to pass into the night. And He is Knower of what is in the hearts.

7 Believe in Allāh and His Messenger, and spend of that whereof He has made you heirs. So those of you who believe and spend — for them is a great reward.

8 And what reason have you that you believe not in Allāh? And the Messenger invites you to believe in your Lord, and He has indeed accepted your covenant, if you are believers.

9 He it is Who sends down clear messages to His servant, that he may bring you forth from darkness into light. And surely Allāh is Kind, Merciful to you.

10 And what reason have you that you spend not in Allāh's way? And Allāh's is the inheritance of the heavens and the earth. Those of you who spent before the Victory and fought are not on a level (with others). They are greater in rank than those who spent and fought afterwards. And Allāh has promised good to all. And Allāh is Aware of what you do.

SECTION 2:
Light and Life given by the Prophet

11 Who is he that will offer to Allāh a good gift, so He will double it for him, and he will have a generous reward.

12 On that day thou wilt see the faithful men and the faithful women, their light gleaming before them and on their right hand. Good news for you this day! — Gardens wherein rivers flow, to abide therein! That is the grand achievement.

13 On the day when the hypocrites, men and women, will say to those who believe: Wait for us, that we may borrow from your light. It will be said: Turn back and seek a light. Then a wall, with a door in it, will be raised between them. Within it shall be mercy, and outside of it chastisement.

14 They will cry out to them: Were we not with you? They will say: Yea, but you caused yourselves to fall into temptation, and you waited and doubted, and vain desires deceived you, till the threatened punishment of Allāh came, and the arch-deceiver deceived you about Allāh.

15 So this day no ransom will be accepted from you, nor from those who disbelieved. Your abode is the Fire; it is your patron and evil is the resort.

16 Has not the time yet come for the believers that their hearts should be humble for the remembrance of Allāh and the Truth that is revealed, and (that) they should not be like those who were given the Book before, but time was prolonged for them, so their hearts hardened. And most of them are transgressors.

17 Know that Allāh gives life to the earth after its death. Indeed, We have made the signs clear for you that you may understand.

18 The men who give in charity and the women who give in charity and set apart for Allāh a goodly portion, it will be doubled for them, and theirs is a generous reward.

19 And those who believe in Allāh and His messengers, they are the truthful and the faithful ones with their Lord. They have their reward and their light. And those who disbelieve and reject Our messages, they are the inmates of hell.

SECTION 3:
Truth shall be Established

20 Know that this world's life is only sport and play and gaiety and boasting among yourselves and a vying in the multiplication of wealth and children. It is as rain, whose causing the vegetation to grow pleases the husbandmen, then it withers away so that thou seest it turning yellow, then it becomes chaff. And in the Hereafter is a severe chastisement, and (also) forgiveness from Allāh and (His) pleasure. And this world's life is naught but a source of vanity.

21 Vie one with another for forgiveness from your Lord and a Garden the extensiveness of which is as the extensiveness of the heaven and the earth — it is prepared for those who believe in Allāh and His messengers. That is the grace of Allāh; He gives it to whom He pleases. And Allāh is the Lord of mighty grace.

22 No disaster befalls in the earth, or in yourselves, but it is in a book before We bring it into existence — surely that is easy to Allāh —

23 So that you grieve not for what has escaped you, nor exult in that which He has given you. And Allāh loves not any arrogant boaster:

24 Such as are niggardly and enjoin niggardliness on

men. And whoever turns back, then surely Allāh is the Self-Sufficient, the Praised.

25 Certainly We sent Our messengers with clear arguments, and sent down with them the Book and the measure, that men may conduct themselves with equity. And We sent down iron, wherein is great violence and advantages to men, and that Allāh may know who helps Him and His messengers, unseen. Surely Allāh is Strong, Mighty.

SECTION 4:
Double Reward for Believers

26 And certainly We sent Noah and Abraham, and We gave prophethood and the Book to their offspring; so among them is he who goes aright, but most of them are transgressors.

27 Then We made Our messengers to follow in their footsteps, and We made Jesus son of Mary to follow, and We gave him the Gospel. And We put compassion and mercy in the hearts of those who followed him. And (as for) monkery, they innovated it — We did not prescribe it to them — only to seek Allāh's pleasure, but they did not observe it with its due observance. So We gave those of them who believed their reward, but most of them are transgressors.

28 O you who believe, keep your duty to Allāh and believe in His Messenger — He will give you two portions of His mercy, and give you a light in which you shall walk, and forgive you. And Allāh is Forgiving, Merciful —

29 That the People of the Book may know that they control naught of the grace of Allāh, and that grace is in Allāh's hand. He gives it to whom He pleases. And Allāh is the Lord of mighty grace.

Part 28

CHAPTER 58

Al-Mujādilah: The Pleading Woman

(REVEALED AT MADĪNAH: 3 *sections*; 22 *verses*)

SECTION 1: Safeguarding Women's Rights

In the name of Allāh, the Beneficent, the Merciful.

1 Allāh indeed has heard the plea of her who pleads with thee about her husband and complains to Allāh; and Allāh hears the contentions of both of you. Surely Allāh is Hearing, Seeing.

2 Those of you who put away their wives by calling them their mothers — they are not their mothers. None are their mothers save those who gave them birth, and they utter indeed a hateful word and a lie. And surely Allāh is Pardoning, Forgiving.

3 And those who put away their wives by calling them their mothers, then go back on that which they said, must free a captive before they touch one another. To this you are exhorted; and Allāh is Aware of what you do.

4 But he who has not the means, should fast for two months successively before they touch one another, and he who is unable to do so should feed sixty needy ones. That is in order that you may have faith in Allāh and His Messenger. And these are Allāh's limits. And for the disbelievers is a painful chastisement.

5 Surely those who oppose Allāh and His Messenger will be humbled as those before them were humbled; and indeed We have revealed clear messages. And for the disbelievers is an abasing chastisement.

6 On the day when Allāh will raise them all together, then inform them of what they did. Allāh records it,

while they forget it. And Allāh is Witness over all things.

SECTION 2:
Secret Counsels condemned

7 Seest thou not that Allāh knows whatever is in the heavens and whatever is in the earth? There is no secret counsel between three but He is the fourth of them, nor between five but He is the sixth of them, nor between less than that nor more but He is with them wheresoever they are; then He will inform them of what they did on the day of Resurrection. Surely Allāh is Knower of all things.

8 Seest thou not those who are forbidden secret counsels, then they return to that which they are forbidden, and hold secret *counsels for sin and revolt* and disobedience to the Messenger. And when they come to thee they greet thee with a greeting with which Allāh greets thee not, and say within themselves: Why does not Allāh punish us for what we say? Hell is enough for them; they will burn in it, and evil is the resort!

9 O you who believe, when you confer together in private, give not to each other counsel of sin and revolt and disobedience to the Messenger, but give to each other counsel of goodness and observance of duty. And keep your duty to Allāh, to Whom you will be gathered together.

10 Secret counsels are only of the devil that he may cause to grieve those who believe, and he can hurt them naught except with Allāh's permission. And on Allāh let the believers rely.

11 O you who believe, when it is said to you, Make room in assemblies, make room. Allāh will give you ample. And when it is said, Rise up, rise up. Allāh will exalt those of you who believe, and those who are given knowledge, to high ranks. And Allāh is Aware of what you do.

12 O you who believe, when you consult the Messenger, offer something in charity before your consultation. That is better for you

THE PLEADING WOMAN

and purer. But if you have not (the means), then surely Allāh is Forgiving, Merciful.

13 Do you fear that you will not (be able to) give in charity before your consultation? So when you do it not, and Allāh has turned to you (mercifully), keep up prayer and pay the poor-rate and obey Allāh and His Messenger. And Allāh is Aware of what you do.

SECTION 3:
Internal Enemy to be guarded against

14 Hast thou not seen those who take for friends a people with whom Allāh is wroth? They are neither of you nor of them, and they swear falsely, while they know.

15 Allāh has prepared for them a severe chastisement. Evil indeed is that which they do!

16 They take shelter under their oaths, so they turn (men) from Allāh's way; for them is an abasing chastisement.

17 Of no avail against Allāh, will be to them their wealth or their children. They are the companions of the Fire; therein they will abide.

18 On the day when Allāh will raise them all up, they will swear to Him as they swear to you, and they think that they have some (excuse). Now surely they are the liars.

19 The devil has gained the mastery over them, so he has made them forget the remembrance of Allāh. They are the devil's party. Now surely the devil's party are the losers.

20 Those who oppose Allāh and His Messenger, they shall be among the most abased.

21 Allāh has written down: I shall certainly prevail, I and My messengers. Surely Allāh is Strong, Mighty.

22 Thou wilt not find a people who believe in Allāh and the latter day loving those who oppose Allāh and His Messenger, even though they be their fathers, or their sons, or their brothers, or their kinsfolk. These are they into whose hearts

He has impressed faith, and strengthened them with a Spirit from Himself, and He will cause them to enter Gardens wherein flow rivers, abiding therein. Allāh is well-pleased with them and they are well-pleased with Him. These are Allāh's party. Now surely it is Allāh's party who are the successful!

Chapter 59

Al-Ḥashr: **The Banishment**

(Revealed at Madīnah: 3 *sections*; 24 *verses*)

SECTION 1:
The Exiled Jews

In the name of Allāh, the Beneficent, the Merciful.

1 Whatever is in the heavens and whatever is in the earth glorifies Allāh; and He is the Mighty, the Wise.

2 He it is Who caused those who disbelieved of the People of the Book to go forth from their homes at the first banishment. You deemed not that they would go forth, while they thought that their fortresses would defend them against Allāh. But Allāh came to them from a place they expected not and cast terror into their hearts — they demolished their houses with their own hands and the hands of the believers. So take a lesson, O you who have eyes!

3 And had it not been that Allāh had decreed for them the exile, He would certainly have chastised them in this world; and for them in the Hereafter is the chastisement of the Fire.

4 That is because they were opposed to Allāh and His Messenger, and whoever is opposed to Allāh, surely Allāh is Severe in retribution.

5 Whatever palm-tree you cut down or leave it standing upon its roots, it is by Allāh's permission, and that He may abase the transgressors.

6 And whatever Allāh restored to His Messenger from them, you did not press forward against it any horse or any riding-camel, but Allāh gives authority to His messengers against whom He pleases. And Allāh is Possessor of power over all things.

7 Whatever Allāh restored to His Messenger from the people of the towns, it is for Allāh and for the Messenger, and for the near of kin and the orphans and the needy and the wayfarer, so that it be not taken by turns by the rich among you. And whatever the Messenger gives you, accept it, and whatever he forbids you, abstain (therefrom); and keep your duty to Allāh. Surely Allāh is Severe in retribution.

8 (It is) for the poor who fled, who were driven from their homes and their possessions, seeking grace of Allāh and (His) pleasure, and helping Allāh and His Messenger. These it is that are the truthful.

9 And those who made their abode in the City and in faith before them love those who have fled to them, and find in their hearts no need of what they are given, and prefer (them) before themselves, though poverty may afflict them. And whoever is saved from the niggardliness of his soul, these it is that are the successful.

10 And those who come after them say: Our Lord, forgive us and our brethren who had precedence of us in faith, and leave no spite in our hearts towards those who believe. Our Lord, surely Thou art Kind, Merciful.

SECTION 2:
The Hypocrites fail in their Promise to the Jews

11 Hast thou not seen the hypocrites? They say to their brethren who disbelieve from among the People of the Book: If you are expelled, we certainly will go forth with you, and we will never obey anyone concerning you; and if you are fought against, we will certainly help you. And Allāh bears witness that they surely are liars.

12 If they are expelled, they will not go forth with them, and if they are fought against, they will not help them; and even if they help them, they will certainly turn (their) backs; then they shall not be helped.

13 Your fear in their hearts is indeed greater than Allāh's. That is because they are a people who understand not.

14 They will not fight against you in a body save in fortified towns or from behind walls. Their fighting between them is severe. Thou wouldst think them united, but their hearts are divided. That is because they are a people who have no sense.

15 Like those before them shortly: they tasted the evil consequences of their conduct, and for them is a painful chastisement.

16 Like the devil when he says to man: Disbelieve. But when he disbelieves, he says: I am free of thee: surely I fear Allāh, the Lord of the worlds.

17 So the end of both of them is that they are both in the Fire to abide therein. And that is the reward of the wrongdoers.

SECTION 3:
An Exhortation

18 O you who believe, keep your duty to Allāh, and let every soul consider that which it sends forth for the morrow, and keep your duty to Allāh. Surely Allāh is Aware of what you do.

19 And be not like those who forget Allāh, so He makes them forget their own souls. These are the transgressors.

20 Not alike are the companions of the Fire and the owners of the Garden. The owners of the Garden are the achievers.

21 Had We sent down this Qur'ān on a mountain, thou wouldst certainly have seen it falling down, splitting asunder because of the fear of Allāh. And We set forth these parables to men that they may reflect.

22 He is Allāh besides Whom there is no God: The Knower of the unseen and the seen; He is the Beneficent, the Merciful.

23 He is Allāh, besides Whom there is no God; the King, the Holy, the Author of Peace, the Granter of Security, Guardian over all, the Mighty, the Supreme, the Possessor of greatness. Glory be to Allāh from that which they set up (with Him)!

24 He is Allāh; the Creator, the Maker, the Fashioner: His are the most beautiful names. Whatever is in the heavens and the earth declares His glory; and He is the Mighty, the Wise.

Chapter 60
Al-Mumtaḥanah:
The Woman Who is Examined

(Revealed at Madīnah: *2 sections*; *13 verses*)

SECTION 1:
Friendly Relations with Enemies

In the name of Allāh, the Beneficent, the Merciful.

1 O you who believe, take not My enemy and your enemy for friends. Would you offer them love, while they deny the Truth that has come to you, driving out the Messenger and yourselves because you believe in Allāh, your Lord? If you have come forth to strive in My way and to seek My pleasure, would you love them in secret? And I know what you conceal and what you manifest. And whoever of you does this, he indeed strays from the straight path.

2 If they overcome you, they will be your enemies, and will stretch forth their hands and their tongues towards you with evil, and they desire that you may disbelieve.

3 Your relationships and your children would not profit you, on the day of Resurrection — He will decide between you. And Allāh is Seer of what you do.

4 Indeed, there is for you a good example in Abraham and those with him, when they said to their people: We are clear of you and of that which you serve besides Allāh. We disbelieve in you and there has arisen enmity and hatred between us and you forever until you believe in Allāh alone — except Abraham's saying to his sire: I would ask forgiveness for thee, and I control naught for thee from Allāh. Our Lord, on Thee do we rely, and to Thee do we turn, and to Thee is the eventual coming.

5 Our Lord, make us not a trial for those who disbelieve, and forgive us, our Lord. Surely Thou art the Mighty, the Wise.

6 Certainly there is for you in them a good example, for him who hopes for Allāh and the Last Day. And whoever turns away, surely Allāh is the Self-Sufficient, the Praised.

SECTION 2:
Friendly Relations with non-Muslims

7 It may be that Allāh will bring about friendship between you and those of them whom you hold as enemies. And Allāh is Powerful; and Allāh is Forgiving, Merciful.

8 Allāh forbids you not respecting those who fight you not for religion, nor drive you forth from your homes, that you show them kindness and deal with them justly. Surely Allāh loves the doers of justice.

9 Allāh forbids you only respecting those who fight you for religion, and drive you forth from your homes and help (others) in your expulsion, that you make friends of them; and whoever makes friends of them, these are the wrongdoers.

10 O you who believe, when believing women come to you fleeing, examine them. Allāh knows best their faith. Then if you know them to be believers send them not back to the disbelievers. Neither are these (women) lawful for them, nor are those (men) lawful for them. And give them what they have spent; and there is no blame on you in marrying them, when you give them their dowries. And hold not to the ties of marriage of disbelieving women, and ask for what you have spent, and let them ask for what they have spent. That is Allāh's judgment; He judges between you. And Allāh is Knowing, Wise.

11 And if any part (of the dowries) of your wives has passed away from you to the disbelievers, then your turn comes, give to those whose wives have gone away the like of what they have spent, and keep your duty to Allāh in Whom you believe.

12 O Prophet, when believing women come to thee giving thee a pledge that they will not associate aught with Allāh, and will not steal, nor commit adultery; nor kill their children, nor bring a calumny which they have forged of themselves, nor disobey thee in what is good, accept their pledge, and ask forgiveness for them from Allāh. Surely Allāh is Forgiving, Merciful.

13 O you who believe, take not for friends a people with whom Allāh is wroth — they indeed despair of the Hereafter, as the disbelievers despair of those in the graves.

CHAPTER 61

Al-Ṣaff: **The Ranks**

(Revealed at Madīnah: 2 *sections*; 14 *verses*)

SECTION 1:
Triumph of Islām

In the name of Allāh, the Beneficent, the Merciful.

1 *Whatever is in the heavens and whatever is in the earth glorifies Allāh; and He is the Mighty, the Wise.*

2 O you who believe, why say you that which you do not?

3 It is most hateful in the sight of Allāh that you say that which you do not.

4 Surely Allāh loves those who fight in His way in ranks, as if they were a solid wall.

5 And when Moses said to his people: O my people, why do you malign me, when you know that I am Allāh's messenger to you? But when they deviated, Allāh made their hearts deviate. And Allāh guides not the transgressing people.

6 And when Jesus, son of Mary, said: O Children of Israel, surely I am the messenger of Allāh to you, verifying that which is before me of the Torah and giving the good news of a Messenger who will come after me, his name being Ahmad. But when he came to them with clear arguments, they said: This is clear enchantment.

7 And who is more unjust than he who forges a lie against Allāh and he is invited to Islām. And Allāh guides not the unjust people.

8 They desire to put out the light of Allāh with their mouths, but Allāh will perfect His light, though the disbelievers may be averse.

9 He it is Who has sent His Messenger with the guidance and the Religion of Truth that He may make it prevail over all religions, though the polytheists are averse.

SECTION 2:
Establishment of Truth needed Sacrifices

10 O you who believe, shall I lead you to a merchandise which will deliver you from a painful chastisement?

11 You should believe in Allāh and His Messenger, and strive hard in Allāh's way with your wealth and your lives. That is better for you, did you but know!

12 He will forgive you your sins and cause you to enter Gardens wherein rivers flow, and goodly dwellings in Gardens of perpetuity — that is the mighty achievement —

13 And yet another (blessing) that you love: help from Allāh and a victory near at hand; and give good news to the believers.

14 O you who believe, be helpers (in the cause) of Allāh, as Jesus, son of Mary, said to the disciples: Who are my helpers in the cause of Allāh? The disciples said: We are helpers (in the cause) of Allāh. So a party of the Children of Israel believed and another party disbelieved; then We aided those who believed against their enemy, and they became predominant.

Chapter 62
Al-Jumu'ah: The Congregation

(Revealed at Madīnah: 2 *sections*; 11 *verses*)

SECTION 1:
Muslims chosen for Divine Favours

In the name of Allāh, the Beneficent, the Merciful.

1 Whatever is in the heavens and whatever is in the earth glorifies Allāh, the King, the Holy, the Mighty, the Wise.

2 He it is Who raised among the illiterates a Messenger from among themselves, who recites to them His messages and purifies them, and teaches them the Book and the Wisdom — although certainly they were before in manifest error —

3 And others from among them who have not yet joined them. And He is the Mighty, the Wise.

4 That is Allāh's grace; He grants it to whom He pleases. And Allāh is the Lord of mighty grace.

5 The likeness of those who were charged with the Torah, then they observed it not, is as the likeness of the ass carrying books. Evil is the likeness of the people who reject the messages of Allāh. And Allāh guides not the iniquitous people.

6 Say: O you who are Jews, if you think that you are the favourites of Allāh to the exclusion of other people, then invoke death, if you are truthful.

7 But they will never invoke it because of what their hands have sent before. And Allāh is Knower of the wrongdoers.

8 Say: The death from which you flee, that will surely overtake you; then you will be sent back to the Knower of the unseen and the seen, so He will inform you of that which you did.

SECTION 2:
Friday Prayer

9 O you who believe, when the call is sounded for prayer on Friday, hasten to the remembrance of Allāh and leave off traffic. That is better for you, if you know.

10 But when the prayer is ended, disperse abroad in the land and seek of Allāh's grace, and remember Allāh much, that you may be successful.

11 And when they see merchandise or sport, they break away to it, and leave thee standing. Say: What is with Allāh is better than sport and merchandise. And Allāh is the best of Providers.

CHAPTER 63
Al-Munāfiqūn: The Hypocrites

(REVEALED AT MADĪNAH: 2 *sections*; 11 *verses*)

SECTION 1:
The Hypocrites

In the name of Allāh, the Beneficent, the Merciful.

1 When the hypocrites come to thee, they say: We bear witness that thou art indeed Allāh's Messenger. And Allāh knows thou art indeed His Messenger. And Allāh bears witness that the hypocrites are surely liars.

2 They take shelter under their oaths, thus turning (men) from Allāh's way. Surely evil is that which they do.

3 That is because they believed, then disbelieved; thus their hearts are sealed, so they understand not.

4 And when thou seest them, their persons please thee; and if they speak, thou listenest to their speech. They are like pieces of wood, clad with garments. They think every cry to be against them. They are the enemy, so beware of them. May Allāh destroy them! How they are turned back!

5 And when it is said to them: Come, the Messenger of Allāh will ask forgiveness for you, they turn away their heads and thou seest them hindering (others), and they are big with pride.

6 It is alike to them whether thou ask forgiveness for them or ask not forgiveness for them — Allāh will never forgive them. Surely Allāh guides not the transgressing people.

7 They it is who say: Spend not on those who are with the Messenger of Allāh that they may disperse. And Allāh's are the treasures of the heavens and the earth, but the hypocrites understand not.

8 They say: If we return to Madīnah, the mightier will surely drive out the meaner therefrom. And

might belongs to Allāh and His Messenger and the believers, but the hypocrites know not.

SECTION 2:
An Exhortation

9 O you who believe, let not your wealth nor your children divert you from the remembrance of Allāh; and whoever does that, these are the losers.

10 And spend out of that which We have given you before death comes to one of you, and he says: My Lord, why didst Thou not respite me to a near term, so that I should have given alms and been of the doers of good deeds?

11 But Allāh respites not a soul, when its term comes. And Allāh is Aware of what you do.

Chapter 64

Al-Taghābun:
The Manifestation of Losses

(Revealed at Madīnah: 2 *sections*; 18 *verses*)

SECTION 1:
Disbelievers Warned

In the name of Allāh, the Beneficent, the Merciful.

1 Whatever is in the heavens and whatever is in the earth glorifies Allāh. His is the kingdom, and His the praise; and He is Possessor of power over all things.

2 He it is Who created you, but one of you is a disbeliever and one of you is a believer. And Allāh is Seer of what you do.

3 He created the heavens and the earth with truth, and He shaped you, then made goodly your shapes; and to Him is the resort.

4 He knows what is in the heavens and the earth, and He knows what you hide and what you manifest. And Allāh is Knower of what is in the hearts.

5 Has there not come to you the story of those who disbelieved before, then tasted the evil consequences of their conduct, and they had a painful chastisement?

6 That is because there came to them their messengers with clear arguments, but they said: Shall mortals guide us? So they disbelieved and turned away, and Allāh is above all need. And Allāh is Self-Sufficient, Praised.

7 Those who disbelieve think that they will not be raised. Say: Aye, by my Lord! you will certainly be raised; then you will certainly be informed of what you did. And that is easy to Allāh.

8 So believe in Allāh and His Messenger and the Light which We have revealed. And Allāh is Aware of what you do.

9 The day when He will gather you for the day of Gathering, that is the day of the Manifestation of losses. And whoever believes in Allāh and does good, He will remove from him his evil and cause him to enter Gardens wherein rivers flow, to abide therein forever. That is the great achievement.

10 And those who disbelieve and reject Our messages, they are the companions of the Fire, abiding therein; and evil is the resort.

SECTION 2:
An Exhortation

11 No calamity befalls but by Allāh's permission. And whoever believes in Allāh, He guides his heart. And Allāh is Knower of all things.

12 And obey Allāh and obey the Messenger; but if you turn away, the duty of Our Messenger is only to deliver (the message) clearly.

13 Allāh, there is no God but He. And on Allāh let the believers rely.

14 O you who believe, surely of your wives and your children there are enemies to you, so beware of them. And if you pardon and forbear and forgive, surely Allāh is Forgiving, Merciful.

15 Your wealth and your children are only a trial, and Allāh — with Him is a great reward.

16 So keep your duty to Allāh as much as you can, and hear and obey and spend; it is better for your souls. And whoever is saved from the greediness of his soul, these it is that are the successful.

17 If you set apart for Allāh a goodly portion, He will double it for you and forgive you. And Allāh is the Multiplier (of rewards), Forbearing,

18 The Knower of the unseen and the seen, the Mighty, the Wise.

CHAPTER 65
Al-Ṭalāq: **The Divorce**

(REVEALED AT MADĪNAH: 2 *sections*; 12 *verses*)

SECTION 1:
Supplementary Divorce Rules

In the name of Allāh, the Beneficent, the Merciful.

1 O Prophet, when you divorce women, divorce them for their prescribed period, and calculate the period; and keep your duty to Allāh, your Lord. Turn them not out of their houses — nor should they themselves go forth — unless they commit an open indecency. And these are the limits of Allāh. And whoever goes beyond the limits of Allāh, he indeed wrongs his own soul. Thou knowest not that Allāh may after that bring about an event.

2 So when they have reached their prescribed time, retain them with kindness or dismiss them with kindness, and call to witness two just ones from among you, and give upright testimony for Allāh. With that is admonished he who believes in Allāh and the Latter Day. And whoever keeps his duty to Allāh, He ordains a way out for him,

3 And gives him sustenance from whence he imagines not. And whoever trusts in Allāh, He is sufficient for him. Surely Allāh attains His purpose. Allāh indeed has appointed a measure for everything.

4 And those of your women who despair of menstruation, if you have a doubt, their prescribed time is three months, and of those, too, who have not had their courses. And the pregnant women, their prescribed time is that they lay down their burden. And whoever keeps his duty to Allāh, He makes his affair easy for him.

5 That is the command of Allāh, which He has

revealed to you. And whoever keeps his duty to Allāh, He will remove from him his evils and give him a big reward.

6 Lodge them where you live according to your means, and injure them not to straiten them. And if they are pregnant, spend on them until they lay down their burden. Then if they suckle for you, give them their recompense, and enjoin one another to do good; and if you disagree, another will suckle for him.

7 Let him who has abundance spend out of his abundance, and whoever has his means of subsistence straitened to him, let him spend out of that which Allāh has given him. Allāh lays not on any soul a burden beyond that which He has given it. Allāh brings about ease after difficulty.

SECTION 2:
Makkah warned

8 And how many a town which rebelled against the commandment of its Lord and His messengers, so We called it to severe account and We chastised it with a stern chastisement!

9 So it tasted the evil consequences of its conduct, and the end of its affair was perdition.

10 Allāh has prepared for them severe chastisement, so keep your duty to Allāh, O men of understanding, who believe. Allāh has indeed sent down to you a Reminder —

11 A Messenger ˋ who recites to you the clear messages of Allāh, so that he may bring forth those who believe and do good deeds from darkness into light. And whoever believes in Allāh and does good deeds, He will cause him to enter Gardens wherein rivers flow, to abide therein forever. Allāh has indeed given him a goodly sustenance.

12 Allāh is He Who created seven heavens, and of the earth the like thereof. The command descends among them, that you may know that Allāh is Possessor of power over all things, and that Allāh encompasses all things in (His) knowledge.

CHAPTER 66
Al-Taḥrīm: The Prohibition

(REVEALED AT MADĪNAH: 2 *sections*; 12 *verses*)

SECTION 1:
Prophet's Domestic Relations

In the name of Allāh, the Beneficent, the Merciful.

1 O Prophet, why dost thou forbid (thyself) that which Allāh has made lawful for thee? Seekest thou to please thy wives? And Allāh is Forgiving, Merciful.

2 Allāh indeed has sanctioned for you the expiation of your oaths; and Allāh is your Patron, and He is the Knowing, the Wise.

3 And when the Prophet confided an information to one of his wives — but when she informed (others) of it, and Allāh informed him of it, he made known part of it and passed over part. So when he told her of it, she said: Who informed thee of this? He said: The Knowing, the One Aware, informed me.

4 If you both turn to Allāh, then indeed your hearts are inclined (to this); and if you back up one another against him, then surely Allāh is his Patron, and Gabriel and the righteous believers, and the angels after that are the aiders.

5 Maybe, his Lord, if he divorce you, will give him in your place wives better than you, submissive, faithful, obedient, penitent, adorers, fasters, widows, and virgins.

6 O you who believe, save yourselves and your families from a Fire whose fuel is men and stones; over it are angels, stern and strong. They do not disobey Allāh in that which He commands them, but do as they are commanded.

7 O you who disbelieve, make no excuses this day. You are rewarded only as you did.

SECTION 2:
Progress of the Faithful

8 *O you who believe, turn to Allāh with sincere repentance. It may be your Lord will remove from you your evil and cause you to enter Gardens wherein flow rivers, on the day on which Allāh will not abase the Prophet and those who believe with him. Their light will gleam before them and on their right hands* — *they will say: Our Lord, make perfect for us our light, and grant us protection; surely Thou art Possessor of power over all things.*

9 *O Prophet, strive against the disbelievers and the hypocrites, and remain firm against them, and their abode is hell; and evil is the resort.*

10 Allāh sets forth an example for those who disbelieve — the wife of Noah and the wife of Lot. They *were both under two of Our righteous servants, but they* acted treacherously towards them, so they availed them naught against Allāh, and it was said: Enter the Fire with those who enter.

11 And Allāh sets forth an example for those who believe — the wife of Pharaoh, when she said: My Lord, build for me a house with Thee in the Garden and deliver me from Pharaoh and his work, and deliver me from the iniquitous people.

12 And Mary, the daughter of Amran, who guarded her chastity, so We breathed into him of Our inspiration, and she accepted the truth of the words of her Lord and His Books, and she was of the obedient ones.

Part 29

CHAPTER 67

Al-Mulk: The Kingdom

(REVEALED AT MAKKAH: 2 sections; 30 verses)

SECTION 1:
The Kingdom of God

In the name of Allāh, the Beneficent, the Merciful.

1 Blessed is He in Whose hand is the Kingdom, and He is Possessor of power over all things,

2 Who created death and life that He might try you — which of you is best in deeds. And He is the Mighty, the Forgiving,

3 Who created the seven heavens alike. Thou seest no incongruity in the creation of the Beneficent. Then look again: Canst thou see any disorder?

4 Then turn the eye again and again — thy look will return to thee confused, while it is fatigued.

5 And certainly We have adorned this lower heaven with lamps and We make them means of conjectures for the devils, and We have prepared for them the chastisement of burning.

6 And for those who disbelieve in their Lord is the chastisement of hell, and evil is the resort.

7 When they are cast therein, they will hear a loud moaning of it as it heaves,

8 Almost bursting for fury. Whenever a group is cast into it, its keepers ask them: Did not a warner come to you?

9 They say: Yea, indeed a warner came to us, but we denied and said: Allāh has revealed nothing; you are only in great error.

10 And they say: Had we but listened or pondered, we should not have been among the inmates of the burning Fire.

11 Thus they will confess

THE KINGDOM

their sins; so far (from good) are the inmates of the burning Fire.

12 Those who fear their Lord in secret, for them is surely forgiveness and a great reward.

13 And conceal your word or manifest it, truly He is Knower of that which is in the hearts.

14 Does He not know Who created? And He is the Knower of subtleties, the Aware.

SECTION 2:
The Disbelievers' Doom

15 He it is Who made the earth subservient to you, so go about in the spacious sides thereof, and eat of His sustenance. And to Him is the rising (after death).

16 Do you feel secure that He Who is in the heaven will not make the earth to swallow you up? Then lo! it shall shake.

17 Or do you feel secure that He Who is in the heaven will not send on you a violent wind? Then shall you know how (truthful) was My warning!

18 And certainly those before them denied, then how (terrible) was My disapproval!

19 Do they not see the birds above them spreading and contracting (their wings)? Naught upholds them save the Beneficent. Surely He is Seer of all things.

20 Or who is it that will be a host for you to help you against the Beneficent? The disbelievers are in naught but delusion.

21 Or who is it that will give you sustenance, if He should withhold His sustenance? Nay, they persist in disdain and aversion.

22 Is, then, he who goes prone upon his face better guided or he who walks upright on a straight path?

23 Say: He it is Who brought you into being and made for you ears and eyes and hearts. Little thanks it is you give!

24 Say: He it is Who multiplies you in the earth and to Him you will be gathered.

25 And they say: When will this threat be (executed), if you are truthful?

26 Say: The knowledge is with Allāh only, and I am only a plain warner.

27 But when they see it nigh, the faces of those who disbelieve will be grieved, and it will be said: This is that which you used to call for.

28 Say: Have you considered if Allāh should destroy me and those with me — rather He will have mercy on us — yet who will protect the disbelievers from a painful chastisement?

29 Say: He is the Beneficent — we believe in Him and on Him do we rely. So you will come to know who it is that is in clear error.

30 Say: Have you considered if your water should subside, who is it then that will bring you flowing water?

CHAPTER 68
Al-Qalam: **The Pen**

(REVEALED AT MAKKAH: 2 *sections*; 52 *verses*)

SECTION 1:
Not a Madman's Message

In the name of Allāh, the Beneficent, the Merciful.

1 (By) the inkstand and the pen and that which they write!

2 By the grace of thy Lord thou art not mad.

3 And surely thine is a reward never to be cut off.

4 And surely thou hast sublime morals.

5 So thou wilt see, and *they (too) will see,*

6 Which of you is mad.

7 Surely thy Lord knows best who is erring from His way, and He knows best those who go aright.

8 So obey not the rejectors.

9 They wish that thou shouldst be pliant, so they (too) would be pliant.

10 And obey not any mean swearer,

11 Defamer, going about with slander,

12 Hinderer of good, outstepping the limits, sinful,

13 Ignoble, besides all that, notoriously mischievous —

14 Because he possesses wealth and sons.

15 When Our messages are recited to him, he says: Stories of those of yore!

16 We shall brand him on the snout.

17 *We shall try them* as We tried the owners of the garden, when they swore to pluck its fruits in the morning,

18 And would not set aside a portion (for the poor).

19 But a visitation from thy Lord came on it, while they slept.

20 So it became as black, barren land —

21 Then they called out one to another in the morning,

22 Saying: Go early to your tilth, if you would pluck (the fruit).

23 So they went, while they said one to another in low tones:

24 No poor man shall enter it today upon you.

25 And in the morning they went, having the power to prevent.

26 But when they saw it, they said: Surely we are in error;

27 Nay, we are made to suffer privation.

28 The best of them said: Said I not to you, Why do you not glorify (Allāh)?

29 They said: Glory be to our Lord! surely we were unjust.

30 Then some of them *advanced against* others, blaming each other.

31 Said they: O woe to us! Surely we were inordinate —

32 Maybe, our Lord will give us instead one better than it — surely to our Lord we make petition.

33 Such is the chastisement. And certainly the chastisement of the Hereafter is greater, did they but know!

SECTION 2:
A Reminder for the Nations

34 Surely the dutiful have with their Lord Gardens of bliss.

35 Shall We then make those who submit as the guilty?

36 What is the matter with you? How do you judge?

37 Or have you a book wherein you read

38 That you shall surely have therein what you choose?

39 Or have you covenants from Us on oath, extending to the day of Resurrection, that yours is surely what *you judge?*

40 Ask them which of them will vouch for that.

41 Or have they associate-gods? Then let them bring their associates, if they are truthful.

42 On the day when there is a severe affliction, and

THE PEN

they are called upon to prostrate themselves, but they are not able —

43 Their looks cast down, abasement will cover them. And they were indeed called upon to prostrate themselves, while yet they were safe.

44 So leave Me alone with him who rejects this announcement. We shall overtake them by degrees, from whence they know not.

45 And I bear with them, surely My plan is firm.

46 Or dost thou ask from them a reward, so that they are burdened with debt?

47 Or is the unseen with them so that they write (it) down?

48 So wait patiently for the judgment of thy Lord, and be not like the Companion of the fish, when he cried while he was in distress.

49 Had not favour from his Lord reached him, he would certainly have been cast down on naked ground, while he was blamed.

50 Then his Lord chose him, and He made him of the righteous.

51 And those who disbelieve would almost smite thee with their eyes when they hear the Reminder, and they say: Surely he is mad!

52 And it is naught but a Reminder for the nations.

Chapter 69
Al-Ḥāqqah: **The Sure Truth**

(Revealed at Makkah: 2 *sections*; 52 *verses*)

SECTION 1:
The Doom

In the name of Allāh, the Beneficent, the Merciful.

1 The sure Truth!

2 What is the sure Truth?

3 And what would make thee realize what the sure Truth is?

4 Thamūd and 'Ād called the calamity a lie.

5 Then as for Thamūd, they were destroyed by the severe punishment.

6 And as for 'Ād, they were destroyed by a roaring, violent wind,

7 Which He made to prevail against them for seven nights and eight days continuously, so that thou mightest have seen the people therein prostrate as if they were trunks of hollow palm-trees.

8 So canst thou see a remnant of them?

9 And Pharaoh and those before him and the overthrown cities wrought evil.

10 And they disobeyed the messenger of their Lord, so He punished them with a vehement punishment.

11 Surely We carried you in the ship, when the water rose high,

12 That We might make it a reminder for you, and that the retaining ear might retain it.

13 So when the trumpet is blown with a single blast,

14 And the earth and the mountains are borne away and crushed with one crash —

15 On that day will the Event come to pass,

16 And the heaven will be cleft asunder; so that day it will be frail,

17 And the angels will be on its sides. And above them

eight will bear that day thy Lord's Throne of Power.

18 On that day you will be exposed to view — no secret of yours will remain hidden.

19 Then as for him who is given his book in his right hand, he will say: Lo! Read my book.

20 Surely I knew that I should meet my account.

21 So he will be in a life of bliss,

22 In a lofty Garden,

23 Its fruits are near.

24 Eat and drink pleasantly for that which you sent on before in bygone days.

25 And as for him who is given his book in his left hand — he will say: O would that my book had not been given to me!

26 And I had not known what my account was!

27 O would that (death) had made an end (of me)!

28 My wealth has not availed me.

29 My authority has gone from me.

30 Seize him, then fetter him,

31 Then cast him into the burning Fire,

32 Then insert him in a chain the length of which is seventy cubits.

33 Surely he believed not in Allāh, the Great,

34 Nor did he urge the feeding of the poor.

35 Therefore he has not here this day a true friend,

36 Nor any food except refuse,

37 Which none but the wrongdoers eat.

SECTION 2:
False Allegations refuted

38 But nay! I swear by that which you see,

39 And that which you see not!

40 Surely, it is the word of an honoured Messenger,

41 And it is not the word of a poet. Little is it that you believe!

42 Nor the word of a soothsayer. Little is it that you mind!

43 It is a revelation from the Lord of the worlds.

44 And if he had fabricated against Us certain sayings,

45 We would certainly have seized him by the right hand,

46 Then cut off his heart's vein.

47 And not one of you could have withheld Us from him.

48 And surely it is a Reminder for the dutiful.

49 And We certainly know that some of you are rejectors.

50 And it is indeed a (source of) grief to the disbelievers.

51 And surely it is the certain Truth.

52 So glorify the name of thy Lord, the incomparably Great.

CHAPTER 70
Al-Ma'ārij: **The Ways of Ascent**

(REVEALED AT MAKKAH: *2 sections; 44 verses*)

SECTION 1:
Certainty of the Punishment

In the name of Allāh, the Beneficent, the Merciful.

1 A questioner asks about the chastisement to befall

2 The disbelievers — there is none to avert it —

3 From Allāh, Lord of the ways of Ascent.

4 To Him ascend the angels and the Spirit in a day the measure of which is fifty thousand years.

5 So be patient with a goodly patience.

6 Surely they see it far off,

7 And We see it nigh.

8 The day when the heaven is as molten brass,

9 And the mountains are as wool;

10 And no friend will ask of friend,

11 (Though) they are made to see them. The guilty one would fain redeem himself from the chastisement of that day by his children,

12 And his wife and his brother,

13 And his kin that gave him shelter,

14 And all that are in the earth — then deliver him —

15 By no means! Surely it is a flaming Fire,

16 Plucking out the extremities —

17 It shall claim him who retreats and turns his back,

18 And hoards then withholds.

19 Surely man is created impatient —

20 Fretful when evil afflicts him,

21 And niggardly when good befalls him —

22 Except those who pray,

23 Who are constant at their prayer,

24 And in whose wealth there is a known right

25 For the beggar and the destitute,

26 And those who accept the truth of the day of Judgment:

27 And those who are fearful of the chastisement of their Lord —

28 Surely the chastisement of their Lord is (a thing) not to be felt secure from —

29 And those who restrain their sexual passions,

30 Except in the presence of their mates or those whom their right hands possess — for such surely are not to be blamed.

31 But he who seeks to go beyond this, these are the transgressors.

32 And those who are faithful to their trusts and their covenant,

33 And those who are upright in their testimonies,

34 And those who keep a guard on their prayer.

35 These are in Gardens, honoured.

SECTION 2:
A New Nation to be raised up

36 But what is the matter with those who disbelieve, that they hasten on to thee,

37 On the right hand and on the left, in sundry parties?

38 Does every man of them desire to be admitted to the Garden of bliss?

39 By no means! Surely We have created them for what they know.

40 But nay! I swear by the Lord of the Eastern lands and the Western lands! that We are certainly Powerful

41 To bring in their place (others) better than them, and We shall not be overcome.

42 So leave them alone to plunge in vain talk and to sport, until they come face to face with that day of theirs which they are promised —

43 The day when they come forth from the graves

THE WAYS OF ASCENT

in haste, as hastening on to a goal,

44 Their eyes cast down, disgrace covering them. Such is the day which they are promised.

CHAPTER 71
Nūḥ: Noah

(REVEALED AT MAKKAH: 2 *sections*; 28 *verses*)

SECTION 1:
Noah preaches

In the name of Allāh, the Beneficent, the Merciful

1 Surely We sent Noah to his people, saying: Warn thy people before there come to them a painful chastisement.

2 He said: O my people, surely I am a plain warner to you:

3 That you should serve Allāh and keep your duty to Him and obey me —

4 He will forgive you some of your sins and grant you respite to an appointed term. Surely the term of Allāh, when it comes, is not postponed. Did you but know!

5 He said: My Lord, I have called my people night and day:

6 But my call has only made them flee the more.

7 And whenever I call to them that Thou mayest forgive them, they thrust their fingers in their ears and cover themselves with their garments, and persist and are big with pride.

8 Then surely I have called to them aloud,

9 Then spoken to them in public and spoken to them in private,

10 So I have said: Ask forgiveness of your Lord; surely He is ever Forgiving,

11 He will send down upon you rain, pouring in abundance,

12 And help you with wealth and sons, and make for you gardens, and make for you rivers.

13 What is the matter with you that you hope not for greatness from Allāh?

14 And indeed He has created you by various stages.

15 See you not how Allāh

has created the seven heavens alike,

16 And made the moon therein a light, and made the sun a lamp?

17 And Allāh has caused you to grow out of the earth as a growth,

18 Then He returns you to it, then will He bring you forth a (new) bringing forth.

19 And Allāh has made the earth a wide expanse for you,

20 That you may go along therein in spacious paths.

SECTION 2:
Destruction of Transgressors

21 Noah said: My Lord, surely they disobey me and follow him whose wealth and children have increased him in naught but loss.

22 And they have planned a mighty plan.

23 And they say: Forsake not your gods; nor forsake Wadd, nor Suwā', nor Yaghūth and Ya'ūq and Nasr.

24 And indeed they have led many astray. And increase Thou the wrongdoers in naught but perdition.

25 Because of their wrongs they were drowned, then made to enter Fire, so they found no helpers besides Allāh.

26 And Noah said: My Lord, leave not of the disbelievers any dweller on the land.

27 For if Thou leave them, they will lead astray Thy servants, and will not beget any but *immoral*, ungrateful ones.

28 My Lord, forgive me and my parents and him who enters my house believing, and the believing men and the believing women. And increase not the wrongdoers in aught but destruction!

Chapter 72
Al-Jinn: The Jinn

(Revealed at Makkah: 2 *sections*; 28 *verses*)

SECTION 1:
Foreign Believers

In the name of Allāh, the Beneficent, the Merciful.

1 Say: It has been revealed to me that a party of the jinn listened, so they said: Surely we have heard a wonderful Qur'ān,

2 Guiding to the right way — so we believe in it. And we shall not set up anyone with our Lord:

3 And He — exalted be the majesty of our Lord! — has not taken a consort, nor a son:

4 And the foolish among us used to forge extravagant lies against Allāh:

5 And we thought that men and jinn did not utter a lie against Allāh:

6 And persons from among men used to seek refuge with persons from among the jinn, so they increased them in evil doing:

7 And they thought, as you *think*, that Allāh would not raise anyone:

8 And we sought to reach heaven, but we found it filled with strong guards and flames:

9 And we used to sit in some of the sitting-places thereof to steal a hearing. But he who tries to listen now finds a flame lying in wait for him:

10 And we know not whether evil is meant for those on earth or whether their Lord means to direct them aright:

11 And some of us are good and others of us are below that — we are sects following different ways:

12 And we know that we cannot escape Allāh in the earth, nor can we escape Him by flight:

13 And when we heard

the guidance, we believed in it. So whoever believes in his Lord, he fears neither loss nor injustice:

14 And some of us are those who submit, and some of us are deviators. So whoever submits, these aim at the right way.

15 And as to deviators, they are fuel of hell:

16 And if they keep to the (right) way, We would certainly give them to drink of abundant water,

17 So that We may try them thereby. And whoever turns away from the reminder of his Lord, He will make him enter into an afflicting chastisement:

18 And the mosques are Allāh's, so call not upon anyone with Allāh:

19 And when the Servant of Allāh stood up praying to Him, they well-nigh crowded him (to death).

SECTION 2:
Protection of Revelation

20 Say: I only call upon my Lord, and associate naught with Him.

21 Say: I control not evil nor good for you.

22 Say: None can protect me against Allāh, nor can I find any refuge besides Him:

23 (Mine is naught) but to deliver (the command) of Allāh and His messages. And whoever disobeys Allāh and His Messenger, surely for him is the Fire of hell, to abide therein for ages,

24 Till when they see that which they are promised, they will know who is weaker in helpers and less in numbers.

25 Say: I know not whether that which you are promised is nigh or if my Lord will appoint for it a distant term.

26 The Knower of the unseen, so He makes His secrets known to none,

27 Except a messenger whom He chooses. For surely He makes a guard to go before him and after him,

28 That He may know that they have truly delivered the messages of their Lord; and He encompasses what is with them, and He keeps account of all things.

CHAPTER 73
Al-Muzzammil:
The one covering himself up

(REVEALED AT MAKKAH: 2 *sections*; 20 *verses*)

SECTION 1:
The Prophet enjoined to pray

In the name of Allāh, the Beneficent, the Merciful.

1 O thou covering thyself up!

2 Rise to pray by night except a little,

3 Half of it, or lessen it a little,

4 Or add to it, and recite the Qur'ān in a leisurely manner.

5 Surely We shall charge thee with a weighty word.

6 The rising by night is surely the firmest way to tread and most effective in speech.

7 Truly thou hast by day prolonged occupation.

8 And remember the name of thy Lord and devote thyself to Him with (complete) devotion.

9 The Lord of the East and the West — there is no God but He — so take Him for Protector.

10 And bear patiently what they say and forsake them with a becoming withdrawal.

11 And leave Me and the deniers, possessors of plenty, and respite them a little.

12 Surely with Us are heavy fetters and a flaming Fire,

13 And food that chokes and a painful chastisement.

14 On the day when the earth and the mountains quake and the mountains become (as) heaps of sand let loose.

15 Surely We have sent to you a Messenger, a witness against you, as We sent a messenger to Pharaoh.

16 But Pharaoh disobeyed the messenger, so

We seized him with a violent grip.

17 How, then, if you disbelieve, will you guard yourselves on the day which will make children grey-headed?

18 The heaven being rent asunder thereby. His promise is ever fulfilled.

19 Surely this is a Reminder; so let him, who will, take a way to his Lord.

SECTION 2:
Prayer enjoined on Muslims

20 Thy Lord knows indeed that thou passest in prayer nearly two-thirds of *the night, and (sometimes)* half of it, and (sometimes) a third of it, as do a party of those with thee. And Allāh measures the night and the day. He knows that (all of) you are not able to do it, so He has turned to you (mercifully); so read of the Qur'ān that which is easy for you. He knows that there are sick among you, and others who travel in the land seeking of Allāh's bounty, and others who fight in Allāh's way. So read as much of it as is easy (for you), and keep up prayer and pay the poor-rate and offer to Allāh a goodly gift. And whatever of good you send on beforehand for yourselves, you will find it with Allāh — that is best and greatest in reward. And ask forgiveness of Allāh. Surely Allāh is Forgiving, Merciful.

CHAPTER 74
Al-Muddaththir:
The one wrapping himself up

(REVEALED AT MAKKAH: 2 *sections*; 56 *verses*)

SECTION 1:
The Prophet is enjoined to Warn

In the name of Allāh, the Beneficent, the Merciful.

1 O thou who wrappest thyself up,

2 Arise and warn,

3 And thy Lord do magnify,

4 And thy garments do purify,

5 And uncleanness do shun,

6 And do no favour seeking gain,

7 And for the sake of thy Lord, be patient.

8 For when the trumpet is sounded,

9 That will be — that day — a difficult day,

10 For the disbelievers, anything but easy.

11 Leave Me alone with him whom I created,

12 And gave him vast riches,

13 *And sons dwelling in his presence,*

14 And made matters easy for him,

15 And yet he desires that I should give more!

16 By no means! Surely he is inimical to Our messages.

17 I will make a distressing punishment overtake him.

18 Surely he reflected and determined,

19 But may he be destroyed how he determined!

20 Again, may he be destroyed how he determined!

21 Then he looked,

22 Then frowned and scowled,

23 Then turned back and

THE ONE WRAPPING HIMSELF UP

was big with pride,

24 Then said: This is naught but magic from of old!

25 This is naught but the word of a mortal!

26 I will cast him into hell.

27 And what will make thee realize what hell is?

28 It leaves naught, and spares naught.

29 It scorches the mortal.

30 Over it are nineteen.

31 And We have made none but angels wardens of the Fire, and We have not made their number but as a trial for those who disbelieve, that those who have been given the Book may be certain and those who believe may increase in faith, and those who have been given the Book and the believers may not doubt; and that those in whose hearts is a disease and the disbelievers may say: What does Allāh mean by this parable? Thus Allāh leaves in error whom He pleases, and guides whom He pleases. And none knows the hosts of thy Lord but He. And this is naught but a Reminder to mortals.

SECTION 2:
The Warning

32 Nay, by the moon!

33 And the night when it departs!

34 And the dawn when it shines!—

35 Surely it is one of the gravest (misfortunes).

36 A warning to mortals,

37 To him among you who will go forward or will remain behind.

38 Every soul is held in pledge for what it earns,

39 Except the people of the right hand.

40 In Gardens, they ask one another,

41 About the guilty:

42 What has brought you into hell?

43 They will say: We were not of those who prayed;

44 Nor did we feed the poor;

45 And we indulged in vain talk with vain talkers;

46 And we called the day of Judgment a lie;

47 Till the inevitable overtook us.

48 So the intercession of intercessors will not avail them.

49 What is then the matter with them, that they turn away from the Reminder.

50 As if they were frightened asses,

51 Fleeing from a lion?

52 Nay, everyone of them desires that he should be given pages spread out —

53 By no means! But they fear not the Hereafter.

54 Nay, it is surely a Reminder.

55 So whoever pleases may mind it.

56 And they will not mind unless Allāh please. He is Worthy that duty should be kept to Him and Worthy to forgive.

Chapter 75
Al-Qiyāmah: **The Resurrection**

(Revealed at Makkah: 2 sections; 40 verses)

SECTION 1:
The Truth of the Resurrection

In the name of Allāh, the Beneficent, the Merciful.

1 Nay, I swear by the day of Resurrection!

2 Nay, I swear by the self-accusing spirit!

3 Does man think that We shall not gather his bones?

4 Yea, We are Powerful to make complete his whole make.

5 Nay, man desires to go on doing evil in front of him.

6 He asks: When is the day of Resurrection?

7 So when the sight is confused,

8 And the moon becomes dark,

9 And the sun and the moon are brought together —

10 Man will say on that day: Whither to flee?

11 No! There is no refuge!

12 With thy Lord on that day is the place of rest.

13 Man will that day be informed of what he sent before and what he put off.

14 Nay, man is evidence against himself,

15 Though he put up excuses.

16 Move not thy tongue therewith to make haste with it.

17 Surely on Us rests the collecting of it and the reciting of it.

18 So when We recite it, follow its recitation.

19 Again on Us rests the explaining of it.

20 Nay, but you love the present life,

21 And neglect the Hereafter.

22 (Some) faces that day will be bright,

23 Looking to their Lord.

24 And (other) faces that day will be gloomy,

25 Knowing that a great disaster will be made to befall them.

26 Nay, when it comes up to the throat,

27 And it is said: *Who will ascend (with it)?*

28 And he is sure that it is the parting,

29 And affliction is combined with affliction —

30 To thy Lord on that day is the driving.

SECTION 2:
The Dead Rise

31 So he accepted not the truth, nor prayed,

32 But denied and turned back,

33 Then he went to his people in haughtiness.

34 Nearer to thee and nearer,

35 Again, nearer to thee and nearer (is woe).

36 *Does man think that he will be left aimless?*

37 Was he not a small life-germ in sperm emitted?

38 Then he was a clot; so He created (him), then made (him) perfect.

39 Then He made of him two kinds, the male and the female.

40 Is not He Powerful to give life to the dead?

Chapter 76
Al-Insān: **The Man**

(REVEALED AT MAKKAH: *2 sections; 31 verses*)

SECTION 1:
Attainment of Perfection

In the name of Allāh, the Beneficent, the Merciful.

1 Surely there came over man a time when he was nothing that could be mentioned.

2 Surely We have created man from sperm mixed (with ovum), to try him, so We have made him hearing, seeing.

3 We have truly shown him the way; he may be thankful or unthankful.

4 Surely We have prepared for the disbelievers chains and shackles and a burning Fire.

5 The righteous truly drink of a cup tempered with camphor —

6 A fountain from which the servants of Allāh drink, making it flow in abundance.

7 They fulfil vows and fear a day, the evil of which is widespread.

8 And they give food, out of love for Him, to the poor and the orphan and the captive.

9 We feed you, for Allāh's pleasure only — We desire from you neither reward nor thanks.

10 Surely we fear from our Lord a stern, distressful day.

11 So Allāh will ward off from them the evil of that day, and cause them to meet with splendour and happiness;

12 And reward them, for their steadfastness, with a Garden and with silk;

13 Reclining therein on raised couches; they will see therein neither (excessive heat of) sun nor intense cold.

14 And close down upon them are its shadows, and

its fruits are made near (to them), easy to reach.

15 And round about them are made to go vessels of silver and goblets of glass,

16 Crystal-clear, made of silver — they have measured them according to a measure.

17 And they are made to drink therein a cup tempered with ginger —

18 (Of) a fountain therein called Salsabīl.

19 And round about them will go youths, never altering in age; when thou seest them thou wilt think them to be scattered pearls.

20 And when thou lookest thither, thou seest blessings and a great kingdom.

21 On them are garments of fine green silk and thick brocade, and they are adorned with bracelets of silver, and their Lord makes them to drink a pure drink.

22 Surely this is a reward for you, and your striving is recompensed.

SECTION 2: **Another Generation Raised up**

23 Surely We have revealed the Qur'ān to thee, in portions.

24 So wait patiently for the judgment of thy Lord, and obey not a sinner or an ungrateful one among them.

25 And glorify the name of thy Lord morning and evening.

26 And during part of the night adore Him, and glorify Him throughout a long night.

27 Surely these love the transitory life and neglect a grievous day before them.

28 We created them and made firm their make, and, when We will, We can bring in their place the like of them by change.

29 Surely this is a Reminder; so whoever will, let him take a way to his Lord.

30 And you will not, unless Allāh please. Surely Allāh is ever Knowing, Wise —

31 He admits whom He pleases to His mercy; and the wrongdoers — He has prepared for them a painful chastisement.

Chapter 77
Al-Mursalāt: Those Sent Forth

(Revealed at Makkah: 2 *sections*; 50 verses)

SECTION 1:
Consequences of Rejection

In the name of Allāh, the Beneficent, the Merciful.

1 By those sent forth to spread goodness!

2 Then those driving off the chaff!

3 And those spreading (goodness), far and wide!

4 Then those making a distinction!

5 Then those offering the Reminder,

6 To clear or to warn! —

7 Surely that which you are promised will come to pass.

8 So when the stars are made to disappear,

9 And when the heaven is rent asunder,

10 And when the mountains are carried away as dust,

11 And when the messengers are made to reach their appointed time,

12 To what day is the doom fixed?

13 To the day of Decision.

14 And what will make thee comprehend what the day of Decision is?

15 Woe on that day to the rejectors!

16 Did We not destroy the former generations?

17 Then We followed them up with later ones.

18 Thus do We deal with the guilty.

19 Woe on that day to the rejectors!

20 Did We not create you from ordinary water?

21 Then We placed it in a secure resting-place,

22 Till an appointed term,

23 So We determined — how well are We at determining!

24 Woe on that day to the rejectors!

25 Have We not made the earth draw to itself

26 The living and the dead,

27 And made therein lofty mountains, and given you to drink of sweet water?

28 Woe on that day to the rejectors!

29 Walk on to that which you called a lie.

30 Walk on to the shadow, having three branches,

31 Neither cool, nor availing against the flame.

32 It sends up sparks like palaces,

33 As if they were tawny camels.

34 Woe on that day to the rejectors!

35 This is the day on which they speak not,

36 Nor are they allowed to offer excuses.

37 Woe on that day to the rejectors!

38 This is the day of Decision; We have gathered you and those of yore.

39 So if you have a plan, plan against me (now).

40 Woe on that day to the rejectors!

SECTION 2:
Consequences of Rejection

41 Surely the dutiful are amid shades and fountains,

42 And fruits such as they desire.

43 Eat and drink pleasantly for what you did.

44 Thus do We reward the doers of good.

45 Woe on that day to the rejectors!

46 Eat and enjoy yourselves for a little; surely you are guilty.

47 Woe on that day to the rejectors!

48 And when it is said to them, Bow down, they bow not down.

49 Woe on that day to the rejectors!

50 In what narration after it, will they believe?

Part 30

CHAPTER 78

Al-Naba': **The Announcement**

(Revealed at Makkah: 2 *sections*; 40 *verses*)

SECTION 1:
The Day of Decision

In the name of Allāh, the Beneficent, the Merciful.

1 Of what do they ask one another?

2 Of the tremendous announcement

3 About which they differ.

4 Nay, they will soon know;

5 Nay, again, they will soon know.

6 Have We not made the earth an expanse

7 And the mountains as pegs?

8 And We have created you in pairs,

9 And made your sleep for rest,

10 And made the night a covering,

11 And made the day for seeking livelihood.

12 And We have made above you seven strong (bodies),

13 And made a shining lamp,

14 And We send down from the clouds water pouring forth in abundance,

15 That We may bring forth thereby grain and herbs,

16 And luxuriant gardens.

17 Surely the day of Decision is appointed —

18 The day when the trumpet is blown, so you come forth in hosts,

19 And the heaven is opened so it becomes as doors,

20 And the mountains are moved off, so they remain a semblance.

21 Surely hell lies in wait,

22 A resort for the inordinate,

23 Living therein for long years.

24 They taste not therein coolness nor drink,

25 But boiling and intensely cold water,

26 Requital corresponding.

27 Surely they feared not the reckoning,

28 And rejected Our messages, giving the lie (thereto).

29 And We have recorded everything in a book,

30 So taste, for We shall add to you naught but chastisement.

SECTION 2:
The Day of Decision

31 Surely for those who keep their duty is achievement,

32 Gardens and vineyards,

33 And youthful (companions), equals in age,

34 And a pure cup.

35 They hear not therein vain words, nor lying —

36 A reward from thy Lord, a gift sufficient;

37 The Lord of the heavens and the earth and what is between them, the Beneficent, they are not able to address Him.

38 The day when the Spirit and the angels stand in ranks; none shall speak except he whom the Beneficent permits and he speaks aright.

39 That is the True Day, so whoever desires may take refuge with his Lord.

40 Truly We warn you of a chastisement near at hand— the day when man will see what his hands have sent before, and the disbeliever will say: O would that I were dust!

CHAPTER 79
Al-Nāzi'āt: Those Who Yearn
(REVEALED AT MAKKAH: 2 sections; 46 verses)

SECTION 1:
The Great Commotion

In the name of Allāh, the Beneficent, the Merciful.

1 By those yearning vehemently!

2 And those going forth cheerfully!

3 And those running swiftly!

4 And those that are foremost going ahead!

5 And those regulating the Affair!

6 The day when the quaking one shall quake —

7 The consequence will follow it.

8 Hearts that day will palpitate,

9 Their eyes downcast.

10 They say: Shall we indeed be restored to (our) first state?

11 What! After we are rotten bones?

12 They say: That would then be a return with loss.

13 It is only a single cry,

14 When lo! they will be awakened.

15 Has not there come to thee the story of Moses,

16 When his Lord called him in the holy valley, Ṭuwā?

17 Go to Pharaoh, surely he has rebelled.

18 And say: Wilt thou purify thyself?

19 And I will guide thee to thy Lord so that thou fear (Him).

20 So he showed him the mighty sign;

21 But he denied and disobeyed.

22 Then he went back hastily,

23 So he gathered and called out.

24 Then he said: I am

your Lord, the most High.

25 So Allāh seized him with the punishment of the Hereafter and of this life.

26 Surely there is in this a lesson for him who fears.

SECTION 2:
The Great Calamity

27 Are you the stronger in creation or the heaven? He made it.

28 He raised high its height, and made it perfect,

29 And He made dark its night and brought out its light.

30 And the earth, He cast it after that.

31 He brought forth from it its water and its pasture.

32 And the mountains, He made them firm,

33 A provision for you and for your cattle.

34 So when the great Calamity comes;

35 The day when man remembers all that he strove for,

36 And hell is made manifest to him who sees.

37 Then as for him who is inordinate,

38 And prefers the life of *this world*,

39 Hell is surely the abode.

40 And as for him who fears to stand before his Lord and restrains himself from low desires,

41 The Garden is surely the abode.

42 They ask thee about the Hour, When will that take place,

43 About which thou remindest?

44 To thy Lord is the goal of it.

45 Thou art only a warner to him who fears it.

46 On the day when they see it, it will be as if they had but tarried for an evening or a morning.

CHAPTER 80

'Abasā: **He Frowned**

(Revealed at Makkah: 42 verses)

In the name of Allāh, the Beneficent, the Merciful.

1 He frowned and turned away,

2 Because the blind man came to him.

3 And what would make thee know that he might purify himself,

4 Or be mindful, so the Reminder should profit him?

5 As for him who considers himself free from need

6 To him thou dost attend.

7 And no blame is on thee, if he purify himself not.

8 And as to him who comes to thee striving hard,

9 And he fears —

10 To him thou payest no regard.

11 Nay, surely it is a Reminder.

12 So let him, who will, mind it.

13 In honoured books,

14 Exalted, purified,

15 In the hands of scribes,

16 Noble, virtuous.

17 Woe to man! How ungrateful is he!

18 Of what thing did He create him?

19 Of a small life-germ. He creates him, then proportions him,

20 Then makes the way easy for him,

21 Then He causes him to die, then assigns to him a grave,

22 Then, when He will, He raises him to life again.

23 Nay, but he does not what He commands him.

24 Then let man look at his food —

25 How We pour down abundant water,

26 Then cleave the earth, cleaving (it) asunder,

27 Then cause the grain to grow therein,

28 And grapes and clover,

29 And the olive and the palm,

30 And thick gardens,

31 And fruits and herbage —

32 A provision for you and your cattle.

33 But when the deafening cry comes,

34 The day when a man flees from his brother,

35 And his mother and his father,

36 And his spouse and his sons.

37 Every man of them, that day, will have concern enough to make him indifferent to others.

38 Faces on that day will be bright,

39 Laughing, joyous.

40 And faces on that day will have dust on them,

41 Darkness covering them.

42 Those are the disbelievers, the wicked.

CHAPTER 81
Al-Takwīr: **The Folding Up**

(REVEALED AT MAKKAH: 29 verses)

In the name of Allāh, the Beneficent, the Merciful.

1 When the sun is folded up,

2 And when the stars are dust-coloured,

3 And when the mountains are made to pass away,

4 And when the camels are abandoned,

5 And when the wild animals are gathered together,

6 And when the cities are made to swell,

7 And when men are united,

8 And when the one buried alive is asked

9 For what sin she was killed,

10 And when the books are spread,

11 And when the heaven has its covering removed,

12 And when hell is kindled,

13 And when the Garden is brought nigh —

14 Every soul will know what it has prepared.

15 Nay, I call to witness the stars,

16 Running their course, (and) setting,

17 And the night when it departs,

18 And the morning when it brightens,

19 Surely it is the word of a bountiful Messenger,

20 The possessor of strength, established in the presence of the Lord of the Throne,

21 One (to be) obeyed, and faithful.

22 And your companion is not mad.

23 And truly he saw himself on the clear horizon.

24 Nor is he niggardly of the unseen.

25 Nor is it the word of an accursed devil —

26 Whither then are you going?

27 It is naught but a Reminder for the nations,

28 For him among you who will go straight.

29 And you will not, except Allāh please, the Lord of the worlds.

CHAPTER 82
Al-Infiṭār: **The Cleaving**

(REVEALED AT MAKKAH: *19 verses*)

In the name of Allāh, the Beneficent, the Merciful.

1 When the heaven is cleft asunder,

2 And when the stars become dispersed,

3 And when the rivers are made to flow forth,

4 And when the graves are laid open —

5 Every soul will know what it has sent before and what it has held back.

6 O man, what beguiles thee from thy Lord, the Gracious?

7 Who created thee, then made thee complete, then made thee in a right good state?

8 Into whatever form He pleases He casts thee.

9 Nay, but you give the lie to the Judgment,

10 And surely there are keepers over you,

11 Honourable recorders,

12 They know what you do.

13 Surely the righteous are in bliss,

14 And the wicked are truly in burning Fire —

15 They will enter it on the day of Judgment.

16 And will not be absent from it.

17 And what will make thee realize what the day of Judgment is?

18 Again, what will make thee realize what the day of Judgment is?

19 The day when no soul controls aught for another soul. And the command on that day is Allāh's.

Chapter 83
Al-Tatfīf: **Default in Duty**

(Revealed at Makkah: 36 *verses*)

In the name of Allāh, the Beneficent, the Merciful.

1 Woe to the cheaters!

2 Who, when they take the measure (of their dues) from men, take it fully,

3 And when they measure out to others or weigh out for them, they give less than is due.

4 Do they not think that they will be raised again,

5 To a mighty day? —

6 The day when men will stand before the Lord of the worlds.

7 Nay, surely the record of the wicked is in the prison.

8 And what will make *thee* know *what the prison* is?

9 It is a written book.

10 Woe on that day to the rejectors!

11 Who give the lie to the day of Judgment.

12 And none gives the lie to it but every exceeder of limits, every sinful one;

13 When Our messages are recited to him, he says: Stories of those of yore!

14 Nay, rather, what they earned is rust upon their hearts.

15 Nay, surely they are that day debarred from their Lord.

16 Then they will surely enter the burning Fire.

17 Then it will be said: This is what you gave the lie to.

18 Nay, surely the record of the righteous is in the highest places.

19 And what will make thee know what the highest places are?

20 It is a written book.

21 Those drawn near (to Allāh) witness it.

22 Surely the righteous

DEFAULT IN DUTY

are in bliss,

23 On raised couches, gazing —

24 Thou recognizest in their faces the brightness of bliss.

25 They are given to drink of a pure drink, sealed.

26 The sealing of it is (with) musk. And for that let the aspirers aspire.

27 And it is tempered with water coming from above —

28 A fountain from which drink those drawn near (to Allāh).

29 Surely they who are guilty used to laugh at those who believe.

30 And when they passed by them, they winked at one another,

31 And when they returned to their people, they returned exulting.

32 And when they saw them, they said: Surely these are in error —

33 And they were not sent as keepers over them.

34 So this day those who believe laugh at the disbelievers —

35 On raised couches, gazing.

36 Surely the disbelievers are rewarded as they did.

CHAPTER 84

Al-Inshiqāq: **The Bursting Asunder**

(REVEALED AT MAKKAH: 25 *verses*)

In the name of Allāh, the Beneficent, the Merciful.

1 When the heaven bursts asunder,

2 And listens to its Lord and is made fit;

3 And when the earth is stretched,

4 And casts forth what is in it and becomes empty,

5 And listens to its Lord and is made fit.

6 O man, thou must strive a hard striving (to attain) to thy Lord, until thou meet Him.

7 Then as to him who is given his book in his right hand,

8 *His account will be* taken by an easy reckoning,

9 And he will go back to his people rejoicing.

10 And as to him who is given his book behind his back,

11 He will call for perdition.

12 And enter into burning Fire.

13 Surely he was (erstwhile) joyful among his people.

14 Surely he thought that he would never return (to Allāh) —

15 Yea, surely his Lord is ever Seer of him.

16 But nay, I call to witness the sunset redness,

17 And the night and that which it drives on,

18 And the moon when it grows full,

19 That you shall certainly ascend to one state after another.

20 But what is the matter with them that they believe not?

21 And, when the Qur'ān is recited to them, they adore (Him) not?

22 Nay, those who disbelieve give the lie —

23 And Allāh knows best what they hide.

24 So announce to them a painful chastisement,

25 Except those who believe and do good — for them is a reward that shall never be cut off.

CHAPTER 85
Al-Burūj: **The Stars**

(REVEALED AT MAKKAH: 22 verses)

1 By the heaven full of stars!

2 And the Promised day!

3 And the bearer of witness and that to which witness is borne!

4 Destruction overtake the companions of the trench! —

5 The fire fed with fuel —

6 When they sit by it,

7 And they are witnesses of what they do with the believers.

8 And they punished them for naught but that they believed in Allāh, the Mighty, the Praised,

9 Whose is the kingdom of the heavens and the earth. And Allāh is Witness of all things.

10 Those who persecute believing men and believing women, then repent not, theirs is the chastisement of hell, and theirs the chastisement of burning.

11 Those who believe and do good, theirs are Gardens wherein flow rivers. That is the great achievement.

12 Surely the grip of thy Lord is severe.

13 Surely He it is Who creates first and reproduces;

14 And He is the Forgiving, the Loving,

15 Lord of the Throne of Power, the Glorious,

16 Doer of what He intends.

17 Has not there come to thee the story of the hosts,

18 Of Pharaoh and Thamūd?

19 Nay, those who disbelieve give the lie —

20 And Allāh encompasses them on all sides.

21 Nay, it is a glorious Qur'ān,

22 In a guarded tablet.

CHAPTER 86
Al-Ṭāriq: **The Comer By Night**

(REVEALED AT MAKKAH: 17 *verses*)

In the name of Allāh, the Beneficent, the Merciful.

1 By the heaven and the Comer by night!

2 And what will make thee know what the Comer by night is?

3 The star of piercing brightness—

4 There is not a soul but over it is a keeper.

5 So let man consider of what he is created.

6 He is created of water pouring forth,

7 Coming from between the back and the ribs.

8 Surely He is Able to return him (to life).

9 On the day when hidden things are manifested,

10 Then he will have no strength nor helper.

11 By the cloud giving rain,

12 And the earth opening (with herbage)!

13 Surely it is a decisive word,

14 And it is not a joke.

15 Surely they plan a plan,

16 And I plan a plan.

17 So grant the disbelievers a respite — let them alone for a while.

Chapter 87
Al-A'lā: **The Most High**

(REVEALED AT MAKKAH: 19 *verses*)

In the name of Allāh, the Beneficent, the Merciful.

1 Glorify the name of thy Lord, the Most High!

2 Who creates, then makes complete,

3 And Who measures, then guides,

4 And Who brings forth herbage,

5 Then makes it dried up, dust-coloured.

6 We shall make thee recite so thou shalt not forget —

7 Except what Allāh please. Surely He knows the manifest, and what is hidden.

8 And We shall make thy way *smooth to a state of* ease.

9 So remind, reminding indeed profits.

10 He who fears will mind,

11 And the most unfortunate one will avoid it,

12 Who will burn in the great Fire.

13 Then therein he will neither live nor die.

14 He indeed is successful who purifies himself,

15 And remembers the name of his Lord, then prays.

16 But, you prefer the life of this world,

17 While the Hereafter is better and more lasting.

18 Surely this is in the earlier scriptures,

19 The scriptures of Abraham and Moses.

CHAPTER 88
Al-Ghāshiyah:
The Overwhelming Event

(REVEALED AT MAKKAH: 26 *verses*)

In the name of Allāh, the Beneficent, the Merciful.

1 Has there come to thee the news of the Overwhelming Event?

2 Faces on that day will be downcast,

3 Labouring, toiling,

4 Entering burning Fire,

5 Made to drink from a boiling spring.

6 They will have no food but of thorns,

7 Neither nourishing nor satisfying hunger.

8 Faces on that day will be happy,

9 Glad for their striving,

10 In a lofty Garden,

11 Wherein thou wilt hear no vain talk.

12 Therein is a fountain flowing.

13 Therein are thrones raised high,

14 And drinking-cups ready placed,

15 And cushions set in rows,

16 And carpets spread out.

17 See they not the clouds, how they are created?

18 And the heaven, how it is raised high?

19 And the mountains, how they are fixed?

20 And the earth, how it is spread out?

21 So remind. Thou art only one to remind.

22 Thou art not a warder over them —

23 But whoever turns back and disbelieves,

24 Allāh will chastise him with the greatest chastisement.

25 Surely to Us is their return.

26 Then it is for Us to call them to account.

CHAPTER 89
Al-Fajr: **The Daybreak**
(REVEALED AT MAKKAH: 30 *verses*)

In the name of Allāh, the Beneficent, the Merciful.

1 By the daybreak!

2 And the ten nights!

3 And the even and the odd!

4 And the night when it departs!

5 Truly in this is an oath for men of understanding.

6 Hast thou not considered how thy Lord dealt with 'Ād,

7 (Of) Iram, having lofty buildings,

8 The like of which were not created in the land;

9 And (with) Thamūd, who hewed out rocks in the valley;

10 And Pharaoh, the lord of hosts,

11 Who exceeded limits in the cities,

12 And made great mischief therein?

13 So thy Lord poured on them a portion of chastisement.

14 Surely thy Lord is Watchful;

15 As for man, when his Lord tries him, then gives him honour and favours him, he says: My Lord honours me.

16 But when He tries him, then straitens to him his subsistence, he says: My Lord has disgraced me.

17 Nay, but you honour not the orphan,

18 Nor do you urge one another to feed the poor,

19 And you devour heritage, devouring all,

20 And you love wealth with exceeding love.

21 Nay, when the earth is made to crumble to pieces,

22 And thy Lord comes with the angels, ranks on ranks;

THE DAYBREAK

23 And hell is made to appear that day. On that day man will be mindful, and of what use will being mindful be then?

24 He will say: O would that I had sent before for (this) my life!

25 But none can punish as He will punish on that day.

26 And none can bind as He will bind on that day.

27 O soul that art at rest,

28 Return to thy Lord, well-pleased, well-pleasing,

29 So enter among My servants,

30 And enter My Garden!

CHAPTER 90
Al-Balad: **The City**

(REVEALED AT MAKKAH: 20 *verses*)

In the name of Allāh, the Beneficent, the Merciful.

1 Nay, I call to witness this City!

2 And thou wilt be made free from obligation in this City —

3 And the begetter and he whom he begot!

4 We have certainly created man to face difficulties.

5 Does he think that no one has power over him?

6 He will say: I have wasted much wealth.

7 Does he think that no one sees him?

8 Have We not given him two eyes,

9 *And a tongue and two lips,*

10 And pointed out to him the two conspicuous ways?

11 But he attempts not the uphill road;

12 And what will make thee comprehend what the uphill road is?

13 (It is) to free a slave,

14 Or to feed in a day of hunger

15 An orphan nearly related,

16 Or the poor man lying in the dust.

17 Then he is of those who believe and exhort one another to patience, and exhort one another to mercy.

18 These are the people of the right hand.

19 And those who disbelieve in Our messages, they are the people of the left hand.

20 On them is Fire closed over.

CHAPTER 91
Al-Shams: **The Sun**

(REVEALED AT MAKKAH: 15 *verses*)

In the name of Allāh, the Beneficent, the Merciful.

1 By the sun and his brightness!

2 And the moon when she borrows light from him!

3 And the day when it exposes it to view!

4 And the night when it draws a veil over it!

5 And the heaven and its make!

6 And the earth and its extension!

7 And the soul and its perfection! —

8 So He reveals to it its way of evil and its way of good;

9 He is indeed successful who causes it to grow,

10 And he indeed fails who buries it.

11 Thamūd rejected (the truth) in their inordinacy,

12 When the basest of them broke forth with mischief —

13 So Allāh's messenger said to them: (Leave alone) Allāh's she-camel, and (give) her (to) drink.

14 But they called him a liar and slaughtered her. So their Lord destroyed them for their sin and levelled them (with the ground);

15 And He fears not its consequence.

Chapter 92
Al-Lail: The Night

(Revealed at Makkah: 21 *verses*)

In the name of Allāh, the Beneficent, the Merciful.

1 By the night when it draws a veil!

2 And the day when it shines!

3 And the creating of the male and the female! —

4 Your striving is surely (for) diverse (ends).

5 Then as for him who gives and keeps his duty,

6 And accepts what is good —

7 We facilitate for him (the way to) ease.

8 And as for him who is niggardly and considers himself self-sufficient,

9 And rejects what is good —

10 We facilitate for him (the way to) distress.

11 And his wealth will not avail him when he perishes.

12 Surely Ours is it to show the way,

13 And surely Ours is the Hereafter and the former.

14 So I warn you of the Fire that flames.

15 None will enter it but the most unfortunate,

16 Who rejects (the truth) and turns (his) back.

17 And away from it shall be kept the most faithful to duty,

18 Who gives his wealth, purifying himself,

19 And none has with him any boon for a reward,

20 Except the seeking of the pleasure of his Lord, the Most High.

21 And he will soon be well-pleased.

CHAPTER 93
Al-Ḍuḥā: **The Brightness of the Day**

(REVEALED AT MAKKAH: 11 *verses*)

In the name of Allāh, the Beneficent, the Merciful.

1 By the brightness of the day!

2 And the night when it is still! —

3 Thy Lord has not forsaken thee, nor is He displeased.

4 And surely the latter state is better for thee than the former.

5 And soon will thy Lord give thee so that thou wilt be well pleased.

6 Did He not find thee an orphan and give (thee) shelter?

7 And find thee groping, so He showed the way?

8 And find thee in want, so He enriched thee?

9 Therefore the orphan, oppress not.

10 And him who asks, chide not.

11 And the favour of thy Lord, proclàim.

CHAPTER 94
Al-Inshirāḥ: **The Expansion**

(REVEALED AT MAKKAH: 8 *verses*)

In the name of Allāh, the Beneficent, the Merciful.

1 Have We not expanded for thee thy breast,

2 And removed from thee thy burden,

3 Which weighed down thy back,

4 And exalted for thee thy mention?

5 Surely with difficulty is ease,

6 With difficulty is surely ease.

7 So when thou art free (from anxiety), work hard,

8 And make thy Lord thy exclusive object.

CHAPTER 95
Al-Tin: **The Fig**

(REVEALED AT MAKKAH: 8 *verses*)

In the name of Allāh, the Beneficent, the Merciful.

1 By the fig and the olive!

2 And mount Sinai!

3 And this city made secure!

4 Certainly We created man in the best make.

5 Then We render him the lowest of the low,

6 Except those who believe and do good; so theirs is a reward never to be cut off.

7 So who can give the lie to thee after (this) about the Judgment?

8 Is not Allāh the Best of the Judges?

Chapter 96
Al-'Alaq: The Clot

(Revealed at Makkah: 19 *verses*)

In the name of Allāh, the Beneficent, the Merciful.

1 Read in the name of thy Lord Who creates —

2 Creates man from a clot,

3 Read and thy Lord is most Generous,

4 Who taught by the pen,

5 Taught man what he knew not.

6 Nay, man is surely inordinate,

7 Because he looks upon himself as self-sufficient.

8 Surely to thy Lord is the return.

9 Hast thou seen him who forbids

10 A servant when he prays?

11 Seest thou if he is on the right way,

12 Or enjoins observance of duty?

13 Seest thou if he denies and turns away?

14 Knows he not that Allāh sees?

15 Nay, if he desist not, We will seize him by the forelock —

16 A lying, sinful forelock!

17 Then let him summon his council,

18 We will summon the braves of the army.

19 Nay! Obey him not, but prostrate thyself, and draw nigh (to Allāh).

CHAPTER 97
Al-Qadr: **The Majesty**

(REVEALED AT MAKKAH: 5 *verses*)

In the name of Allāh, the Beneficent, the Merciful.

1 Surely We revealed it on the Night of Majesty —

2 And what will make thee comprehend what the Night of Majesty is?

3 The Night of Majesty is better than a thousand months.

4 The angels and the Spirit descend in it by the permission of their Lord — for every affair —

5 Peace! it is till the rising of the morning.

Chapter 98
Al-Bayyinah: The Clear Evidence
(Revealed at Makkah: 8 *verses*)

In the name of Allāh, the Beneficent, the Merciful.

1 Those who disbelieve from among the People of the Book and the idolaters could not have been freed till clear evidence came to them —

2 A Messenger from Allāh, reciting pure pages,

3 Wherein are (all) right books.

4 Nor did those to whom the Book was given become divided till clear evidence came to them.

5 And they are enjoined naught but to serve Allāh, being sincere to Him in obedience, upright, and to keep up prayer and pay the poor-rate, and that is the right religion.

6 Those who disbelieve from among the People of the Book and the idolaters will be in the Fire of hell, abiding therein. They are the worst of creatures.

7 Those who believe and do good, they are the best of creatures.

8 Their reward is with their Lord: Gardens of perpetuity wherein flow rivers, abiding therein forever. Allāh is well pleased with them and they are well pleased with Him. That is for him who fears his Lord.

CHAPTER 99
Al-Zilzāl: **The Shaking**
(REVEALED AT MAKKAH: 8 *verses*)

In the name of Allāh, the Beneficent, the Merciful.

1 When the earth is shaken with her shaking,

2 And the earth brings forth her burdens,

3 And man says: What has befallen her?

4 On that day she will tell her news,

5 As if thy Lord had revealed to her.

6 On that day men will come forth in sundry bodies that they may be shown their works.

7 So he who does an atom's weight of good will see it.

8 And he who does an atom's weight of evil will see it.

CHAPTER 100
Al-'Ādiyāt: **The Assaulters**

(REVEALED AT MAKKAH: 11 *verses*)

In the name of Allāh, the Beneficent, the Merciful.

1 By those running and uttering cries!

2 And those producing fire, striking!

3 And those suddenly attacking at morn!

4 Then thereby they raise dust,

5 Then penetrate thereby gatherings —

6 Surely man is ungrateful to his Lord.

7 And surely he is a witness of that.

8 And truly on account of the love of wealth he is niggardly.

9 Knows he not when that which is in the graves is raised,

10 And that which is in the breasts is made manifest?

11 Surely their Lord this day is Aware of them.

CHAPTER 101
Al-Qāri'ah: **The Calamity**

(REVEALED AT MAKKAH: 11 *verses*)

In the name of Allāh, the Beneficent, the Merciful.

1 The calamity!

2 What is the calamity?

3 And what will make thee know how terrible is the calamity?

4 The day wherein men will be as scattered moths,

5 And the mountains will be as carded wool.

6 Then as for him whose measure (of good deeds) is heavy,

7 He will live a pleasant life.

8 And as for him whose measure (of good deeds) is light,

9 The abyss is a mother to him.

10 And what will make thee know what that is?

11 A burning Fire.

Chapter 102

Al-Takāthur:
The Abundance of Wealth

(REVEALED AT MAKKAH: 8 *verses*)

In the name of Allāh, the Beneficent, the Merciful.

1 Abundance diverts you,

2 Until you come to the graves.

3 Nay, you will soon know,

4 Nay, again, you will soon know.

5 Nay, would that you knew with a certain knowledge!

6 You will certainly see hell;

7 Then you will see it with certainty of sight;

8 Then on that day you shall certainly be questioned about the boons.

Chapter 103
Al-'Aṣr: **The Time**

(Revealed at Makkah: 3 *verses*)

In the name of Allāh, the Beneficent, the Merciful.

1 By the time! —

2 Surely man is in loss,

3 Except those who believe and do good, and exhort one another to Truth, and exhort one another to patience.

Chapter 104
Al-Humazah: **The Slanderer**

(Revealed at Makkah: 9 *verses*)

In the name of Allāh, the Beneficent, the Merciful.

1 Woe to every slanderer, defamer!

2 Who amasses wealth and counts it —

3 He thinks that his wealth will make him *abide*.

4 Nay, he will certainly be hurled into the crushing disaster;

5 And what will make thee realize what the crushing disaster is?

6 It is the Fire kindled by Allāh,

7 Which rises over the hearts.

8 Surely it is closed in on them,

9 In extended columns.

CHAPTER 105
Al-Fīl: **The Elephant**

(REVEALED AT MAKKAH: 5 *verses*)

In the name of Allāh, the Beneficent, the Merciful.

1 Hast thou not seen how thy Lord dealt with the possessors of the elephant?

2 Did He not cause their war to end in confusion?

3 And send against them birds in flocks?

4 Casting at them decreed stones —

5 So He rendered them like straw eaten up?

CHAPTER 106
Al-Quraish: **The Quraish**

(REVEALED AT MAKKAH: 4 *verses*)

In the name of Allāh, the Beneficent, the Merciful.

1 For the protection of the Quraish —

2 Their protection during their journey in the winter and the summer.

3 So let them serve the Lord of this House,

4 Who feeds them against hunger, and gives them security against fear.

Chapter 107
Al-Mā'ūn: **Acts of Kindness**

(Revealed at Makkah: 7 *verses*)

In the name of Allāh, the Beneficent, the Merciful.

1 Hast thou seen him who belies religion?

2 That is the one who is rough to the orphan,

3 And urges not the feeding of the needy.

4 So woe to the praying ones,

5 Who are unmindful of their prayer!

6 Who do (good) to be seen,

7 And refrain from acts of kindness!

Chapter 108
Al-Kauthar: **The Abundance of Good**

(Revealed at Makkah: 3 *verses*)

In the name of Allāh, the Beneficent, the Merciful.

1 Surely We have given thee abundance of good.

2 So pray to thy Lord and sacrifice.

3 Surely thy enemy is cut off (from good).

Chapter 109
Al-Kāfirūn: **The Disbelievers**

(Revealed at Makkah: 6 *verses*)

In the name of Allāh, the Beneficent, the Merciful.

1 Say: O disbelievers,

2 I serve not what you serve,

3 Nor do you serve Him Whom I serve,

4 Nor shall I serve that which ye serve,

5 Nor do you serve Him Whom I serve.

6 For you is your recompense and for me my recompense.

Chapter 110
Al-Naṣr: **The Help**

(Revealed at Makkah: 3 *verses*)

In the name of Allāh, the Beneficent, the Merciful.

1 When Allāh's help and victory comes,

2 And thou seest men entering the religion of Allāh in companies,

3 Celebrate the praise of thy Lord and ask His protection. Surely He is ever Returning (to mercy).

CHAPTER 111
Al-Lahab: **The Flame**

(REVEALED AT MAKKAH: 5 *verses*)

In the name of Allāh, the Beneficent, the Merciful.

1 Abū Lahab's hands will perish and he will perish.

2 His wealth and that which he earns will not avail him.

3 He will burn in fire giving rise to flames —

4 And his wife — the bearer of slander;

5 Upon her neck a halter of twisted rope!

CHAPTER 112
Al-Ikhlāṣ: **The Unity**

(REVEALED AT MAKKAH: 4 *verses*)

In the name of Allāh, the Beneficent, the Merciful.

1 Say: He, Allāh, is One.

2 Allāh is He on Whom all depend.

3 He begets not, nor is He begotten;

4 And none is like Him.

Chapter 113
Al-Falaq: The Dawn
(REVEALED AT MAKKAH: 5 *verses*)

In the name of Allāh, the Beneficent, the Merciful.

1 Say: I seek refuge in the Lord of the dawn,

2 From the evil of that which He has created,

3 And from the evil of intense darkness, when it comes,

4 And from the evil of those who cast (evil suggestions) in firm resolutions,

5 And from the evil of the envier when he envies.

Chapter 114
Al-Nās: The Men
(REVEALED AT MAKKAH: 6 *verses*)

In the name of Allāh, the Beneficent, the Merciful.

1 Say: I seek refuge in the Lord of men,

2 The King of men,

3 The God of men,

4 From the evil of the whisperings of the slinking (devil),

5 Who whispers into the hearts of men,

6 From among the jinn and the men.

INDEX

Explanation: The chapter number is placed before a colon (:), and the numbers of the verses in that chapter are given after the colon. For instance, 20:29–34 represents chapter 20, verses 29 to 34. A semi-colon (;) closes the references to one particular chapter. The reader's attention is drawn to the following headings of this Index in which reference is made to certain important subjects as dealt with in the Holy Qur'ān: *Allāh, Civic Life, Human Soul, Intellectual Development, Knowledge, Man, Morals, Muḥammad, Muslims, Nature, Prayer, Qur'ān, Revelation, Science, State Polity* and *Women.*

Aaron, Moses' request for help of, 20:29–34; 26:13; 28:34; is made a prophet, 4:163; 6:84; 10:75; 19:53; 21:48; 23:45; 25:35; leader of Israelites in Moses' absence, 7:142; not guilty of making the calf, 20:90, 95; his excuse, 7:150, See also *Moses.*

Ablution, 5:6

Abraham, entire submission of, to Allāh, 2:124, 131; 3:67; 4:125; 16:120; 37:83–84; made a prophet and model of virtue, 2:124, 130; 16:120–122; 21:73; 38:45–47; prophethood granted to descendants of, 3:33; 29:27; 37:113; 57:26; preaches against idolatry, 6:74; 19:42–48; 21:52–56, 62–67; 26:69–82; 29:16–17; 37:85–96; 43:26–27; preaches against worship of heavenly bodies, 6:75–83; 37:88–89; breaks the idols, 21:57–67; 37:91–93; plans against, to cast into fire, 21:68; 29:24; 37:97; is delivered, 21:69–71; 29:24–26; 37:98–99; controversy with a sun-worshipper, 2:258; seeks to understand law of rise and fall of nations,

INDEX

2:260; asks forgiveness for his sire, 9:114; 19:47; 60:4; is the progenitor of Arabs, 90:3; prays for a righteous son, 37:100; given good news of Ishmael, 37:101; vision of, to sacrifice his son, 37:102; settles Ishmael near the Ka'bah, 14:37; prays for a secure city to be raised there, 2:126; 14:35; prays for Makkah to be made the spiritual centre of the world, 14:37–38; enjoined to purify the Sacred House of idols, 2:125; 22:26; prays for a nation keeping up prayer to be raised in Arabia, 2:128; 14:37, 40; prays, with Ishmael, for a messenger to be raised in Makkah, 2:129; with Ishmael rebuilds Ka'bah, 2:127; covenant made with, 2:124; Place (*Maqām*) of, 2:125; 3:97; scriptures of, 87:19; messengers come to, 11:69–70; 15:51–52; 51:24–25; informed of birth of a son, 15:53–56; 37:112; 51:28–30; and a grandson, 6:84; 11:71; 19:49; 21:72; 29:27; pleads for Lot's people, 11:74–76; enjoins Unity on his descendants, 2:132; 43:28; severs connection with enemies, 60:4–5; an exemplar, 16:120; 60:4; to be remembered with goodness among later generations, 37:108–111; Islām as the religion of, 3:67; Muḥammad and his followers are nearest to, 3:68; faith of, followed by Muslims, 4:125; 16:123

Abū Bakr, accompanies the Prophet in his flight, 9:40; enjoined to show forgiveness, 24:22

Abū Lahab, 111:1–3; wife of, 111:4–5

Abuse, must be borne with patience, 3:186; 20:130; 33:48; 50:39; 73:10; withdrawing from company of abusers, 4:140; 6:68; turning away from the ignorant, 7:199; 28:55; showing forgiveness in face of, 2:109

Actions, each responsible for own, 3:30; 4:111; 6:52; 10:41; 29:12; 52:21; see *Burden*, *Deeds*, *Evil*, *Good works*, and *Life after death*.

'Ād, successors of Noah's people, 7:69; their punishment, 7:72; see also 9:70; 50:13

Adam, created to rule on earth, 2:30; is created from dust,

3:59; 15:28; 17:61; 38:71; is taught the names, 2:31; is made complete and granted inspiration, 15:29; 38:72; angels ordered to make submission to, 2:34; 7:11; 15:28–29; 17:61; 18:50; 20:116; 38:72; *Iblis* refuses to submit to, 2:34; 7:11; 15:31; 17:61; 18:50; 20:116; 38:73–74; is made to live in the garden with Eve, 2:35; 7:19; 20:117–119; both forbidden to approach the tree, 2:35; 7:19; is misled by the devil, 2:36; 7:20–22; 20:120–121; result of tasting the tree, 7:22; 20:121; fault of, due to forgetting, 20:115; repentance of, 2:37; 7:23; excels the whole creation, 2:34; Adam and his descendants chosen, 3:33; two sons of, 5:27–31

Adoption, 33:4

Adornment, 7:31; not prohibited, 7:32

Adultery, punishment for, 24:1–2; interdict against, 24:3; strong evidence required to establish the charge, 24:4, 13; preventives against, 23:5–6; 24:27, 30–31; 70:29–30; punishment for indecency short of, 4:15–16; see *Morals: chastity*.

Agreement, fulfilment of, 5:1; 16:91–92; see *Morals: true to promises;* may be repudiated in case of treachery, 8:58

Aḥmad, prophecy about, 61:6

'Ā'ishah, slander against, 24:11–20

Alcohol, see *Intoxicants*.

Allāh, is above limitations, 6:103; 42:11; has the best, most beautiful names, 7:180; 17:110; 20:8; 59:24; everything in universe glorifies Him, 17:44; 24:41; 59:24; everything submits to, 3:83; 13:15; 16:48–49; 22:18; evidence for the existence of, 2:28; 7:172; 10:31–35; 27:60–64; 35:3, 11–14; 40:61–68; 52:35–36; 56:57–73

— Unity of: is One, 2:163; 6:19; 14:52; 16:22; 21:108; 22:34; 37:4; 38:65; 41:6; 112:1; no god besides, 2:255; 3:2; 4:87; 47:19; 52:43; 64:13; not two or three gods,

INDEX

16:51; 4:171; 5:73; has no associates, 6:163; 17:111; 25:2; has no son, 6:101; 17:111; 25:2; 112:3; see also under *Sonship;* error of ascribing daughters to, 37:149–158; see also *Feminine divinities;* service is due to Him, 1:4; 13:36; 18:110; 36:60–61; 39:64–66; pray to Him alone, 1:4; 10:105–107; 25:68; 26:213; 28:88; 72:18–20; doctrine of Unity, borne witness to, 3:18; Unity of law bears witness to, 21:22; declared by diversity in nature, 2:164; absolute Unity proclaimed, 112:1–4; see also *Gods* and *Polytheism.*

— is Loving: 11:90; 85:14; loves those who do good to others, 2:195; 3:134, 148; 5:13, 93; loves those who turn to Him, 2:222; loves the steadfast, 3:146; loves the dutiful, 3:76; 9:4, 7; loves those who trust in Him, 3:159; loves the equitable, 5:42; 49:9; 60:8; love of, gained by following Holy Prophet, 3:31; loves and is loved, 5:54; to be loved by man, see *Human soul: man to love God;* is pleased with the righteous, and they with Him, 5:119; 9:100; 58:22; 89:28; 93:5; 98:8

— is Merciful: (every ch. except 9th starts with this declaration); has ordained it upon Himself to show mercy, 6:12, 54, 133; most Merciful of all merciful ones, 7:151; 12:64, 92; 21:83; 23:118; mercy is preponderant quality of, 6:160; 17:54; embraces all in mercy, 40:7; 6:147; 7:156; all should rejoice in mercy of, 10:58; has created all for mercy, 11:119; none should despair of His mercy, 12:87; 39:53; mercy of, to wrongdoers, 3:128; two portions of mercy of, 57:28

— is Forgiving, 39:53; 40:3; 42:5, 25, 30, 34; 74:56; 3:135, 155; 4:64, 99, 106, 110, 149; 5:101; 6:54; 7:153, 155; 12:98; 14:36; 20:82; 25:70; 33:71; 53:32; 57:28; accepts repentance, *ibid.,* and see also *Repentance.*

— is Compassionate: to all, 2:143; 22:65; to believers, 2:207; 3:30; 9:117, 128; 24:20

— is Good to all, 2:243, 251; 10:60; 12:38; 27:73

— is Omniscient: knows all things, 2:29; 6:101; 24:35;

29:62; 42:12; comprehends all things in knowledge, 6:80; 7:89; 20:98; His knowledge reaches heaven and earth, 2:255; 29:52; 57:4; knows unseen and seen, 13:9; 32:6; 35:38; 49:18; knows atom and less than that, 10:61; 34:2–3; 57:3–4; knows what is in hearts and minds, 2:235; 11:5; 29:10; 33:51; 35:38; knows suggestions of mind, 50:16; knows the secret and yet more hidden, the subconscience, 20:7; knows secret thoughts and open words, 2:77; 6:3; 11:5; 16:23; 27:74; knows the Hour and all in wombs, 13:8; 31:34; 41:47; knows every falling leaf, 6:59; knows secret counsels, 58:7

— is Omnipotent: has power over all things, 2:20, 106, 284 etc.; 25:54; is Knowing and Powerful, 30:54; 35:44; 42:50; powerful to give spiritual life, 75:4, 40; 36:81; 42:29; powerful to change old order, 70:40–41; powerful to send sign, 6:37; 23:95; powerful to chastise, 6:65; controls all, 4:85

— is Omnipresent: nearer to man than life-vein, 50:16; is nigh, 2:186; 11:61; 34:50; is with you wherever you are, 57:4; 58:7; in all directions you face God, 2:115; none can hide himself from God, 4:108; is the fourth in every three, 58:7

— is the Creator: Creator of all things, 6:101; 13:16; 20:50; 25:2; 39:62; none else can create, 13:16; 16:20; 31:11; 35:40; created what you know not, 16:8; 36:36; created heavens and earth, 6:1; 14:32; 27:59–60; created with truth, 6:73; 16:3; 29:44; not fatigued by creation of, 46:33; 50:38; see also under *Heaven;* as sending down things for man, 7:26; 15:21; 39:6; 57:25; Creator, Maker and Fashioner, 59:24; see *Evolution;* Creator of man, 55:3; 39:6; see also under *Man;* creates then reproduces creation, 10:4; 29:19–20; 30:11, 27; 85:13; Creator and Sustainer, 56:58–74; Sustainer of all, 11:6; for other acts of creation, see under *Pairs* and *Nature.*

— gives life and causes death, 2:28; 7:158; 9:116; 23:80; 57:2

INDEX

— above every need, 6:14; 29:6; 35:15; 39:7; 47:38; 51:57

— man's relation with, see *Human soul;*

— ever-enduring, 28:88; 55:27; ever-living, 2:255; 3:2; 20:111; 25:58; 40:65; the First, Last, Manifest and Hidden, 57:3; the Truth, 31:30; ultimate cause of all things, 6:1; other attributes of, 59:22–24; meeting with, 84:6; remembrance of, sets heart at rest, 13:28; coming of, 2:210; 6:158; no change in course of, 17:77; 35:43; 48:23; does not lead man astray, 9:115; 13:27; 14:27; 16:37

Allegiance, oath of, 5:7; 48:10, 18; from women converts, 60:12

Allies, Battle of, 33:9; assistance of angels at, 3:125; prophecy relating to, 38:11; 67:17; 85:4; prophecy fulfilled, 33:9, 22

Amran, 3:33, 35

Angels, submit to Adam, see *Adam;* opponents' demands for coming of, 6:8; 15:7–8; 25:21–22; 17:94–95; meaning of coming of, 2:210; 6:111, 158; 16:33; could not be messengers to people, 6:8–9; assistance of, 3:123–125; 8:9–10; 33:9; make believers firm, 8:12; ask forgiveness for people, 40:7–9; 42:5; coming of, with inspiration, 16:2; descend upon believers, 41:30–31; coming with revelation to the Holy Prophet, 19:64; guardian angels, 13:11; recording angels, 82:10–12; the wings of, 35:1; looked upon as female divinities and called daughters of Allāh, 37:149–159; 43:16, 19; 53:27–28; 17:40; and see *Feminine divinities.*

Animals, benefits for man in use of, 16:5–8, 66, 80; 23:21–22; 36:71–72; 40:79–80; 43:12–13; 5:4; 6:142; 39:6; slaughter of, see *Food.*

Apostates, 2:217; 5:54

Arabia, granting of life to, 29:63; insecurity in, 29:67; towns destroyed on borders of, 46:27–28 ns, 6:156–157; bearers of Prophet's message to other nations, 16:89; made masters of mighty empires, 18:31; Abraham was progenitor of, 90:3

— pre-Islamic Arabs: in a state of mutual warfare, 3:103; denied inheritance to women and children, 89:19; took women as heritage, 4:19; married mothers, 4:22; custom of *ẓihār* among, see *Ẓihār;* liberating animals in honour of idols, 5:103; making sacrifice to idols, 6:137; superstitions of, 6:138–139; practice of postponing pilgrimage, 9:36; birth of daughter regarded a misfortune, 16:58–59; 43:17; buried daughters alive, 6:137, 140; 16:59; powerful tribes set agreements at naught, 16:92; denied beneficence of God, 17:110; 21:36; 25:60; see also *Polytheists.*

— A'rāb (desert Arabs), 9:90, 97–99, 101; 48:11–12; 49:14–17

Aram, 89:7

Arrows, dividing by, forbidden, 5:3, 90

'*Arsh,* 7:54; 11:7; bearers of, 40:7; 69:17.

Ascension (*Mi'rāj*) of the Prophet, 17:1, 60

Atonement, refutation of the doctrine of, 5:18; 6:164; 17:15; how sins are forgiven, 29:7; see also *Burden.*

Backbiting, 49:12

Badr, prophecies relating to battle of, 8:7; 25:25–27; 44:16; 54:44–48; 64:9–10; 78:18–20; prophecy as to when it will take place, 34:30; appointed time of punishment of enemy, 18:58; force of persecution to be broken at, 20:128–130; enemy demanded a judgment in the battle of, 8:19; afforded a distinction, 8:41; sign in the battle of, 3:13; Divine help at, 3:123; 8:9; encounter necessary to manifest truth, 8:6–8; Muslims strengthened at, 8:11; Allāh's hand in the fighting at, 8:17; situation of parties at, 8:42; as a proof of truth, 8:42;

INDEX

unbelievers marching to, in exultation, 8:47–48; how unbelievers were smitten at, 8:50–51; *prisoners of war at, to be released, 8:70*

Bakkah, 3:96

Ba'l, 37:125

Balance, the, of good deeds, 7:8–9; 23:102–103; 101:6–9; 21:47; as measuring measure and justice, 42:17; 55:7–9; 57:25

Banī Naḍīr, 59:2

Banī Quraiẓah, 33:26–27

Baptism, the Divine, 2:138

Begging, disapproved, 2:273

Belief: fundamental beliefs of Islām, 2:3–4; 2:177, 2:285; 4:136; belief in Allāh and all revelation, 2:136; *and see under Revelation;* in Allāh and all messengers, 4:152; *and see under Prophets;* in Allāh and Prophet, 7:158; 47:2; 57:7; 61:11; 64:8; in Allāh and Last Day or Hereafter, 2:8, 62, 126; 4:39; 9:99; novices in belief, 49:14; waverers in, 4:137; true believers, 8:2–4, 74; 9:111–112; 23:1–11; 32:15–16; 49:15; spiritual distinctions promised to, 8:29; 10:2; 14:27; 39:33–35; 46:16; 48:5; 58:11; see also *Faith* and *Good works*.

Bequest, for charitable purposes, 2:180; law of, not abrogated, 2:182; 2:240; 4:11–12; 5:106

Bible, corruption of, 2:75, 79; 3:77–78; 4:46; 5:13, 44–47, 68; for differences with Qur'ān, see *Qur'ān;* see also *Gospel* and *Torah;* for prophecies about Prophet in, see *Muḥammad: Prophecies about*.

Birds, in Abrahah's invasion of Makkah, 105:3–5; subjugated by Solomon, 27:17

Blind and deaf, metaphors used in spiritual sense, 22:46; 7:179; 8:22; 17:72, 97; 2:18, 171; 5:71; 6:39; 25:73; 41:17; sealing of ears and eyes, 2:7; 6:46; 16:108; 45:23; 47:23; Prophet's rejectors do not see or listen,

7:198; 10:42–43; 27:80–81; 30:52–53; 43:40; 21:45; 36:9; 67:10; blind compared with those who see, 6:104; 11:24; 13:16, 19; 35:19; 40:58; see also under *Dead* and *Heart*.

Blind, the lame and the sick and the, 24:61; 48:17

Blind man, incident of the, 80:1–4,

Bloodwit, 2:178

Book, as signifying laws of nature, 10:61; 11:6; 22:70; 27:75; 35:11; 57:22; as signifying previous revelation, 2:85, 177; 3:78; 5:15; 10:37, 94; Book of Deeds, 17:13–14; 18:49; 23:62; 34:3; 36:12; 39:69; 45:28; 50:4; 54:52–53; 69:19–20, 25–27; 78:29; 83:7–9, 18–20; 84:7–15; and see *Life after death*: grows out of ...; as signifying Qur'ān, see *Qur'ān*.

Book, People of the, see *People of the Book*.

Books, circulation of, prophesied, 81:10

Bribery, 2:188

Brotherhood, of man, see *Humanity*; of Islām, see *Muslims*.

Burden, each one to bear his own, 29:12–13; 35:18; 39:7; 53:38; on the day of Resurrection, 6:31; 16:25; 20:100; 29:13; see also *Actions* and *Atonement*; imposed on man only to extent of ability, 2:286; 6:152; 7:42; 23:62; 65:7; prayer for relief from, 2:286; of law, lightened in Islām, 4:28; removed by Prophet, 7:157; of anxiety for humanity, felt by Prophet, 94:2–3

Burnt-offering, 3:183

Cain, 5:27–31

Calf, the golden, 2:51, 54; 7:148, 152; 20:87–97.

Camels, 7:40; 22:27, 36; prophecy relating to their abandonment, 81:4

Cave, story of dwellers of, 18:9–26

INDEX

Charity, as a basic principle of Islām, 2:177; 4:36–37; 30:38–39; 32:16; 51:19; 70:24–25; to withhold is to deny religion, ch. 107; fruit of, 2:261; 30:39; leads to success, 2:274; not to be followed by reproach or injury, 2:262–264; strong condemnation of giving in order to be seen, 2:264; 4:38; for Allāh's pleasure, 2:265; for love of Allāh, 76:8–9; 2:177; only good things to be given in, 2:267; the things one loves, 3:92; open and secret, 2:271, 274; 13:22; 14:31; 35:29; object of secret charity, 2:273; 4:114; various acts of charity: feeding the poor, 76:8–9; 90:14–16; 36:47; 69:33–34; 89:18; 107:3; caring for orphans, 4:5–6; 17:34; 89:17; 93:9; 107:2; and see *Orphans;* speaking kind words, 2:83; 2:263; 4:8; 17:23, 28; charity towards dumb creation, 51:19; contrasted with usury, 2:274–276, 30:39

— *Zakāt* (Poor rate), as basic principle of faith, 2:110, 177, 277; 9:11, 18; 22:78; 31:2–5; 98:5; enjoined on Israelites, 2:43, 83; objects of expenditure of, 9:60

Chastity, see *Morals.*

Children, as a worldly gain, like wealth, 18:46; 17:6; 18:39–40; 23:55–56; 68:13–14; 71:12, 21; as a source of trial, 8:28; 64:14–15; no difference if one has females only or males only or cannot have any, 42:49–50; no disgrace in birth of female, see *Daughters;* to be loved, 25:74; bearing and bringing up of, 31:14; 46:15; suckling of, 2:233; killing of, prohibited, see *Infanticide;* not to divert one from duty to God, 63:9; possession of, cannot avail against Allāh and His Judgment, 3:10, 116; 26:88; 31:33; 58:17; see also *Parents* and *Relationship.*

Christianity, belief in death of Christ on cross, fundamental doctrine of, 4:159; history of, referred to in story of dwellers of cave, 18:9–26; early followers of were Unitarians, 18:14; saint-worship in, 17:57; early refutation of by Qur'ān, 112:3; see also *Atonement, Trinity* and *Sonship.*

INDEX

Christians (see also *People of the Book*), how they can attain salvation, 2:62, 111–112; love of life of, 2:96; challenged to test truth of claims by means of prayer, 3:61; invited to common principles for mutual understanding, 3:64; take a man for God, 5:17, 72; 18:102; exceeding bounds in deifying a mortal, 4:171; only following earlier people in deifying a man, 5:77; 9:30; belief of, in Jesus as son of God, 9:30; 18:4–5; and see *Sonship;* worship of Mary by some, 5:116; take their religious leaders for gods, 9:31; 17:57; invented monkery, 57:27; try to control God's grace, 57:29; told of true baptism, 2:138; covenant with, 5:14; nearest to Islām, 5:82; humility of, *ibid.;* compassion in hearts of, 57:27; professing Islām, 5:83; prophecy of acceptance of Islām by later generations, 5:118; 21:97; wealth of, contrasted with Muslim poverty, 18:32–44; engrossment in materialism and neglect of spiritual needs by modern Christians, 18:102–104; chastisement of, for pursuit of materialism, 5:115; 18:7–8, 99–101; world-domination by Christian nations prophesied, 21:96–97; mutual enmity and hatred of, 5:14

Civic Life, work and striving: no good work is wasted, 3:195; 12:56, 90; 18:30; striving shall be rewarded fully, 6:135; 39:39–40; 79:34–41; 92:4; striving hard even to meet the Lord, 84:6; going deep into matters, 79:1–5; reward of labourers is excellent, 3:136; 29:58; 39:74; earning of wealth, 2:267; 4:32; 30:23; 62:10; 78:11; travelling recommended to earn wealth, 34:18; 67:15; 73:20; wealth to be obtained from the sea, 16:14; 17:66; 35:12; from cattle, 16:5–7; from mountains, 16:15–18; 79:32–33; trade to be carried on, 2:198, 275; 4:29; wealth not to be earned by false means, 2:188; 4:29; 5:62; earth is full of abundant resources, 4:100; 7:10; 15:20; inheritance of wealth, see *Inheritance;* proper use of wealth: wealth neither to be squandered nor withheld, 17:26–29; 25:67; hoarding of wealth denounced, 9:34; 70:18; 104:1–3; see *Niggardliness*; to be given away for love of God, 2:177; to be spent for parents, offspring, kindred, needy and wayfarers, 2:215; 30:38; spending of wealth for others brings abundance, 2:268; see *Charity*; love of wealth, 89:17–20; 100:6–8; diverts man from real object of life, 62:11; 102:1–2; attention drawn to higher values of life, 3:14; 18:46, 105; 57:20–21; 63:9; honesty in dealing, 7:85; 17:35; 83:1–6; contracts, debts, security, 2:280, 282–283; evidence, see *Evidence*; social relations with other communities, 5:2, 5; 60:8

Clothing, of inner piety, 7:26; purification of, as well as heart, 74:4; required of women, see *Women*; of evildoers as symbolising punishment, 14:50; 22:19

Companions, see *Muḥammad: Companions of*.

Contracts, writing of, 2:282

Controversy, principle of, 16:125; 29:46

Counsel, 3:159; 42:38; see also *Secret counsels*.

Covenant, of Allāh, 2:27; 3:77, 81, 187; 6:152; 13:20, 25; 16:91, 95; 33:15, 23; 48:10; covenants with people, see *Morals: true to covenants*.

Cow, Israelites told to slaughter, 2:67–71

Creation, see *Allāh: Creator, Earth, Heaven, Man* and *Science*.

Dābbat al-arḍ (creature from the earth), 27:82, 34:14

Daughters (see also *Children* and *Parents*), given by God, just like sons, 42:49–50; condemnation of those who feel ashamed at birth of, 16:58–59; 43:17; killing of, at birth, among pre-Islamic Arabs, see under *Arabs*; idolators' ascribing of, to God, see under *Angels* and *Feminine divinities*.

David, kills Goliath and is made king, 2:251; made a prophet and granted scripture, 4:163; 6:84; 17:55;

granted wisdom, knowledge and judgment, 2:251; 21:78–79; 27:15; 38:20; curses Israelites, 5:78; significance of mountains and birds being made subservient to, 21:79; 34:10; 38:17–19; making of coats of mail by, 21:80; 34:11; iron made pliant to, 34:10–11; and the two litigants, 38:21–26

Day, as equal to a thousand years, 22:47; 32:5; of fifty thousand years, 70:4; see *Heaven* for creation in six periods; days of Allāh, 14:5; 45:14

Day and night, alternation of, 2:164; 3:190; 10:6; one passing into the other, 3:27; 22:61; 25:62; 31:29; benefits of the two, 28:71–73; 30:23; 40:61; 78:10–11

Day, the Last, (see also *Belief, Hour* and *Life after Death*), of Judgment and Requital, 1:3; 26:82; 37:20–21; 51:12–14; 56:56; 82:15–19; of Gathering, 42:7; 64:9; of Reckoning, 14:41; 38:16, 26

— of Resurrection: God will judge differences of religion on, 2:113; 10:93; 16:92, 124; 22:17, 69; 45:17; happy position of believers on, 2:212; 3:185; 7:32; punishment for evil-doers on, 2:174; 3:180; 11:98; 16:25, 27; 17:97; 18:105; 20:100–102, 124–127; 22:9; justice done on, 3:161; deeds brought before man on, 17:13–14; relationships will not avail on, see *Relationship*; see also 7:172; 19:95; 23:16; 28:61; 30:56; 39:15; 75:6–13

Dead, the physically, cannot return to life in this world, 21:95; 23:100; 39:42; the spiritually dead, 27:80; 30:52; 35:22; as speaking, 6:111; raising of, to life, 6:36, 122; 22:7; 30:19; 41:39; 75:40; dead nations raised to life, 2:258–260; those killed in Allāh's way, not dead, 2:154; 3:169–170; reward of, 3:156–158; 4:74; 22:58–59

Deafness, spiritual, 31:7; 41:44; see also *Blind and deaf* and *Heart.*

Death, man must face, see *Man;* see also *Dead* and *Life after death.*

INDEX

Debts, see *Usury*.

Deeds (see also *Actions* and *Good works*), all bear results, 31:16; 99:7–8; 21:47; and see under *Book of deeds* and *Life after death;* how rendered null, 3:22; 7:147; 9:17, 69; 25:23; 47:1, 8–9

Defamatory speech, 4:148

Defaulters, 9:90–98; 48:11–17; 83:1–6

Democracy, see *Counsel* and *State Polity*.

Desert, dwellers of, see *Arabs: A'rāb*.

Devil, the, in human form, 3:175; 8:48; 14:22; 22:3; standing for wicked opponents, 23:97; as applied to foreign tribes, 38:37–38; applied to soothsayers, 15:16–18; 37:7; 67:5; creation of, from fire, 7:12; 38:76; sees man but man does not see him, 7:27; is open enemy to man, 12:5; 17:53; 35:6; 36:60; has no authority over man, 14:22; 15:42; 17:65; has no authority except over those who befriend him, 16:99–100; 34:20–21; friend of unbelievers, 2:257; 7:27; promptings of, cease to affect with growth of spiritual life, 38:79; stealing a hearing, 15:16–18; respited, 7:14–15; 15:36–37; 38:79–80; made abject, 7:13; is disappointed, 7:16; misleads both Adam and Eve, 2:36; 7:20; 20:120; leads man to evil, 36:62; as a tempter, 7:17; 15:39; 17:64; suggests evil practices, 4:119–120; changes the natural religion of man, 4:119; gives false promises, 14:22; 17:64; disowns responsibility for having misled, 59:16; threatens to mislead humanity, 15:39; 17:62; 38:82; sows dissension among people, 17:53; incites unbelievers, 19:83; descends upon the sinful, 26:221–223; opposes prophets, 22:52–53; causes mischief against the righteous, 41:36; makes evil deeds look attractive, 6:43; 16:63; 27:24; 29:38; 35:6–8; whisperings of, 114:1–6; struggle of, shall fail, 4:76; seeking refuge from, 7:200; 16:98; 23:97–98; 41:36; visitation from, how guarded against, 7:201; party of the, 58:18–20

INDEX

Dhu-l-Kifl, 21:85; 38:48

Dhu-l-Qarnain, 18:83–98

Ditch, the Battle of, see *Allies*.

Divorce, cannot be pronounced in menstruation, 65:1; arbiters to be appointed as preliminary to, 4:35; witnesses of, 65:2; period of waiting, 2:228; 65:4; may be revoked twice, 2:229; when it becomes irrevocable, 2:230; liberality to be shown when divorcing, 2:231; becomes necessary if injury is caused to wife, 2:231; remarriage with first husband allowed, 2:232; provision for divorced women, 2:236; in case of ill-usage or desertion of wife, 4:128; before consummation of marriage, 2:236–237; 33:49; divorced women to be treated kindly, 65:1–2, 6–7

Dowry (*Mahr* — given by husband to wife on marriage), necessary to be settled on wife, 4:4; not to be taken back, 4:19; amount not limited, 4:20; remissible in case of *Khul‘*, 2:229; when not payable in case of divorce, 2:236; when half is payable, 2:237; in former marriages with unbelievers, 60:10–11

Dumb, the spiritually, 2:18, 171; 6:39; 8:22; 17:97; see also *Blind and deaf*.

Earth, creation of, in six periods, 41:9–10; made after heaven, 79:30; see also under *Heaven;* a resting-place for man, 2:22; 27:61; 40:64; 43:10; a wide expanse, 20:53; 71:19; 78:6; made subservient to man, 67:15; 2:29; 22:65; man grows out of and returns to, 71:17–18; 77:25–26; bringing out of treasures of, 99:2

— spiritual transformation of: life given to, after death, 57:17; 7:57; 16:65; 22:5; 29:63; 30:19, 50; 35:9; 36:33; 41:39; changing into a different earth, 14:48; beaming with Divine light, 39:69; cleaving asunder of, 13:31; 50:44; 80:26; crumbling of, 89:21; and mountains, quacking and crumbling of, 56:4–5; 69:14; 73:14; stretching of, 84:3–5; inheriting of, by righteous, see *Land;*

INDEX

— earthquakes, as indicating great transformation, 99:1; 79:6

East and West, Allāh is master of both, 2:115, 142; 26:28; 70:40; 73:9; Islām to illumine both, 24:35; meaning of facing, 2:177; two of, 43:38; 55:17

Egypt, vision of the king of, 12:43; interpreted by Joseph, 12:47–48; Pharaoh's arrogant rule in, 43:51; Israelites pray in houses in, 10:87

Elephant, possessors of, 105:1

Elias, 6:85

Elisha, 6:86

Enoch, see *Idrīs*.

Eve, see *Adam*.

Evidence, should be given truthfully without fear or favour, 4:135; 5:106; 6:152; 70:33; to be given justly even if it favours enemy, 5:8; sin of concealing, 2:140, 283; circumstantial, is admissible, 12:26–28; for contracts of debt, 2:282; for divorce, 65:2; for charge of indecency or adultery, 4:15; 24:4; of non-Muslims, 5:106; witnesses not to suffer loss, 2:282; rebuttal of, by opposing evidence, 5:107; of ears, eyes and skin, 41:20–22; of tongue, hands and feet, 24:24

Evil, consequences of, 2:81; 30:9–10; removal of, 4:31; 64:9; 2:271; 5:65; 8:29; 66:8; annuled by good deeds, 11:114; 25:70; should be repelled with good, 13:22; 23:96; 28:54; 41:34; requital of, 4:123; 27:90; 28:84; 37:39; 53:31; punishment should be similar to, 6:160; 10:27; 40:40; forgiveness of, 42:40; see *Allāh: is forgiving* and *Morals: forgiveness;* hatred for, 40:10; doers of, must not be supported, 4:85, 105–107; 5:2; 11:113; 24:16; see also *Good Works*.

Evolution, 1:1; 71:14, 17; 87:1–3; 22:5; travelling in earth to find first creation, 29:20

Exultation, 17:37; 31:18

Ezekiel, vision of, 2:259

Ezra, called son of God, 9:30

Faith, endeared to true believers, 49:7; impressed into their hearts, 58:22; heart-felt faith in God, 67:29; see *Human soul: faith in God;* increase in, 3:173; 8:2; 9:124; 33:22; 48:4; 74:31; not wasted, 2:143; possession of knowledge and, 30:56; the Crier calling to, 3:193; prayer for brethren in faith, 59:10; initial stage of, 49:14; forced denial of, 16:106; selling faith for disbelief, 3:177; those loving disbelief more than, 9:23; when faith does not profit, 6:158; 32:29; 40:85; when it does, 10:98; turning back from, 2:108–109; 3:100, 106; 9:66; see also *Apostates;* light of, see *Light;* see also 6:82; 40:28; 42:52; 52:21

Fasting, enjoined, 2:183; those exempt, 2:184–185; limits and requirements, 2:187; as expiation, 2:196; 4:92; 5:89, 95; 58:3–4

Fatalism, see *Predestination;* necessity of striving to attain object, see under *Civic Life.*

Female slaves, marriage with, 2:221; conditions for marrying, 4:25; must not be forced into prostitution, 24:33

Feminine divinities, 4:117; 6:100; 16:57, 62; 53:19–23; see also under *Angels.*

Fig, 95:1

Fire, Abraham saved from, 21:69; seen by Moses in a vision, 20:10; burnt offerings, 3:183; parable of one who kindles, 2:17; from the green tree (photosynthesis), 36:80; illegal gain likened to eating of, 2:174; 4:10; in heart of man, 104:6–7; see also *Hell;* creation from, 7:12; 15:27; 38:76; use of, by man, 13:17; 56:71–73

Flight, the, (*Hijrah*), 9:40; 8:33; prophetical reference, 17:80; 25:54; 43:89

Food, good and lawful things to be consumed, 2:168, 172;

INDEX

5:4–5, 87–88, 96; 16:114; of People of the Book, 5:5; moderation in, 7:31; forbidden foods, 2:173; 5:3; 6:121, 145; 16:115; allowed in case of unavoidable necessity, *see all last refs.*; forbidden to Israelites, 6:146; slaughter of animals, 6:118, 121, 142; 2:173; 5:3

Forgiveness, see *Allāh: is Forgiving* and *Morals: forgiveness.*

Fornication, 17:32; 24:2; 25:68; see *Adultery.*

Friday service, 62:9–11

Gabriel, 2:97–98; 66:4; conveys Divine messages, 42:51; see *Spirit.*

Gambling, 2:219; 5:90; reason of prohibition, 5:91

Garden, standing for success, 36:26; 55:46; see *Paradise.*

God, see *Allāh.*

Gods, false: no proof of existence of, 6:19; 21:24; 23:117; 35:40; 46:4; and see *Polytheists: have no authority;* disorder if any existed, 21:22; 23:91; are falsehood, 22:62; 31:30; can neither harm nor benefit, 5:76; 10:18; 22:12–13; 25:55; 39:38; do not hear or answer, 13:14; 18:52; 19:42; 28:64; 35:14; 46:5; 7:148; 20:89; cannot guide, 7:148; 10:35; cannot judge, 40:20; cannot avail or help, 6:40, 94; 7:197; 11:101; 34:22; 41:48; cannot create anything, 7:191; 10:34; 13:16; 16:20; 22:73; 35:40; 46:4; have no faculties, 7:195; cannot give life or cause death, 2:258; 25:3; 30:40; are slaves to laws of nature, 7:194; have no power, 16:73; themselves seeking nearness to God, 17:57; not to be feared, 6:81; the Prophet to dissociate himself from, 6:19; 10:104–105; ch. 109; Muslims must not abuse, 6:108; see also *Idols, Polytheism,* and *Polytheists.*

Gog and Magog, 18:94; prophecy of prevalence of, over whole world, 18:98–99; 21:96

Goliath, 2:249–251

Good works, doing of is essential corollary to belief, 2:25, 82; 4:173; 7:42; 10:4; 13:29; 28:80; 34:37; 64:9; 103:3; success attained by those who believe and do, 20:75–76; 24:55; 29:7; 35:10; 38:28; 41:8; 42:26; 47:2; 5:12; doing good to others, 2:112, 195; 3:134; 16:90; 29:69; 39:34–35; 51:15–16; vying with one another in doing, 2:148; 3:114; 5:48; 21:90; chosen ones must be foremost in doing, 35:32; help progress of man while evil retards it, 91:9–10; 92:5–10; doing of, benefits one's soul while evil harms it, 2:265, 286; 10:23; 17:7; 30:44; 41:46; 45:15; reward for, is good, 16:30, 97; 39:10; 53:31; 55:60; bring tenfold and more reward, 4:40; 6:160; 10:26; 27:89; 28:84; 42:23; annul evil deeds, 11:114; 25:70; contrast between good and evil, 14:24–26; 16:75–76; weighing of good and evil, 7:8–9; 23:102–103; 101:6–9; abide for ever, 18:46; 19:76; motive in doing is to seek pleasure of Allāh, 92:19–21; 2:207, 265, 272; 4:74, 114; 5:16; 6:162; 60:1

Gospel, revelation of, 3:3–4; current gospels not the Gospel spoken of by the Qur'ān, see *Bible*; as containing light and guidance, 5:46–47; promises success for sacrifices made, 9:111; gives good news of Holy Prophet's advent, see *Muḥammad: prophecies about*; see also 3:48, 65; 5:66, 68, 110; 48:29; 57:27

Gossip, 17:36; gossip-mongers, 24:23

Government, to be entrusted to fit persons, 4:58; government by parliament, 42:38; see also *State Polity*.

Graves, those in, as referring to the spiritually dead, 22:7; 35:22; 36:51; 54:7–8; 70:43–44; 82:4; see also *Dead*.

Grove, dwellers of the, 15:78; 26:176; 38:13; 50:14

Ḥadīth, authority of, 4:59; called as Wisdom, 33:34; 2:151; 3:164; 62:2; Prophet as exemplar, 33:21

Ḥajj, see *Pilgrimage*.

Hāmān, 28:6, 8, 38; 29:39; 40:24, 36

INDEX

Hārūt and Mārūt, 2:102

Heart, sealing of, 2:7; 4:155; 6:46, 110; 7:100–101; 9:87, 93; 10:74; 16:108; 30:59; 40:35; 45:23; 47:16; 63:3; veils and coverings on, and deafness in ears, 17:46; 18:57; 41:5; 6:25; blindness of, 22:46; 41:17; those not using it to understand, 7:179; 47:24; taking heed by heart and hearing, 50:37; hardening of, 2:74; 57:16; 5:13; 6:43; 22:53; 39:22; contentment and tranquillity of the, 13:28; 2:248; 3:126; 5:113; 8:10; 48:4; see also *Tranquility*; a sound heart, 26:89; 37:84

Heaven (*samā'*, physical heaven), a vapour, 41:11; vastness of, 55:7; 57:21; 79:28; 88:18; coming down of portion of, 34:9; 52:44; sustenance coming from, 40:13; rolling up of, 21:104; bursting asunder of, 25:25; 73:18; 77:9; 82:1; 84:1; 19:90–91; 55:37; 69:16; commotion of, 52:9; removal of covering of, 81:11; opening of, 78:19; 15:14; 54:11; creation of, in six periods, 7:54; 10:3; 32:4; 41:9–12; see also *Science* and *Allāh: Creator*; the seven heavens, 17:44; 23:86; 67:3; 71:15; called seven ways, 23:17; described as being full of paths, 51:7; raised without pillars, 13:2; 31:10; rotation of heavenly bodies, 21:33; 36:40; livings beings in, 16:49; 17:44; 19:93; 27:87; 42:29; 55:29

Hell, who shall go to, 2:81; 23:103; not eternal, 6:128; 11:107; purges of evil, 57:15; fitting man for spiritual progress, 101:8–11; a manifestation of spiritual realities, 39:48; 76:4; is hidden from the eye, 26:91; compared to spiritual blindness, 17:72; 20:124–126; life in, begins here, *ibid.*; intense regret for evil done is hell, 2:167; a state of being gnawed by grief, 14:17; 22:22; being debarred from the Lord is, 83:15; 3:87–88; fire of, arises within the heart, 104:6–7; is neither a state of life nor of death, 20:74; 87:12–13; a punishment corresponding to sin, 78:21–30; manifestation of, in this life, 14:49; 32:21; 54:48; 79:36; 89:23; as applied to punishment of this life, 29:54; 81:12; righteous shall not go to, 21:101–102; only for the wicked, 19:68–72;

continuance of the punishment of, 4:56; seven gates of, 15:44; the parable of nineteen relating to, 74:30–31; inmates of, call out to dwellers of garden, 7:50; covering of, 77:30–33; various forms of punishment in, 11:106; 18:29; 21:100; 22:19–22; 38:56–58; 40:71–72; 73:12–13; 88:2–7

Hereafter, see *Life after death, Resurrection, Hell, Paradise,* and *Day, the Last.*

Hijrah, see *Flight.*

Holy Ghost, the, 2:87; see *Spirit.*

Homicide, see *Murder.*

Homosexuality, denounced, 4:16; 7:80–81; 26:165–166; 27:54–55; 29:28–29

Hour, the, as signifying doom of opponents, 6:31; 7:187; 16:77; 18:36; 19:75; 20:15; 22:1; 43:66; 47:18; 54:46; 79:42–44; as signifying Day of Judgment, 21:49; 25:11; 30:12, 55; 40:46; knowledge of the, 7:187; 31:34; 33:63; 41:47; 43:85; as departure of prophethood from Israel, 43:61

Hūd 7:65–72; 11:50–60, 89; 26:123–140; 46:21–26

Ḥudaibiyah, truce at, was a victory for Muslims, 48:1; oath of allegiance at, 48:10, 18; terms of truce, 48:24; truce was necessary for safety of Muslims in Makkah, 48:25; Prophet's vision later fulfilled, 48:27

Hudhud, 27:20

Human soul: Divine Soul is breathed into man, 15:28–29; 32:7–9; 38:72; purity of, 30:30; 95:4; 7:172; 14:22; 15:42; three stages in progress of, 12:53; 75:2; 89:27–30; man to love God, 2:165, 177; 3:31; 5:54; 76:8–9; man pleased with God, see under *Allāh: is loving;* faith in God, 2:256–257; 10:9; 19:96; 33:47; 48:18; 49:7; 57:12, 19; 58:22; trust in God, 3:159; 9:51, 129; 11:88, 123; 12:67; 13:30; 14:12; 25:58; 42:36; 60:4; 65:3; refuge in God, ch. 113; ch. 114; 2:67; 7:200; 16:98; 23:97–98; 41:36; contentment in God, 13:28;

INDEX 597

57:23; 89:27–28; meeting with God, 2:45–46, 223; 6:31; 32:10, 23; 33:44; 53:42; 84:6; God is man's friend, 2:257; 3:68; 4:45; 5:55–56; 6:14; 10:62–64; 45:19; whom God loves, see *Allāh: is loving*; whom God does not love, 2:190; 3:57, 140; 5:64; 6:141; 8:58; 16:23; 28:76; 57:23

Humanity, oneness of, 2:213; 4:1; 10:19; diversity of, 30:22; 35:28; brotherhood of, 49:13; service of, 2:177; 4:36; 51:19; 76:8–9; 89:17–18; 90:11–16; ch. 107

Humility, see under *Morals*.

Ḥunain, battle of, 9:25–27

Hunting, by trained beasts and birds of prey, 5:4

Ḥūr, see *Paradise*.

Hypocrites, detailed accounts of, 2:8–16; 3:154–180; 4:60–147; 9:38–127; ch. 63

— evils of: practise deception, 2:9; 4:142–143; false oaths of, 9:56, 62, 74, 95–96; 58:14–19; 63:1–2; dishonesty of, 4:105–112; fears of, 4:77; 5:52; 9:64, 74; desire to run away, 9:57; break promise with God, 9:75–76; 33:15; enjoin evil and forbid good, 9:67; do not accept Prophet's judgment, 4:60–64; 24:47–50; secret counsels of, 4:81, 114; 9:78; spread false reports, 4:83; spread evil reports, 33:60–61; slander 'Ā'ishah, 24:11; efforts of, to destroy Muslims, 4:113; 63:7–8; bear ill-will towards Muslims, 9:50; molest the Prophet, 9:61; their plots, 9:48; their carpings, 9:58–59; their mocking, 2:14–15; 9:65; they taunt believers, 9:79; their opposition doomed to failure, 4:115; 5:53; acting as spies, 5:41; seeking friendship with enemies of Islām, 4:139; 5:52; obey enemies of Islām, 47:25–26; build mosque to cause harm, 9:107–110

— and battles: refuse to fight, 3:167–168; 4:77; 47:20; do not go to Tabūk, 9:42–45; their presence a source of weakness, 9:47; are glad to remain behind in battles, 9:81, 86–87, 93; false excuses of, 9:90, 94; 48:11–12; show cowardice on account of strength of allies,

33:12–20; refuse to bear hardship, 9:49; untrue to their promise to Jews, 59:11–14

— punishment of, from God, 2:10; 4:137–139, 141, 145; 9:52, 63; 48:6; must be separated, 3:179; 29:11; 47:29–31; their uncleanness increased, 9:125; their trials, 9:126; their hearts turned away, 9:127; their spending not acceptable to Allāh, 9:53–54; are cursed, 9:68; works rendered null, 9:69; 33:19; 47:28; their property and children a source of torture, 9:55, 85; are deprived of light, 57:13–15; shall not be forgiven, 9:80; 63:6

— how dealt with by Muslims, 4:88–91; not to be taken as friends, 4:144; prayer not to be offered for, 9:84; not allowed to go forth with Muslims in wars, 9:83; 48:15; punished twice, 9:101; meaning of *jihād* against, 9:73; 66:9

— those who confessed their faults, 9:102–103; repentance of, shall be accepted, 4:146–147; 33:24; a party of them pardoned, 9:66

Iblīs, see under *Adam;* is not an angel but one of the jinn, 18:50; see also *Devil.*

Idols, stones set up for, 5:3; superstitions of worshippers of, about cattle, 6:138–139, 143–144; offerings to, 6:136; 16:56; belief in the intercession of, 10:18; 30:13; 36:23; 43:86; bedecked with ornaments, 43:18; are only names, 12:40; 53:23; are only a lie, 29:17; filth of, 22:30; worshipped by Abraham's people, 26:70–74; see also *Gods, Polytheism* and *Polytheists.*

Idrīs, 19:56–57; 21:85

Immunity, declaration of, 9:1–3

'Imrān, see *Amran.*

Incarnation, doctrine of, refuted, 42:11

Individual responsibility, doctrine of, see *Actions* and *Atonement: refutation of.*

INDEX   599

Infanticide, forbidden, 6:152; 17:31; 60:12; as custom of idolators, see under *Arabs*

Inheritance, law of, 4:7, 11–12, 176; only actual relatives to inherit, 33:6

Injīl, see *Gospel*.

Intellectual development (see also *Knowledge*), man urged to use reason and understanding, 2:73, 242; 3:190–191; 6:151; 30:24; 45:5; 67:10; to reflect and ponder, 3:191; 7:176, 184; 10:24; 16:44; 30:8; 34:46; 59:21; 4:82; 23:68; 38:29; 47:24; signs in nature for those who reflect, 2:164; 3:190; 13:3; 16:11–13, 67–69; 30:21–24; 39:42; 45:5, 13; see also *Signs: in nature;* blind following condemned, 2:170–171; 5:104; 7:179; 31:21; 43:22–23; condemnation of failure to use reason, 2:44; 5:58; 8:22; 25:44; 36:62; proof required to establish truth, 2:111; 6:143, 150; 27:64; 37:157; 46:4

Intercession, 2:48, 255; 4:85; 43:86; only by Allāh's permission, 2:255; 10:3; 19:87; 20:109; 21:28; 34:23; 53:26; entirely in Allāh's hands, 6:70; 32:4; 39:44; 40:18; see also *Idols*.

Interest, from banks, see *Usury*.

Intoxicants, prohibited, 2:219; 5:90; reason of prohibition, 5:91; first step in the prohibition of, 4:43

Iron, 57:25; 34:10; 18:96

Isaac, 2:133, 136, 140; 3:84; 4:163; 37:112–113; 38:45

Ishmael (see also *Abraham*), 2:125, 127–129; rebuilding Ka'bah along with Abraham, 2:127; settled in Arabia, 14:37; Abraham's prayer for, 14:39–41; 2:128; Abraham's vision of sacrificing, 37:101–107; was a prophet, 19:54–55

Islām (see also *Belief, Faith, Muslims* and *Religion*), significance of, 2:112; 3:19, 85; 4:125; 6:162–163; 31:22; fundamental principles of, 2:3–4; principle of brotherhood of man laid down by, 49:13; as the natural religion of man, 3:83; 29:49; 30:30; 34:6; religion of all prophets, 2:132; 42:13; accepts all the prophets of the world, 2:4; high ideal of, 6:162; a perfect religion, 5:3; compared to a seed sown, 48:29; 80:24—32; propagation of, made obligatory, 3:104; 9:122; unparalleled tolerance of, 22:40; forbids compulsion in religion, see *Religion: freedom of;* inculcates humility in the hour of triumph, 110:1—3; leniency of the martial and criminal laws of, 5:34; does not impose hardship on man, 2:286; 22:78; 2:185; 5:6; gives man scope to frame laws himself, 5:101—102; recognizes a law being given to every people, 5:48; levels all distinctions, 6:52; superstitions swept off by, 2:189; 6:136—139, 143—144; introduces a new meaning into the principle of sacrifice, 22:36—37; disallows vows of celibacy, 24:32; moderation inculcated by, 42:40

— success of: opposition to, shall be brought to naught, 61:8; steady progress of, notwithstanding severest opposition, 41:53; signs of the advancement of, 7:57—58; victories promised for, 48:21; progress of, shall be hampered for 1000 years, 32:5; prophecy of its firm establishment, 32:5; prevalence of, over all religions, 9:33; 48:28; 61:9; sacrifices necessary for the triumph of, 61:10—13; prophecy of establishment of the kingdom of, 24:55; 28:5, 58; 67:1; resplendent light of, 24:35—38; light of, shall be spread in East and West, see *Light*.

Israelites (see also *People of the Book*)

— History of: favours bestowed on, 2:40, 47, 122; 28:5—6; 44:32; 45:16; subjected to severe torment by Pharaoh, 2:49; 7:127; 28:4; 40:25; 44:30—31; pray to be delivered from persecution, 10:85—86; made to cross the Red Sea, 2:50; 7:138; 10:90; 20:77; 44:24; made rulers in the Holy Land, 7:129, 137; 17:104; 28:5; granted kingdom and prophethood, 5:20; refuse to march on Holy Land, 5:21—24; in the wilderness, 5:26; go after false gods, 7:138; how raised to life after death, 2:243; make and worship a calf, 2:51, 92—93; 4:153;

INDEX

7:148; led astray by Sāmirī, 20:85–97; repent of calf-worship, 7:149; not punished for calf-worship, 2:54; 7:152–153; demand sight of Allāh, 2:55; 4:153; cloud giving shade to, 2:57; 7:160; receive manna and quails, 2:57; 7:160; settling in a city, 2:58; punished with plague, 2:59; 7:161–162; ask for water in the wilderness, 2:60; 7:160; demand for food in wilderness, 2:61; abasement of, 2:61; twelve leaders and tribes of, 5:12; 7:160; seventy elders chosen from, 7:155; covenant of God with, 2:40, 83; 5:70; making of covenant and raising of mountain, 2:63, 93; 4:154; 7:171; break the covenant, 4:155; 5:12–13; overtaken by earthquake, 2:55; 4:153; 7:155, 171; break Sabbath, see *Sabbath;* made apes, 2:65; 7:165–166; made apes and swine, 5:60; malign Moses, 33:69; 61:5; ask for a king to be raised up, 2:246; hundred years' death of, 2:259; try to kill prophets, 2:61, 91; 3:21, 112, 183; 4:155; 5:70; falsely charge Mary with adultery, 4:156; reject Jesus, 3:52; 61:14; attempt to kill Jesus, 3:54; 4:157; 2:72; believe that Jesus was cursed, 4:159; turn blind and deaf to truth twice, 5:71; make mischief twice, 17:4; cursed by David and Jesus, 5:78; resettling of, 17:6; kingdom of God departs from, 3:26–27; 4:53; prophecy of persecution of, by tyrants, 3:112; 7:167

— evils of: hard-heartedness of, 2:74; corruption of scriptures by, 2:75; 4:46; 5:13, 41; hypocrisy of, 2:44; ignorance of, 2:78; claim of, to exemption from punishment, 2:80; 3:24; 5:71; claim to be favourites of God, 2:94; 5:18; 62:6; insolence of, 2:88; hate Gabriel, 2:97; forbidden foods to, 3:93; 4:160; 6:146; iniquity of, 4:160; take usury, 4:161; devour property falsely, 4:161; sinful utterances and doings of, 5:62–63; treachery among, 2:85; 5:13; deny resurrection, 60:13; likened to ass carrying books, 62:5; the good among, 3:113–115; 4:162; 7:159, 168

— and Islām: invited to accept the Prophet, 2:40; hopes of, in the Promised Prophet, 2:89; recognise but reject the

Prophet because not an Israelite, 2:89—91; 26:198—200; learned men of, know of prophecies relating to Prophet, 26:197; persist in rejection of the Prophet, 2:101; hatred to the Prophet, 2:104; plans against the Prophet, 2:87; 3:21—22; two tribes of, betray alliance and punished for backing enemy, 33:26—27; 59:2—4; given a chance at the Prophet's advent, 17:8; their law abrogated by Islām, 2:106; plots of, to make Muslims apostatize, 3:72; acting as spies, 5:41; hypocritical towards Muslims, 2:76; 5:61; call Allāh poor, 3:181; mock Muslims for raising subscriptions for national defence, 5:64; do not like good to befall Muslims, 2:105; worship Arab idols, 4:51; befriend idolaters, 5:80—81; most stern in hatred towards Islām, 5:82; Muslims should pardon and forgive, 2:109; 5:13

Jacob, prophecy of birth of, 11:71; enjoins Unity and true religion on his descendants, 2:132—133; was a prophet, 6:84; 19:49; 38:45—47; religion of, 2:140; 12:38; and forbidden food, 3:93; revelation of, 2:136; 3:84; 4:163; 21:72—73; told of dream by Joseph, 12:4—6; removal of Joseph from, 12:11—18; sends Benjamin with brothers, 12:63—68; has hope in grief, 12:83—87; goes to Egypt, 12:99

Jerusalem, destruction of, by Babylonians, 17:5; destroyed by Romans, 17:7; earlier *qiblah* of Muslims, 2:142; in *Miʿrāj* of Holy Prophet, 17:1

Jesus Christ, prophecy of birth of, 3:45; 4:171; 19:19; only a messenger, 4:171; 5:75; 43:59; a servant of God, 19:30; 21:26; 43:59; birth of, 3:47; 19:22—26; mentioned among prophets who had fathers, 6:85—87; an ordinary mortal, 3:59; 5:75; strengthened with Holy Spirit, 2:87, 253; 5:110; taught Torah and Gospel, 3:48; 5:110; verifies Torah and modifies Mosaic law, 3:50; 5:46; 61:6; taught same basic principles as other prophets, 42:13; 3:51; 5:117; 19:31, 36; 43:63—64; revelation of, like that of other prophets, 2:136; 3:84;

INDEX

4:163; sent only to Israelites, 3:49; 61:6; was not rude to his mother, 19:32; denies claim to Godhead, 5:116–117; belief in divinity of, denounced, 5:17, 72; 18:102; 9:30–31; doctrine of Sonship of, refuted, see *Sonship*; Arab unbelievers object to honouring of, 43:57–59; is rejected by the Jews, 3:52; as a sign for the Jews, 19:21; 43:61; curses Israelites, 5:78; helped by disciples, 3:52-53; 61:14; revelation to disciples of, 5:111; they ask for food from heaven, 5:112–113; prays for food, 5:114–115; followers of, promised triumph over rejectors, 3:55; 61:14; compassion in hearts of followers of, 57:27; Jewish plans against life of, 3:54; enemies of, withheld, 5:110; cleared of false charges, 3:55; is promised deliverance from death on cross, 3:55; did not die while on the cross, 4:157; only apparently killed, 2:72–73; 4:157; granted spiritual exaltation, not raised bodily, 3:55; 4:158; died a natural death, 3:55; 5:117; is not alive, further proof, 3:144; 5:75; 21:7–8, 34; 16:20–21; 7:25; finds shelter, 23:50; prophesies advent of Holy Prophet, 36:14; 61:6

Jews, see *Israelites*.

Jibrīl, see *Gabriel*.

Jihād, as meaning spiritual striving to attain nearness to God, 22:78; 29:69; applied to the bearing of persecution at Makkah, 29:6; as struggle in a general sense, 2:218; 8:72, 74; excellence and importance of, 3:142; 4:95; 9:20, 88; 49:15; 61:11; see also *Muslim wars*.

Jinn, creation of, from fire, 15:27; 55:15; as signifying leaders of evil, 34:41; listen to the Qur'ān, 46:29; 72:1; as leaders of some Jewish tribes, 46:30–31; as future Christian nations, 72:1–14; subjugated by Solomon, 27:17

Job, 21:83–84; 38:41–44; 4:163; 6:84

John the Baptist, 3:39; 6:85; 19:7–15; 21:90; sinlessness of, 19:13–14

Jonah, 37:139–148; 21:87–88; 68:48–50; 10:98; 4:163; 6:86

Joseph, sees the vision, 12:4–6; his brothers plot against him, 12:7–18; taken out of the pit by travellers, 12:19–20; in Potiphar's house, 12:21; granted wisdom, 12:22; remains firm under temptations, 12:23–25; his innocence established, 12:26–29; further temptations, 12:30–34; cast into prison, 12:35; Joseph and the two prisoners, 12:36; preaches to them, 12:37–40; interprets their visions, 12:41; interprets the king's vision, 12:43–49; cleared of false charges, 12:50–53; raised to dignity, 12:54–56; his brothers go to him and he helps them, 12:58–62; the youngest brother, 12:63–69; incident of the cup, 12:70–77; Jacob's grief for, 12:84–86; reveals himself to his brothers, 12:88–91; forgives them, 12:92; prayer of, 12:101; history of, repeated in Prophet's history, 12:102–103; see also 6:84; 40:34

Judgment, day of, see *Day, the Last*.

Jūdī, 11:44

Justice, to be done between people, 4:58; 38:26; 42:15; to be done between Muslims and non-Muslims, 4:105–106; towards enemy, 5:2, 8, 42; to be done in Muslim disputes, 49:9; no partiality even for relatives, 4:135; 6:152; broadest possible conception of, 7:29; 16:90; see also *Evidence*.

Ka'bah, made a resort for people, 2:125; as House of God, 2:125; 22:26; first House of worship on earth, 3:96; rebuilt by Abraham, 2:127; *Maqām* (Place) of Abraham, 2:125; 3:97; see also *Abraham*; appointed as *Qiblah*, 2:142–145; to become the Muslim centre, 2:144; reasons for, 2:148; a support for men, 5:97; shall not be approached by unbelievers, 9:28; service of, cannot compare with struggle to propagate truth, 9:19–22; sacrifice of animals at, 22:33, 36; 5:95

Kingdom of God, 3:26–27; 6:73; 67:1

Kingdom of heaven, granted to Muslims, 4:54; inaccessible to unbelievers, 7:40

INDEX

Knowledge (see also *Intellectual development*), Reading and use of pen recommended, 68:1; 96:1–5; raises man in dignity, 39:9; 58:11; possessors of, recognize the truth of revelation, 4:162; 17:107–109; 22:54; 29:49; 34:6; they testify to Divine unity, 3:18; they fear God, 35:28; acting without proper knowledge, condemned, 3:66; 4:83; 6:100, 119, 140, 148; 11:46–47; 17:36; 22:3–4; 24:15; 31:20; 49:6; travelling in search of knowledge, 3:137; 18:65–66; 29:20; Prophet told to pray for increase of, 20:114; given to man from God, 2:31; 96:3–5; 55:1–4; given to prophets and other elect, 2:247; 12:22; 18:65; 21:74, 79–80; 27:15; 28:14; Prophet raised to be a Teacher, 2:151; 62:2–3; wisdom is a great good, 2:269; study of nature, 3:190–191; 10:5–6; 13:3–4; 16:10–16, 66–69, 78–81; 17:12; 30:22; 45:3–5; study of the conditions of different countries, 22:46; 29:20; 35:27–28; gain knowledge of diversity of mankind, 30:22; 49:13; study of histories of different nations, 12:109–111; 30:9; 33:62; 35:43–44; 40:21, 82; man can rule forces of nature with, 2:30, 34; see also under *Man;* mankind excels other creation, on account of, 7:140; 17:70; three degrees of, 102:5–8

Korah, 28:76–82; 29:39; 40:24

Lailat al-Qadr, 97:1–5

Land, inheriting of the, by the righteous, 7:128; 21:105; 39:74; 70:40–41; see also 7:100; 19:40

Lāt, 53:19

Life (see also *Civic Life*), seriousness and great purpose of, 21:16; 23:115; 30:8; 67:2; 75:36; see also *Humanity: service of;* a struggle with difficulties, 90:4; greed for material life, 2:96; 3:14; 18:103–104; material life, a sport, 6:32; 29:64; 47:36; 57:20; material life deceives man, 6:70, 130; 7:51; 45:35; ultimate decay of physical life, 16:70; 30:54; 36:68; 10:23–24; 18:45; water as source of, see *Water;* created in pairs, see

Pairs; man's physical life, see *Man;* physical and spiritual life, created by God, 2:28; 22:5–6; 23:12–14; spiritual life given by Qur'ān, 8:24; transitory physical life contrasted with spiritual, 2:212; 3:14–15; 9:38; 11:15–16; 17:18–21; 18:45–46, 103–108; 28:61; 40:39; 79:37–41; 87:16–17

Life after death, grows out of record of man's deeds, 17:13–14; 17:71; 50:3–4, 18; 82:10–12; 83:7–20; 13:11; 21:94; 43:80; 45:28–29; 50:17–18; 58:6; see also *Book;* begins in this life, 89:27–30; 3:198; 17:72; 41:30–32; 55:46; complete manifestation of hidden spiritual realities of this life, 6:28; 20:124–126; 24:24; 39:69–70; 50:22; 57:12; 69:18; 86:8–9; 99:6–8; a higher reality than this life, 17:21; 29:64; 40:39; progress in higher life is unceasing, 39:20; 66:8; see also *Hell* and *Paradise.*

Light, of faith, 57:12, 28; 66:8; 2:257; 5:16; 6:122; 14:1; 33:43; 65:11; of the religion of Islām, 24:35; 9:32; 39:22; 61:8; Prophet called Light, 5:15; 33:46; Prophet sent with, 4:174; 7:157; 42:52; 64:8; contrasted with spiritual darkness, 13:16; 35:19–22; both light and darkness created by Allāh, 6:1

Lot, was a prophet, 6:86; righteousness of, 21:74; preaches and is rejected, 7:80–82; 26:160–168; 27:54–56; 29:28–30; evils of his people, 7:80–81; 26:165–166; 27:55; 29:28–29; coming of messengers to, 11:77; 15:61–64; 29:33–34; his people demand the guests, 11:78; 15:67–69; forbidden to shelter strangers, 15:70; offers his daughters as hostages, 11:78; 15:71; leaves the city, 11:81; 15:65–66; delivered along with his followers, while rejectors destroyed, 7:83–84; 11:82; 15:73–74; 26:169–173; 27:57–58; 37:133– 138; 54:33–39; wife of, exemplified evil, 66:10; wife destroyed with rejectors, 7:83; 11:81; 26:171; 27:57; 29:33; 37:135; see also 11:89; 21:71; 50:13

Love, of Allāh for man, see *Allāh: is Loving;* of man for Allāh, see *Human soul.*

INDEX 607

Luqmān, 31:12–19

Madīnah, 9:101; 59:9; 63:8

Magians, 22:17

Magog, see *Gog*.

Mahr, see *Dowry*.

Makkah (see also *Ka'bah*), called Bakkah, 3:96; Abraham's prayer for, and its security, 2:126; 14:35; inviolability of, 2:191; inviolability of things relating to, 2:194; made sacred, 27:91; 29:67; made secure, 95:3; unproductive of fruit, 14:37; not warned before Holy Prophet, 32:3; 36:6; warned by Prophet, 6:92; 7:4; 65:8–10; prophecy of punishment of, by famine, 44:10–15; famine overtakes, 16:112–113; Prophet's Flight from, see *Flight;* drives out Prophet, 47:13; prophecy of Prophet's return to, 28:85; prophecy of the conquest of, by Muslims, 14:14; 17:76; security of, prophesied, 28:57; a guidance for the nations, 3:96; three prophecies relating to the future of, 3:97; called mother of towns, 6:92; 42:7

Mālik, the angel, 43:77

Man (see also *Human soul*), creation of: from dust or clay, 6:2; 7:11–12; 22:5; 32:7; 35:11; 37:11; 40:67; 55:14; from extract of clay, 23:12; from clay giving sound and fashioned in shape, 15:26–28, 33; from insignificant origin, 16:4; 32:8; 36:77; 53:46; 75:37; 76:1–2; 80:18–19; 96:2; from water, 25:54; 77:20; 86:5–7; see also *Water;* from a male and female, 42:11; 49:13; from single being, and its mate of same, 4:1; 7:189; 39:6; grows out of earth, 71:17; creation of, from haste, 21:37; impatience of, 70:19; object of creation of, 11:7; 23:115; 51:56–57; 75:36; 76:2; 90:4; stages in the physical growth of, 22:5; 23:14; 40:67; in womb, 3:6; 39:6; 53:32; made complete, 18:37; 32:9; 38:72; 75:38; 82:6–8; made in goodly form, 40:64; 64:3; made to rule universe, 2:29; everything made subservient to,

13:2; 14:32–33; 16:12–14; 21:81; 22:65; 31:20; 43:12–13; 45:12–13; attains to perfection by Divine inspiration, 15:29; Divine spirit breathed into, see *Human soul;* greatness and vast capabilities of, 95:4–6; is taught language, 55:3–4; turns to Allāh in affliction but forgets Him in ease, 7:189–190; 10:12; 16:53–55; 39:49; and is ungrateful in ease, 6:63–64; 10:22–23; 17:67, 83; 30:33–34; 31:32; 39:8; 41:49–51; ungratefulness of, 11:9; 22:66; 42:48; 43:15; 100:6; unfaithfulness of, to trust, 33:72; threefold duty of, 5:93; spiritual needs of, must be provided for, 6:38; must face death, 3:185; 7:25; 23:15; 55:26–27; 56:60; 80:21; best clothing granted to, is piety, 7:26

Manāt, 53:20

Marriage (see also *Wives* and *Women*), union of two natures one in essence, 4:1; a contract requiring free consent of both parties, 4:21; obligatory, 24:32–33; to be performed after maturity is attained, 4:6; divorced women and widows free to remarry, 2:232, 234–235; see also *Divorce;* women whom it is forbidden to marry, 4:23; conditions for marriage with slave girls, 4:25; intermarriages: with idolaters forbidden, 2:221; 60:10–11; with followers of scriptures, 5:5; polygamy, when allowed, see *Polygamy.*

— relation of husband and wife: of love and compassion, 25:74; 30:21; comfort each other, 7:189; apparel for *one another*, 2:187; mutual obligations: good fellowship and kindness, 2:228–229, 231; 4:19; giving of free gifts to each other, 2:237; lodge wife according to means, 65:6; dowry a free gift, 4:4; even if a heap of gold is given to wife it is hers, 4:19–21, 24; see also *Dowry;* men are maintainers of women, 4:34

— privacy of home life, 24:27–28, 58–59; 33:53

— intermingling of sexes, 24:30–31, 60; 33:59

— respect and love for parents and offspring, 6:151;

25:74; and see *Parents* and *Children*.

Mārūt, see *Hārūt*.

Marwah, see *Ṣafā*.

Mary, mother of Jesus, 3:35; birth of, 3:36; given in charge of Zacharias, 3:37; faith of, in God, 3:37; is chosen, 3:42; her marriage, 3:44; receives news of birth of a son, 3:45–47; 19:16–21; received news in vision, 19:17; conceives and gives birth, 19:22–26; suffers pains of child-birth, 19:23; guarding of chastity by, 21:91; 66:12; falsely charged with fornication, 4:156; lived and died like mortals, 5:17, 75; a truthful woman, 5:75; erroneous belief in divinity of, 5:116; given a shelter with Jesus, 23:50; set as an example to believers, 66:11–12; see also *Women*.

Meekness, see *Morals: Humility*.

Menstruation, 2:222; see also *Divorce*.

Mercy, see *Allāh: is merciful*.

Michael, angel, 2:98

Midian, Moses' stay in, 28:22–28; 20:40; likeness of, to Madīnah, 28:45; see also 7:85; 9:70; 11:84; 22:44; 29:36

Miracles, see *Signs*.

Miʿrāj, see *Ascension*.

Monkery, 5:87; a Christian innovation, 57:27

Months, number of, 9:36; sacred months, 2:189; 9:36–37

Moon, rending asunder of, 54:1; darkening of, 75:8; as standing for the Prophet's cause, 36:39; 84:18–19; see also *Sun and Moon*.

Morals: picture of moral qualities, 3:134–135; 6:151–152; 17:23–39; 23:1–9; 25:63–76; 31:12–19; 33:35; 70:22–35

— truth: truthful ones, 5:119; 9:119; 33:24, 35, 70; bearing true witness, 4:135; 5:8; 6:152; 70:33; true to promises and covenants, 2:177; 3:75–76; 5:1; 8:27; 16:91; 17:34; 23:8; 33:23; 70:32; falsehood to be shunned, 16:116; 22:30; 25:72; liars condemned, 3:61; 24:7; 39:3, 32

— honest dealing, 4:105–107; 6:152; 17:35; 83:1–3

— sincerity, 2:139; 7:29; 39:2–3, 14; 74:6; 98:5; insincerity and show condemned, 107:4–6; 2:44; 2:264; 3:167; 4:142, 145–146; 61:2–3

— purity, 9:103, 108; 24:21; 33:33; 74:4–5; 87:14; 91:9; 2:222; 5:6; *not to be ascribed to oneself,* 4:49; 53:32

— unselfishness, 2:207, 262; 3:92; 4:53; 6:162; 11:51; 12:104; 25:57; 59:9; 64:16; 76:8–9; 92:19–20

— humility, 17:37–38; 25:63; 28:83; 31:18–19; 2:45–46; 4:63; 7:13, 55, 146, 205; 16:23, 29; 40:35; 57:16

— patience, 103:2–3; 2:153–157, 177, 249–250; 3:120, 146, 186, 200; 11:11; 13:22; 16:126–127; 28:80; 29:58–59; 39:10; 42:43; 49:5; perseverance, 11:112; 30:43; 41:6, 30–31

— thankfulness, 2:152, 172, 185, 243; 4:147; 5:6, 89; 14:7–8, 34; 16:18, 114; 25:62; 27:19, 40; 28:73; 31:12, 31; 34:13; 39:7, 66; 46:15

— self-control, 3:134; 4:135; 7:201; 18:28; 30:29; 38:26; 42:37; 79:40–41

— chastity, 17:32; 21:91; 23:5; 24:30–33; 25:68; 70:29

— *courage,* 3:172–175; 5:54; 6:80–82; 9:40; 20:46; 33:39; 39:36

— forgiveness, 2:109; 3:134, 159; 4:149; 5:13; 7:199; 12:92; 15:85; 24:22; 41:34–35; 42:37, 40, 43; 64:14

Mortgage, 2:283

Moses, revelation to mother of, 20:38–39; 28:7; cast into river, 20:39; 28:7; picked up by Pharaoh's people, 20:39; 28:8; brought back to his mother, 20:40; 28:12–13; journey of, to Khartum, 18:60–82; travels of, in search of knowledge, *ibid.*; kills an Egyptian, 20:40; 26:14, 19–21; 28:15–21, 33; goes to Midian, 20:40; 28:22–28; sees fire (in vision) in return journey, 20:10; 27:7; 28:29; is called, 19:52; 20:11–14; 27:8–9; 28:30; 79:16; sees in the visionary state that his staff has become a serpent and his hand is white, 20:17–23; 27:10–12; 28:31–32; commanded to go to Pharaoh, 7:103; 10:75; 11:96–97; 20:24; 23:45–46; 26:15; 27:12; 40:23–24; 51:38; 79:17; asks for a helper, Aaron, 20:25–35; 26:12–14; 28:33–34; commanded to demand deliverance of the Israelites, 7:104–105; 20:47; 26:16–17; 44:17–18; controversy with Pharaoh, 20:49–55; 26:18–31; shows signs to Pharaoh, 7:107–108; 20:56; 26:32–33; 43:46–47; 79:20; Pharaoh consults his chiefs and calls enchanters, 7:109–112; 10:76–79; 20:57–59; 26:34–37; Moses and the enchanters, 7:113–126; 10:80–82; 20:60–73; 26:38–51; nine signs of, 17:101; 27:12; Pharaoh's people plead with, to avert plague, 7:134–135; 43:48–50; exhorts his people to patience and prayer, 7:128; 10:84, 87; only few believe in, 10:83; a secret believer in, 40:28–45; commanded to depart by night, 20:77; 26:52; 44:23–24; crosses the sea, 7:138; 10:90; 20:78; 26:53–66; people of, ask him to make idols, 7:138–140; appointment of forty nights, 2:51; 7:142; retires to the mountain to receive the law, 7:143–145; 20:83–84; desires to see Allāh, 7:143; is granted the Torah, 7:143–145; a book revealed to, 2:53; 6:91, 154; 11:110; 17:2; returns with the law and finds his people worshipping a calf, 7:150; 20:86–90; is wroth with Aaron, 7:150; 20:92–94; prays for forgiveness of his people, 2:54; 7:155–156; burns the calf, 20:97; orders slaughter of a cow, 2:67–71; prays for drinking-water in the wilderness, 2:60; finds twelve springs, 2:60; commands his people to march on Holy Land, and their response, 5:21–26; false imputations against, 33:69; 61:5; granted distinction or criterion, 2:53; 21:48; gives promise of delivery and the promised land, 7:129; fol-

INDEX

lowed by other Israelite messengers, 2:87; transgression of Israelites prophesied by, 7:145−147; Holy Prophet appeared in likeness of, 73:15; see also *Muḥammad: Prophecies about;* book of, bears testimony to truth of Qur'ān, 11:17. See also 4:164; 6:84; 19:51−53; 25:35−36; 29:39; 42:13; 53:36; 87:19

Mosques, 2:114; 22:40

Mountains, creation of, 16:15; 13:3; 15:19; 21:31; 27:61; 31:10; 50:7; 77:27; as pegs of the earth, 78:7; provide food, 79:32−33; declaring Allāh's glory, 21:79; 34:10; 38:18; 22:18; passing away, crumbling or crushing of, as signifying fall of great opponents, 93:1−5; 18:47; 20:105−106; 27:88; 52:10; 56:5; 69:14; 70:9; 73:14; 77:10; 78:20; 81:3; 101:5; habitations in, 7:74; 15:82; 16:68, 81; 26:149; trust offered to, 33:72; see also 35:27; 88:19

Muḥammad, the Holy Prophet:

— Mission of: raised to settle differences of all nations, 2:213; a mercy to the whole world, 21:107; brings men from darkness to light, 14:1; 57:9; 65:11; a light for the world, see *Light;* as a torch to wayfarers, 33:46; resplendence of the light of, 53:7; 81:23; is the corner by night, 86:1−4; truth of his cause to shine forth gradually, 93:1−5; as an exemplar, 33:21; asks no reward, 6:90; 12:104; 25:57; 34:47; 38:86−87; 42:23; bearer of good news and warner, 33:45−46; 2:119; 5:19; 11:1−2; 17:105; as teacher and purifier, 2:129, 151; 3:164; 62:2−3; a teacher of his immediate followers and those coming later, 62:2−3; as the Clear Evidence, 98:1−2; raising the dead to life, 6:122; 13:31; commanded to warn, 74:1−2; as a plain warner, 7:184; 15:89; 22:49; denies possession of superhuman powers, 6:50; 7:188; 10:49; 46:9; only a mortal, 17:93; 18:110; 41:6; stands above all low motives, 6:162; charged with the heaviest task, 73:5; corruption prevailing before advent of, 30:41; great anxiety and untiring zeal of, for bringing about a transformation of humanity, 9:128;

10:99; 12:103; 18:6; 26:3; 35:8; 94:3; must deliver the message, 5:67; 46:35; only delivers message, 3:20; 5:92; 16:35; 24:54; 72:21–23; strives hard in the cause of truth, 9:73, 88; 25:52; 66:9; commanded to fight alone, 4:84; to remain upright, 10:105; sufferings of, 14:13; consolation to, 20:1–4; told to seek comfort in prayer, 20:130; 50:39–40; enjoined to pray by night, 73:1–9, 20; 17:79; to be steadfast in preaching, 42:15; 46:35; to be patient, 11:49; 30:60; 38:17; 70:5; 74:7; sinlessness of, 53:2; enjoined to ask protection from faults, 40:55; preaching of, shakes belief in idols, 25:42; hatred of false gods entertained by, 109:1–5; cannot guide whom he loves, 28:56; not to care for carpers, 33:1, 48; special Divine protection granted to, 3:145; 86:4; Divine help shall be granted to, 6:34; 22:15; eminence to which he was to be raised, 94:4; 96:3; is entitled to intercede, 43:86; good manners to be observed towards, 33:53; 49:1–5; manners in assembly of, 58:11; consultation with, 58:12–13; obedience necessary to, 4:59, 64, 80; 24:54, 56; 64:12; 81:21; fruits of obedience to, 4:69; 3:31, 132; call of, to be strictly obeyed, 24:62–63; made free from obligation with respect to Makkah, 90:2; holds out justice between Muslims and non-Muslims, 4:105; spiritual resurrection brought about by, 17:51–52; transformation wrought by, 14:48; 25:63–75; prophecy of final triumph of, 14:14; 20:2; *mi'rāj* of, see *Ascension;* marvellous faith of, in ultimate triumph, 6:5, 10; all nations should submit to, 22:67; universality of the message of, 6:19, 90; 7:158; 13:7; 25:1–2; 34:28; 42:7; 68:52; 81:27; the last of prophets, 33:40

— and other prophets: excellence of, above other prophets, 2:253; truth of, testified to by all prophets, 3:81; requires faith in all prophets, 3:84; and see *Prophets;* coming after a cessation of the mission of prophets, 5:19; 23:130; to follow Abraham's faith, 4:125; 16:123; likeness of, to Moses, 46:10; 73:15; comparison drawn between Moses and, 52:1–7; see

INDEX

also under *Moses;* must be judged as a prophet, 46:9

— revelation of: received revelation through Gabriel, 2:97; 16:102; 26:192–195; revelations of, not outcome of desire, 53:3–4; given a mighty revelation, 53:10; to judge by Divine revelation, 5:49; never forgot revelation, 87:6–7; relief afforded to by revelation, 94:1–8; faithfully delivered the Qur'ān, 10:15; 46:9; could not give up the Qur'ān, 11:12; 17:73–74; 28:87

— Prophecies about: Abraham and Ishmael pray for appearance of, 2:129; covenant with prophets regarding advent of, 3:8; 33:7; appearance of, waited for by Jews, 2:89; recognized like son, 2:146; 6:20; prophecies about, in all ancient scriptures, 26:195–196; 37:37; prophecy of being an Arab, 26:198–199; 41:44; prophecies of Moses, 28:43–46; prophecies of Moses and Jesus as to the advent of, 7:157; advent of, prophesied by Jesus, 61:6

— Life of: an orphan, 93:6; could not read or write, 7:157; 29:48; previous life of, a testimony to truth, 10:16; warns his relatives, 26:214; the blind man's incident, 80:1–10; flies to Madīnah, see *Flight;* passing three days in a cave, 9:40; prophecy of his return to Makkah after Flight, 28:85; vision of, regarding performing Pilgrimage, 48:27; allegiance sworn to, 48:10; triumph of, in Arabia, 110:1–3

— Qualities of: gentle dealing with opponents, 3:159; compassion for believers, 9:128; gentle to his followers, 15:88; wealth had no attraction for, 15:88; 20:131; simplicity of life of, 25:7; sublime morals of, 68:4; purity and perfection of, 33:45–46; heroic fortitude of, 43:88; attainment of perfection by, 53:6–7; nearness of, to Allāh, 53:8–9; utmost possible Divine knowledge of, 53:11–14; greatness of, 81:19–21

— false allegations against: his refuge in Allāh from false imputations, 7:200; heart of, sealed against their abuses, 42:24; allegation against, as to learning the Qur'ān from others, 16:103; 25:5; 44:14; charged with forgery, 10:37–38; 11:35; 25:4–6; 46:8; 52:33–34; called an enchanter, a dreamer, a forger, a poet, 21:3–5; conjectures regarding, 52:29–34; charges of being a poet or soothsayer refuted, 52:29–30; 69:38–52; not a poet, 36:69; 37:36–37; called mad: the answer, 68:1–7; 68:51; 7:184; 15:6–8; 23:70; 81:22; false imputations against, 33:56–57

— Companions of: loved virtue and hated evil, 49:7; were purified from sins, 24:21; 98:7–8; were strengthened with Holy Spirit, 58:22; followers of Prophet: to be raised to greatness, 95:6; has a greater claim on the faithful than themselves, 33:6; mercy specially ordained for, 7:156

— Wives of: marriages of the Prophet, 33:50; not to divorce his wives, 33:52; wives of, not to be remarried, 33:53; are mothers of believers, 33:6; should retain simplicity, 33:28–29; should not display their finery, 33:33–34; purity enjoined on, 33:30–32

— Opposition to: to judge with equity among enemies, 5:42, 42:15; secret counsels against, see *Secret counsels;* forgives enemies, 5:13; 15:85; enjoined to ask forgiveness for his oppressors, 110:3; to bear abuse with patience and take no notice, 20:130; 33:48; 46:35; 50:39; 73:10; protection granted to, against all enemies, 5:67; should strive against unbelievers and hypocrites, 9:73; 66:9; plans against, by opponents, 12:102; 16:26; 77:39; plans to tempt, 17:73; Quraish plan to kill, 8:30; 27:49; attempts on life of, 3:21–22; 5:11; doom of opponents of, 7:182–187; 18:59; 38:67; 51:59–60; 69:1–10; 77:12–40; opposition to, shall be brought to naught, 18:47; 22:47–54; 23:62–67, 93–95; 52:42; 68:17–33; 75:10–13; 79:7–9; 84:16–18; abasement of opponents of, 27:87; 42:45; 73:11–14

Murder, 2:178–179; 5:32; 6:151; 17:33; 4:92–93

Muslim, meaning of, 2:112

Muslims, believe in all the prophets, see *Prophets and Revelation;* true followers of Abraham, 3:68; 4:125; 16:123; love Allāh most, 2:165; 9:24; see also under *Human soul;* spend in the way of Allāh, 2:195; should always have a missionary force, 3:104; 9:122; should study causes of rise and fall of nations, 3:137–138; are persecuted, 3:195; 4:75; 16:41–42; 22:39–40; 29:2–3; comforted in persecution, 29:56, 60; should be steadfast under persecutions, 29:10; those recanting under compulsion, 16:106; should forgive persecutors when they overcome, 22:60

— excellent qualities of: granted good visions, 10:62–64; strengthened by Holy Spirit, 16:102; 58:22; angels bring good news to, 41:30–32; strengthened by revelation, 9:124; Divine light to be met with in houses of, 24:36; see also *Light;* follow a middle course between worldliness and monkery, 57:27–29; 2:201; should be true to promises, see *Morals: truth;* should fulfil agreements with idolaters, 9:4; should practise highest good, 16:90; should help one another in goodness, not in sin, 5:2; should be just even against themselves and relatives, 4:135; should be strictly truthful, see *Morals: truth;* enjoined to respect each other, 49:11–12; to treat as Muslims those who offered Islamic salutation, 4:94; brotherhood of, 6:52; 9:11,71; 49:10; to help each other in religious matters, 8:72–73; not to kill one another intentionally, 4:92; should remain united, 3:103; divisions among, to be deprecated, 3:105; 16:92; should not become sects, 6:159; 30:31–32; peace to be made between quarrelling parties of, 49:9–10; must sacrifice their lives in the cause of truth and suffer privations, 2:154–156, 177, 214; 3:186, 200; 9:24; should strive hard in the cause of truth, 9:88; 22:78; 49:15; 61:11; exhorted to make sacrifices, 63:9–11; must undergo trials, 3:142; 29:2–3; 33:11; 47:31; vastness of the sympathy of, 4:36; limits of obedience to authority, 4:59; greetings of, to each other, 4:86; social relations with non-Muslims, 5:5; see also *Belief: true believers* and *Morals.*

— greatness of nation, and prophecies relating to its eminence: a most exalted nation, 2:143; the best of nations, 3:110; 98:7; shall be made a great nation, 22:65–66; three classes of, 35:32; made leaders for others, 22:78; grand kingdom granted to, 4:54; shall be exalted and granted kingdom, 3:26–27; prophecy that they shall be made eminent, 2:152; promise of conquests for, 2:115; shall be made guardians and masters of Sacred Mosque, 8:34; 22:25; prophecy that they shall inherit the land, see *Land;* conquests promised to, outside Arabia, 33:27; 48:16, 21; prophecy that they shall be masters of the Holy Land, 21:105; prophecy of their being made rulers on earth, 24:55; 27:62; prophecy relating to the supremacy of, over unbelievers, 83:34–35

— dealings of, with enemies: friendly relations of, with non-Muslims who are not enemies, not disallowed, 60:8–9; friendly relations with enemies forbidden, 60:1–3; 3:28, 118–120; not to take enemy Jews and Christians for friends, 5:51; not to be misled by Jews and Christians, 3:100–101; should be just to enemies, 5:2; should be upright and act equitably towards enemies, 5:8; not to turn their backs when facing enemy, 8:15–16; to meet tenfold numbers in battle, 8:65–66; to give protection to idolaters, 9:6; to be kind to unbelievers and not to mind their abuses, 17:53; see also *Abuse;* to be firm against enemies, compassionate among themselves, 48:29; some other guiding rules of life for, 3:15–17; 6:151–153; 13:19–22; 23:57–61; 25:63–75; 51:15–19; 61:2–3; 64:11–18; 70:22–35; 74:3–7

Muslim wars, permission given, 2:190; 22:39–40; were defensive, 3:167; 22:39; undertaken because enemy fought to force Muslims back from their faith, 2:217; necessary to establish peace, 2:251; 8:60; and religious freedom for all, 22:40; persecutors to be punished,

2:191; to cease when persecution stops and religious liberty is established, 2:193; 8:39; Muslims to accept peace if enemy sued for it, 8:61–62; to be continued till Makkah was taken, 2:191; not to be carried on within the precincts of Makkah unless enemy does it first, 2:191; against idolaters, due to violation of treaties, 9:4–5; with followers of the Book, aim of, 9:29; what unbelievers were to be fought against, 9:123; acquisitions made in, 8:1, 41, 69; 59:7–8; an early prophecy relating to, 79:1–9; prophecy of Makkans waging war against Muslims, 100:1–6; prisoners taken in, released by Holy Prophet, 8:67–70; 47:4; see also names of individual battles.

Naml, valley of, 27:18

Nasr, idol, 71:23

Nations, doom of, 7:34; raising of, to life after death, 2:258–260; how and why punished, 6:42–45; 7:94–96; not punished until warned by a messenger, 6:131; 17:15; 26:208; 28:59; 30:47; term of, 7:34; 10:49; 15:4–5; destroyed when they transgress, 17:16; do not rise until they amend themselves, 13:11; to be called to their record, 45:28

Nature (and ecology): the natural environment, 2:164; 13:17; growth of vegetation, 6:99, 141; 7:57–58; 10:24; 18:45; importance of climate, 24:43; 29:63; 35:9; 45:5; 78:14–16; survival of all creatures: all creatures are communities, 6:38; earth for all, 55:10; sustenance for all provided by God, 15:19–20; 20:53–54; 29:60; 50:7–11; 79:31–33; 80:24–32; sustenance and places of habitation provided by God, 11:6; animal species are a "sign" for man, 42:29; 45:4; variety of animals, 24:45; trees, importance and function of, 14:24–25; 16:10–11; 27:60; 36:79–80; 56:71–72; benefit of whole grain, 55:12; signs in, for man to ponder, see *Signs;* see also under *Knowledge.*

INDEX

Nicknames, 49:11

Niggardliness, condemned, 2:268; 3:180; 4:37; 9:75–77; 47:37–38; 57:23–24; 59:9; 92:8–11; 100:8

Noah, main accounts of history of, 7:59–64; 10:71–73; 11:25–49; 23:23–29; 26:105–122; 37:75–82; 54:9–16; 71:1–28; and the ark, 11:37–41; 23:27–29; 29:15; 54:13–15; a son of, is drowned, 11:42–43; prayer of, for his son, 11:45–47; history of, is a history of the Prophet and a warning to his opponents, 11:49

Oaths, 2:224–225; 5:89; 16:91–94; 24:53; 66:2

Olive, 24:35; 95:1

Orphans, stress on kind treatment of, 89:17; 90:12–16; 93:9; 107:1–3; care of, 2:220; 8:41; 59:7; property of, not to be wasted, 4:2; 6:152; 17:34; should be educated and examined, 4:6; warning against swallowing property of, 4:10; justice should be done to, 4:127

Pairs, creation of things in, 36:36; 43:12; 51:49; in vegetation, 13:3; 20:53; in animals, 42:11; in mankind, 35:11; 42:11; 53:45; 78:8

Parable, setting forth of, 2:26; of the gnat, 2:26; of fire kindled, 2:17–18; of rain and lightning, 2:19–20; of one calling out to the deaf, 2:171; of birds obeying call, 2:260; of seed yielding manifold fruit, 2:261; of seed sown on stone, 2:264; of garden on elevated land, 2:265; of garden smitten by whirlwind, 2:266; of cold wind destroying harvest, 3:117; of one perplexed, 6:71; of one who rejects messages, 7:175–176; of the dog, 7:176; of rain producing luxuriant herbage and its withering away, 10:24; 18:45; 57:20; of the scum, 13:17; of ashes blown by wind, 14:18; of the good tree, 14:24–25; of the evil tree, 14:26; of milk and of wine, 16:66–67; of the bee, 16:68–69; of slave and master, 16:75; 30:28; 39:29; of the dumb man, 16:76; of one who unravels her yarn, 16:92; of a secure town, 16:112; of the rich man and the poor man, 18:32—44; of one who falls from on high, 22:31; of a fly, 22:73; of the pillar of light, 24:35; of mirage, 24:39; of intense darkness, 24:40; of the spider, 29:41; of the people of the town, 36:13—32; of the garden with rivers of milk, etc., 47:15; of the ass, 62:5; of the owners of the garden, 68:17—33

Paradise (see also *Life after Death*), fruits of, 2:25; 37:41—42; 69:23; blessings of, not conceivable, 32:17; 52:23; purity, beauty and spiritual nature of blessings of, 37:41—49; description of blessings of, is only a parable, 13:35; 47:15; blessings tasted by righteous in this life, 37:41; 47:6; extensiveness of, 3:133; 57:21; drinks of, 37:45—47; 47:15; 56:18—19; 76:5—6, 17—18, 21; 83:25—28; highest bliss of, is sight of Allāh, 50:35; nearness to Allāh is a blessing of, 54:54—55; 56:11—12, 88—89; 83:21, 28; pleasure of Allāh attained in, 3:15; 5:119; 9:21—22, 72, 100; 58:22; 89:27—30; 92:19—21; 98:8; perfect peace prevailing in, 6:127; 10:10, 25; 14:23; 19:62—63; 36:55—58; 50:34; 56:25—26; all one desires in, 25:16; 41:31; 42:22; 50:35; women equally entitled to blessings of, along with men, 4:124; 9:72; 13:23; 36:55—56; 40:8, 40; 43:70; 57:12; a true picture of, 15:45—48; is a place where there is no grief, toil, or fatigue, 7:49; 15:48; 35:34—35; 43:68; talk of those in paradise with those in hell, 37:50—60; unceasing progress in, 39:20; 66:8; wives and children of the faithful shall go to, 40:8; 52:21; *ḥūr* in, 52:20; 55:70; 44:54; 56:22; everlasting, 11:108; 15:48; 38:54; 41:8; 44:56; stands for achievement of object, 78:31; a manifestation of, in this life, 81:13; when granted in this life, 89:27—30. See also 55:46—78; 76:5—22; 88:8—16

Parents, doing good to and giving thanks to, 17:23—24; 29:8; 31:14—15; 46:15; duty to God higher than duty to, 29:8; 31:15; see also *Relationship*.

INDEX

Peace, in Islamic concept of paradise, see *Paradise;* of mind, see *Heart: contentment of;* to be accepted in war if offered, see *Muslim wars;* as the Muslim salutation, 4:94

Pen, 31:27; 68:1; 96:4

People of the Book (see also *Christians* and *Israelites*), claim exclusive salvation, 2:111, 135; 4:123; 5:18; denounce each other, 2:113; corruption of scriptures by, 2:75, 79; 3:78; 5:15; transgressions of, 3:187–188; 5:59–66; deviated from simple faith of Abraham, 3:65–68; early prophets of, were not Jews or Christians, 2:140; not true in following own scriptures, 5:66, 68; believe that Jesus died on the cross, 4:159; both good and bad among, 3:75, 113–115; 5:66; Holy Prophet appeared for, 5:15–16, 19; 98:1; recognize Prophet like their sons, 2:146; 6:20; called to submit to God, 3:20; recognize but reject truth, 2:144, 146; lead astray and hide truth, 3:69–71; disbelief of, 2:145; 3:19–20, 70, 98, 110; how they can attain salvation, 2:62; 5:69; those who accepted Islām, 3:199; 13:36; 28:52–53; 29:47; hostility of, towards Muslims, 2:105, 109; 3:99–100, 186; Muslims not to take hostile as friends, 5:51, 57; Muslims to show forgiveness to, 2:109; Muslim wars against, 9:29; invited to common principles by Islām, 3:64; 42:15; how Muslims should argue with, 29:46; food of, allowed to Muslims, 5:5; chaste women among, may be married, 5:5

Persia, prophecy relating to vanquishment of, by Romans, 30:2–4

Pharaoh, 7:103–141; 10:75–92; 20:24, 39, 43–79; 26:10–68; 28:3–9, 38–42; 40:24–37; 43:46–56; follows Israelites and is drowned, 10:90; 20:78; 26:63–66; acknowledges truth while drowning, 10:90; body of, cast ashore and preserved as sign, 10:92; prayer of wife of, 66:11

Pilgrimage, 2:158; 2:196–203; 5:1–2; 5:94–96;

22:26–33; the greater, 9:3; proclaimed, 3:97; 22:27; see also *Sacrifice*.

Planets, see *Heaven* and *Solar System*.

Poets, 26:224–227; see *Muḥammad: false allegations against*.

Polygamy, permitted under exceptional circumstances, 4:3; allowed for the care of widows and orphans, 4:127; justice between wives, 4:129

Polytheism (*shirk*, associating others with One God), the gravest sin, 4:48, 116; 5:72; 31:13; blind following of desires is included in, 25:43; 45:23; not taught by any prophet, 3:79–80; 25:17–18; 34:44; 43:20–21, 45; prohibition of, 4:36; 6:56, 151; 17:22, 39; 18:110; 29:8; 31:15; 40:66; 51:51; 60:12; see also *Idols* and *Gods*.

Polytheists, great error of, 46:5, have no authority for their beliefs, 7:33; 12:40; 22:71; 30:35; 42:21; follow only conjecture, 10:36, 66; blindly follow their forefathers, 7:70; 11:62, 87, 109; 14:10; 26:74; 34:43; 43:22–24; and see under *Intellectual development*; compared to slaves, 16:75; claim their idol-worship is God's will, see *Predestination*; claim their gods bring them near Allāh, 17:42; 39:3; asked to "name" gods, 13:33; call on One God when in distress, 6:41; uncleanness of, 9:28; degradation of, 22:31; greed of, 2:96; devil's authority over, 16:100; do not help poor, 41:6–7; works of, rendered null, 6:88; 39:65; idolatrous customs of, see under *Arabs*; denial of gods on Day of Judgment, 6:22–23; 7:37; 10:28; 16:27, 86; 28:62–64; 35:14; 40:73–74; 41:47–48; 46:6. See also 33:73; 42:13; 48:6; 68:41; 98:1–3

— relations of with Muslims: their hostility towards Muslims, 2:105; 3:186; 5:82; marriage with, prohibited, 2:221; Prophet to turn away from, 6:106–107; 15:94; war with, 9:5, 36; agreements made with, 9:1–12; and Sacred House, 9:17–19; forgiveness not to be asked for those who die as, 9:113

INDEX

Poor, the care of, 90:11–16; 59:8–9; 69:33–34; 74:44; 89:18; 107:1–3; see also *Charity*.

Poor-rate (*Zakāt*), a fundamental principle of Islām, see under *Charity*.

Prayer, is answered, 2:186; 3:195; 40:60; 14:39; 19:4; 21:84, 88, 90; 27:62; 37:75; 42:26; benefit of, 29:45; 9:99, 103; 10:87; 11:52; 19:48; 25:77; 52:27–28; 71:10–12; to pray is in man's nature, 1:4; 6:41; 41:49–51; man's ungratefulness after acceptance of his, 6:63–64; 7:189–190; 10:12, 22–23; 16:53–54; 30:33–34; 39:8, 49; true spirit of, 2:45; 2:177; 2:238; 6:63, 162; 7:55–56, 205; 19:3; 23:1–2; 32:15–16; 57:16; 73:8; sincerity in, 7:29; 29:65; 31:32; 40:14, 65; when devoid of spirit, 107:4–5; is a glorification of God, 20:130; 50:39–40; 76:25–26; restrains from sins, 29:45; 2:186; a fundamental duty in Islām, 2:3, 177, 277;, 7:170; 9:71; 13:22; 24:56; 30:31; meaning of, must be understood, 4:43; in danger, 2:239; to be shortened when travelling, 4:101; when actually fighting, 4:102; must be performed at fixed times, 4:103; the five times, 11:114; 17:78; 20:130; 30:17–18; the *tahajjud*, 17:79; 73:6, 20; 32:16; 51:17; middle course to be adopted with regard to, 17:110

— some prayers from the Qur'ān: the ideal prayer, 1:1–7; prayers for guidance, 3:8; 5:83; for forgiveness and protection from sin and evil, 2:286; 3:191–194; 7:23; 7:155–156; 11:47; 21:87; 23:97–98, 118; 28:16; 40:7–9; 59:10; 71:28; for seeking refuge in Allāh, ch. 113; ch. 114; for joining the righteous, 3:193; 7:47; 12:101; for help against enemy, 2:250, 286; 3:147; for seeking of good, 2:201; 7:156; for help in affairs, 17:80; 18:10; 20:25–28; for family, 3:38; 14:40–41; 25:74; 46:15; for believers, 14:41; 59:10; 71:28; when oppressed and persecuted, 4:75; 7:126; 10:85–86; 60:5; when in distress, 21:83, 87–88; 54:10; for a journey, 11:41; 23:29; for knowledge, 20:114; in gratitude, 27:19; 46:15; for acceptance of prayer, 2:127

Predestination, see *Religion: one is free;* idol-worshippers try to use as argument, 6:148–149; 16:35; 43:20–22

Priests, taken as gods, 3:64; 6:137; 9:31; 17:57; devouring people's property falsely, 9:34; falsely claim purity, 4:49; hypocrisy of, 2:44

Privacy, see under *Marriage.*

Promised land, see under *Israelites.*

Property, to be treated as a means of support, 4:5; not to be acquired illegally, 4:29; respect for property rights, 2:188; see *Civic Life.*

Prophethood, finality of, 33:40

Prophets (see also *Revelation*), belief in, is essential, 2:177, 285; 3:179; 4:171; 57:19; raised among all nations, 2:213; 10:47; 16:36, 84, 89; 35:24; all prophets are not mentioned in the Qur'ān, 4:164; 40:78; no distinction between, as regards belief in, 2:136, 285; 3:84; 4:150–152; all sent as part of one system, 2:87; 3:33–34; 5:19; 23:44; 57:26–27; granted book, judgment and prophecy, 6:89; sent with arguments and scriptures, 3:184; 16:43–44; 35:25; 57:25; as warners and bearers of good news, 2:213; 4:165; 6:48; 18:56; basic religion of all was submission to One God, 2:132–133; all taught Unity of God, 21:24–25; 39:65–66; 43:45; 6:88; could not claim divinity, 3:79–80; 21:29; choice of, is made by Allāh, 6:124; 22:75; 28:68; 40:15; sinlessness of, 21:25–28; cannot act *unfaithfully,* 3:161; Divine secrets are made known to, 72:26–27; revelation to, specially guarded, 72:27–28; had wives and children, 13:38; were mortals, 14:11; 36:15; and ate food, 21:7–8; 23:33; 25:20; mocked at by enemies, 6:10; 13:32; 15:10–11; 21:41; 36:30; Divine promise of help to, 2:214; 14:13–20; receive Divine help, 12:110; 21:9; 30:47; 40:51; doom of the opponents of, 6:42–45; 14:13–20; 17:77; 43:6–8; 77:7; histories of, meant as a warning, 12:111; slaying of, see *Israelites: try to kill prophets;* from among jinn, 6:130; teachings of, corrupted by evil generations, 16:63–64; 19:59; 57:16; false prophets would not prosper, 69:44–47; differences of degrees of excellence, *2:253; 17:55;* covenant with, *3:81; 33:7;* all prophets testified to the truth of the Holy Prophet, 3:81

Prostitution, 24:33

Qiblah, change in, 2:142; afforded a distinction, 2:143; differences of Jews and Christians with regard to, 2:145; see *Ka'bah*.

Quraish, 106:1; trade of, 106:2; advantages enjoyed by, 106:4; doom of, 53:57; prophecy of the defeat of, 70:40–44; see also *Muḥammad: Opposition to*.

Qur'ān, the Holy, is a revelation to Prophet from Allāh, 20:2–4; 27:6; 39:41; 53:10; original or basis of, 43:4; 13:39; opponents challenged to produce the like of, 2:23–24; 10:37–38; 11:13–14; 17:88, 52:33–34; a book whose blessings shall not be intercepted, 6:92; a warning for the whole world, 6:19; 25:1; settles all differences, 16:64; a book to be pondered over, 4:82; 23:68; 38:29; 47:24; a complete collection of best moral and spiritual teachings, 17:89; 39:27; 18:54; 30:58; a collection of all that is best in any religion and scripture, 98:3; contains the highest conceivable ideas, 29:49; is perfect and right-directing, 18:1–2; 39:28; is the truth, 6:66; 17:105; 23:90; 32:3; 35:31; truth of, recognized through knowledge, 22:54; 34:6; contains the best narratives, 12:1–3; explains everything necessary, 6:114; 10:37; 12:111; 16:89; 17:12; is a guidance, 2:2; 3:138; 39:23; 45:11; is a guidance and mercy, 10:57; 29:51; 7:52; 27:77; 31:3; is a guidance and good news, 2:97; 16:89, 102; 27:2; guides to what is upright, 17:9; contains guidance and arguments and affords a criterion, 2:185; contains answers to objections as well as arguments, 25:33; gives clear evidence and proof, 6:104; 7:203; 45:20; consists of clear messages, 2:99; 22:16; 24:1; 57:9; makes manifest, 15:1; 26:2; called Reminder, 15:6, 9; 16:43–44; 20:99; 21:50; 80:4, 11;

Reminder for all nations, 6:90; 12:104; 38:87; 68:52; 81:27; is free from every discrepancy, 4:82; uniformity in, 39:23; rule of interpretation of, 3:7; falsehood shall not prevail against, 41:41–42; is a purifier, 29:45; gives life to dead hearts, 10:57; 17:82; 41:44; a healing for spiritual diseases, 10:57; 17:82; 41:44; to be listened to with silence, 7:204; opponents of, try to prevent its hearing, 41:26; a book of wisdom, 10:1; 3:58; 11:1; 31:2; 36:2; knowledge of, taught by God, 55:1–2; 75:19; to be taught gradually, 17:106; duty of explaining message of, to people, 3:187; brings forth men from darkness into light, 14:1; 57:9; 65:11; not the work of a poet, 26:224–226; 36:69; 69:41; cannot be the work of devil, 26:210–212; 81:25; must achieve its object, 20:2–5; revealed to the Prophet's heart, 2:97; 26:193–194; revealed on a blessed night, 44:3; 97:1; revelation of, began in Ramaḍān, 2:185; revealed piecemeal, 25:32; 76:23; made to enter into hearts, 26:200; revealed in Arabic, 12:2; 16:103; 20:113; 26:195; 41:3, 44; 42:7; 43:3; 46:12; made easy in Arabic, 19:97; 44:58; made easy to remember, 54:40; *Fātiḥah* is essence of whole, 15:87; Divine promise to guard it against corruption, 15:9; 56:77–80; 85:21–22; revelation of, was requirement of beneficence of Allāh, 55:1–2; Christian nations of future believing in truth of, 72:1–14; transformation wrought by, 13:31; 59:21; 84:1–5; will make its followers eminent, 21:10; scribes of, shall be honoured, 80:13–16

— and previous revelation: verifies previous revelation, 2:41, 89, 101; 6:92; 10:37; 35:31; fulfils previous prophecy, 10:94; 20:133; 26:196–197; 28:52–53; 46:12; verifies and guards all previous revelations, 5:48; abrogation, refers to abrogation of previous scriptures, 2:106; 16:101; connection of, with previous revelation, 28:51; borne testimony to by Moses, 11:17; 46:10

— collection of, internal evidence of collection of, 75:17–18; evidence of the writing of, 68:1; 80:13–16;

98:2; recited by Muslims in day and night prayers, 73:20; arrangement of, by revelation, 25:32

Ramaḍān, 2:185; see also *Fasting*.

Rass, 25:38; 50:12

Relationship: ties of, to be respected, 4:1; 8:75; 9:10; 24:61; 25:54; 33:6; 42:23; doing good to relatives, 2:83, 177; 4:8, 36; 16:90; 17:26; 24:22; 30:38; must bear true witness even against relatives, 4:135; 6:152; duty to Allāh above, 9:23–24, 113; 58:22; 63:9; 64:14–16; of no avail on Day of Judgment, 23:101; 60:3; 70:11–14; 80:33–37

Religion: differences of, should not be a cause of dispute, 2:139; 22:17; 22:67–69; 29:46; 42:15; to be judged on Day of Judgment, see *Day: of Resurrection;* freedom of, 2:193; 2:256; 8:39; 10:99; 22:40; one is free to accept or reject truth, 6:104; 10:41, 108; 18:29; 27:92; 39:41; 73:19; 74:54–55; 76:3, 29; study of, 9:122; not to be followed blindly, see under *Intellectual development;* spirit of, more important than form of, 2:177; 3:92; 22:37; ch. 107

Religious leaders, see *Priests*.

Reminder, see under *Qur'ān*.

Repentance, what is meant by, 2:160; 3:89; 4:145–146; 5:39; 16:119; 24:5; 28:67; 66:8; when not acceptable, 3:90; 4:17–18; see also *Allāh: Forgiving*.

Resurrection, a manifestation of hidden realities, see under *Life after death;* a new growth, 23:14–16; 32:10–11; 36:78–81; 50:3–4; 56:60–61; 71:17–18; 75:36–40; 80:21–22; preservation of what is necessary for, 50:4; the spiritual resurrection, 30:19; 36:33; see also *Day, the Last*.

Retaliation, law of, 2:178; in Torah, 5:45

Revelation, is a universal experience of humanity, 4:163–165; and see *Prophets: raised among all nations;* Muslims must believe in all revelation, 2:4, 136, 285; 3:84; 4:136; 5:59; 29:46; a requirement of Divine attributes, 6:91; helps man to overcome evil, 2:38, 151; 5:65–66; 7:35; 17:82; 41:44; 47:2; 62:2; effect of, likened to rain on earth, 7:57; 16:65; 22:5; 29:63; 35:9; 36:33; 41:39; in broad sense granted to objects and beings other than man, 8:12; 16:68–69; 41:12; 99:4–5; granted to man in three ways, 42:51; descends upon the heart, 2:97; 26:192–194; 53:10–11

— revelation to non-prophets: to Moses' mother, 20:38; 28:7; to Mary, 3:42–43, 45–47; 19:17–21, 24–26; to disciples of Jesus, 5:111; granted to companions of the Prophet, 58:22; granted to true believers, 10:62–64; 41:30–32; 12:108

Righteousness, what it consists of, 2:177; 3:92; the righteous, 4:69; 76:5

Rock, dwellers of the, 15:80; hearts likened to, 2:74

Romans, the, 30:2–4

Saba', 27:22; 34:15

Sabbath, violation of, by Israelites, 2:65; 4:47, 154; 7:163; 16:124

Sabians, 2:62; 5:69; 22:17

Sacred months, wars not to be carried on in, except when enemy is aggressive, 2:194, 217; their postponement, 9:36–37

Sacrifice, 22:28; meaning underlying, 22:34–37; as the means of obtaining great good, 108:2

Ṣafā, and Marwah, 2:158

Saints, worship of, 17:57; see also *Priests.*

Ṣāliḥ, his preaching to T̲h̲amūd, their rejection and destruction, 7:73–79; 11:61–68; 14:9–14; 26:141–159; 27:45–53; she-camel of, as a sign, 7:73; 11:64–65; 17:59; 26:155–158; 54:27–31; 91:13–14; see also *T̲h̲amūd.*

Salsabīl, 76:18,

Salvation, how attained, 2:38, 112; 89:27–30; 91:9–10

Sāmirī, leads Israelites astray, 20:85; makes a calf, 20:87–88; confesses, 20:96; is punished by Moses, 20:97

Samuel, 2:246–248

Saul, 2:247–249

Scandal, preventions against, 24:58–59

Science, study of nature urged and man to conquer nature, see under *Intellectual development, Knowledge* and *Man;* see also *Nature;* law and order in nature, 67:3–4; unity in diversity of nature, 13:3–4; scientific disclosures in Qur'ān: prophecy about spread of books and making of scientific discoveries, 81:10–11; laws of gravitation, 13:2; 31:10; 77:25–26; moon does not possess original light, 17:12; 91:2; life created from water, see *Water;* orbits of planetary bodies, 21:33; 23:17; 36:40; 51:7; sun's movement in space, 36:38; creation of universe and its stages, 21:30; 41:9–12; 79:30; unlimited creation, 31:27; heaven originally vapour, 41:11; geological convulsions in earth's history, 16:15; future forms of transport, 36:41–42; space travel, 15:14–15; 29:22; 55:33; 78:19; 81:11; creation of all things in pairs, see *Pairs;* growth of child in womb, 23:13–14; existence of sub-conscious mind, 20:7; existence of what is smaller than atom, 10:61; 34:3; work of honey bee, 16:68–69; evolution of man, see *Evolution;* atomic warfare, 17:58; 22:1–2; 55:35; 70:8–9; 73:14–18

Sea, man to derive advantage from, 16:14; 35:12; ships running in, for man's benefit, 2:164; 14:32; 17:66; 22:65; 31:31; see also *Ships;* the two seas, 25:53; 35:12; 55:19–25

Seal of prophets, 33:40; see also *Prophethood.*

Secret counsels, condemned, 4:81, 108; 9:78; 17:47;

58:7–8, 10; private counsels for good causes, 4:114; 58:9

Sectarianism, condemned, 3:103; 6:159; 30:31–32

Seeds, growth of, brought about by God, 56:63–65; truth likened to sowing of, 6:95; 48:29; see also under *Parable*.

Sheba, queen of, 27:20–44

Ships, 36:41; 42:32–33; 43:12–14; see also *Sea*.

<u>Shirk</u>, see *Polytheism*.

Shu'aib, 7:85–93; 11:84–95; 15:78–79; 26:176–191; 29:36–37

Signs, demanded by unbelievers, 2:118; 6:35–37; 6:109; 10:20; 13:7, 27; 20:133; 21:5; shown in support of Islām, 13:38; 21:37; 26:4; 27:93; 41:53; 3:12; denied and scoffed at, 2:145; 6:25, 109, 111; 17:59; 30:58–59; 37:14–15; 54:2; punishment of opponents as, 11:103; 15:75; 26:67, 103 etc.; 27:52; 34:9; of spiritual revival, 16:65; 36:33, 37

— in nature, 10:6; 12:105; 17:12; 29:44; 45:3–4; 51:20–21; see also *Intellectual development: signs in nature*.

Sin, open and secret denounced alike, 6:120, 151; 7:33; see *Atonement, Evil,* and *Allāh: Forgiving*.

Slander, 4:112; 24:4, 23; 68:10–13; 104:1

Slaughter, of animals, see *Food*.

Slaves, freedom of, enjoined, 2:177; 9:60; 24:33; 47:4; 90:13; liberating, as expiation for sin, 4:92; 5:89; 58:3; see also *Female Slaves*.

Sodom, 25:40; 29:34–35; 15:74–76; see also *Lot*.

Solar system, 78:12–13; see also *Heaven*.

Solomon, was a prophet, 4:163; 6:84; fabrications against, 2:102; did not worship idols, 2:102; wind being made subservient to, refers to fleet of, 21:81; 34:12; jinn and devils working for, 38:37–38; understands speech of

INDEX

birds, 27:16; granted abundance, 27:16; and the Naml, 27:18–19; reviews birds, 27:20; and the Queen of Sheba, the story of, 27:20–44; shows her the error of sun-worship by metaphor of palace of glass, 27:44; death of, 34:14; weak rule of the successor of, 34:14; 38:34–35; prays for a spiritual kingdom, 38:35

Son, adopted is not real, 33:4; see also *Parents*.

Sonship, doctrine of, rejected, 2:116; 6:101; 9:30; 10:68; 18:4–5; 19:35, 88–93; 21:26–27; 23:91; 43:81–82; 112:3; term son of God, metaphorical use of, 21:26; 39:4; use as meaning favourite, 5:18

Soothsayers, 37:7–10

Soul, see *Human soul*.

Spirit, as meaning Gabriel, 2:87; 16:102; 26:193; awakening of Divine, in man, 70:4; 78:38; descent of, 97:4; as meaning revelation, 4:171; 17:85; 40:15; 42:52; believers strengthened with, 58:22; Divine spirit breathed into man, see *Human soul*.

Spirit of truth, Jesus' prophecy of coming of, 17:81; 61:6

Spiritual growth, three stages of: animal stage, 12:53; self-accusing spirit, 75:2; final stage, soul at rest, 89:27–30

Spiritual majority, attained at forty, 46:15

Star, the, disappearance of, 53:1

Stars, as means of conjectures for astrologers, 67:5; disappearance of, 77:8; darkening of, 81:2; dispersal of, 82:2; as direction guides for man, 6:97; 16:16; made subservient to man, 7:54; 16:12; worship of, condemned, 6:76; 37:88–89; make submission to God, 22:18; in Joseph's vision, 12:4

State Polity: Inter-communal relations, 3:186; 60:8–9; form of government, 42:38; 3:159; who should be placed in authority, 4:58; fitness to rule, 2:247; 12:55–56; 22:41; 24:55; 38:17–20; those unfit to rule, 4:53; 38:34–35; rulers on trial, 10:14; obedience to authority, limits of, 4:59; 12:76; justice as the basis of rule, 4:58, 105–107, 135; 5:2, 8; 6:152; 16:90; 38:26; 42:15; faithfulness to treaties, 5:1; 9:4, 7; 16:92, 94; when war becomes necessary, 2:190–193, 246, 251; 4:75; 8:39; 9:13, 29; 22:39–40; peace, 8:61–62; 8:58; 9:1–4

Submission, to God, see *Islām: significance of.*

Sun, course of the, 36:38; folding up of, 81:1; Holy Prophet as sun of righteousness, 33:46; 91:1; see also *Sun and moon.*

Sun and moon, function of, in nature, 6:96; 7:54; 10:5; 21:33; 36:38–40; 55:5; 71:15–16; submit to God, 22:18; made subservient to man, 13:2; 14:33; 16:12; 29:61; 31:29; 35:13; 39:5; not to be worshipped, 6:77–78; 41:37; in Joseph's vision, 12:4; brought together, 75:9; perfect man likened to, 91:1–2

Sunnah, see *Ḥadīth.*

Suwā', 71:23

Tabūk, expedition to, 9:41–42; brought about clear distinction between believers and hypocrites, 9:43–110

Taqdīr, significance of, as meaning making to a measure, 80:19; 87:3; 25:2; 54:49; as referring to measure in laws of nature, 15:21; 23:18; 43:11; see also *Fatalism* and *Predestination.*

Taurāt, see *Torah.*

Tayammum, 4:43; 5:6

T̲h̲amūd, reject Ṣāliḥ and are destroyed, see *Ṣāliḥ* and 15:80–84; 17:59; 25:38; 29:38; 41:13–14, 17–18; 51:43–45; 53:51; 54:23–31; 69:4–5; 85:18; 89:9; 91:11–15

Theft, 5:38

Throne, see *'Arsh.*

Time, testimony of, that truth shall prosper, 103:1–3

Torah, 3:3; corruption of, see under *Bible;* retaliation in,

INDEX

5:45; Jesus verified but made changes in law of, see *Jesus;* promises success for sacrifices made, 9:111; not observed by its followers, 5:43, 66, 68; 62:5; see also 3:65, 93; 7:157; 48:29; see *Bible.*

Trade, is work and not like usury, 2:275; see topics under *Civic Life;* not to divert man from duty to God, 24:37; 62:9; high regard for honesty in, see *Civic Life:honesty.*

Tranquility, see under *Heart;* see also 9:26, 40; 48:18, 26

Treaties, stress laid on regard for, as opposed to modern loose views on, see *Morals:true to covenants* and *State Polity.*

Trees, good and evil likened to, 14:24–26; metaphor of all being pens, 31:27; function of in nature, see *Nature.*

Trench, companions of the, 85:4

Trinity, doctrine of, refuted, 4:171; 5:73

Trumpet, blowing of, 6:73; 18:99; 27:87; 39:68; 20:102; 36:51; 50:20; 78:18

Trust(s), to be given to those worthy of holding, 4:58; one must be faithful to, 8:27; 23:8; nature faithful to, but not so man, 33:72

Tubba', people of, 44:37; 50:14

Uḥud, battle of, 3:121; hypocrites desert Muslims at, 3:122; assistance of angels at, 3:124; enemy returns disappointed, 3:127; served as a distinction, 3:140–143, 154–168; causes of the misfortune, 3:152–153; victory was first obtained, 3:152; enemy assumes offensive after retreat and Muslims in disorder, 3:153; Muslims rally round the Prophet at his call and defend themselves, 3:154; murmurings of hypocrites, 3:154; delinquents pardoned, 3:152, 155; Prophet's gentle dealing, 3:159

Universe, beginning and end of, 46:3; see also topics under *Science* and *Heaven.*

Usury, 2:275–280; 3:130; 30:39

'Uzzā, idol, 53:19

Veil, spiritual, 7:46; 50:22

Visions, instances of, seen by Abraham, Joseph, Moses and Mary, see under their names; *Mi'rāj* was a vision, see *Ascension*; seen by ordinary people and unbelievers, 12:36–41, 43–49

Wadd, idol, 71:23

Wall, to keep out Gog and Magog, 18:94–98; between hypocrites and believers, 57:13

Wars, modern, spoken of in Qur'ān, 18:99; see also *Muslim Wars* and under *State Polity*.

Water, as source of life, 21:30; 24:45; 11:7; 25:54

Wealth, see *Civic Life*.

Widows, period of waiting for, 2:234; remarriage permitted, 2:234–235; provision for, in addition to share of inheritance, 2:240

Wills, see *Bequest*.

Wine, see *Intoxicants*; spiritual, in Paradise, see *Paradise: drinks of*.

Witnesses, see *Evidence*.

Wives (see also *Marriage, Widows* and *Women*), rights of, 2:228; 4:34; may claim divorce, 2:229; see also *Divorce*; as bringer up of children, 2:223; dowry must be given to, by husband, 4:4; see also *Dowry*; what women it is forbidden to marry, 4:23; must not be abused but treated kindly, 4:19–20; relation of husband and wife, 2:187; 30:21

Women (see also *Marriage* and *Wives*), can receive revelation, 3:42; 19:17; 20:38; 28:7; Mary is listed with prophets, 21:91–92 in context of 21:76–90; is mentioned in terms for prophets, 19:16; is set as example to all believers, 66:11–12; women given equal reward to men, 3:195; 4:124; 16:97; 40:40; have same moral qualities as men, 33:35; equals in Muslim fraternity, 9:71–72; equally entitled to blessings of Paradise as men, see under *Paradise;* complaint of ordinary woman against husband heard by Allāh, 58:1–4; take pledge with Prophet, 60:12; daughters given precedence over sons, 42:49–50; earning and property rights of, 4:4, 7, 32; injunction regarding dress of, 24:31, 60; 33:59; position of, in pre-Islamic Arabia, 33:4; 58:1–4; burying alive of infant girls before Islām, see under *Arabs;* prophecy of greater awareness of women's rights in future times, 81:8–9

Word(s) of Allāh, as meaning prophecy fulfilled by John, 3:39; and by Jesus, 3:45; 4:171; as meaning prophecies sure to be fulfilled, 6:34, 115; 10:64; 18:27; as creation, 18:109; 31:27

Wuḍū', see *Ablution.*

Yaghūth, idol, 71:23

Yathrib, 33:13; see *Madīnah.*

Ya'ūq, idol, 71:23

Zacharias, was a prophet, 6:85; Mary given into charge of, 3:37; prays for a son, 3:38; 19:2–6; 21:89–90; birth of John announced to, 3:39–40; 19:7–9; a sign granted to, 3:41; 19:10.

Zaid, son of Ḥārithah, divorces Zainab, 33:37

Zakāt, see under *Charity.*

Zaqqūm, tree of, 17:60; 37:62; 44:43

Zihār, 33:4; 58:1–4